TRANSFORMATIONAL AND CHARISMATIC LEADERSHIP:
THE ROAD AHEAD

MONOGRAPHS IN LEADERSHIP AND MANAGEMENT

Series Editor: James G. (Jerry) Hunt

MONOGRAPHS IN LEADERSHIP AND MANAGEMENT
VOLUME 2

TRANSFORMATIONAL AND CHARISMATIC LEADERSHIP:
THE ROAD AHEAD

EDITED BY

BRUCE J. AVOLIO

*Department of Management,
College of Business Administration,
University of Nebraska – Lincoln, USA*

FRANCIS J. YAMMARINO

*Center for Leadership Studies,
School of Management,
State University of New York at Binghamton, USA*

JAI

United Kingdom – North America – Japan – India – Malaysia – China – Australasia

JAI Press is an imprint of Emerald Group Publishing Limited
Howard House, Wagon Lane, Bingley BD16 1WA, UK

First edition 2007

Copyright © 2008 Emerald Group Publishing Limited

Reprints and permission service
Contact: booksandseries@emeraldinsight.com

British Library Cataloguing in Publication Data
A catalogue record for this book is available from the British Library

ISBN: 978-0-76-230962-7

Awarded in recognition of
Emerald's production
department's adherence to
quality systems and processes
when preparing scholarly
journals for print

INVESTOR IN PEOPLE

CONTENTS

PART V. THE ROAD AHEAD

ABOUT THE EDITORS

Bruce J. Avolio, Ph.D, is the Donald and Shirley Clifton Chair in Leadership at the University of Nebraska in the College of Business Administration. Dr. Avolio has an international reputation as a researcher in leadership having published over 80 articles and book chapters. He consults with a large number of organizations in North America, South America, Africa, Europe, South-east Asia, Australia, New Zealand, and Israel. His research and consulting include work with the militaries of the USA, Singapore, Sweden, Finland, Israel, South Africa, and Europe. His latest book is entitled "Full Leadership Development: Building the Vital Forces in Organizations" (Sage, 1999). His forthcoming book with Erlbaum is entitled, "Made/Born: Leadership Development in Balance", which is Forthcoming 2003. Professor Avolio is on the editorial boards of the *Academy of Management Journal, Journal of Organizational Behavior*, and the *Leadership Quarterly*.

Francis J. Yammarino, Ph.D., is a Professor of Management and Director and Fellow of the Center for Leadership Studies at the State University of New York at Binghamton. He received his Ph.D. from the State University of New York at Buffalo in Organizational Behavior (Management). Dr. Yammarino has extensive research experience in the areas of superior-subordinate relationships, leadership, self-other agreement processes, and multiple levels of analysis issues. He serves on the editorial review boards of seven scholarly journals, including the *Academy of Management Journal, Journal of Applied Psychology,* and the *Leadership Quarterly*. Dr. Yammarino is a Fellow of the American Psychological Society and the Society for Industrial and Organizational Psychology. He has published six books and over 80 articles. Dr. Yammarino has received several research and teaching awards, and has served as a consultant to numerous organizations, including IBM, Textron, TRW, Lockheed Martin, Medtronic, United Way, and the U.S. Army, Navy, Air Force, and Department of Education.

LIST OF CONTRIBUTORS

John Antonakis	Department of Psychology, Yale University, USA
Bruce J. Avolio	Department of Management, University of Nebraska – Lincoln, USA
Bernard M. Bass	Center for Leadership Studies, State University of New York at Binghamton, USA
Shane Connelly	Department of Psychology, University of Oklahoma, USA
Richard A. Couto	Program in Leadership and Change, Antioch University, USA
Fred Dansereau	School of Management, State University of New York at Buffalo, USA
Rex Dumdum	Center for Leadership Studies, State University of New York at Binghamton, USA
Dov Eden	Faculty of Management, Tel Aviv University, Israel
Blaine Gaddis	Department of Psychology, University of Oklahoma, USA
Whitney Helton-Fauth	Department of Psychology, University of Oklahoma, USA
Robert J. House	Wharton School of Management, University of Pennsylvania, USA
Mansour Javidan	Faculty of Management, University of Calgary, Canada

Ronit Kark   Departments of Psychology and Sociology,
                        Bar-Ilan University, Israel

Insook Kim   College of Nursing, Yonsei University,
                        South Korea

Kyoungsu Kim   College of Business Administration,
                        Chonnam National University, South Korea

Kevin Lowe   Bryan School of Business, University of
                        North Carolina at Greensboro, USA

Ofra Mayseless   Faculty of Education, University of Haifa,
                        Israel

John B. Miner   Writer and Consultant, Eugene, OR, USA

Michael D. Mumford   Department of Psychology, University of
                        Oklahoma, USA

Ken W. Parry   Centre for the Study of Leadership, Victoria
                        University of Wellington, New Zealand

Micha Popper   Department of Psychology, University of
                        Haifa, Israel

Boas Shamir   Department of Anthropology and Sociology,
                        Hebrew University of Jerusalem, Israel

Johannes Steyrer   Department of Management and
                        Organizational Behavior, Vienna University
                        of Economics and Business Administration,
                        Austria

Jill M. Strange   Department of Psychology, University of
                        Oklahoma, USA

Roni Sulimani   Faculty of Management, Tel Aviv University,
                        Israel

David A. Waldman   School of Management, Arizona State
                        University West, USA

Francis J. Yammarino   School of Management/Center for Leadership
                               Studies, State University of New York at
                               Binghamton, USA

PREFACE

For three days in the spring of 2001, about 100 of the world's leadership scholars, both junior and senior in the discipline, gathered on the campus of the State University of New York at Binghamton. The purpose of this gathering of scholars was twofold. First, it served as a *festschrift* to honor Bernard M. Bass for his over 50 years of contributions to leadership theory, research, and practice. Second, the *conference* sought to review and push to the next level the state of the art of transformational and charismatic leadership.

The festschrift began with an opening reception and dinner to honor Bernie Bass for his career of work on leadership, culminating in his over 20-year effort to understand transformational and charismatic leadership. For the next two days, speakers, presenters, and discussants not only reminisced about their interactions and work with Bernie over the years, but also offered their latest thoughts on transformational and charismatic leadership. Keynote addresses were delivered by Jeff Sonnenfeld, Don Clifton, Walt Ulmer, Jim Burns, Georgia Sorenson, and Wayne Casio, and many of the other contributors to the conference are listed in this book. Key sessions and themes of the leadership conference included: the meaning of the constructs of transformational and charismatic leadership; moral and ethical aspects of such leadership; measurement and analysis of transformational and charismatic leadership; related forms of leadership; and the future of leadership research.

This book, focusing on the past, present, and future state of transformational and charismatic leadership theory, is a result of the festschrift/conference. We would like to thank all the many people who made this event and book possible. Individuals and organizations we wish to thank include the conference sponsors: Center for Leadership Studies (Bruce Avolio & Fran Yammarino, Co-Directors), School of Management (Glenn Pitman, Dean & Richard Reeves-Ellington, Associate Dean), Broome-Tioga BOCES (Larry Kiley, Superintendent), United Health Services (Pete McGinn, CEO), and Universal Instruments (Paul Slobodian, Vice President). We thank all the keynote speakers, conference participants, and contributors to this book. Their ideas have inspired us and will move the field forward further and faster.

We also wish to thank members of the Binghamton administrative staff – Wendy Clark, Bernadette Cencetti, Mary Ellen Engard, Myra Demming, and Marie Iobst – for their hard work in helping to organize the conference and to produce this book. Several Binghamton doctoral students – John Garger, Paul Jacques, and Mike Eom – and faculty members – Don Spangler, Shelley Dionne, Surinder Kahai, Kim Jaussi, Rex Dumdum, Ron Kwok, and Naga Sivasubramanian – also contributed greatly to the success of the conference. We wish especially to thank Ruth Bass, whose life-long friendship and support have provided us all with more quality time with Bernie that has, no doubt, enriched all of our work on leadership. Finally, we wish to thank Jerry Hunt and all the production people at Elsevier Science who facilitated the publication of this book.

We now invite you, the readers, to sit back, relax, and enjoy "Transformational and Charismatic Leadership: The Road Ahead." We believe that the more people travel this road, the wider it will become, and the more we will learn and develop what constitutes the most profound aspects of leadership and human potential.

Bruce J. Avolio and Francis J. Yammarino
Binghamton, NY

Editors

INTRODUCTION TO, AND OVERVIEW OF, TRANSFORMATIONAL AND CHARISMATIC LEADERSHIP

Bruce J. Avolio and Francis J. Yammarino

Transformational and charismatic leadership represent the "new leadership genre." While there are nearly as many definitions of these notions as there are researchers in the field, we believe that all these views have a core common element. Specifically, transformational and charismatic leadership theory and models broadly represent a set of approaches to understanding leadership (not management) that can help us understand how certain leaders foster performance beyond expected standards by developing an emotional attachment with followers and other leaders, which is tied to a common cause, which contributes to the "greater good" or larger collective. We define such leadership as Burns (1978) did, as representing the moral high road of leadership. It is also leadership that is individually considerate, intellectually stimulating, inspirationally motivational, visionary, and of high ethical standards. Transformational and charismatic leadership involve a unique bonding among leaders and followers – emotional attachment, respect, and trust form the basis of these approaches.

The purpose of this book is to assess the state of the art of transformational and charismatic leadership theory and methods. The contributors to this volume review the past, critique the present, and speculate about the future of transformational and charismatic leadership theory. In brief, our intent is to set the research agenda for the field for at least the next 10 years.

In this book, we examine all aspects of transformational and charismatic leadership: the past, present, and future; antecedents and consequences; initiation and development; mediators and moderators; and multiple levels of analysis issues. Our goal is to cover not only "the road well-traveled," but also "the road ahead", in order to expand the lanes that will be traveled by colleagues who are just entering the field of leadership. To accomplish this purpose, this volume is organized into five thematic sections: transformational leadership, charismatic leadership, psychological perspectives on these theories, related perspectives on these theories, and the future.

OVERVIEW

Section I, "Transformational Leadership", begins with an article by Antonakis and House on the Full-range Leadership Theory (FRLT). In their chapter, they highlight the history of the FRLT as a key part of the neo-charismatic movement. Antonakis and House then identify the FRLT as an integrative platform for the field, specify conditions that can moderate the factor structure of the Multifactor Leadership Questionnaire (MLQ), assess its validity, and suggest "instrumental leadership" as a needed addition to make the full range model even "fuller".

In the next article, Dumdum, Lowe, and Avolio present a meta-analysis of the MLQ and outcomes. In an update of earlier work, they found confirming evidence in support of prior meta-analyses. These results held for both primary linkages of leadership dimensions and outcomes as well as moderated relationships.

The final article in this section, by Kark and Shamir, in contrast, focuses more on the followers of transformational leaders, ironically a neglected component of most theories of leadership. By integrating theories of the self-concept and transformational leadership, they propose that transformational leaders influence the *relational* and *collective* selves of followers. This influence in turn fosters followers' personal identification with the leader and social identification with the organizational unit, which goes to the core of how transformational leaders energize followers to achieve extraordinary levels of performance.

Section II, "Charismatic Leadership", begins with an article by Couto. In the form of a letter to Publius, the authors of the "Federalist Papers," Couto addresses the Founding Fathers' views and fears regarding charismatic leadership. He points out that the Founding Fathers opposed some forms of charisma, endorsed other forms of it, and sought socialized charismatic leaders to govern. Couto links these issues to more current problems with presidential elections, including the recent one of 2000.

Mumford and Strange, in the next article, focus on the articulation of a vision as part of charismatic leadership. They view leaders' visions as prescriptive mental models of their beliefs about optimal organizational functioning. In their work, they identified "ideologues," whose mental models stress the maintenance of extant standards, and "charismatics," whose mental models stress adaptive change.

The third chapter in this section, by Kim, Dansereau, and Kim, extends the concept of a single charismatic style to multiple styles. They identify three dimensions of charismatic leader behaviors – vision-related, personal, and empowering – and eight styles of charismatic leadership (e.g. entrepreneurial jungle fighter, intellectual leader, servant leader, strategic leader) based on various combinations of these behaviors. Further, they explain how socialized vs. personalized power motives of charismatic leaders, as moderated by follower self-esteem and environmental constraints, can lead to followers' voluntary acceptance vs. unquestioning obedience to a leader.

In the final chapter of this section, Waldman and Javidan examine the connections between charismatic leadership and upper echelons theory. They explore charismatic leadership at the strategic level, and offer theory and data in support of two alternative models involving strategic change, CEO charisma, and perceived environmental uncertainty.

Section III, "Psychological Perspectives", begins with a chapter by Popper and Mayseless focusing on the "internal world" of transformational leaders. They argue that the psychological substructure of such leaders includes a motivation to lead, leadership self-efficacy, motivation and capacity to relate to others pro-socially, optimism, and openness to new ideas and experiences. They discuss the origins of these characteristics in earlier childhood experiences, as explained by psychological attachment theory, and how these experiences shape the leader followers meet later in life.

In the next chapter, Steyrer continues this internal exploration with a focus on stigma, charisma, and the narcissistic personality. Using social-cognitive and psycho-dynamic theories, he discusses the emergence of charismatic leaders based on attributes, exhibited consciously or unconsciously, that are stigmatized by society. He then explains charismatic relationships in terms of intra-personal and interpersonal feedback processes based on theories of narcissistic behavior.

In the final chapter of this section, Connelly, Gaddis, and Helton-Fauth explore the role of emotions in transformational and charismatic leadership. Beyond relationships of global emotions such as emotional intelligence and positive and negative affect to leadership, they identify relevant positive and negative emotion categories as well as their antecedents and consequences and specific emotions linked to transformational and charismatic leadership. These detailed and intricate ideas are applied to transformational and personalized and socialized charismatic leadership theories to understand how emotions influence leader communication, motivation, and interpersonal relations with followers.

Section IV, "Related Perspectives", begins with a chapter by Eden and Sulimani on the effectiveness of Pygmalion leadership training. In this work, they report results of a controlled field experiment in which means efficacy, in addition to self-efficacy, is used to induce Pygmalion effects of instructors (leaders) on trainees (followers). This is the first experimental confirmation of the effectiveness of Pygmalion training among instructors of adults, and has broad implications for leadership development training efforts.

In the next chapter, Miner reviews work on role motivation theories of leadership. His key point is that leadership can only be fully understood within organizational systems (context). Such systems are hierarchic (managerial), professional (specialized), task (entrepreneurial), and group (team). Leadership and organizational forms are thus linked in role motivation theory in a way that brings the third piece of the leadership triangle into focus – the context.

In the final chapter of this section, Parry provides additional support for the construct of transformational leadership through phenomenologically determined social processes. Using full-grounded theory method and questionnaires, he identifies a model of social processes of leadership with four lower-order social processes subfactors (i.e. active management, team goal alignment, resolving uncertainty, and reciprocity) linked to transformational and transactional leadership.

Section V, "The Road Ahead", begins with how much leadership research in general and transformational and charismatic leadership in particular began – with the work of Bass. In this thoughtful and interesting essay, Bass first looks back at an address he gave to the American Management Association in 1967, looking ahead to the year 2000 to make predictions about management, leadership, and organizations. He then looks ahead from the present (2001, when his essay was written) to 2034 to forecast 24 ideas and trends about leadership and organizations. His predictions about the first 33-year window were fairly accurate; we suspect that his forecasts about the second 33-year window will be similarly profound.

In the concluding chapter of this section and this book, we (Avolio and Yammarino) first identify the key contributions of Bass to the literature on transformational and charismatic leadership. Next, through a review of the contributions, we note some main themes of this volume and the literature on transformational and charismatic leadership. We then challenge the field of leadership researchers to push down "the road ahead" and advance theory, research, methods, and practice in the realm of transformational and charismatic leadership.

WHAT'S MISSING?

While this book has attempted to be comprehensive in its coverage of transformational and charismatic leadership, we might ask, "What's missing?" We identify below a half-dozen issues, questions really, to begin this discussion among scholars in the transformational and charismatic leadership field.

First, where are the *data*? Like many "young" fields of study, transformational and charismatic leadership *theories* are ahead of *data* about the theories. We have many more conceptualizations about, and theories of, transformational and charismatic leadership than rigorous empirical studies about them. The possible exception may be the empirical studies of Avolio, Bass, and colleagues involving the MLQ. More importantly, there is a dearth of empirical studies that are longitudinal in nature, or combine quantitative and qualitative methods, or pit rival theories against one another in rigorous empirical tests. Moreover, there are relatively few experimental lab or field studies that have been done, attempting to systematically manipulate transformational and charismatic leadership to study how these theories can be used to explain causal impact on motivation and performance. It is through these latter types of work that the field of transformational and charismatic leadership studies will advance more rapidly.

Second, where are the *levels of analysis*? With the possible exception of the work of Yammarino and colleagues, most theoretical and empirical work on transformational and charismatic leadership fails to address multiple levels of analysis issues. Theories, constructs, variables, and relationships must specify levels of analysis; measures and analyses must account for levels of analysis; and these ideas must be addressed *explicitly*, not implicitly, assumed, or ignored. As levels of analysis issues are understood, incorporated, and tested in the realm of transformational and charismatic leadership, rapid advances in the field will occur.

Third, where is *culture*? Despite Bass' work on the universality of leadership and the GLOBE project of House and colleagues, the universality vs. cultural-specificity of transformational and charismatic leadership is still subject to debate. More clearly, we do not have a good theoretical feel for, or enough empirical results about, which dimensions or aspects of transformational and charismatic leadership are universal vs. specific to only a culture or a limited set of cultures. The articulation of emic and etic approaches to transformational and charismatic leadership and the culture-levels analysis linkage would help clarify these issues in the future, especially if supported by data.

Fourth, where are the *fundamental underlying processes*? At present, transformational and charismatic leadership theories still seem to emerge from a "black box," but some progress has been made over the last five years in terms of examining the personality of such leaders, life experiences, moral perspective, problem-solving capabilities, emotions, attitudes and implicit models of leadership. Yet, the field has only begun to explore underlying personality characteristics and basic human interpersonal relationships that may foster transformational and charismatic leadership. We do not have, however, well articulated theories of what underlies transformational and charismatic leadership to enhance or inhibit their development; and empirical studies of such phenomena are basically non-existent. Clearly, more research is needed on these topics.

Fifth, where's the *context*? As with the culture-related debate, another key issue is whether transformational and charismatic leadership are context-free, context-specific, or context-dependent. Does the key driver of the emergence and success of transformational and charismatic leadership lie in strong vs. weak situations, or strong vs. weak leaders, or both? This harkens back to an old notion presented by Bass of great times (contexts or situations) vs. great leaders to explain leadership processes and outcomes. The field has only begun to explore these issues in the new genre realm. Future research on these topics is critical for the advancement of understanding transformational and charismatic leadership.

Sixth, where's the *distinction or interface* between transformational and charismatic leadership? Throughout this introduction, and at many points in this book, transformational and charismatic leadership are used interchangeably or as synonyms. Are they the same or different constructs? The "new genre" scholars argue that they are the same; the "transformational" scholars argue that they are different; the "charisma" scholars argue that they are addressing the important and unique component; and the "leadership" and other scholars are just confused! There are numerous theoretical, measurement, and levels of analysis issues to address here to begin to resolve this multi-faceted debate. Maybe, on "the road ahead," we'll discover that the more appropriate title for this book should have been, "Transformational vs. Charismatic Leadership: The Fork in the Road!" Or, to paraphrase Yogi Berra, when you come to a fork in the road take it, or at the very least, think that there is a potential fork.

Seventh, if we simply "fired" all followers, where would the *field of leadership* be? Obviously, there is a critical need to explore the dynamics between the leader and follower. In addition, we must begin to explore the leadership triangle in much greater depth, which includes the leader, the follower, and the context in which their interactions are embedded over time. Why not conduct a study where we examine every aspect of the follower and then predict the type of leader that he or she must have worked with over time? There needs to be much greater attention paid to what the followers bring to the leadership triangle, especially as we go more deeply into the identification processes associated with transformational and charismatic leadership.

Eighth, in what ways do leaders interact with followers in the dramatically *changing "e-economy"* that is emerging? Although there has been some work done on "e-leadership" by Kahai, Avolio, Sosik and their colleagues, this whole area of leadership and virtual interactions is wide open to exploration.

Regardless of where we travel, in closing, we wish to thank all the contributors to this volume for broadening and challenging our understanding of transformational and charismatic leadership. We believe that the future of theory, research, and method in this area is very bright indeed. The "new genre" of leadership is rapidly becoming the "established genre" of leadership, and we are delighted to be a small part of it. With that in mind, we welcome you, the readers, to join us on "the road ahead" to transformational and charismatic leadership, not only to walk with us, but to run ahead!

PART I:
TRANSFORMATIONAL LEADERSHIP

THE FULL-RANGE LEADERSHIP THEORY: THE WAY FORWARD

John Antonakis and Robert J. House

ABSTRACT

In this chapter, we briefly trace the history of the neo-charismatic movement and review Bass and Avolio's full-range leadership theory (FRLT). We present the FRLT as the flame bearer of the movement, and argue that it should be used as a platform to integrate similar leadership theories. We identify conditions that may moderate the factor structure of the FRLT, and review the validity of the Multifactor Leadership Questionnaire – the instrument underlying the FRLT. Furthermore, we identify theoretical deficiencies in the FRLT and propose the addition of a broad class of behaviors labeled instrumental leadership, *which, we argue, is distinct from transformational, transactional, and laissez-faire leadership. Finally, we discuss the utility of dispositional variables in predicting the emergence of leadership.*

INTRODUCTION

Hunt (1991) quoted an unknown author stating: "Once I was active in the leadership field. Then I left it for about ten years. When I returned it was as if I had been gone only ten minutes" (p. 1). Admittedly, leadership research was threatened in its early stages by seemingly inconsistent results and marginal advances in theory. Now, the voluminous amounts of disparate findings threaten leadership research in a different way. Are we leadership researchers cursed to chasing an ever-more elusive phenomenon? Where do we go from here?

Transformational and Charismatic Leadership, Volume 2, pages 3–33.
© 2002 Published by Elsevier Science Ltd.
ISBN: 0-7623-0962-8

The time has now come to place some of the scattered and fragmented dots into a picture, much like an impressionist painter uses seemingly disparate colors, dots, and strokes to produce a cohesive painting. We are ready to begin "painting" a new picture and frame a theory that has the potential to explain the leadership phenomenon, its consequences, and antecedent conditions. In 1985, Bass proposed a theory of leadership that, 17 years later, appears to be leading the way in what Bryman (1992) has characterized as the "new leadership" models. These approaches moved the leadership field forward from the trait approaches of the 1930s, the behavioral approaches of the 1950s, and contingency approaches of the 1970s, to account for the predominantly emotional and inspirational effects of leaders on followers. Bass's theory and the instrument that purports to measure it – the Multifactor Leadership Questionnaire (Avolio, Bass & Jung, 1995; Bass & Avolio, 1995) – are very popular in the leadership arena (Hunt, 1999; Yukl, 1998), and Bass's theory has played a salient role in shifting the leadership paradigm to what it is today (Conger, 1999; Hunt, 1999).

Given the wide attention that Bass's theory has received, social scientists and practitioners need to be informed whether:

(1) this theory has been justifiably propelled to the forefront of the leadership field;
(2) future research and training efforts that use this theory are justified; and
(3) this theory can be used as a foundation to integrate other theories of leadership.

The Bass (1985) theory, the precursor to the Bass and Avolio (Bass, 1998; Bass & Avolio, 1994, 1997) theory of transactional, transformational, and laissez-faire leadership, appears to be a solid platform from which to launch future research inquiries. We believe that this theory – currently referred to as the full-range leadership model – holds substantial promise to explain leadership and render its multidimensional nature into tangible and empirically measured behaviors useful for predicting leadership outcomes. Although attempts have been made in the past to present an integrative theory of leadership, we believe that our approach will be more successful than prior approaches, because the full-range leadership theory (FRLT)[1]:

(1) has achieved unprecedented acceptance in the management and leadership literatures;
(2) is supported by a large number of empirical findings; and
(3) has been developed in an integrative manner.

In this chapter, we focus on individual-level leadership by briefly reviewing the theories that predated the FRLT, and which are fundamental for its explanation.

Then, we discuss the components of the FRLT and examine its universality and the conditions under which it is moderated. Next, we review the validity of the Multifactor Leadership Questionnaire – the instrument underlying the FRLT. We link the FRLT to related theories of leadership, demonstrate why those approaches should be subsumed in the FRLT, and, based on these approaches, propose possible additions of factors to FRLT. Last, we link the FRLT to dispositional variables to explain the possible emergence of leadership.

THE CONCEPTION OF THE FRLT

The reason that the FRLT holds promise as an integrative theory of leadership is because it is built on, or can be explained by, theories, which, in their time, took a bold approach and questioned traditional notions of leadership. We have selected five theories that we feel are instrumental to explaining the FRLT and its overarching components. Theories that were not directly related to the FRLT in the manner specified above were not selected.

Weber (1924/1947) originally conceived of the notion of the charismatic leader, who arises in times of crisis. For Weber, charisma in leaders referred to special powers that leaders had that allowed them to undertake great feats that appealed to followers. Weber (1968) believed that followers of a charismatic leader willingly place their destiny in their leader's hands and support the leader's mission that may have arisen out of "enthusiasm, or of despair and hope" (p. 49). Weber (1968) argued that the core of charisma is an emotional appeal whose "attitude is revolutionary . . . transcends everything" (p. 24) and breaks with tradition. Finally, Weber (1968) stated that the charismatic effect of the leader may continue as artifacts of the organizational culture, but then wanes as the organization loses its emotional character, and is enveloped in the rational processes of the bureaucracy.

Following Weber, Downton (1973) proposed a theory of transactional, charismatic, and inspirational rebel political leadership. Downton referred to the term transactional as being an economic exchange process, and believed that the fulfillment of mutual transactional commitments forms the basis of trust. Positive transactions occur when followers receive rewards contingent on achieving desired outcomes, whereas negative transactions (i.e. punishment) are applied in response to followers' non-compliance. Downton argued that charismatic leaders have potent effects on followers because of their transcendental ideals and authority that facilitate the followers' identification with, and trust in, the leader, which is further augmented by inspirational leadership. The inspirational leader is persuasive and encourages followers to make sacrifices toward the identified ideals, gives followers a sense of purpose, and creates meaning for actions distinct from the charismatic process. Finally, Downton proposed that all sources of leadership, whether transactional, inspirational, or charismatic should be used in varying degrees.

Based on Weber's explication of the charismatic leader, House (1977) was the first to present an integrated theoretical framework and testable propositions to explain the behaviors of charismatic leaders. House also presented a detailed explanation of the psychological impact of charismatic leaders on followers; an element lacking from previous theories. House proposed that the basis for the charismatic appeal is the emotional interaction that occurs between followers and their leader. Depending on mission requirements, charismatic leaders arouse followers' power, affiliation, and achievement motives to accomplish the leader's vision. Followers in turn display affection and admiration for the leader, in whom their sentiments and ideals are expressed. According to House, charismatic leaders set high expectations for themselves and their followers, and show confidence that these expectations can be achieved. As a result, House argued that these leaders become role models and objects of identification for followers, who in turn emulate their leader's ideals and values, and are enthusiastically inspired and motivated. Charismatic leaders are also seen as courageous, because they challenge a status quo that is seen as undesirable. Finally, in focusing on the personal characteristics of charismatic leaders, House argued that they display a high degree of self-confidence, pro-social assertiveness, and moral conviction.

Similar to Downton's typology of charismatic and transactional leadership, Zaleznik (1977/1992) was the first to draw a distinction between the concepts of management and leadership. Zaleznik (1989) stated that managers typically follow rational, bureaucratized processes, are passive and reactionary, and use formal structures to control and influence behaviors of followers. Under these types of conditions, follower satisfaction is derived primarily from material rewards. Managers do not develop creativity, nor do they strive to cultivate emotional attachments with their followers lest predetermined role and task requirements be disturbed. In contrast, Zaleznik (1989) described leaders as eschewing the status quo, and providing vivid images and visions of the future to their followers. These leaders use emotional means and charisma to inspire followers, and shift their followers' values and belief systems. Leaders develop their followers emotionally and cognitively, and emphasize moral conviction in their mission. As a consequence, followers identify with, and idealize, these types of leaders.

Using an approach comparable with that of Downton (1973) and Zaleznik (1977/1992), Burns (1978) proposed that the leader-follower interaction could be either:

(1) transactional, which entailed a relationship based on the exchange of valued items, whether political, economic or emotional; or
(2) transforming where the motivation, morality, and ethical aspirations of the leader and followers are raised.

According to Burns, transforming leadership – focused on transcendent and far-reaching goals – has a greater effect on followers and collectives than does transactional leadership, which in turn is focused on promoting self-interest and is thus limited in scope and impact. Transforming leaders create follower awareness of moral and ethical implications and convince them to transcend their self-interest for that of the greater good.

INTEGRATION OF THE THEORIES

As is evident, a striking dichotomy is articulated in the above theories: the grouping of the *charismatic-transforming-leadership* approach, vs. the *bureaucratic-transactional-management* approach. The former focuses on vision, ideals, values, risk, change, and charismatic leadership, and the latter on control, contracts, rationality, norms, conservatism, and stability. An elevation and arousal of motives, ideals, and values characterizes the charismatic-transforming-leadership approach, whereas exchanges and self-interest characterize the bureaucratic-transactional-management approach. This schism could be viewed from several perspectives, the most important of which deals with moral and ethical conviction. Morals and ethics were central to Burn's (1978) theory, and evident too in House's (1977) and Zaleznik's (1989) frameworks. Morals and ethics, and their implications to *ideals* and *values*, are in essence what effects the decisions individuals make. Ideals and values guide how priorities to interpersonal and organizational tasks are assigned, and thus ultimately govern behavioral outcomes. Theoretically, if those in power care about their followers – and understand the impact of their actions on the collective and other social systems – they adopt ideals that arouse motives of followers, thus facilitating the leader's charismatic appeal. Those individuals are *transforming* leaders, and lead followers that are intrinsically motivated and intimately attached to the leader's mission. Leaders that do not use such means are left to influence their followers through rewards and sanctions. They are *transactional* leaders who have a limited influence on higher-order motives of followers.

The Distinction Between Revolutionary and Organizational Charisma

Before introducing the FRLT, we first distinguish "revolutionary" charisma conceived by Weber (1924/1947) from "organizational" charisma conceived by the neo-charismatic theorists. As noted by Beyer (1999), current views of charisma have departed from Weber's perspective, and many theorists (e.g. Bass, 1985; Conger & Kanungo, 1998; Sashkin, 1988) view charisma in a "tame" way. House (1999) referred to the above distinction as the Weberian (sociological) vs. the organizational (behavioral) view. As noted by Shamir (1999), the taming of charisma has advantages in that it can be found and studied in a variety of settings. Thus, following Bass (1999), Conger and Kanungo (1998), and Sashkin (1988), our thinking of charisma is directed toward organizational leadership, and leaders who use symbolic means to motivate followers, are sensitive to follower needs, and in whom followers can express their ideals. Charismatic leaders are viewed as strong and confident based on attributions that followers make of these leaders. Followers respect and trust these leaders, who in turn arouse follower motives to achieve transcendent ideals. Theoretically, these types of leaders display moral conviction and are idealized and highly respected by followers. This perspective contrasts with the "take-it-or-leave-it" radical perspective of revolutionary leaders, who are usually idolized by followers who accept the leader or despised by those who do not believe in the leader's mission.

THE BIRTH OF THE FRLT

Bass's (1985) theory is largely built on the above approaches. The central core of his theory is the ideals of leaders, which, following House (1977), is that which ignites charisma. We present an extension of Bass's theory, which emanated from work of Bass and Avolio (1994, 1997), as presented in Bass (1998) and Avolio (1999). This revised theory includes the leader's ethical and moral orientation as the core of *authentic transformational leadership*. Bass (1998) described personalized and self-aggrandizing leaders who are ethically and morally empty as *pseudo-transformational* and *inauthentic*.

Extending Burn's (1978) theory, and using the term *transformational* instead of transforming, Bass (1985) proposed an integrative theory of organizational leadership. For Bass, transformational leaders act as agents of change by arousing and transforming followers' attitudes, beliefs, and motives from a lower to a higher level of arousal. They provide vision, develop emotional relationships with followers and make them aware of, and believe in, superordinate goals that go beyond self-interest. Transactional leaders clarify role and tasks requirements, and provide followers positive and negative rewards contingent on successful performance.

However, in contrast to Burns, Bass argued that transactional leadership is an essential prerequisite to effective leadership, and that leaders need to display both transformational and transactional behaviors to certain degrees. Accordingly, transformational leadership yields superior performance when augmenting transactional leadership, referred to as the "augmentation hypothesis" by Bass. This proposition refers to the increase in effect when transformational leadership is added to transactional leadership in predicting outcomes, and has been empirically supported (e.g. Bycio et al., 1995; Geyer & Steyrer, 1998; Hater & Bass, 1988; Waldman, Bass & Yammarino, 1990). Transactional leadership is typical of management, whereby objectives are set and outcomes monitored to ensure that resources yield intended outcomes. Bass predicted that this method of individual influence is effective, but limited, and stated that transformational leadership is needed to take the process beyond mere goal attainment, to a higher meaning and purpose. This assertion remains to be tested empirically.

Below, we present Bass and Avolio's (1994, 1997) FRLT, which evolved from Bass's (1985) transactional/transformational theory, and which reflects Bass (1998) and Avolio's (1999) current thinking. The updated theory, and the way it has been explicated and measured (Avolio et al., 1995; Bass & Avolio, 1995, 1997) resulted in a broader array of factors, from the six factors of the original 1985 theory. According to Bass (1998), and Bass and Avolio (1995, 1997), the FRLT comprises nine factors reflecting three broad classes of behavior of transformational, transactional, and laissez-faire leadership. Transformational leadership comprises the following five factors:

(1) *Idealized influence (attributed),* or attributed charisma, refers to follower attributions about the leader as a result of how they perceive the leader's power, confidence, and transcendent ideals. This is the emotional component of leadership, which theoretically shifts follower self-interest toward the interest of the greater good.
(2) *Idealized influence (behaviors),* or behavioral charisma, refers to specific leader behaviors that reflect the leaders' values and beliefs, their sense of mission and purpose, and their ethical and moral orientation.
(3) *Inspirational motivation* refers to leaders who inspire and motivate followers to reach ambitious goals that may have previously seemed unreachable, by raising followers' expectations, and communicating confidence that followers can achieve ambitious goals, thus creating a

self-fulfilling prophecy (i.e. a *Pygmalion effect*). Refer to Eden's chapter (this volume) for further details on Pygmalion Leadership.

(4) *Intellectual stimulation* refers to how leaders question the status quo, appeal to followers' intellect to make them question their assumptions, and invite innovative and creative solutions to problems.

(5) *Individualized consideration* refers to leaders who provide customized socio-emotional support to followers, while developing and empowering them. This outcome is achieved by coaching and counseling followers, maintaining frequent contact with them, and helping them to self-actualize.

Transactional leadership comprises the following three factors:

(1) *Contingent reward* leadership is based on economic and emotional exchanges, by clarifying role requirements, and rewarding and praising desired outcomes. Contingent reward leadership is a constructive transaction and is reasonably effective in motivating followers, but to a lesser degree than is transformational leadership.

(2) *Management-by-exception active* is a negative transaction, because the leader monitors deviations from norms and provides corrective action. It is similar to contingent reward in terms of focusing on outcomes; however, in this case, the leader actively watches for, and acts on, mistakes or errors.

(3) *Management-by-exception passive* is similar to management-by-exception active; however, passive leaders wait until deviations occur before intervening.

Finally, to fully account for all potential full-range leadership behaviors, a scale of non-leadership called *laissez-faire leadership* was added to indicate an absence of leadership (i.e. a non-transaction). These types of leaders avoid taking positions or making decisions, and abdicate their authority. After management-by-exception passive, this factor is the most inactive form of leadership.

Relation of FRLT to Leadership Outcomes

Based on empirical evidence and theoretical reasoning (Avolio et al., 1995; Bass & Avolio, 1993), Bass (1998) stated that the leadership scales of the FRLT are hierarchically related to outcomes of leadership in the following way: the transformational constructs and contingent reward are positive predictors of effectiveness, and the passive constructs are negative predictors. There is substantial and consistent support for this hierarchy of effects of leader behaviors based on the results of numerous studies (a small sample of these studies includes Avolio et al., 1999b; Barling, Weber & Kelloway, 1996; Coad & Berry, 1998; Druskat, 1994; Geyer & Steyrer, 1998; Howell & Avolio, 1993; Sosik, Kahai & Avolio, 1998; Yammarino, Dubinsky, Comer & Jolson, 1997).

According to Avolio (1999) and Bass (1998), management-by-exception active has been found to be a weak positive predictor in some instances, and a zero or negative predictor in other instances. Empirical evidence provided by Avolio et al. (1995) and Lowe et al. (1996) supports this proposition. Avolio and Bass argued that in situations where risk is prevalent, management-by-exception might be necessary to ensure successful outcomes. In these types of situations, the role of the leader is to ensure that predetermined standards are met, by being actively vigilant for erroneous actions that may lead to detrimental outcomes.

The passive-avoidant factors of the FRLT have been found to be ineffective. According to Bass (1998), laissez-faire leadership is the most inactive form of leadership, and typically the most ineffective. Management-by-exception passive, although required in some situations (e.g. when supervising a large amount of followers), has generally been found to be ineffective and, when overused, can create anxiety, hostility or stress in followers (Bass, 1998). Thus, Bass and Avolio (1997) argued that leaders should incorporate the passive-avoidant behaviors in their repertoire, as long as the active components – transformational and contingent reward leadership – are the most dominant behaviors.

In other words, leaders should display transformational behaviors most often, then contingent reward leadership, then management-by-exception active, then management-by-exception passive, and seldom, if ever, laissez-faire leadership. This hierarchical framework has also found support in a meta-analysis by Lowe et al. (1996), who stated that the relation of transformational leadership was greater to outcome measures, whether organizationally or subjectively determined, as compared with transactional leadership. Refer to Dumdum, Lowe and Avolio's chapter (this volume) for current meta-analytic results.

The Universality of the FRLT

Bass (1996, 1997) stated that the FRLT is universal and that situational variables, to some extent, play a role in determining the type of leadership that emerges. Bass (1998) argued further that the hierarchical relation of the full-range constructs remain stable irrespective of situational variables. This proposition is supported by the studies that we listed above relating the FRLT to outcomes. These studies reflected a variety of conditions and environmental settings. The literature includes many other studies and dozens of doctoral dissertations that support the notion that transformational leadership is more positively associated with organizational effectiveness and follower satisfaction than is transactional or non-leadership.

The issue of the universality of the FRLT previously caused confusion in the leadership literature. We refer to the factor structure of the Multifactor Leadership Questionnaire that with the exception of Avolio et al. (1995) and Bass and Avolio (1997) could not be validated in its entirety by other researchers, but whose factor structure has emerged in various combinations. According to Antonakis (2001), situational variables moderate the inter-factor relations of the FRLT and also the manner in which the factors are related to outcomes of leadership. However, *the full nine-factor model is still valid in various conditions.* Lowe et al. (1996) originally raised a similar point in a meta-analysis of 39 studies and demonstrated that the effect sizes of the MLQ factors are moderated by leader-level and type of organization. Moderators are variables that have an impact on the strength of the independent variables, and "can and integrate seemingly irreconcilable theoretical positions" (Baron & Kenny, 1986, p. 1173). Zaccaro and Klimoski (2001) stressed that some of the confusion in the leadership literature is because of a lack of understanding of contextual boundaries of leadership. Following a similar argument, Antonakis noted that leaders display different sets of behaviors as a function of environmental conditions, and tentatively concluded that transformational leadership may be consistently related to outcome measures across a vast array of conditions, as proposed by Bass (1998).

After synthesizing the data of independent studies into homogenous groups using structural-equation modeling, Antonakis (2001) confirmed the validity of the nine factors comprising the FRLT. This procedure, referred to as a multisample analysis (see Jöreskog, 1971), can be used to determine whether parameter estimates are invariant within samples. Within each homogenous group, the covariances between the factors, and the loadings of the latent and residual variables on the manifest variables, were set to equality. This procedure is referred to as strict factorial invariance (Byrne, 1994) and provides the most conservative estimates for a model's invariance across data sets.

When using all the data sets, the nine-factor model indicated a moderate fit, but was, however, not the best representative of the data (e.g. $\chi^2(684, n = 6,525) = 5437.38$, $p < 0.01$; Normed Fit Index (NFI) = 0.895; Incremental Fit Index (IFI) = 0.907; Root Mean Square Error of Approximation (RMSEA) = 0.033; Akaike Information Criteria (AIC) = 5869.379; Expected Cross-Validation Index (ECVI) = 0.902). The fit indices for an eight-factor model, which included passive management-by-exception and laissez-faire leadership into one first-order factor, indicated a better fit (e.g. $\chi^2(652, n = 6,525) = 5117.64$, $p < 0.01$; NFI = 0.901; IFI = 0.912; RMSEA = 0.032; AIC = 5613.643; ECVI = 0.863). Because the models were not hierarchically related, as indicated by the lower AIC and ECVI values, the eight-factor model was deemed to fit the data better. Several other fit indices also indicated a better fit for the eight-factor model.

When grouping the data into homogenous sets, the nine-factor model consistently fitted the data better than eight competing models that were tested based on the propositions and previous results in the literature. For instance, in the high risk/unstable conditions data set, the results of the nine-factor model indicated a good fit (e.g. $\chi^2(36, n = 502) = 75.24$, $p < 0.01$; NFI = 0.984; IFI = 0.992; RMSEA = 0.047; AIC = 183.244; ECVI = 0.366). The eight-factor model, which was the second-best fitting model indicated a worse fit (e.g. $\chi^2(41, n = 502) = 93.85$, $p < 0.01$; NFI = 0.980; IFI = 0.989; RMSEA = 0.051; AIC = 191.847; ECVI = 0.384). When non-homogenous samples were added to moderator groups, the fit indices worsened, which provided further evidence for the moderator categories. Similar results were reported in other moderating conditions, which included various environmental and organizational settings, leader gender, and the hierarchical level of the leader. Thus, moderating conditions may affect the factor structure of the FRLT as well as the hierarchical relation of the constructs to outcome variables. Yet, the nine-factor model does receive relatively strong support.

Does Organizational Context Matter?

Bass (1998) – in following the Weberian tradition – surmised that in contrast to transactional leadership, transformational leadership is *more likely* to emerge in times of crises or periods of major turbulence. Theoretically, this is because, in those conditions, a leader can seize the opportunity to identify the deficiencies of the status quo, and promote a future state that will appeal to followers. Leaders allay follower fears in crisis conditions. Thus, it is more likely that transformational leadership will emerge in such conditions. Bass also stated that transactional leadership is more likely to emerge in stable environments, the hypothesis here being that the routine tasks and functions of the bureaucracy stifle the emergence of transformational leadership. Furthermore, Bass stated that transformational leaders are more likely to emerge in organic types of organizations that are not highly structured and do not have routine tasks and functions, again, in contrast to transactional leaders who prevail in steady environmental sets.

We believe, however, that crises and organic environments are sufficient but not necessary conditions for transformational leadership to emerge. The majority of empirical data support the proposition that the transformational constructs are related to outcome measures in a variety of environmental conditions, as do theoretical propositions advanced by Etzioni (1961), Shamir and Howell (1999), and Shils (1965). Conger and Kanungo (1998) also argued that crisis, although an important antecedent to charisma does not *necessarily* trigger charisma, and that a leader's identification of opportunities to change the status quo, whether crisis-induced or not, is charisma's catalyst. House (1977) acknowledged that the ideals and values of a leader, and not necessarily environmental turbulence, are catalysts to the charismatic effect. Furthermore, as indicated by the results of Gasper's (1992) meta-analysis, the correlations of transformational leadership with follower measures of effectiveness, satisfaction, and extra effort were higher in military (e.g. 0.76, 0.71, and 0.88) than in civilian organizations (e.g. 0.27, 0.22, and 0.32) (Bass, 1998).

Following House's (1977) propositions that the emergence and effectiveness of charismatic leaders occur most frequently under conditions where the role of followers includes moral involvement, we presume that in military conditions where patriotism and a sense of duty prevail, leaders have more opportunities to engage followers in value-based goals. Moreover, given the large amount of contact that leaders and followers have in military organizations, we would expect that leaders have more opportunities to influence followers. Also, because of the frequency of crisis conditions in the military settings (e.g. combat, combat training, etc.), it is likely that followers may have more opportunity to identify with leaders that communicate transcendent ideals and show confidence in their own and their followers' abilities.

House, Spangler and Woycke (1991), reported that crises have fostered the rise of charisma among U.S. presidents. Waldman, Ramirez, House and Puranam (2000) reported a positive relation between CEO charisma and financial performance under conditions of uncertainty over a 4-year period of time. In post-hoc analyses, Waldman et al. speculated that charisma may be negatively related to performance under conditions of certainty, presumably because, in these conditions, the change that charisma may invoke is unnecessary, and may even cause confusion. The results of Waldman et al. suggest that the relationship of charisma to performance measures of high-level leaders may be moderated by environmental context. These findings need to be replicated in future research before any definitive conclusions can be drawn.

Similar to the arguments advanced above about the universality of charisma, bureaucracies are not necessary conditions for the emergence of transactional leadership. In fact, one could argue that in those conditions, transformational leadership may well emerge, especially if followers perceive the bureaucratic conditions as unfavorable. Lowe et al. (1996) showed the existence of transformational leadership to be more prevalent in public – and hence bureaucratic – than in private organizations. Antonakis (2001) also reported that transformational leadership was prevalent in bureaucracies, and that the relations of the transformational factors to leader outcomes were positive, whereas the relations of corrective transactional, and laissez-faire leadership to outcome measures were negative. These findings suggest that transformational leadership may serve to offset the constraining conditions of bureaucratic organizations. This possibility warrants further investigation.

Does Gender Matter?

There is some support for differences in the manner that leaders operate as a function of gender (e.g. Bass, Avolio & Atwater, 1996; Carless, 1998a; Druskat, 1994; Eagly & Johannesen-Schmidt, in press). Typically, these studies show men to use transactional leadership more frequently than do women, who in turn used transformational leadership, especially individualized consideration, more frequently than do men. The differences that were reported could be because women are socialized to display nurturing and developmental behaviors, which are essential elements of transformational leadership (Bass, 1998; Bass et al., 1996; Eagly & Johannesen-Schmidt, in press).

Furthermore, Eagly and Johannesen-Schmidt argued that women are more transformational than are men, because women may have to meet higher standards of performance than do men, to enable them to establish and maintain their legitimacy as leaders. Maher (1997) stated that potential gender differences may not be universal and could be attributable to situational or contextual variables. Antonakis (2001), who reported a potential gender effect that stated that it could be a function of situational variables, given that the samples he analyzed were from situational conditions that traditionally appealed to a specific gender. Thus, it is possible that gender, context, or a gender-context interaction causes differences in leadership styles of men and women, or how those leaders are perceived by their followers.

Does National Culture Matter?

Bass (1996, 1997) proposed that the concept of leadership, based on his theory, is universal regardless of national culture constraints. Although leadership behaviors may vary as a function of national culture (Bjerke, 1999; Hofstede, 1991), leadership as a phenomenon may be universal across cultures (Dorfman, Howell, Hibino, Lee, Tate & Bautista, 1997; Gibson & Marcoulides, 1995). In support of Bass's contentions, Den Hartog, House, Hanges, Ruiz-Quintanilla, and Dorfmann (1999) confirmed that elements of transformational and charismatic leadership were universally reported as highly effective across 62 cultures.

An issue that we believe is central in possibly explaining differences in leadership styles across cultures may be how leaders differentially enact their full-range behaviors across cultures. Bass (1998) stated that leaders can display the full range of leadership behaviors in a directive or participative manner. We thus propose that the FRLT may be universal, but the manner in which leaders enact the full-range of leader behaviors will vary. For example, leaders could be individually considerate by simply paying attention to followers' needs and including followers' wishes in developmental plans (i.e. a participative approach). In other cultures, leaders may make all the decisions and build follower developmental plans irrespective of what followers may want (i.e. a directive approach). The leader, however, is displaying individualized consideration in both situations.

Regarding the link between leadership and culture, Meade (1967) determined that directive leadership is more related to follower performance than is participative leadership in countries that have prevalent authoritarian social structures. Hofstede (1991) argued that leadership style varies as a function of culture, as expressed in his cultural dimensions. Theoretically, leadership may be affected by the following Hofstede variables:

(1) power distance (i.e. the acceptance of unequal power differentials and how they are distributed in society);
(2) uncertainty avoidance (i.e. the degree to which people can cope with an uncertain future); and
(3) individualism vs. collectivism (i.e. the degree to which individuals are motivated by self-interest or that of the collective).

Thus, it can be inferred that in high power-distance societies, a directive leadership style may be supported. This proposition has found support in Hofstede's speculations, and in empirical results (e.g. Bochner & Hesketh, 1994; Offermann & Hellmann, 1997; Pavett & Morris, 1995).

In collectivist cultures, Triandis (1993) argued that a charismatic-type leader who shows concern for the values of the collectivity would be supported. Bass also stated that a collectivist society would more likely support a transformational leader than would individualist societies; however, this does not preclude the emergence of transformational leadership in individualist societies. The claim that transformational leaders can emerge more readily in collectivist societies results from the proposition that it may be easier to promote a collective vision in such cultures, because collective goals are highly valued in those cultures. A leader in a collectivist (and high power-distance) society may also use management-by-exception often to maintain social stability. Using corrective transactional leadership may be necessary, because group norms must be respected and maintained (Hofstede, 1991). For example, Singer and Singer (1990) reported that transformational and transactional leadership were used equally in Chinese organizations and that, in a Taiwanese sample, management-by-exception was displayed most frequently; however, the difference in frequency of transactional and transformational leader behaviors was non-significant. Furthermore, Singer and Singer showed that Taiwanese employees actually preferred transformational over transactional leadership. Thus, it is likely that culture may operate as a moderator on the patterns of relationships of the FRLT factors.

Do Followers and Tasks Matter?
Based on the propositions of the path-goal theory of leadership, House (1971) argued that leaders function as catalysts to motivate followers by helping them achieve work-related tasks. This may be valid for the manner in which contingent reward leadership operates, which is somewhat related to House's path-goal theory. Furthermore, individualized consideration is by nature contingency-based, that is, leaders pay attention to the individual needs of followers, coach and mentor them as required, and help them develop their potential. Similarly, all other factors of the FRLT are to a degree a function of the individual needs of followers and environmental conditions in general, and leaders must infer or "read" these conditions and act accordingly to ensure desirable outcomes (cf. Kenny & Zaccaro, 1983; Zaccaro, Foti & Kenny, 1991). Effective leaders most likely customize their behaviors by anticipating and reacting to follower needs and other environmental contingencies, and facilitate the path to follower goals. Goal facilitation, however, appears to be missing from the FRLT. This proposition is discussed later in our attempt to expand the FRLT.

In conclusion, Shamir and Howell (1999) noted, "charismatic leadership principles and processes potentially apply across a wide variety of situations; however, there are situations in which they apply more than in others" (p. 258). This reflects our argument for the moderator propositions above that the FRLT is likely to be universal and hierarchically related to leader outcomes, but that the combinations of behaviors that leaders use in various conditions will vary somewhat to match those conditions. Furthermore, the strength of the relation of leader behaviors to outcomes may also vary as a function of contextual conditions (c.f., Antonakis, 2001; Gasper, 1992; Jung & Avolio, 1999; Waldman et al., 2000).

Next, we examine the validity of the instrument that purports to measure the FRLT, the MLQ5X.

The Multifactor Leadership Questionnaire (MLQ)

The MLQ has come a long way since being introduced by Bass in 1985. As a result of a decade of research, the latest version of the MLQ – the MLQ5X (Bass & Avolio, 1995) – is the best-validated instrument to represent the FRLT. Although it is also the most popular instrument for measuring transformational leadership, previous versions have not escaped criticism (Hunt, 1999; Yukl, 1998). For example, earlier versions of the MLQ bundled behaviors and attributions in the charisma scale, and also leadership behaviors with outcomes (Hunt, 1991; Yukl, 1998). Yukl argued further that the instrument lacked discriminant validity.

Many of these criticisms have been rebutted or addressed by Bass and Avolio (1993), and have been taken into account in the development of the MLQ5X (Avolio et al., 1995). Indeed, using confirmatory methods and pooled samples of data ($n = 1,394$), Avolio et al. demonstrated that the MLQ5X is reliable and valid, and offered evidence for its discriminant validity using the full nine-factor model. Similar validation results have been reported in Bass and Avolio (1997) using pooled samples of data ($n = 1,490$). Researchers, though, using different versions of the MLQ in various organizational and national culture settings have presented varied factor structures of the theory (e.g. Avolio, Bass & Jung, 1999a; Avolio et al., 1999b; Bycio et al., 1995; Carless, 1998b; Den Hartog et al., 1997; Druskat, 1994; Geyer & Steyrer, 1998). Most of these studies either tested more limited models or failed to validate the nine-factor MLQ model, although various combinations of the factors did emerge.

According to Antonakis (2001), most studies testing the factor-structure of the MLQ were limited in that moderating conditions were not considered in sampling and grouping considerations. This proposition is based on the assumption that the process of leadership is affected by the context in which it is embedded. In other words, the factor structure of the MLQ varies across settings, which therefore influences the pattern of relationships among the constructs. Some of these studies are also limited to the extent that they did not include all of the MLQ scales, or they modified certain items.

Baron and Kenny (1986) noted that moderators might affect the way a relation holds in different subpopulations, which is precisely what Antonakis discovered. Furthermore, many studies used exploratory techniques for construct validation where, clearly, confirmatory techniques would be more suitable, especially when testing latent variables (Bollen, 1989). In support of the contextual hypothesis, and as mentioned previously, Antonakis affirmed that the nine-factor model consistently represented the data better in homogenous conditions than eight other competing models. Thus, the nine-factor model was found to be invariant – a very strong test for the construct validity of a psychometric instrument – within homogenous conditions, suggesting that the FRLT is context-sensitive, but universal across conditions.

The latest evidence suggests that the MLQ5X is valid and reliable, and adequately gauges the FRLT. Although we believe that to be the case, as social scientists, we still view the MLQ5X and the FRLT with some skepticism, as we do any measurement instrument and theoretical model. This is because the MLQ5X does not capture all possible leadership behaviors, and because other models could disconfirm the nine-factor model suggested by the FRLT. We believe that this is not merely possible, but highly likely, and to move the field forward, it is necessary to explore these possibilities. To look over the current peaks of our knowledge, we must stand on sturdy theoretical scaffolding. We believe that this scaffolding is the FRLT, to which other theories of leadership should be compared and attached, so that lacunae in the FRLT are identified and filled. In this way, a more complete full-range theory will emerge.

EXTENDING THE FRLT

In this section, we briefly review three neo-charismatic-type theories that are well regarded in the leadership domain, to determine whether any of their factors can fill a deficiency in the FRLT. We also refer to House's path-goal theory, and similar theories, to advance theoretical propositions that reflect a general class of leader behavior we call *instrumental leadership*.

As in the introductory review, we are purposely not casting our nets wide. To consolidate and move the new leadership arena forward, we are required first to look within, so that in the future, a more general theory of leadership is developed from the FRLT. The theories we review generally provide support for the factors of FRLT, but also identify gaps that potentially explain an aspect of leadership that may not be included in the FRLT. In proposing additional constructs to the FRLT, we are admittedly rather conservative for two reasons.

First, we strive to attain theoretical parsimony. Adding factors to an established model may not be of practical value unless these new factors are theoretically different and account for additional unique variance in dependent variables. We thus have erred on the side of caution and wait for future empirical results before we attempt to extend the FRLT further.

Second, the FRLT has passed some major empirical tests. Proposing the addition of factors that may be already captured by the MLQ directly or indirectly may be deleterious to the theory's validity. As social scientists, however, we are skeptical of any theory that purports to represent reality, as we do not know if another theory can better gauge this reality; nor are we aware of all possible constructs that represent leadership. The existence of a more inclusive theory is dependent on expanding the FRLT, so in this sense, we were obliged to theorize with our assumptions suspended. We review the three theories below chronologically.

Conger and Kanungo (1988, 1998) proposed a theory of charismatic leadership to explain the legitimization of a leader through an attributional process based on the perceptions that followers have of the leader's behaviors. Conger and Kanungo (1998) proposed that individuals are validated as leaders by their followers through a three-stage behavioral process. First, effective charismatic leaders assess the status quo to determine the needs of followers, evaluate the resources that are available within the constituency, and articulate a compelling argument to arouse follower interest. Second, leaders articulate a vision of the future that inspires follower action to achieve the vision. The idealized vision creates follower identification and affection for the leader, because the vision embodies a future state of affairs that is valued by followers.

Third, leaders create an aura of confidence and competence by demonstrating conviction that the mission is achievable. This three-stage process is hypothesized to engender high trust in the leader, and follower performance that enables the organization to reach its goals. According to Conger and Kanungo (1998), the aforementioned processes comprise five factors. These five factors are compared with the nine factors of the FRLT in Table 1. Conceptually, the propositions of the Conger and Kanungo (1998) theory are highly congruent with those of the FRLT – as indicated in Table 1 – and the FRLT could possibly benefit from the addition of the sensitivity to the environment factor (which we call environmental monitoring), because it is not addressed by any of the FRLT factors.

House and Shamir (1993) proposed an integrative theory of leadership based on Shamir, House, and Arthur's (1993) propositions that charismatic leaders use their vision and mission as a platform to implicate the self-concept of followers. In this way, leaders have exceptional effects on followers who are motivated by increased levels of self-esteem, self-worth, self-efficacy, and identification with the leader. Shamir et al. stated that these exceptional leaders affect followers as a result of motivational mechanisms that are induced by the leader's behaviors. These behaviors include providing an ideological explanation for action, emphasizing a collective purpose, referring to historical accounts related to ideals, referring to the self-worth and efficacy of followers,

Table 1. Comparison of FRLT Factors with Factors of Three Competing Models.

Factor of Other Models	FRLT Factors	IIA	IIB	IM	IS	IC	CR	MBEA	MBEP	LF
Formulation and articulation of a strategic vision (CK)			X	X						
Sensitivity to the environment (CK)										
Sensitivity to member needs (CK)						X				
Personal risk (CK)		X								
Unconventional behavior (CK)		X			X					
Visionary behavior (HS)			X	X						
Positive self-presentation (HS)		X								
Empowering Behaviors (HS)				X		X				
Calculated risk taking and self-sacrificial behavior (HS)		X								
Adaptive behavior (HS)										
Strategic organizational philosophy (S)										
Tactical policies and programs (S)										
Focusing attention (S)			X	X						
Communicating personally (S)			X	X		X				
Demonstrating trustworthiness (S)		X		X						
Displaying respect (S)		X				X				
Taking risks (S)		X								

Note: CK = Conger and Kanungo (1998) model; HR = House and Shamir (1993) model; S = Sashkin's (1988) model; IIA = idealized influence attributed; IIB = idealized influence behavior; IM = inspirational motivation; IS = intellectual stimulation; IC = individualized consideration; CR = contingent reward; MBEA = management-by-exception active; MBEP = management-by-exception passive; LF = laissez-faire leadership; X = FRLT factors that theoretically correspond with factors of other models.

and expressing high performance expectations of followers and confidence that they are capable of fulfilling the mission. As a result of the leader's behavior, the motivational mechanisms trigger the self-concept effects that lead to personal commitment to the leader's mission, self-sacrificial behavior, organizational citizenship, and task meaningfulness.

In identifying patterns and gaps in the theoretical frameworks they reviewed, House and Shamir proposed a seven-factor model of leadership to account for the above leader behaviors. These factors are listed in Table 1 and are compared with the factors of the FRLT. As is evident from Table 1, these factors largely overlap with the FRLT factors apart from adaptive behavior – borrowed from Conger and Kanungo's (1998) theory – which reflects the environmental monitoring factor discussed earlier.

Sashkin's (1988) theoretical framework focused on the key components of visionary leadership in higher-level leaders. Sashkin proposed that leaders have a high need for socialized power (McClelland, 1985) and tacit knowledge of what vision to project as a function of environmental conditions. That is, by virtue of their cognitive skills, they are able to take advantage of situational conditions, and seek opportunities to create or adapt to the future. Sashkin stated that visionary leaders are able to express their vision and expand it to a broader context. Visionary leaders carve their vision into operational components (i.e. strategic and tactical) that can be translated into action at all organizational levels. As demonstrated in Table 1, the factors underlying Sashkin's model are conceptually comparable with the FRLT, except for the propositions regarding the strategic functions of leaders.

We believe that an addition of a broad class of leader behavior, referred to as *instrumental leadership*, could be included in the FRLT. Instrumental leadership is distinct from transformational, transactional, and laissez-faire leadership. Instrumental leadership does not engage followers in ideals-based behavior or in fulfilling transactional obligations. The conception of instrumental leadership is based, in part, on Nadler and Tushman's (1990) explication of leader behaviors that go beyond charismatic (or transformational) leadership, and on propositions specified by Bowers and Seashore (1966), House (1971), Sashkin (1988), and Antonakis (2001). We believe that instrumental leadership consists of two subclasses of behaviors. The first is *strategic leadership* (consisting of environmental monitoring, and strategy formulation and implementation) – which influences organizational performance indirectly though actions and decisions taken by the leader and his or her followers. The second subclass of instrumental leadership is *follower work facilitation* (path-goal facilitation, and outcome monitoring) – which influences follower performance achievement directly. Refer to Antonakis and House

(2001) for the propositions and implications underlying instrumental leadership.

DISPOSITIONAL VARIABLES AND THE FRLT

Zaccaro et al. (1991) – staunch defenders of linking dispositional variables to leadership – noted "Trait explanations of leader emergence are generally regarded with little esteem" (p. 308). According to Lord, De Vader, and Alliger (1986), and House and Aditya (1997), this negative view has been prompted in part by Stogdill's (1948) review of the trait literature. They noted that, although Stogdill's review did highlight some inconsistencies, it was largely misunderstood, and his comments about conflicting findings misinterpreted. House and Aditya stated further that Stogdill did not consider moderating conditions that may have caused some of the inconsistent findings. Contrary to popular belief among scholars, Stogdill called for further research on the interaction of traits and contextual variables, and *did not* call for a moratorium on the study of traits. Other flaws in the pioneering personality literature could be attributed to a lack of theory-driven research designs, ill-developed test measures, ignorance of situational effects, failure to differentiate between management and leadership, and mixing of sample units (House & Baetz, 1979; House & Aditya, 1997).

As a consequence of the above, House and his associates (e.g. House, 1988, 1996; House & Howell, 1992; House, Shane & Herold, 1996; Howell, 1988) have made repeated calls for the continuation of personality-based approaches to studying leadership. Indeed, House et al. (1996) asserted that "the predictive validity of [personality] dispositions is too strong to dismiss and that this evidence represents a compelling case for incorporating dispositional arguments and evidence into theories of behavior in organizations" (p. 204). Personality has been linked to many behavioral outcomes. As summarized by Spangler, House, and Palrecha (2001), personality-based approaches to studying leadership appear to be useful, and interest in the relation of dispositional variables to leadership continues. In establishing the usefulness of this research, House et al. (1991) mentioned, "effective leaders may be identifiable at a relatively early age on the basis of their personality profile" (p. 391).

House and his colleagues have established a line of research based on individual motives that appear to be reliably associated with the emergence of leadership – particularly charismatic leadership – as established by McClelland (1975, 1976), and his explication of the leadership motive pattern (LMP). Winter, John, Stewart, Klohnen, and Duncan (1998) defined motives as referring to individuals' "wishes and desires – states of affairs that they would like to bring about . . . or, in the case of avoidance motives, states of affairs that they would like to prevent" (p. 231). Winter et al. stated that motives may be held implicitly (i.e. not subject to introspection) or may be held explicitly (i.e. are self-attributed).

As such, it may be possible to tap into explicit motives through self-reports, but since implicit motives are held subconsciously, they can only be measured indirectly. Implicit motives and explicit motives seldom correlate with each other. The former appear to predict long-term behavior, and the latter short-term behavior (McClelland, Koestner & Weinberger, 1989). Similarly, Argyris (1994) illustrated the incongruence between espoused (i.e. self-attributed values) and actual values (i.e. implicit values that guide behavior). Because motives "drive, direct and select behavior" (McClelland, 1980, p. 13), and are held implicitly, they are instrumental in determining what choices individuals make in their daily lives. McClelland (1975) proposed three types of individual motives that affect human behavior.

Need for power. For McClelland (1975), need for power influences individuals to have an impact on others and systems. McClelland argued that individuals with a high need for power can express this need by being leaders. The way power is enacted depends on whether a leader conceives of power as an instrument to further his or her goals, or as an instrument to serve others. This depends on the leader's responsibility disposition (Winter & Barenbaum, 1985). Individuals who have a strong responsibility disposition theoretically use power to serve others in a morally responsible way. Power motivation in the absence of at least a moderate if not strong responsibility disposition, can be dissolute when it is manifested in leaders. McClelland referred to such enactment as the exercise of personalized, as opposed to socialized, power.

Need for achievement. Achievement motivation is defined as a non-conscious concern for achieving excellence in accomplishments through one's individual efforts (McClelland, Atkinson, Clark & Lowell, 1958). Achievement-motivated individuals set challenging goals for themselves, assume personal responsibility for goal accomplishment, and are highly persistent in the pursuit of goals. McClelland and Boyatzis (1982) found that a high need for achievement was associated with managerial success at low levels of management where promotion depended less on influencing others and more on individual contribution. In management positions at higher levels in organizations, managerial effectiveness depends on the extent to which managers delegate effectively, and motivate and coordinate others. Theoretically, high achievement motivated managers are strongly inclined to be personally involved in performing or meddling in the work of their followers. Individuals high on the need for achievement would be ineffective delegators and micromanagers (House & Aditya, 1997; Winter, 2002).

Need for affiliation. Individuals with a high need for affiliation are motivated to make friends with others, and strive to be accepted in a social group. McClelland (1975) stated that such a need is not conducive to leadership, because it "places the well-being of individuals above the well-being of the system," or of the greater good (p. 274). These types of individuals tend to be submissive, and are unwilling to take positions on difficult matters. Furthermore, McClelland reported that "someone who is eager for power is *less* likely to be friendly with others" – need for power is thus typically negatively correlated with need for affiliation (p. 322). As House and Aditya (1997) stated, high-affiliation individuals are ineffective in management positions as they are non-confrontational, reluctant to communicate negative feedback to others, submissive, and unwilling to exert discipline when needed.

Based on the above descriptions, McClelland (1975) proposed the following profile for effective leadership (i.e. the LMP): high socialized power, high responsibility disposition, and low need for affiliation. McClelland also mentioned that effective leaders score low on need for achievement. These propositions have found empirical support (e.g. McClelland & Boyatzis, 1982). House et al. (1991), also reported that need for power positively related to charisma, that need for achievement was negatively related to charisma, and that need for affiliation was negatively but not significantly related to charisma. House et al. also reported that in the political arena, need for power would generally be positively related to leadership outcomes, while need for achievement and affiliation were negatively related to leadership outcomes. Spangler and House (1991) reported similar results.

Based on the above, it may be possible that the LMP can be related to the extended FRLT. Relating the LMP to the transformational factors is logically derived from McClelland's (1975) theorizing and the literature we reviewed. For example, individuals with a high need for power, high responsibility disposition, low need for affiliation, and low need for achievement would likely be transformational leaders. Charisma, as discussed above, is predicted by the LMP.

Similarly, inspirational motivation, intellectual stimulation, and individualized consideration should be associated with the profile. McClelland, for instance, described socialized leaders as being inspirational leaders who communicate as follows: "Here are the goals which are true and right and which we share. Here is how we can reach them. You are strong and capable.

You can accomplish these goals" (McClelland, 1975, p. 260). The leader is articulating idealized vision, high expectations, and confidence that the expectations can be met, which is precisely how inspirational motivation is described in the FRLT. Intellectual stimulation is also theoretically related to high LMP leaders, as noted by Howell (1988), who stated "Through intellectual stimulation, the socialized charismatic leader coaches followers to think on their own and to develop new ventures that will further the group's goals" (p. 224). Howell further stated, "Another distinctive behavior of socialized leaders is individualized consideration" (p. 223), in terms of the degree to which they focus on the developmental needs of their followers. Lastly, individuals with a high need for power are risk takers (Winter, 2002), which is comparable with our definition of transformational leaders. We also speculate that the LMP may be extendable to transactional, instrumental, and laissez-faire leadership. Refer to Antonakis and House (2001) for a detailed discussion on the full-range leadership motive profile (FRLMP).

Another important dispositional element underlying successful leadership is the leader's cognitive skills (Kenny & Zaccaro, 1983; Sashkin, 1988; Sternberg et al., 2000; Zaccaro, Foti & Kenny, 1991). From a cognitive perspective, leadership can be conceived as a higher-order process that allows individuals to make sense of vast amounts of information, and to use that information to make effective decisions and to demonstrate effective behaviors. Making sense entails conceptualizing the problem, constructing a model of causal relations between variables implicated in the problem, and applying this knowledge to solve the types of ill-conceived, unstructured practical problems that individuals, including leaders, face on a daily basis (Orasanu & Connolly, 1995; Sashkin, 1988; Schön, 1983; Sternberg et al., 2000).

The cognitive processes and knowledge structures discussed above are generally held tacitly (Wagner & Sternberg, 1990), and an individual's ability to gain such knowledge is a function of their practical intelligence, that is, "the ability to acquire – experientially – tacit knowledge that is relevant to solving practical problems" (Antonakis, Hedlund, Pretz & Sternberg, 2001). Based on a series of studies of military leaders, Sternberg et al. (2000) have found evidence for the operation of a *tacit knowledge* construct, that is, a construct representing knowledge that is implicit and rooted in action. Sternberg et al. reported that such knowledge accounts for additional variation in performance outcomes beyond that of general intelligence. The above suggests that the enactment of successful leadership behaviors may be a function of leaders' cognitive resources and knowledge derived from their experiences. We hope that as a result of the above assertions, research will be stimulated to determine whether the FRLMP and practical intelligence/tacit knowledge predict the emergence and effectiveness of leadership.

CONCLUSIONS

As was evident in this chapter, there are ample theoretical arguments and empirical results to support the validity of the FRLT. The theory appears to be universally valid, and its factor structure and strength of predictive validity a function of moderating conditions. Moderators are gaining prominence in leadership research (e.g. Antonakis, 2001; Antonakis & Avolio, 2001; Howell, Dorfman & Kerr, 1986; Pawar & Eastman, 1997; Shamir & Howell, 1999), and further empirical work is required to better explain the boundary conditions of theoretical frameworks such as the FRLT. The evidence reviewed above demonstrates that MLQ is an appropriate gauge of the FRLT. However, it could be modified to accommodate the addition of a broad class of behaviors that we called instrumental leadership. Whether instrumental leadership proves to be practically useful, and whether the extended FRLT can be validated will be determined in subsequent research. Finally, we have stretched theoretical arguments concerning the leadership motive pattern to fit the extended FRLT, and we hope that our speculations will be put to the test. Although our hope was to lay the foundations for a consolidation of leadership theory, our approach was limited, because our integration strategy was restrictive. For example, we did not include LMX theory or other leader-member exchange-type theories.

Furthermore, we hope to see longitudinal research that establishes that transformational leaders have the ability to actually transform individuals and organizations. This notion implicitly pervades the theories and assumptions of leadership scholars of the new paradigm (Beyer, 1999; House, 1999). We have evidence that behaviors of transformational leaders are associated with improved organizational effectiveness, follower satisfaction, and follower motive arousal, but this evidence does not imply that transformational leaders caused transformations in organizations and followers. Although causal links could be theorized, up to this point, we have seen no empirical evidence to make that deduction.

In conclusion, Bass made the following opening remarks in his 1985 book: "The hope is that this book will represent a major breakthrough in understanding what it takes for leaders to have great effects on their followers" (p. xiii). Bass can look back with knowledge that his work did represent a major breakthrough, and that in its current form, the FRLT holds much promise as the flame bearer for the new leadership paradigm. We hope that we have made a contribution to augmenting the FRLT and have moved the field forward so that, one day, a general theory of leadership can be constructed. We have uncovered our "painting" and hope that our dots, colors, and strokes blend well, into a telling picture. We look forward to seeing similar types of paintings in the future.

NOTE

1. We refer to the "model" as a theory, because it reflects the explanation of a phenomenon, and has a structural framework and measurement model that is empirically testable.

REFERENCES

Antonakis, J. (2001). The validity of the transformational, transactional, and laissez-faire leadership model as measured by the Multifactor Leadership Questionnaire (MLQ5X). *Dissertation Abstracts International* (University Microfilms No. 3000380).

Antonakis, J., & Avolio, B. J. (2002). The contextual nature of leadership: Moderating conditions of the full-range leadership theory as measured by the Multifactor Leadership Questionnaire (Unpublished Manuscript).

Antonakis, J., Hedlund, J., Pretz, J., & Sternberg, R. J. (2001). Exploring the nature and acquisition of tacit knowledge for military leadership (Under review; Army Research Institute for the Behavioral and Social Sciences).

Antonakis, J., & House, R. J. (2001). A reformulated full-range leadership theory (Unpublished manuscript).

Argyris, C. (1994). *On organizational learning*. Oxford: Blackwell Publishers.

Avolio, B. J. (1999). *Full leadership development: Building the vital forces in organizations*. Thousand Oaks, CA: Sage Publications.

Avolio, B. J., Bass, B. M., & Jung, D. I. (1995). *MLQ Multifactor leadership questionnaire: Technical Report*. Redwood City, CA: Mindgarden.

Avolio, B. J., Bass, B. M., & Jung, D. I. (1999a). Re-examining the components of transformational and transactional leadership using the Multifactor Leadership Questionnaire. *Journal of Occupational and Organizational Psychology, 72*, 441–462.

Avolio, B. J., Howell, J. M., & Sosik, J. J. (1999b). A funny thing happened on the way to the bottom line: Humor as a moderator of leadership style effects. *Academy of Management Journal, 42*(2), 219–227.

Barling, J., Weber, T., & Kelloway, E. K. (1996). Effects of transformational leadership training on attitudinal and financial outcomes: A field experiment. *Journal of Applied Psychology, 81*(6), 827–832.

Baron, R. M., & Kenny, D. A. (1986). The moderator-mediator variable distinction in social psychological research: Conceptual, strategic, and statistical considerations. *Journal of Personality and Social Psychology, 51*(6), 1173–1182.

Bass, B. M. (1985). *Leadership and performance beyond expectations*. New York: The Free Press.

Bass, B. M. (1996). Is there universality in the full range model of leadership? *International Journal of Public Administration, 19*(6), 731–761.

Bass, B. M. (1997). Does the transactional-transformational leadership paradigm transcend organizational boundaries? *American Psychologist, 52*(2), 130–139.

Bass, B. M. (1998). *Transformational leadership: Industrial, military, and educational impact.* Mahwah, NJ: Lawrence Erlbaum Associates.

Bass, B. M. (1999). Weber and the neo-charismatic leadership paradigm: A response to Beyer. *Leadership Quarterly, 10*(4), 563–574.

Bass, B. M., & Avolio, B. J. (1993). Transformational leadership: A response to critiques. In: M. M. Chemers & R. Ayman (Eds), *Leadership theory and research: Perspectives and directions* (pp. 49–80). San Diego: Academic Press.

Bass, B. M., & Avolio, B. J. (Eds) (1994). *Improving organizational effectiveness through transformational leadership.* Thousand Oaks, CA: Sage Publications.

Bass, B. M., & Avolio, B. J. (1995). *MLQ Multifactor leadership questionnaire for research: Permission set.* Redwood City, CA: Mindgarden.

Bass, B. M., & Avolio, B. J. (1997). *Full range leadership development: Manual for the multifactor leadership questionnaire.* Palo Alto, CA: Mindgarden.

Bass, B. M., Avolio, B. J., & Atwater, L. (1996). The transformational and transactional leadership of men and women. *Applied Psychology: An International Review, 45*(1), 5–34.

Beyer, J. M. (1999). Taming and promoting charisma to change organizations. *Leadership Quarterly, 10*, 30–330.

Bjerke, B. (1999). *Business leadership and culture: National management styles in the global economy.* Cheltenham, U.K.: Edward Elgar Publishing.

Bochner, S., & Hesketh, B. (1994). Power distance, individualism/collectivism, and job-related attitudes in a culturally diverse work group. *Journal of Cross-Cultural Psychology, 25*(2), 233–257.

Bollen, K. A. (1989). *Structural equations with latent variables.* New York: John Wiley & Sons.

Bowers, D. G., & Seashore, S. E. (1966). Predicting organizational effectiveness with a four-factor theory of leadership. *Administrative Science Quarterly, 11*, 238–263.

Bryman, A. (1992). *Charisma and leadership in organizations.* London: Sage Publications.

Burns, J. M. (1978). *Leadership.* New York: Harper & Row.

Bycio, P., Hackett, R. D., & Allen, J. S. (1995). Further assessments of Bass's (1985) conceptualization of transactional and transformational leadership. *Journal of Applied Psychology, 80*(4), 468–478.

Byrne, B. M. (1994). *Structural equation modeling with EQS and EQS/Windows: Basic concepts, applications and programming.* Thousand Oaks, CA: Sage Publications.

Carless, S. A. (1998a). Gender differences in transformational leadership: An examination of superior, leader, and subordinate perspectives. *Sex Roles, 39*(11/12), 887–902.

Carless, S. A. (1998b). Assessing the discriminant validity of transformational leader behavior as measured by the MLQ. *Journal of Occupational and Organizational Psychology, 71*(4), 353–358.

Coad, A. F., & Berry, A. J. (1998). Transformational leadership and learning orientation. *Leadership and Organization Development Journal, 19*(4), 164–172.

Conger, J. A. (1989). *The charismatic leader: Behind the mystique of exceptional leadership.* San Francisco: Jossey-Bass Publishers.

Conger, J. A. (1999). Charismatic and transformational leadership in organizations: An insider's perspective on these developing streams of research. *Leadership Quarterly, 10*(2), 145–179.

Conger, J. A., & Kanungo, R. N. (Eds) (1988). *Charismatic leadership: The elusive factor in organizational effectiveness.* San Francisco: Jossey-Bass Publishers.

Conger, J. A., & Kanungo, R. N. (1988). Introduction: Problems and prospects in understanding charismatic leadership. In: J. A. Conger & R. N. Kanungo (Eds), *Charismatic leadership: The elusive factor in organizational effectiveness* (pp. 1–11). San Francisco: Jossey-Bass Publishers.

Conger, J. A., & Kanungo, R. N. (1998). *Charismatic leadership in organizations.* Thousand Oaks, CA: Sage Publications.

Den Hartog, D. N., House, R. J., Hanges, P. J., Ruiz-Quintanilla, S. A., & Dorfmann, P. W. (1999). Culture specific and cross-cultural generalizable implicit leadership theories: Are attributes of charismatic/transformational leadership universally endorsed? *Leadership Quarterly, 10*(2), 219–256.

Den Hartog, D. N., Van Muijen, J. J., & Koopman, P. L. (1997). Transactional vs. transformational leadership: An analysis of the MLQ. *Journal of Occupational and Organizational Psychology, 70*(1), 19–34.

Dorfman, P. W., Howell, J. P., Hibino, S., Lee, J. K, Tate, U., & Bautista, A. (1997). Leadership in western and Asian countries: Commonalties and differences in effective leadership processes across cultures. *Leadership Quarterly, 8*(3), 233–274.

Downton, J. V. (1973). *Rebel leadership: Commitment and charisma in the revolutionary process.* New York: The Free Press.

Druskat, V. U. (1994). Gender and leadership style: Transformational and transactional leadership in the Roman Catholic Church. *Leadership Quarterly, 5*(2), 99–119.

Eagly, A. H., & Johannesen-Schmidt, M. C. (2001). The leadership styles of women and men. *Journal of Social Issues, 57*(4, Winter), 781–797.

Etzioni, A. (1961). *A comparative analysis of complex organizations.* New York: The Free Press.

Gasper, J. M. (1992). Transformational leadership: An integrative review of the literature. *Dissertation Abstracts International* (University Microfilms No. 9234203).

Gibson, C. B., & Marcoulides, G. A. (1995). The invariance of leadership styles across four countries. *Journal of Managerial Issues, 7*(2), 176–193.

Geyer, A. L. J., & Steyrer, J. M. (1998). Transformational leadership and objective performance in banks. *Applied Psychology: An International Review, 47*(3), 397–420.

Hater, J. J., & Bass, B. M. (1988). Superiors' evaluations and subordinates' perceptions of transformational and transactional leadership. *Journal of Applied Psychology, 73*(4), 695–702.

Hofstede, G. (1991). *Cultures and organizations: Software of the mind.* Maidenhead, UK: McGraw-Hill Book Company.

House, R. J. (1971). A path-goal theory of leadership effectiveness. *Administrative Science Quarterly, 16*, 321–328.

House, R. J. (1977). A 1976 theory of charismatic leadership. In: J. G. Hunt & L. L. Larson (Eds), *Leadership: The cutting edge* (pp. 189–207). Carbondale: Southern Illinois University Press.

House, R. J. (1996). Path-goal theory of leadership: Lessons, legacy, and a reformulated theory. *Leadership Quarterly, 7*(3), 323–352.

House, R. J. (1999). On the taming of charisma: A reply to Janice Beyer. *Leadership Quarterly, 10*(4), 541–553.

House, R. J., & Aditya, R. N. (1997). The social scientific study of leadership: Quo vadis? *Journal of Management, 23*(3), 409–474.

House, R. J., & Baetz, M. L. (1979). Leadership: Some empirical generalizations and new research directions. *Research in Organizational Behavior, 1*, 341–423.

House, R. J., & Howell, J. M (1992). Personality and charismatic leadership. *Leadership Quarterly, 3*(2), 81–108.

House, R. J., Howell, J. M., & Shamir, B. (2001). Charismatic leadership: A values identification and potency theory. (Manuscript in preparation).

House, R. J., & Shamir, B. (1993). Toward the integration of transformational, charismatic, and visionary theories. In: M. M. Chemers & R. Ayman (Eds), *Leadership theory and research: Perspectives and directions* (pp. 167–188). San Diego: Academic Press.

House, R. J., Shane, S. A., & Herold, D. M. (1996). Rumors of the death of dispositional research are vastly exaggerated. *Academy of Management Review, 21*(1), 203–224.

House, R. J., Spangler, W. D., & Woycke, J. (1991). Personality and charisma in the U.S. presidency: A psychological theory of leaders effectiveness. *Administrative Science Quarterly, 36*(3), 364–397.

Howell, J. M. (1988). Two faces of charisma: Socialized and personalized leadership in organizations. In: J. A. Conger & R. N. Kanungo (Eds), *Charismatic Leadership: The Elusive Factor in Organizational Effectiveness* (pp. 213–236). San Francisco: Jossey-Bass Publishers.

Howell, J. M., & Avolio, B. J. (1993). Transformational leadership, transactional leadership, locus of control, and support for innovation: Key predictors of consolidated-business-unit performance. *Journal of Applied Psychology, 78*(6), 891–902.

Howell, J. P., Dorfman, P. W., & Kerr, S. (1986). Moderator variables in leadership research. *Academy of Management Review, 11*(1), 88–102.

Hunt, J. G. (1991). *Leadership: A new synthesis.* Newbury Park, CA: Sage Publications.

Hunt, J. G. (1999). Transformational/charismatic leadership's transformation of the field: An historical essay. *Leadership Quarterly, 10*(2), 129–144.

Jöreskog, K. G. (1971). Simultaneous factor analysis in several populations. *Psychometrika, 36*(4), 409–426.

Jung, D. I., & Avolio, B. J. (1999). Effects of leadership style and followers' cultural orientation on performance in group and individual task conditions. *Academy of Management Review, 42*(2), 208–228.

Kenny, D. A., & Zaccaro, S. J. (1983). An estimate of variance due to traits in leadership. *Journal of Applied Psychology, 68*, 678–685.

Lord, R. G., De Vader, C. L., & Alliger G. M. (1986). A meta-analysis of the relation between personality traits and leadership perceptions. An application of validity generalization procedures. *Journal of Applied Psychology, 71*(3), 402–410.

Lowe, K. B., Kroeck, K. G., & Sivasubramaniam, N. (1996). Effectiveness correlates of transformational and transactional leadership: A meta-analytic review of the literature. *Leadership Quarterly, 7*(3), 385–425.

McClelland, D. C. (1975). *Power: The inner experience.* New York: Halsted Press.

McClelland, D. C. (1976). Power is the great motivator. *Harvard Business Review, 54*(2), 100–110.

McClelland, D. C. (1980). Motive dispositions: The merits of operant and respondent measures. In: L. Wheeler (Ed.), *Review of Personality and Social Psychology* (pp. 10–41). Beverly Hills, CA: Sage Publications.

McClelland, D. C. (1985). How motives, skills, and values determine what people do. *American Psychologist, 40*(7), 812–825.

McClelland, D. C., Atkinson, J. W., Clark, R. A., & Lowell, E. L. (1958). A scoring manual or the achievement motive. In: J. W. Atkinson (Ed.), *Motives in fantasy, action, and society* (pp. 179–204). New York: Van Nostrand.

McClelland, D. C., & Boyatzis, R. E. (1982). Leadership motive pattern and long-term success in management. *Journal of Applied Psychology, 67*(6), 737–743.

McClelland, D. C., Koestner, R., & Weinberger, J. (1989). How do self-attributed and implicit motives differ? *Psychological Review, 96*(4), 690–702.

Maher, K. J. (1997). Gender-related stereotypes of transformational and transactional leadership. *Sex Roles, 37*(3/4), 209–225.

Mead, R. D. (1967). An experimental study in India. *Journal of Social Psychology, 72*(1), 35–43.

Nadler, D. A., & Tushman, M. L. (1990). Beyond the charismatic leader: Leadership and organizational change. *California Management Review, 32*, 77–97.

Offermann, L. R., & Hellmann, P. S. (1997). Culture's consequences for leadership behavior: National values in action. *Journal of Cross-Cultural Psychology, 28*(3), 342–351.

Orasanu, J., & Connolly, T. (1995). The reinvention of decision making. In: G. A. Klein, J. Orasanu, R. Calderwood & C. E. Zsambok (Eds), *Decision making in action: Models and methods* (pp. 3–20). Norwood, NJ: Ablex Publishing Corporation.

Pavett, C., & Morris, T. (1995). Management styles within a multinational corporation: A five country comparative study. *Human Relations, 48*(10), 1171–1191.

Pawar, B. S., & Eastman, K. K. (1997). The nature and implications of contextual influences on transformational leadership: A conceptual examination. *Academy of Management Review, 22*(1), 80–109.

Sashkin, M. (1988). The visionary leader. In: J. A. Conger & R. N. Kanungo (Eds.), *Charismatic leadership: The elusive factor in organizational effectiveness* (pp. 122–160). San Francisco: Jossey-Bass Publishers.

Schön, D. A. (1983). *The reflective practitioner: How professionals think in action*. New York: Basic Books.

Shamir, B. (1999). Taming charisma for better understanding and greater usefulness: A response to Beyer. *Leadership Quarterly, 10*(4), 555–562.

Shamir, B., House, R. J., & Arthur, M. B. (1993). The motivational effects of charismatic leadership: A self-concept based theory. *Organization Science, 4*(4), 577–594.

Shamir, B. & Howell, J. M. (1999). Organizational and contextual influences on the emergence and effectiveness of charismatic leadership. *Leadership Quarterly, 19*(2), 257–283.

Shils, E. (1965). Charisma, order, and status. *American Sociological Review, 30*(2), 199–213.

Singer, M. S., & Singer, A. E. (1990). Situational constraints on transformational versus transactional leadership behavior, subordinates' leadership preference, and satisfaction. *The Journal of Social Psychology, 130*(3), 385–396.

Sosik, J. J., Kahai, S. S., & Avolio, B. J. (1998). Transformational leadership and dimensions of creativity: Motivating idea generation in computer-mediated groups. *Creativity Research Journal, 11*(2), 111–121.

Spangler, W. D., & House, R. J. (1991). Presidential effectiveness and the leadership motive profile. *Journal of Personality and Social Psychology, 60*(3), 439–455.

Spangler, W. D., House, R. J., & Palrecha, R. (2001). Personality and leadership (Unpublished manuscript).

Sternberg, R. J., Forsythe, G. B., Hedlund, J., Horvath, J. A., Wagner, R. K., Williams, W. M., Snook, S. A., & Grigorenko, E. L. (2000). *Practical intelligence in everyday life*. New York: Cambridge University Press.

Stogdill, R. M. (1948). Personal factors associated with leadership: A survey of the literature. *Journal of Psychology, 25*, 35–71.

A META-ANALYSIS OF TRANSFORMATIONAL AND TRANSACTIONAL LEADERSHIP CORRELATES OF EFFECTIVENESS AND SATISFACTION: AN UPDATE AND EXTENSION

Uldarico Rex Dumdum, Kevin B. Lowe and Bruce J. Avolio

INTRODUCTION

One of the core arguments made by Bass (1985) was that transformational leadership would account for a greater share of the variance in performance outcomes when compared with more traditional transactional styles of leadership. Over the last 15 plus years, considerable evidence has been accumulated supporting Bass' original contention with studies conducted in a very broad range of organizational settings (Avolio, 1999; Bass, 1998). Transformational leadership has been shown to correlate positively with performance outcome measures ranging from growth in church membership (Onnen, 1987) to the performance of platoons operating in near-combat conditions (Bass, Avolio, Jung & Berson, in press).

Transformational and Charismatic Leadership, Volume 2, pages 35–66.

The growing attention in the literature to transformational and charismatic leadership has rejuvenated the field of leadership and attracted a number of new scholars to the field (Hunt, 1999). For example, in a comprehensive 10-year review of the articles published in *The Leadership Quarterly*, Lowe and Gardner (2000) found that the charismatic/transformational leadership paradigm was the most researched area of leadership over the last decade, surpassing attention given any other single leadership paradigm. A further analysis of the Lowe and Gardner data conducted for this chapter showed that the 1995–1999 period produced more published studies on the paradigm than the 1990–1994 period, suggesting a growing interest among leadership scholars in researching charismatic and transformational leadership.

Over the time span since Bass published his (1985) book, there have been three quantitative reviews of the literature conducted on the neocharismatic/ transformational leadership paradigm (DeGroot, Kiker & Cross, 2000; Gaspar, 1992; Lowe, Kroeck & Sivasubramainiam, 1996). Gasper's work focused primarily on educational settings, in which he aggregated a number of study variables later shown to be important moderators of the leadership and effectiveness relationship. Lowe and his colleagues focused on the five-factor model of transformational leadership as measured by the Multi-Factor Leadership Questionnaire (MLQ) to guide their meta-analysis. Lowe et al. examined the relationship between transformational and transactional leadership with individual and organizational-level measures of effectiveness. Lowe et al. (1996) also included three different moderators of the transformational leadership to effectiveness relationship: type of criterion, level of leader, and type of organization. DeGroot, Kiker and Cross (2000) focused more narrowly on the charismatic component of transformational leadership, including in their meta-analysis a wider variety of instruments including the MLQ, which all assessed charismatic leadership.

The primary purpose of the current study was to update and extend the work of Lowe et al. (1996). Specifically, we set as our goal to examine all research using the MLQ that was not included in the Lowe et al. (1996) review, by going back to 1995 and reviewing all published and unpublished research on the MLQ up to and including research published in 2002. The focus of the current meta-analysis was on empirical research using the MLQ to measure transformational leadership and its relationship with measures of performance effectiveness and satisfaction. We settled on this strategy for several reasons. First, transformational leadership research utilizing the full-range leadership model and the MLQ provides the most widely researched empirical assessment of the paradigm available. Alternative measures such as that of Podsakoff,

Triandis, H. C. (1993). The contingency model in cross-cultural perspective. In: M. M. Chemers & R. Ayman (Eds.), *Leadership theory and research: Perspectives and directions* (pp. 167–188). San Diego: Academic Press.

Wagner, R. K., & Sternberg, R. J. (1990). Street smarts. In: K. E. Clark & M. B. Clark (Eds), *Measures of leadership* (pp. 493–504). West Orange, NJ: Leadership Library of America.

Waldman, D. A., Bass, B. M., & Yammarino, F. J. (1990). Adding to contingent-reward behavior: The augmenting effect of charismatic leadership. *Group and Organization Studies, 15*(4), 381–395.

Waldman, D. A., Ramirez, G. G., House, R. J., & Puranam, P. (2001). Does leadership matter? CEO leadership attributes and profitability under conditions of perceived environmental uncertainty. *Academy of Management Journal, 44*(1), 134–143.

Weber, M. (1947). *The theory of social and economic organization* (T. Parsons, Trans.). New York: The Free Press. (Original work published 1924).

Weber, M. (1968). *Max Weber on charisma and institutional building* (S. N. Eisenstadt, Ed.). Chicago: The University of Chicago Press.

Winter, D. G. (2002). The motivational dimensions of leadership: Power, achievement and affiliation. In: R. E. Riggio, S. E. Murphy & F. J. Pirozzolo (Eds.), *Multiple intelligences and leadership* (pp. 119–138). Mahwah, NJ: Lawrence Erlbaum Associates.

Winter, D. G., & Barenbaum, N. B. (1985). Responsibility and the power motive in women and men. *Journal of Personality, 53*, 335–355.

Winter, D. G., John, O. P., Stewart, A. J., Klohnen, E. C., & Duncan, L. E. (1998). Traits and motives: Toward an integration of two traditions in personality research. *Psychological Review, 105*(2), 230–250.

Yammarino, F. J., Dubinsky, A. J., Comer, L. B., & Jolson, M. A. (1997). Women and transformational and contingent reward leadership: A multiple-levels-of-analysis perspective. *Academy of Management Journal, 40*(1), 205–222.

Yukl, G. (1998). *Leadership in organizations* (4th ed.). Englewood Cliffs, NJ: Prentice Hall.

Zaccaro, S. J., Foti, R. J., & Kenny, D. A. (1991). Self-monitoring and trait-based variance in leadership: An investigation of leader flexibility across multiple situations. *Journal of Applied Psychology, 76*, 308–315.

Zaccaro, S. J., & Klimoski, R. J. (2001). The nature of organizational leadership. In: S. J. Zaccaro & R. J. Klimoski (Eds), *The nature of organizational leadership* (pp. 3–41). San Francisco: Jossey-Bass Publishers.

Zaleznik, A. (1989). *The managerial mystique: Restoring leadership in business.* New York: Harper & Row.

Zaleznik, A. (1992). Managers and leaders: Are they different? *Harvard Business Review,* (March–April), 126–135 (Original work published 1977).

MacKenzie, Moorman and Fetter (1990) provide a narrower assessment of the dimensions comprising the full-range model.

Second, an initial review of the literature back to 1995 showed that the MLQ was by far the most frequently used measure for studying transformational leadership, and therefore the number of studies available with this instrument allowed us to conduct more robust tests of moderator variables. The survey developed by Podsakoff et al. (1990) has rarely appeared in the literature, so we decided to abandon its use in the current study.

Third, the Lowe et al. (1996) paper is by far the most widely cited quantitative review of the transformational leadership literature, accumulating over 100 citations in the 6 years since publication. Thus, we felt that using it as point of departure for the current meta-analysis would provide an interesting and helpful update to their original study and offer some continuity to examining the linkages between transformational leadership and performance.

The strategy we adopted can be described as a replication of the theoretical arguments of Bass and extension with respect to data analysis and interpretation. Consequently, we will not focus here on providing an extensive discussion of the origins and evolution of the charismatic/transformational leadership paradigm, which appears in a number of other sources, including other chapters in this book (cf. Antonakis & House, in press; Avolio, 1999; Bass, 1995, 1998; Conger & Kanungo, 1998; House & Aditya, 1997). Our primary purpose is to conduct a meta-analysis of studies published since Lowe et al. (1996) to determine if the relationships they reported still hold. We also extend their analysis by examining the relationship between leadership style and satisfaction. Since the two most widely used criterion measures are performance and satisfaction, we felt that this extension could help provide a more comprehensive picture of the charismatic/transformational leadership paradigm.

We chose to explore satisfaction in this meta-analysis since there is a substantial literature that has showed linkages between satisfaction and performance, a relationship that was described by Landy (1989) as the "Holy Grail" of industrial psychologists. Yet evidence concerning this linkage indicates that the association, although typically significant, is weaker than initially thought and in need of further research (Judge, Thoresen, Bono & Patton, 2001). Hence, our primary purpose is to explore the "true" association between various leadership styles measured by the MLQ and the "big two" criterion measures that are repeatedly used as benchmarks for determining the impact of leadership in organizations. Thus, based on prior leadership research and three previous meta-analyses, we will examine the following broad propositions:

- Transformational leadership will be positively associated with measures of performance effectiveness and satisfaction.
- Transactional contingent reward leadership will be positively associated with measures of performance effectiveness and satisfaction, but less so than transformational.
- Passive-avoidant transactional leadership will be negatively associated with measures of performance effectiveness and satisfaction.

In an attempt to re-examine the findings reported by Lowe et al. (1996), we will explore whether the relationships between leadership style and performance are moderated by organizational type. Specifically, we examined the degree to which the leader × outcome relationships varied between public/government and private organizations.

We also intend to explore how the type of outcome measure moderates the relationship between leadership style and satisfaction. Prior evidence indicates that the leadership styles measured by the MLQ tend to be more highly correlated with subjective vs. more objective or external outcome measures. We intend to examine how the leadership styles measured by the MLQ relate to satisfaction with the leader vs. satisfaction with the job.

Examining the Full-range Model

Prior to reporting our methods and results, we provide a quick overview of the dimensions contained in the full-range leadership development model, which again is covered in more detail by Antonakis and House in the previous chapter. The full-range model of leadership may be broadly classified as transformational leadership, transactional leadership, and nontransactional leadership (Avolio, 1999). Transformational leaders engender trust, seek to develop leadership in others, exhibit self-sacrifice and serve as moral agents, focusing themselves and followers on objectives that transcend the more immediate needs of the work group. Transformational leaders typically engender higher levels of commitment, trust, and loyalty in their followers that may lead to performance beyond expectations. Transformational leadership scales in this meta-analysis included Attributed Charisma, Idealized Influence, Inspirational Motivation, Intellectual Stimulation, and Individualized Consideration. We also conducted a meta-analysis of a global scale of transformational leadership comprising selected items from the dimensional scales, since a number of studies have included this higher-order construct, vs. reporting results for the individual component scales.

Transactional leaders address the self-interest concerns of followers by exchanging rewards or recognition for cooperation and compliance behaviors

consistent with task requirements. The more effective transactional relationships are constructive and often result in achieving defined performance
requirements. Transactional leadership scales in this meta-analysis included the
Contingent Reward, Management-by-Exception, and a more global Transactional Leadership Scale comprising selected items from the component scales.

Non-transactional leadership styles represent leadership behaviors that are
neither transformational nor contingent on the exchange of rewards for effort or
performance. The non-transactional scale used in this meta-analysis has been
labeled in the MLQ as Laissez-Faire.

In sum, our primary goal in conducting this latest meta-analysis of literature
accumulated using the MLQ survey was to update the results of Lowe et al.
(1996), by extending the period of review of their initial study to the year 2002.
Thus, in combination, these two meta-analyses will provide a review of the last
15 years of data collected on Bass's (1985) originally proposed model of
transformational, transactional and non-transactional leadership and the
extended model labeled the full range of leadership.

METHOD

The central purpose for conducting a meta-analysis is to statistically analyze
the results of many empirical studies in order to reveal a summary set of
findings. Among the several available techniques for conducting a meta-
analysis, we chose the method offered by Hunter and Schmidt (1990), which
has become the most widely used approach in the organizational behavior
literature. We followed the guidelines suggested by Schmitt and Klimoski
(1991) in our approach to the coding of studies and gave careful consideration
to the many judgment calls required in meta-analysis as outlined by Wanous,
Sullivan and Malinak (1989). We highlight two of these judgment calls here to
enable an accurate interpretation of our results.

First, we elected to include dissertations and "file drawer" studies in an effort
to capture as broad a sample as possible. We felt some comfort in doing so,
since Lowe et al. (1996) found that few differences existed between published
and unpublished studies in this domain. Indeed, when unpublished studies do
have an impact on the results it is generally to reduce observed correlations.
Thus, the inclusion of unpublished studies typically results in a more
conservative test of significance.

Second, many studies reported multiple measures of effectiveness and
satisfaction, which came from the perspective of a single group of raters. To
report each of these correlations with the associated sample size attributed to
each correlation would overweight studies correlating leadership ratings with

multiple effectiveness criteria, while underweighting other studies that may have included only one outcome measure. If we used the strategy of coding multiple leader-outcome relationships including the same leadership scales collected within a single study, the correlations would not be independent, thus also violating a basic assumption required for conducting a meta-analysis.

There are two basic options one can pursue to deal with the problem of dependent correlations. The research coder can determine the best correlation coefficient to be included in the meta-analysis, eliminating the other correlations from consideration. Alternatively, one can choose to average multiple correlation coefficients to form a composite measure of the variable of interest. In this study, we were interested in effectiveness and satisfaction as multi-faceted constructs and therefore decided to use the averaging strategy to develop composite correlation coefficients in studies where multiple measures of effectiveness and satisfaction were collected.

Selection of Studies for the Meta-analysis

We selected the cutoff date for the Lowe et al. (1996) study as the beginning date for the current study by going back to 1995, when their study was in the publication pipeline. We conducted a full literature search, as described in detail below, and included all articles that were not included in the prior study.

Five criteria were used for inclusion of studies in the meta-analysis:

(1) The study must have used the MLQ to measure leadership style;
(2) The study must have reported a measure of leader effectiveness;
(3) The sample size must have been reported;
(4) A Pearson correlation coefficient (or some other test statistic that could be converted into a correlation) between leadership style and effectiveness must have been reported; and
(5) The leader must have been a direct leader of the subordinate (not an idealized or hypothetical leader).

Studies were located using a variety of methods, including:

(1) Computer searches of ABI-INFORM, Web of Science, Expanded Academic ASAP, Sociological Abstracts, PsychInfo, PA Research II Peer Reviewed, Francis, Emerald, and Dissertation Abstracts;
(2) Manual searches of Academy of Management Proceedings;
(3) Reference lists of published and unpublished sources;
(4) Request for all "file drawer" articles from the Center for Leadership Studies (CLS) at Binghamton University and from the personal library of Bernard M. Bass.

The literature search yielded over 100 studies. Forty-nine studies met the five criteria for inclusion. Twenty-four of these studies were published in journals and books, 13 were unpublished dissertations, and 12 were file-drawer articles. File-drawer articles include working papers, internal reports or articles sent to the CLS (through one or more of the CLS fellows), papers sent to Bernard M. Bass, and papers under revision for journals.

Coding of Information

Studies meeting the five criteria were reviewed, and relevant performance effectiveness and satisfaction data were extracted and coded. The studies were coded twice by six students in three teams comprising two members on each team. The two members of each team independently coded the article and then compared and discussed their coded information. Students were trained on meta-analysis procedures and were taken through several practice articles that had appeared in the meta-analysis reported by Lowe et al. (1996). The training period was discontinued once the pairs of raters had achieved a minimum coding agreement level of 80%.

Initial intercoder agreement well exceeded 90% for all study variables included in the current meta-analysis. Where disagreement did exist, they were found to be a result of clerical error. Subsequent discussion led to corrections of these clerical errors and agreement on the appropriate criterion variables for coding and coefficient signage (need for reverse coding).

For studies in which multiple measures of effectiveness and satisfaction were reported, the coding policy was to code all measures of effectiveness (i.e. individual performance, team performance, extra effort, turnover, cycle time, percentage of goals met) and to code all measures of satisfaction (i.e. satisfaction with leader, job satisfaction). In the overall meta-analysis (see Table 1), these coefficients were averaged (as described above) within a study to obtain a composite measure of effectiveness/satisfaction. This process was repeated in subsequent moderator analyses with relevant coefficients (e.g. effectiveness criterion only, objective measures of effectiveness) within a study averaged to form a composite coefficient. As the specification of the relevant criterion becomes more specific, the need to construct a composite measure is obviated by the specificity of the criterion variable.

Meta-analytic Procedures

Sample weighted means and standard deviations were first calculated. Following the approach of Lowe et al. (1996), correlations were first subjected

Table 1. Overall Meta-analysis.

Scale[1]	Sample Size[2]	Mean[3]	Std Dev.[3]	Scale Alpha[3]	Number of r Coefficients[4]	Number of Studies[4]	Range of r Coefficients	Mean Raw r	Mean Corrected r	95% Credibility Interval[5]	95% Confidence Interval[6]
Attributed Charisma (AC)	9538	2.75	0.79	0.82	65	17	0.93 to −0.67	0.54	0.66	1.00 to 0.08	0.77 to 0.56
Idealized Influence (II)	8608	2.76	0.75	0.72	68	16	0.87 to −0.16	0.50	0.66	1.00 to −0.22	0.75 to 0.58
Inspirational Motivation (IM)	12,009	2.74	0.77	0.86	101	22	0.93 to −0.14	0.46	0.56	1.00 to 0.02	0.66 to 0.46
Intellectual Stimulation (IS)	14,290	2.43	0.79	0.83	113	26	0.90 to −0.25	0.42	0.52	1.00 to −0.03	0.60 to 0.43
Individualized Consideration (IC)	14,842	2.61	0.85	0.82	116	27	0.93 to −0.31	0.44	0.55	1.00 to −0.02	0.64 to 0.46
Transformational Ldrshp (TFL)	9721	3.05	0.89	0.93	79	23	0.87 to −0.19	0.40	0.46	1.00 to −0.14	0.65 to 0.42
Contingent Reward (CR)	18,682	2.42	0.75	0.80	120	27	0.89 to −0.34	0.41	0.51	1.10 to −0.10	0.60 to 0.41
Mgmt-by-Except Active (MBEA)	13,895	1.93	0.81	0.75	90	20	0.50 to −0.62	0.04	0.05	0.38 to −0.29	0.11 to −0.02
Mgmt-by-Except Passive (MBEP)	12,386	1.70	0.67	0.69	68	17	0.43 to −0.76	−0.26	−0.34	0.04 to −0.73	−0.27 to −0.42
Mgmt-by-Except (MBE)	3036	2.12	0.29	0.76	17	5	0.50 to −0.53	−0.16	−0.21	0.11 to −0.52	−0.01 to −0.36
Laissez Faire (LF)	11,564	0.79	0.63	0.76	92	21	0.55 to −0.72	−0.30	−0.38	−0.02 to −0.75	−0.36 to −0.51
Transactional Ldrshp (TRL)	2667	2.94	0.76	0.87	33	10	0.55 to −0.18	0.17	0.20	0.46 to −0.06	0.31 to 0.15

Table 1. Continued.

[1] Because only one coefficient was reported for the scales (1) Management-by-exception and Laissiez-Faire and (2) Charismatic Leadership, they cannot be meta-analyzed and are thus not reported here.

[2] Unique sample size across all studies.

[3] Mean, standard deviation, and reliability weighted by sample size.

[4] Coefficients exceeds number of studies due to multiple criterion variables. For studies correlating one set of leadership ratings to multiple criteria, coefficients are averaged to obtain a composite correlation coefficient. Composite criteria maintain assumptions of sample independence required in the meta-analysis. The impact of different criterion measures on the correlation of leadership ratings to outcomes may be investigated further if credibility interval analysis suggests that moderators may be present (see footnote 6).

[5] Corrected for attenuation due to measurement of the independent and dependent variable.

[6] Credibility intervals indicate the extent to which validity findings can be generalized and indicate moderators when large or include zero. Confidence intervals assess the accuracy of the mean effect size.

to a meta-analysis to eliminate the effects of sampling error. Reliability data were not reported for all of the studies, but the available reports were sufficient to allow for corrections due to unreliability using the artifact distribution method (Hunter & Schmidt, 1990). Credibility and confidence intervals were constructed around the mean effect sizes to make inferences regarding the extent to which moderators might be present and to determine the accuracy and significance of the estimated mean effect size. Credibility intervals indicate the extent to which the corrected coefficient might be generalized and indicate tests for moderators when they are large or include zero, whereas confidence intervals assess the accuracy of the mean effect size.

RESULTS

Overall Meta-analysis Findings

Results of the overall meta-analysis combining effectiveness and satisfaction measures are provided in Table 1. All transformational scales had internal consistency reliabilities exceeding 0.70, the conventional level for acceptance as internally consistent (Nunnally, 1978). All transformational leadership scales were highly and positively correlated with the effectiveness/satisfaction criteria. The corrected and uncorrected coefficients were 0.66 (0.54) for Attributed Charisma, 0.66 (0.50) for Idealized Influence, 0.56 (0.46) for Inspirational Motivation, 0.52 (0.42) for Intellectual Stimulation, 0.55 (0.44) for Individualized Consideration, and 0.46 (0.40) for Transformational Leadership.

Sample weighted scale means and standard deviations were similar for the five transformational scales ranging from 2.43 to 2.76 and 0.72 to 0.86, respectively. The composite Transformational Leadership scale had a mean of 3.05 and a standard deviation of 0.93. All credibility intervals were large, and several included zero, indicating that further analysis for moderators was warranted. This finding is not surprising given the diverse set of subjective and objective criterion measures included in this meta-analysis. Yet, such an initial broad brush does help answer the question of what is the relationship between leadership and desired outcomes. A broad approach also prevents an a priori conclusion regarding the presence of moderators.

For the transactional scales, all of the reliability estimates exceeded 0.70, except a 0.69 for the Management-by-Exception Passive scale. The corrected and uncorrected correlation coefficients were 0.51 (0.41) for Contingent Reward, 0.05 (0.04) for Management-by-Exception Active, –0.34 (–0.26) for Management-by-Exception Passive, and –0.21 (–0.16) for the combined Management-by-Exception scale. The composite scale mean and standard deviation for the transactional scale was 2.94 and 0.76, respectively.

For the non-transactional leadership scale Laissez-Faire, the corrected and uncorrected correlations were –0.30 and –0.38, respectively. Consequently, this scale had the strongest negative relationship with effectiveness/satisfaction among the full-range leadership scales examined in this study. This finding is consistent with that advanced by Avolio (1999), who describes Laissez-faire as ". . . by definition, [the] most inactive, as well as most ineffective, according to almost all prior research on the style (p. 50)". The mean, standard deviation, and reliability of the scale were consistent with those reported for the transformational and transactional scales. The credibility interval was narrower than for most other scales but included zero, suggesting that further exploration for moderators was warranted.

Overall, these preliminary results provide some support for the three basic propositions stated up front, except that the overall transformational scales relationship with the performance outcome (0.46) was similar to the relationship between contingent reward and the performance outcomes (0.51). It is important to note that the composite transformational scale did not include all of the scales, or necessarily all of the items. However, these results generally support Bass' (1998) contention that there is a hierarchical relationship between transformational, transactional, non-transactional and performance effectiveness, especially at the individual scale level.

Based on the wide credibility intervals observed for the overall meta-analysis, we proceeded to investigate moderators. The first natural dichotomy was to separate the criterion measures into effectiveness and satisfaction.

Examining Outcome Measures of Satisfaction and Effectiveness

Table 2 reports two meta-analyses, one for effectiveness and one for satisfaction, which are subsets of the overall meta-analyses discussed above. The careful reader will note that the sum of the effectiveness and satisfaction sample sizes in Table 2 exceed the sample size reported in Table 1. This increase occurs where composite criterion coefficients were initially constructed and then decomposed and assigned the study sample size in each moderator subgroup.

The means and standard deviations for the 12 scales were nearly identical for the effectiveness and satisfaction sub-samples, and consistent with results

Table 2. Relationship of MLQ Scales with Effectiveness and Satisfaction.

Scale[1]	Moderator	Sample Size[2]	Mean[3]	Std Dev.[3]	Scale Alpha[3]	Number of r Coefficients[4]	Number of Studies[4]	Range of r Coefficients	Mean Raw r	Mean Corrected r	95% Credibility Interval[5]	95% Confidence Interval[6]
AC	Effectiveness	9201	2.76	0.78	0.82	45	16	0.89 to -0.20	0.55	0.68	1.00 to 0.12	0.80 to 0.57
	Satisfaction	5966	2.74	0.85	0.78	18	10	0.93 to -0.14	0.72	0.90	1.00 to 0.54	1.00 to 0.81
II	Effectiveness	8196	2.78	0.74	0.72	43	14	0.87 to -0.16	0.52	0.68	1.00 to 0.25	0.77 to 0.59
	Satisfaction	6818	2.77	0.73	0.68	20	12	0.83 to -0.14	0.54	0.73	1.00 to 0.35	0.82 to 0.65
IM	Effectiveness	11,898	2.75	0.76	0.86	70	19	0.85 to -0.14	0.46	0.55	1.00 to 0.00	0.66 to 0.44
	Satisfaction	6600	2.72	0.85	0.85	24	14	0.93 to -0.12	0.62	0.75	1.00 to 0.38	0.83 to 0.67
IS	Effectiveness	13,392	2.43	0.79	0.84	76	23	0.90 to -0.19	0.47	0.57	1.00 to 0.17	0.68 to 0.48
	Satisfaction	8570	2.37	0.84	0.81	26	16	0.86 to -0.12	0.58	0.73	1.00 to 0.31	0.81 to 0.65
IC	Effectiveness	14,364	2.61	0.85	0.82	82	24	0.89 to -0.27	0.47	0.59	1.00 to 0.04	0.68 to 0.49
	Satisfaction	8570	2.58	0.87	0.78	26	16	0.93 to -0.24	0.64	0.81	1.00 to 0.36	0.90 to 0.72
TFL	Effectiveness	7262	3.08	0.84	0.93	45	18	0.87 to -0.19	0.43	0.50	1.00 to -0.17	0.63 to 0.36
	Satisfaction	4034	3.04	0.88	0.95	19	13	0.87 to -0.02	0.35	0.40	0.95 to -0.15	0.53 to 0.26
CR	Effectiveness	16,578	2.36	0.76	0.81	80	24	0.87 to -0.34	0.45	0.56	1.00 to -0.03	0.66 to 0.46
	Satisfaction	9672	2.46	0.79	0.77	30	17	0.89 to 0.08	0.60	0.76	1.00 to 0.31	0.85 to 0.68
MBEA	Effectiveness	12,638	1.91	0.82	0.74	65	18	0.50 to -0.39	0.06	0.08	0.41 to -0.25	0.15 to 0.02
	Satisfaction	7523	1.79	0.88	0.77	19	13	0.35 to -0.62	-0.07	-0.09	0.30 to -0.49	-0.01 to -0.18
MBEP	Effectiveness	11,761	1.50	0.69	0.67	44	15	0.36 to -0.76	-0.28	-0.38	-0.11 to -0.65	-0.32 to -0.43
	Satisfaction	7335	1.72	0.72	0.72	18	12	0.43 to -0.69	-0.35	-0.46	0.13 to -1.00	-0.33 to -0.59
MBE	Effectiveness	3006	2.06	0.45	0.75	8	4	0.50 to -0.53	-0.23	-0.30	-0.06 to -0.54	-0.20 to -0.40
	Satisfaction	1550	2.76	0.51	0.62	5	3	0.13 to -0.36	-0.31	-0.44	-0.08 to -0.80	-0.28 to -0.60
LF	Effectiveness	11,547	0.81	0.63	0.76	70	21	0.51 to -0.69	-0.29	-0.37	-0.03 to -0.70	-0.31 to -0.43
	Satisfaction	7199	0.82	0.68	0.76	19	13	0.55 to -0.73	-0.41	-0.53	0.07 to -1.00	0.40 to -0.66
TRL	Effectiveness	1646	2.74	0.64	0.83	18	7	0.55 to -0.18	0.15	0.19	0.47 to -0.09	0.29 to 0.09
	Satisfaction	1347	3.64	0.73	0.81	5	4	0.41 to 0.04	0.17	0.21	0.39 to 0.02	0.31 to 0.11

Table 2. Continued.

[1] Because only one coefficient was reported for the scales (1) Management-by-exception & Laissez-Faire and (2) Charismatic Leadership, they cannot be meta-analyzed and are thus not reported here.

[2] Unique sample size across all studies.

[3] Mean, standard deviation, and reliability weighted by sample size.

[4] Coefficients exceeds number of studies due to multiple criterion variables. For studies correlating one set of leadership ratings to multiple criteria, coefficients are averaged to obtain a composite correlation coefficient. Composite criteria maintain assumptions of sample independence required in the meta-analysis. The impact of different criterion measures on the correlation of leadership ratings to outcomes may be investigated further if credibility interval analysis suggests that moderators may be present (see footnote 6).

[5] Corrected for attenuation due to measurement of the independent and dependent variable.

[6] Credibility intervals indicate the extent to which validity findings can be generalized and indicate moderators when large or include zero. Confidence intervals assess the accuracy of the mean effect size.

reported for the overall sample. The scale reliabilities for both subgroups were also consistently in the acceptable range with the exception of the Management-by-Exception scale with satisfaction where the alpha was 0.62. Thus, the population parameters for the two subgroups were quite similar. The number of studies in most subgroups exceeded the minimum five recommended for conducting a meta-analysis, and the number of coefficients across the studies was more than sufficient to conduct a proper meta-analysis.

Correlations of the transformational leadership scales with effectiveness and satisfaction were consistently high and positive. For each of the transformational subscales, the coefficient for Satisfaction was greater than for Effectiveness. Corrected coefficients for Effectiveness and Satisfaction respectively were 0.68 (0.90) for Attributed Charisma, 0.68 (0.73) for Idealized Influence, 0.55 (0.75) for Inspirational Motivation, 0.57 (0.73) for Intellectual Stimulation and 0.59 (0.81) for Individualized Consideration. For the Transformational scale used in a smaller number of studies, the Effectiveness and Satisfaction coefficients were 0.50 (0.40). For the transactional leadership scales, the coefficient for Satisfaction was again higher than for Effectiveness when the coefficients were positive and more negative when the coefficients were negative. Corrected coefficients for Effectiveness and Satisfaction, respectively, were 0.76 (0.56) for Contingent Reward, −0.09 (0.08) for Management-by-Exception-Active, −0.46 (−0.38) for Management-by-Exception-Passive, −0.44 (−0.30) for Management-by-Exception, and 0.21 (0.19) for Transactional Leadership.

For the non-transactional Laissez-Faire scale the same pattern was observed, the corrected coefficient was stronger for Satisfaction (−0.53) than for Effectiveness (−0.37). An analysis of the credibility and confidence intervals shows that the intervals remain large but are less likely to include zero than in the overall meta-analysis. In general, the credibility intervals for the transformational subscales and the Contingent Reward scale have higher positive lower bounds, while credibility intervals for the transactional and non-transactional scales have more negative lower bounds. Although the wide confidence intervals continue to suggest the presence of moderators, the decreasing presence of zero in these intervals suggests that improvement was realized through separating these two outcome measures.

Based on results reported in Table 2, we decided to probe the Effectiveness and Satisfaction measures for moderators. Two promising moderators for Effectiveness identified by Lowe et al. (1996) included the type of criterion measure and type of organization. We turn our attention to these two moderators of the leadership to effectiveness relationship first and then examine the leadership to satisfaction relationship by dichotomizing satisfaction into satisfaction with the leader and satisfaction with the job.

Public and Private Organizations

Comparing public with private organizations, we found that the means and standard deviations for these two subgroups across the 12 scales were statistically different owing to the large sample sizes, but there was relatively little practical difference observed. For example, the means for the transformational scales were typically between 2.5 and 2.8 with standard deviations between 0.60 and 0.80. For the transactional scales and non-transactional leadership scales, the means were generally lower, but still comparable scale to scale.

Internal consistency reliabilities met conventional thresholds with the exception of Idealized Influence for Public organizations (0.69) and Laissez-Faire for Private organizations (0.67). The number of studies in most of the subgroups exceeded the minimum five recommended for conducting a meta-analysis, except for four of the 24 subgroups (Idealized Influence-Public, Management-by-Exception-Private (and Public), Transactional Leadership-Private had fewer than five, and one Transformational Leadership-Private had exactly five. Concerns regarding the number of unique studies are ameliorated to some extent by the relatively high number of coefficients garnered from these studies, which often utilized multiple samples or measures within a study.

Correlations between transformational leadership scales and effectiveness were moderately high and positive for all scales. In contrast to the effectiveness/satisfaction subgroup analyses, neither the Public nor Private subgroup consistently had a higher coefficient. Corrected coefficients for Public and Private Organizations, respectively, were 0.76 (0.65) for Attributed Charisma, 0.66 (0.70) for Idealized Influence, 0.48 (0.60) for Inspirational Motivation, 0.50 (0.58) for Intellectual Stimulation, 0.48 (0.61) for Individualized Consideration, and 0.53 (N/A) for the Transformational Leadership scale.

Like the findings for the transformational scales, neither Public/Private subgroup had a consistently higher correlation with effectiveness when we examined the transactional scales. For Contingent Reward, the public subgroup had a marginally higher coefficient (0.56) than the private subgroup (0.53). Management-by-Exception-Active was positively correlated with effectiveness for both subgroups with coefficients of 0.13 and 0.04 in the Private and Public subgroups, respectively. Of the remaining scales, only Management-by-

Table 3. Moderating Effect of Type of Organization on the Relationship of the MLQ Scales and Effectiveness.

Scale[1]	Moderator	Sample Size[2]	Mean[3]	Std Dev.[3]	Scale Alpha[3]	Number of r Coefficients[4]	Number of Studies[4]	Range of r Coefficients	Mean Raw r	Mean Corrected r	95% Credibility Interval[5]	95% Confidence Interval[6]
AC	Public	2633	2.70	0.82	0.78	21	7	0.86 to -0.20	0.60	0.76	1.00 to 0.19	0.93 to 0.59
	Private	6432	2.78	0.77	0.85	21	8	0.89 to -0.19	0.53	0.65	1.00 to 0.09	0.81 to 0.49
II	Public	2307	2.67	0.82	0.69	18	4	0.75 to -0.12	0.49	0.66	1.00 to 0.22	0.83 to 0.49
	Private	5753	2.83	0.71	0.73	23	9	0.87 to -0.16	0.53	0.70	1.00 to 0.26	0.81 to 0.58
IM	Public	4522	2.61	0.90	0.86	42	7	0.79 to -0.09	0.40	0.48	1.00 to -0.16	0.68 to 0.28
	Private	7239	2.79	0.72	0.86	26	11	0.85 to -0.14	0.50	0.60	1.00 to 0.12	0.72 to 0.48
IS	Public	4446	2.51	0.77	0.79	44	9	0.76 to -0.11	0.40	0.50	1.00 to -0.16	0.68 to 0.33
	Private	7435	2.59	0.73	0.85	28	12	0.90 to -0.19	0.48	0.58	1.00 to 0.08	0.70 to 0.46
IC	Public	4446	2.77	0.84	0.79	44	9	0.78 to -0.33	0.38	0.48	1.00 to -0.16	0.65 to 0.31
	Private	8406	2.63	0.85	0.83	34	13	0.89 to -0.27	0.50	0.61	1.00 to 0.09	0.73 to 0.49
TFL	Public	5561	3.02	0.74	0.92	34	13	0.83 to -0.19	0.45	0.53	1.00 to -0.10	0.68 to 0.38
	Private	1701	3.25	1.09	0.93	11	5	0.87 to 0.02	0.32	0.37	1.00 to -0.32	0.64 to 0.10
CR	Public	7330	2.28	0.78	0.82	45	9	0.83 to -0.08	0.43	0.53	1.00 to -0.11	0.71 to 0.36
	Private	7737	2.64	0.75	0.81	31	13	0.87 to -0.34	0.45	0.56	1.00 to -0.01	0.69 to 0.43
MBEA	Public	5289	1.78	0.91	0.74	18	7	0.50 to -0.11	0.10	0.13	0.47 to -0.22	0.23 to -0.02
	Private	7213	2.04	0.72	0.76	45	10	0.33 to -0.39	0.03	0.04	0.37 to -0.29	0.13 to 0.04
MBEP	Public	5584	1.84	0.64	0.80	21	6	0.01 to -0.76	-0.30	-0.38	-0.34 to -0.41	-0.35 to -0.41
	Private	6041	1.11	0.75	0.64	21	8	0.36 to -0.62	-0.26	-0.36	0.01 to -0.73	-0.26 to -0.46
MBE	Public	N/A	N/A	N/A	N/A	N/A	N/A	N/A	N/A	N/A	N/A	N/A
	Private	1630	N/A	N/A	0.77	6	3	0.50 to 0.53	-0.18	-0.23	0.05 to -0.51	-0.09 to -0.37
LF	Public	4635	0.78	0.53	0.78	43	10	0.14 to -0.66	-0.30	-0.38	-0.29 to -0.46	-0.34 to -0.41
	Private	6687	0.75	0.72	0.67	25	10	0.51 to -0.69	-0.28	-0.36	0.07 to -0.80	-0.26 to -0.47
TRL	Public	1552	2.74	0.64	0.83	15	6	0.55 to -0.18	0.16	0.20	0.49 to -0.09	0.31 to 0.09
	Private	94	N/A	N/A	N/A	3	1	N/A	N/A	N/A	N/A	N/A

Table 3. Continued.

[1] Because only one coefficient was reported for the scales (1) Management-by-Exception and Laissez-Faire and (2) Charismatic Leadership, they cannot be meta-analyzed and are thus not reported here.

[2] Unique sample size across all studies.

[3] Mean, standard deviation, and reliability weighted by sample size.

[4] Coefficients exceeds the number of studies due to multiple criterion variables. For studies correlating one set of leadership ratings to multiple criteria, coefficients are averaged to obtain a composite correlation coefficient. Composite criteria maintain assumptions of sample independence required in meta-analysis. The impact of different criterion measures on the correlation of leadership ratings to outcomes may be investigated further if credibility interval analysis suggests that moderators may be present (see footnote 6).

[5] Corrected for attenuation due to measurement of the independent and dependent variable.

[6] Credibility intervals indicate the extent to which validity findings can be generalized and indicate moderators when large or include zero. Confidence intervals assess the accuracy of the mean effect size.

Exception-Passive (–0.38) –0.36 and Laissez-Faire (–0.38) –0.36 for public and private organizations, respectively, had sufficient subgroup sample sizes to make these comparisons.

An analysis of the credibility intervals identifies that although the range of the credibility intervals declined marginally, the number excluding zero continued to improve. The credibility intervals for the private subgroup excluded zero for all transformational subscales. A review of the 95% confidence intervals reveals that all scales excluded zero for all subgroups except Management-by-Exception-Active in Public organizations. Thus, it seems reasonable to conclude that there is a relationship between leadership styles, as measured by the MLQ scales and effectiveness criteria in both public and private organizations with the five transformational subscales, Contingent Reward, and Management-by-Exception-Active scales exhibiting positive relationships and the combined Management-by-Exception scale, Management-by-Exception-Passive and Laissez-Faire scales producing negative relationships with effectiveness. We can also conclude from the large credibility intervals that a continued search for moderators is warranted. Based on prior meta-analyses of the transformational leadership literature, we next considered the impact of the type of criterion on the leadership and effectiveness relationship

Type of Criterion: Leadership Style and Effectiveness

A review of Table 4 reveals a now familiar pattern in means, standard deviations and internal consistency reliabilities. Corrected correlation coefficients were dramatically different across subgroups for the five transformational leadership subscales and the Contingent Reward scale. In general, many more studies utilized subjective measures of effectiveness than utilized objective measures of effectiveness, and thus, there were in some cases insufficient sample sizes in the objective subgroup to examine these relationships.

Corrected correlation coefficients for the subjective and objective groups, respectively, were 0.85 (0.23) for Attributed Charisma, 0.76 (N/A) for Idealized Influence, 0.74 (0.21) for Inspirational Motivation, 0.71 (0.21) for Intellectual Stimulation, 0.75 (0.20) for Individualized Consideration, and 0.70 (0.16) for Contingent Reward. The objective subgroup coefficient for Inspirational Motivation must be interpreted with considerable caution, given the relatively low number of studies, even though they were based on a relatively large aggregated sample size across these few studies.

The findings for the objective subgroup for Intellectual Stimulation, Individualized Consideration, and Contingent Reward are more robust. These findings are consistent with earlier meta-analyses (Lowe et al., 1996) and are based on a sufficiently large number of independent studies.

Corrected correlation coefficients for the remaining transactional and non-transactional scales were 0.10 (0.00) for Management-by-Exception-Active, 0.10 (–0.07) for Management-by-Exception-Passive, –0.32 (N/A) for Management-by-Exception, –0.47 (–0.15) for Laissez-Faire, and 0.32 (–0.05) for Transactional Leadership for the subjective and objective subgroups respectively. However, most of the objective subgroup coefficients should be interpreted cautiously owing to the small number of studies. The notable exception to the small number of studies concern was for the Laissez-Faire scale. Our results are consistent with the argument that Laissez-Faire is the least effective form of leadership.

Credibility interval analysis suggests that a further search for moderators is warranted. This is not surprising since the disappointing number of studies incorporating objective measures of effectiveness hampers our ability to test for these effects. An analysis of the 95% confidence intervals reveals that most do not include zero, and thus we can posit that leadership behavior, as measured by the MLQ, is associated with subjective effectiveness in the direction indicated. For objective measures of effectiveness, we can make this claim for a limited set of scales.

Type of Criterion: Leadership Style and Two Satisfaction Measures

The means, standard deviations, and internal consistency reliabilities were similar to our findings for earlier subgroups. This provides some reassurance that differences in correlations regarding leadership styles and various outcome measures are determined by something other than response bias differences across subgroups. Consistent with our expectations, the transformational leadership scales were more highly correlated with satisfaction with the leader than with satisfaction with the job. Corrected correlations for satisfaction with the leader and satisfaction with the job subgroups, respectively, were 0.92 (0.57) for Attributed Charisma, 0.77 (0.41) for Idealized Influence, 0.78 (0.35) for Inspirational Motivation, 0.71 (0.21) for Intellectual Stimulation, and 0.83 (0.43) for Individualized Consideration. For the Transformational Leadership scale, the subgroup coefficients were 0.57 and 0.30, respectively.

For transactional and non-transactional scales, the subgroup correlations were 0.82 (0.52) for Contingent Reward, –0.12 (–0.05) for Management-by-Exception-Active, –0.47 (–0.39) for Management-by-Exception-Passive,

Table 4. Moderating Effect of Type of Criterion Measurement on the Relationship Between MLQ Scales and Effectiveness.

Scale[1]	Moderator	Sample Size[2]	Mean[3]	Std Dev.[3]	Scale Alpha[3]	Number of r Coefficients[4]	Number of Studies[4]	Range of r Coefficients	Mean Raw r	Mean Corrected r	95% Credibility Interval[5]	95% Confidence Interval[6]
AC	Subjective	6826	2.80	0.84	0.79	39	14	0.89 to −0.20	0.68	0.85	1.00 to 0.48	0.93 to 0.77
	Objective	2375	2.66	0.59	0.91	6	4	0.33 to −0.08	0.19	0.23	0.39 to 0.06	0.31 to 0.14
II	Subjective	7450	2.80	0.73	0.71	39	14	0.87 to −0.12	0.58	0.76	1.00 to 0.39	0.84 to 0.69
	Objective	632	2.56	0.89	0.75	4	1	N/A	N/A	N/A	N/A	N/A
IM	Subjective	7766	2.79	0.82	0.85	57	18	0.85 to −0.09	0.61	0.74	1.00 to 0.38	0.82 to 0.67
	Objective	4132	2.61	0.50	0.88	13	3	0.35 to −0.14	0.17	0.20	0.44 to −0.04	0.33 to 0.10
IS	Subjective	9944	2.42	0.83	0.82	62	21	0.90 to −0.11	0.58	0.71	1.00 to 0.25	0.79 to 0.63
	Objective	3658	2.48	0.55	0.90	14	5	0.58 to −0.19	0.18	0.21	0.42 to 0.01	0.32 to 0.08
IC	Subjective	10,216	2.62	0.85	0.80	65	22	0.89 to −0.27	0.60	0.75	1.00 to 0.30	0.83 to 0.67
	Objective	4034	2.56	0.90	0.89	17	6	0.50 to −0.14	0.17	0.20	0.43 to −0.02	0.29 to 0.12
TFL	Subjective	5474	3.03	0.80	0.93	26	13	0.87 to 0.04	0.52	0.61	1.00 to −0.06	0.77 to 0.45
	Objective	1560	3.31	1.00	0.93	19	10	0.49 to −0.19	0.10	0.11	0.26 to −0.04	0.19 to 0.04
CR	Subjective	12,475	2.30	0.79	0.78	62	21	0.87 to −0.31	0.56	0.70	1.00 to 0.16	0.80 to 0.61
	Objective	4104	2.58	0.60	0.89	18	7	0.43 to −0.34	0.13	0.16	0.32 to 0.00	0.22 to 0.09
MBEA	Subjective	10,621	1.89	0.81	0.74	53	17	0.50 to −0.39	0.08	0.10	0.44 to −0.25	0.17 to 0.03
	Objective	2017	2.18	0.96	0.77	12	3	0.13 to −0.05	0.00	0.00	0.00 to 0.00	0.04 to −0.04
MBEP	Subjective	10,621	1.89	0.81	0.74	53	17	0.50 to −0.39	0.08	0.10	0.44 to −0.25	0.17 to 0.03
	Objective	1097	1.36	0.88	0.68	6	3	0.04 to −0.20	−0.05	−0.07	0.03 to −0.17	−0.01 to −0.13
MBE	Subjective	1550	1.87	0.80	0.71	7	3	0.50 to −0.53	−0.24	−0.32	0.03 to −0.68	−0.16 to −0.49
	Objective	1456	2.15	0.00	0.77	1	1	N/A	N/A	N/A	NA	NA
LF	Subjective	7852	0.90	0.67	0.76	53	18	0.51 to −0.69	−0.37	−0.47	−0.09 to −0.86	−0.40 to −0.55
	Objective	3582	0.50	0.49	0.75	17	6	−0.09 to −0.28	−0.12	−0.15	0.03 to −0.17	−0.10 to −0.21
TRL	Subjective	1049	1.58	0.48	0.84	9	4	0.55 to −0.05	0.27	0.32	0.52 to 0.13	0.43 to 0.22
	Objective	597	3.54	0.73	0.82	9	4	0.12 to −0.18	−0.04	−0.05	0.14 to −0.24	0.01 to −0.11

Table 4. Continued.

[1] Because only one coefficient was reported for the scales (1) Management-by-Exception and Laissez-Faire and (2) Charismatic Leadership, they cannot be meta-analyzed and are thus not reported here.

[2] Unique sample size across all studies.

[3] Mean, standard deviation, and reliability weighted by sample size.

[4] Coefficients exceeds number of studies due to multiple criterion variables. For studies correlating one set of leadership ratings to multiple criteria, coefficients are averaged to obtain a composite correlation coefficient. Composite criteria maintain assumptions of sample independence required in the meta-analysis. The impact of different criterion measures on the correlation of leadership ratings to outcomes may be investigated further if credibility interval analysis suggests that moderators may be present (see footnote 6).

[5] Corrected for attenuation due to measurement of the independent and dependent variable.

[6] Credibility intervals indicate the extent to which validity findings can be generalized and indicate moderators when large or include zero. Confidence intervals assess the accuracy of the mean effect size.

Table 5. Moderating Effect of Type of Criterion Measurement on the Relationship Between MLQ Scales and Satisfaction.

Scale[1]	Moderator	Sample Size[2]	Mean[3]	Std Dev.[3]	Scale Alpha[3]	Number of r Coefficients[4]	Number of Studies[4]	Range of r Coefficients	Mean Raw r	Mean Corrected r	95% Credibility Interval[5]	95% Confidence Interval[6]
AC	Leader	5659	2.76	0.85	0.78	17	9	0.93 to −0.14	0.73	0.92	1.00 to 0.69	1.00 to 0.83
	Job	307	2.38	0.93	0.77	1	1	0.45	0.45	0.57	N/A	N/A
II	Leader	6511	2.81	0.71	0.68	17	11	0.83 to −0.14	0.57	0.77	1.00 to 0.42	0.85 to 0.69
	Job	907	2.60	0.72	0.82	3	3	0.40 to 0.29	0.33	0.41	0.49 to 0.32	0.46 to 0.35
IM	Leader	6293	2.73	0.85	0.85	21	13	0.93 to −0.12	0.64	0.78	1.00 to 0.47	0.85 to 0.70
	Job	907	2.83	0.75	0.83	3	3	0.38 to 0.24	0.29	0.35	0.39 to 0.32	0.43 to 0.28
IS	Leader	8167	2.38	0.84	0.80	23	15	0.86 to −0.12	0.60	0.75	1.00 to 0.38	0.83 to 0.67
	Job	907	2.47	0.72	0.78	3	3	0.42 to 0.22	0.29	0.36	0.54 to 0.20	0.47 to 0.26
IC	Leader	8263	2.59	0.86	0.78	23	15	0.93 to −0.24	0.66	0.83	1.00 to 0.42	0.91 to 0.74
	Job	907	2.58	0.80	0.77	3	3	0.48 to 0.26	0.33	0.43	0.63 to 0.22	0.54 to 0.31
TFL	Leader	2547	3.48	0.92	0.92	10	9	0.87 to −0.02	0.49	0.57	0.96 to 0.18	0.69 to 0.45
	Job	2175	2.95	1.03	0.96	9	6	0.68 to 0.07	0.27	0.30	0.76 to −0.15	0.47 to 0.13
CR	Leader	8513	2.47	0.80	0.77	22	16	0.89 to 0.08	0.64	0.82	1.00 to 0.46	0.89 to 0.74
	Job	2351	2.85	0.63	0.71	8	5	0.69 to 0.09	0.39	0.52	0.95 to 0.09	0.67 to 0.37
MBEA	Leader	6371	1.73	0.92	0.77	15	11	0.35 to −0.62	−0.10	−0.12	0.31 to −0.55	−0.02 to −0.23
	Job	1752	1.86	0.67	0.76	4	4	0.10 to −0.18	−0.04	−0.05	0.14 to −0.23	0.05 to −0.14
MBEP	Leader	7028	1.59	0.71	0.69	15	11	0.43 to −0.69	−0.35	−0.47	0.15 to −1.00	−0.32 to −0.61
	Job	907	1.60	0.69	0.76	3	3	−0.12 to −0.66	−0.31	−0.39	−0.23 to −1.00	−0.10 to −0.68
MBE	Leader	1550	2.26	0.51	0.62	5	3	0.13 to −0.36	−0.31	−0.44	−0.08 to −0.80	−0.28 to −0.60
	Job	N/A	N/A	N/A	N/A	N/A	N/A	N/A	N/A	N/A	N/A	N/A
LF	Leader	7025	0.80	0.68	0.76	16	12	0.55 to −0.73	−0.43	−0.56	0.07 to −1.00	−0.41 to −0.70
	Job	774	0.82	0.56	0.74	3	3	−0.10 to −0.21	−0.19	−0.24	−0.09 to −0.39	−0.19 to −0.29
TRL	Leader	1347	3.64	0.73	0.81	5	4	0.41 to 0.04	0.17	0.21	0.39 to 0.02	0.31 to 0.11
	Job	642	2.60	0.90	0.90	4	3	0.33 to 0.05	0.20	0.24	0.42 to 0.06	0.37 to 0.11

Table 5. Continued.

[1] Because only one coefficient was reported for the scales (1) Management-by-Exception and Laissez-Faire and (2) Charismatic Leadership, they cannot be meta-analyzed and are thus not reported here.

[2] Unique sample size across all studies.

[3] Mean, standard deviation, and reliability weighted by sample size.

[4] Coefficients exceeds number of studies due to multiple criterion variables. For studies correlating one set of leadership ratings to multiple criteria, coefficients are averaged to obtain a composite correlation coefficient. Composite criteria maintain assumptions of sample independence required in the meta-analysis. The impact of different criterion measures on the correlation of leadership ratings to outcomes may be investigated further if credibility interval analysis suggests that moderators may be present (see footnote six).

[5] Corrected for attenuation due to measurement of the independent and dependent variable.

[6] Credibility intervals indicate the extent to which validity findings can be generalized and indicate moderators when large or include zero. Confidence intervals assess the accuracy of the mean effect size.

–0.44 (N/A) for Management-by-Exception, and –0.56 (–0.44) for Laissez-Faire. For the Transactional Leadership scale, the coefficients were 0.21 (0.24). A review of these coefficients reveals a clear pattern of MLQ scale scores being more strongly correlated with Satisfaction with the Leader than with Satisfaction with the job. This is true for both positive correlations (e.g. Attributed Charisma, Contingent Reward) and negative correlations (e.g. Laissez-Faire).

Again, these subgroup analyses must also be viewed with some degree of caution, given the relatively small number of studies in each grouping. Perhaps, the strongest conclusions can be drawn for the Contingent Reward and Transformational Leadership scales and, to a lesser extent, the Management-by-Exception Active scale, given the larger sample sizes representing these different subgroups.

DISCUSSION

With most leadership paradigms, it would be helpful to update results periodically to determine whether the hypothesized relationships change over time. Changes in organizational structure and how performance is measured may affect relationships between leadership style and performance. For example, as more leaders work with followers at a distance and via advanced information technology, one wonders what impact that may have on the relationship between leadership style and performance (Avolio, Kahai & Dodge, 2000). Also, as new cohorts of workers enter organizations, one wonders how the relationship between leadership style and performance may change over time. This leads one to question the extent to which the new cohort of employees, who have been described in the media as more independent and challenging, may view directive leadership as a more negative style of leadership than previous cohorts of employees.

The meta-analysis conducted for this study extends the work of Lowe et al. (1996) by examining 12 scales comprising the MLQ as opposed to the five reported in their study. The inclusion of all 12 scales provides a more comprehensive assessment of the full range of leadership styles, which Antonakis and House (in press) advocate using as the "scaffold" for building a broader and fuller range model of leadership. We have also included in this meta-analysis an examination of the relationship between leadership style and satisfaction, which was not included in the earlier meta-analysis.

Generally speaking, the results of the overall meta-analysis and subsequent examination of moderators confirmed what has been reported in earlier individual studies and meta-analyses. The hierarchical pattern proposed in the full-range model of leadership has received consistent support over these last 15 years, with the current study reflecting prior trends linking transformational, transactional and non-transactional leadership to performance. This consistent pattern of results is encouraging in that it suggests that these relationships are enduring and are not episodic in the sense that they are tied to one period in history, a particular version of the MLQ, or artifacts of the cohort or type of outcome measures being evaluated. Indeed, the corrected correlations reported for effectiveness with the various transformational scales presented in Table 2 are remarkably similar to those reported by Lowe et al. (1996) in their overall meta-analysis of effectiveness. Specifically, the corrected correlations in the current and 1996 study were 0.68 (0.73) for Charisma, 0.59 (0.62) for Individualized Consideration, and 0.57 (0.60) for Intellectual Stimulation, respectively. Contingent Reward was somewhat different 0.56 (0.41), but would lead to the same conclusion, that Contingent Reward is positively and moderately correlated with effectiveness. Perhaps the main difference is that the Contingent Reward scale tended to have a similar positive relationship with performance effectiveness and satisfaction as compared with transformational leadership.

Yet, there were also some notable exceptions comparing the results of the two meta-analyses. For example, there was a significant between-study difference in the corrected correlation coefficient for Management-by-Exception, 0.05 (–0.30). Presently, it is not clear why such a large difference exists. However, it is worth noting that the number of studies utilizing this scale decreased by two-thirds relative to the meta-analysis conducted in 1996. This has been due to an increased use of the subscales representing Management-by-Exception-Active and Management-by-Exception-Passive. The similarity that should be noted is that that the coefficient for Management-by-Exception-Passive in this study was approximately the same as the Management-by-Exception coefficient in the 1996 meta-analysis.

The differences regarding the overall Management-by-Exception scale may be due to a variety of factors. Possibly as organizations de-level, the span of control has increased affecting how leaders actively and passively manage-by-exception with their followers. Alternatively, the earlier meta-analysis conducted by Lowe et al. (1996) was based on an earlier version of the MLQ, which did not distinguish active and passive management-by-exception as clearly. Thus, the item composition of the two instruments may have affected the outcomes that are reported in each respective study.

The differences in MLQ forms between 1996 and 2002 may also help explain the lower positive correlation noted between Contingent Reward leadership and effectiveness reported by Lowe et al. (1996). Specifically, the earlier MLQ Form 5R contained contingent reward items that were more exchange-oriented or based on quid pro quo criteria. The MLQ Form 5X used in most of the research contained in this meta-analysis contains a shorter contingent reward scale (4 vs. 10 items), and that scale taps more of the higher-order transactions associated with recognition and exchange of agreements (Avolio, 1999). Along these lines, Goodwin et al. (2001) have argued that some of the transactional contingent reward items are of a lower-order type, which they associate with more explicit contracting with followers. The remaining items are more of the higher-order transactional type and are generally associated with recognition and forming of implicit contracts. In the newer MLQ Form 5X, two of the contingent reward items appear to represent more of the lower-order transactional-type items. For example one of the items is "rewards us when we do what we are supposed to do". Goodwin et al. (2001) reported that the lower-order transactional scale had a higher discriminant validity vs. the higher-order transactional scale when correlated with the transformational leadership scale

Bass et al. (in press) also showed that when only the lower-order transactional Contingent Reward items were included in a hierarchical regression analysis, the transformational scale augmented the Contingent Reward scale in predicting unit performance over time. However, when the recognition items were included in the Contingent Reward scale, the transformational scale did not significantly augment that Contingent Reward scale in predicting unit performance.

The MLQ has gone through a number of revisions to address concerns about its psychometric properties (Yukl, 1999). Yet, by revising the items and scales to address these concerns, we also run into the potential problem of not being able to replicate earlier findings due to different items being included across survey instruments. However, we do need to reiterate that, by and large, our results remain consistent with the earlier meta-analytic findings. However, we would recommend that future research examine the components of the transactional scales to see if the lower- and higher-order distinction can be reliably obtained across different samples and organizational contexts.

Confirming earlier findings, our results are consistent with Lowe et al. (1996), who reported consistently higher correlations with effectiveness in Public as compared with Private organizations. In the current meta-analysis, the relationships for Public vs. Private were higher for Attributed Charisma, although the coefficients were very close on an absolute basis. However, the relationships reported for Idealized Influence, Inspirational Motivation, Intellectual Stimulation, and Individualized Consideration were higher in private organizations in the present study.

Limitations and Future Directions

As careful as one can be, a meta-analysis is only as good as the studies that are available to conduct an empirical review of the literature. Since the last meta-analysis was conducted, there has been less emphasis in this literature on collecting more 'objective' measures of performance effectiveness. We suggest that future research on the full-range model and MLQ must now begin to focus on collecting a broader range of independent and objective measures collected at the same time as the leadership scales, as well as over time, allowing future research to examine the links explored in this study using a longitudinal framework.

In addition to collecting measures of objective performance, it also will be helpful for the next meta-analysis to have measures of performance that tap both individual and group levels of extra effort or performance beyond expectations. Of course, building a broader database with objective measures is the primary goal, but over time, tapping measures that might be more sensitive to the influence of transformational vs. transactional leadership may help to advance this theory more rapidly. Specifically, a fundamental proposition in Bass's (1985) writings is that transformational leadership will augment transactional in predicting performance. Gathering objective measures that tap into performance around stretch goals or extreme criteria will allow future researchers to examine this fundamental proposition in Bass's work.

There is also sufficient theoretical justification to suggest that transformational leadership impacts on followers in ways that are different than transactional styles of leadership. Thus, to examine the black box in which followers are 'transformed', we suggest that future research concentrate on measuring some of the following outcome measures:

- Using per person productivity (ppp) rates and trends over time to track fundamental improvements and changes in performance.
- Examining growth rates in followers' knowledge, learning capacity, motivation to lead, self and collective-efficacy.
- Examining as outcome measure(s) followers' levels of moral reasoning, willingness to self-sacrifice, ethical standards, and concern for the community, which are all outcomes that Burns (1978) and Bass (1985) used to differentiate transformational vs. transactional leaders. Specifically, if transforming leaders are morally uplifting, self-sacrificing, etc. we should examine moral reasoning as an outcome measure.

- To the extent that transformational leaders develop followers into leaders, we should be examining the leadership qualities/styles of followers over time, as an outcome measure.
- As more leaders lead virtually and at a distance, we need to begin to examine how each of the styles of leadership is related to performance over time and distance.
- As noted by Lowe and Gardner (2000), the field of leadership studies is still by and large dominated by work completed with samples in the USA. Future research needs to explore how the relationships between these leadership styles and outcomes vary as a consequence of culture.
- There are only a handful of studies that have examined the relationship between leadership style and strategic organizational performance (see Waldman and Javidan in this volume for a review). Future research needs to examine the relationship between the full range of leadership styles and various measures of firm performance over time, at the most senior levels of both public and private organizations.

CONCLUSIONS AND IMPLICATIONS

Any researcher going through this coding exercise cannot help but be struck by the fact that there are still too few experimental studies, studies using objective measures, studies exploring distant rather than proximal leaders, studies considering work unit maturity, hierarchical level and other environmental factors such as the rate of change, technology intensity, cross-cultural differences and gender differences to perform a meta-analysis. However, each time one goes through this exercise and points to what is missing, the current and future generations of scholars are alerted to the areas that require further attention and data collection. We suspect that the results reported here, and the areas that we could not explore, will in combination provide further impetus to fill in the blanks to offer yet another assessment of this emerging paradigm of leadership. And in so doing, we hope to advance the field of leadership and broaden potentially what constitutes the full range of styles and criterion measures that can be explored.

REFERENCES

Antonakis, J., & House, R. J. (2002). The full-range leadership theory: The way forward. In: B. J. Avolio & F. J. Yammarino (Eds), *Transformational and charismatic leadership: The road ahead*. New York: Elsevier Science Inc.

Avolio, B, J. (1999). *Full leadership development: Building the vital forces in organizations*, Thousand Oaks: Sage.

Bass, B. M. (1985). *Leadership and performance beyond expectations*. New York: Free Press.

Bass, B. M. (1998). *Transformational leadership: Industrial, military and educational impact*. Hillsdale, NJ: Lawrence Erlbaum Associates

Bass, B. M., Avolio, B. J., Jung, D. I., & Berson, Y. (2002). Predicting unit performance by assessing transformational and transactional leadership. *Journal of Applied Psychology*, in press.

Burns, J. M. (1978). *Leadership*. New York: Free Press.

Conger, J. A., & Kanungo, R. N. (1998). *Charismatic leadership in organizations*. Thousand Oaks, CA: Sage.

DeGroot, T., Kiker, D. S., & Cross, T. C. (2000). A meta-analysis to review organizational outcomes related to charismatic leadership. *Canadian Journal of Administrative Sciences*, *17*, 357–371.

Gaspar, R. (1992). Transformational leadership: An integrative review of the literature. Unpublished doctoral dissertation, Western Michigan University, Kalamazoo.

Goodwin, V. L., Wofford, J. C., & Whittington, J. L. (2001). A theoretical and empirical extension to the transformational leadership construct. *Journal of Organizational Behavior*, *22*, 759–774.

House, R. J., & Aditya, R. N. (1997). The social scientific study of leadership: Quo vadis? *Journal of Management*, *23*, 409–473.

Hunt, J. G. (1999). Transformational/Charismatic leadership's transformation of the field: an historical essay. *The Leadership Quarterly*, *10*, 129–144.

Judge, T. A., Thoresen, C. J., Bono, J. E., & Patton, G. K. (2001). The job satisfaction–job performance relationship: A qualitative and quantitative. *Psychological Bulletin*, *127*, 376–407.

Landy, F. J. (1989). *Psychology of work behavior*. Pacific Grove, CA: Brooks/Cole.

Lowe, K. B., & Gardner, W. L. (2000). A decade of The Leadership Quarterly: Contributions and challenges for the future. *The Leadership Quarterly*, *11*, 459–514.

Lowe, K. B., Kroeck, K. G., & Sivasubramaniam, N. (1996). Effectiveness correlates of transformation and transactional leadership: A meta-analytic review of the MLQ literature. *The Leadership Quarterly*, *7*, 385–425.

Nunally, J. C. (1978). *Psychometric theory*. New York: McGraw-Hill.

Onnen, M. K. (1987). The relationship of clergy leadership characteristics to growing or declining churches. Unpublished doctoral dissertation, University of Louisville, Louisville.

Podsakoff, P. M., MacKenzie, S. B., Moorman, R. H., & Fetter, R. (1990). Transformational leader behaviors and their effects on followers' trust in leader, satisfaction, and organizational citizenship behaviors. *The Leadership Quarterly*, *1*, 107–142.

Schmidt, N. W., & Klimoski, R. J. (1991). *Research methods in human resources management*. Cincinnati: Southwestern Publishing.

Waldman, D. A., & Javidan, M. (2002). Charismatic leadership at the strategic level: Taking a new look at upper echelons theory. In: B. J. Avolio & F. J. Yammarino (Eds), *Transformational and charismatic leadership: The road ahead*. New York: Elsevier Science Inc.

Wanous, J. P., Sullivan, S. E., & Malinak, J. (1989). The role of judgment calls in meta-analysis. *Journal of Applied Psychology*, *74*, 259–264.

Yukl, G. (1999). An evaluation of conceptual weaknesses in transformational and charismatic leadership theories. *Leadership Quarterly*, *10*, 285–305.

REFERENCE STUDIES IN META-ANALYSES

Avolio, B. J., Bass, B. M., & Berson, Y. (2000). Leadership and its impact on platoon readiness at Joint Readiness Training Center (JRTC). Unpublished manuscript.

Avolio, B. J., Howell, J. M., & Sosik, J. J. (1999). A funny thing happened on the way to the bottom line: humor as a moderator of leadership style effects. *Academy of Management Journal, 42*, 219–227.

Avolio, B. J., Jung, D., Murry, W., & Sivasubramaniam, N. (1996). Building highly developed teams: Focusing on shared leadership processes, efficacy, trust, and performance. *Advances in interdisciplinary studies of work teams* (Vol. 3, pp. 173–209). Oxford: JAI Press.

Avolio, B. J., Sivasubramaniam, N., Murry, W. D., & Jung, D. I. (1996). Assessing team leadership and predicting group performance. Unpublished manuscript.

Bass, B. M., Avolio, B. J., Jung, D., & Berson, Y. (1999). Predicting unit performance by assessing transformational and transactional leadership. Unpublished manuscript.

Bayless, R. R. (1996). The identification of leadership styles of large group music ensemble leaders and their use as predictors of teacher effectiveness. Unpublished Dissertation. Kent State University, USA.

Brown, F. W., & Dodd, N. G. (1999). Rally the troops or make the trains run on time: The relative importance and interaction of contingent reward and transformational leadership. *Leadership & Organization Development Journal, 20*, 291–299.

Bycio, P., Hackett, R. D., & Allen, J. S. (1995). Further Assessments of Bass's (1985) Conceptualization of Transactional and Transformational Leadership. *Journal of Applied Psychology, 80*, 468–478.

Commer, L. B., Jolson, M. A., Dubinssky, A. J., & Yammarino, F. J. (1995). When the sales manager is a woman: An exploration into the relationship between salespeople's gender and their responses to leadership styles. *Journal of Personal Selling & Sales Management, 15*, 17–32.

Daughtry, L. H. (1995). Vocational administrator leadership effectiveness as a function of gender and leadership style. Unpublished Dissertation. Virginia Polytechnic Institute and State University, USA.

Doherty, A. J., & Danylchuk, K. E. (1996). Transformational and transactional leadership in interuniversity athletics management. *Journal of Sport Management, 10*, 292–309.

Dubinsky, A. J., Yammarino, F. J., Jolson, M. A., & Spangler, W. D. (1995). Transformational leadership: An initial investigation in sales management. *Journal of Personal Selling & Sales Management, 15*, 17–31.

Elliot, R., & Albert, K. (2000a). An investigation of the Australian MLQ norms database [Draft Document for Internal Research Review]. MLQ Pty Ltd., Australia.

Elliot, R., & Albert, K. (2000b). Predicting performance outcomes from transformational behaviors and rater congruence. Unpublished manuscript.

Garcia, J. L. (1995). Transformational leadership processes and salesperson performance effectiveness: A theoretical model and partial empirical examination. Unpublished Dissertation. The Fielding Institute. USA.

Geyer, A. L. J., & Steyrer, J. M. (1998). Transformational leadership and objective performance in banks. *Applied Psychology: An International Review, 47*, 397–420.

Geyer, A. L. J., & Steyrer, J. M. (undated). Transformational leadership, classical leadership dimensions and performance indicators in savings-banks. Unpublished manuscript.

Gunigundo, M. S. T. (1998). An exploration of the relationship between principal leadership style and student academic achievement in the Philippines. Unpublished Dissertation. Louisiana State University and Agricultural and Mechanical College, USA.

Howell, J. M., & Hall-Merenda, K. E. (1999). The ties that bind: the impact of leader-member exchange, transformational and transactional leadership, and distance on predicting follower performance. *Journal of Applied Psychology, 84*, 680–694.

Hult, G. T. M., Ferrell, O. C., & Schul, P. L. (1998). The effect of global leadership on purchasing process outcomes. *European Journal of Marketing, 32*, 1029–1050.

Judge, T. A., & Bono, J. E. (2000a). Five-factor model of personality and transformational leadership. *Journal of Applied Psychology, 85*, 751–765.

Judge, T. A., & Bono, J. (2000b). Personality and transformational leadership. Unpublished manuscript.

Jung, D., & Avolio, B. J. (1998a). An experimental investigation of the mediating effects of trust and value congruence on transformational and transactional leadership: A multicultural perspective. Unpublished manuscript.

Jung, D., & Avolio, B. J. (1998b). Transformational leadership and it's effects on group processes and performance among Caucasian- and Asian-Americans. Unpublished manuscript.

Jung, D., & Avolio, B. J. (2000). Opening the black box: an experimental investigation of the mediating effects of trust and value congruence on transformational and transactional leadership. *Journal of Organizational Behavior, 21*, 949–964.

Jung, D. I. (1997). Effects of different leadership styles and followers' cultural orientations on performance under various task structure and reward allocation conditions. Unpublished Dissertation. State University of New York at Binghamton, USA.

Kane, T. D., & Tremble, T. R. (2000). Transformational leadership effects at different levels of the army. *Military Psychology, 12*, 137–160.

Koh, W. L., Steers, R. M., & Terborg, J. R. (1995). The effects of transformational leadership on teacher attitudes and student performance in Singapore. *Journal of Organizational Behavior, 16*, 319–333.

Medley, F., & Larochelle, D. R. (1995). Transformational leadership and job satisfaction. *Nursing Management, 26*, 9.

Muenjohn, N. (2000). The effect of culture on the leadership behavior of Australian expatriate managers in Thailand. Unpublished Dissertation. Victoria University of Technology, Australia.

Nischan, T. P. (1997). Transformational leadership as a predictor of effectiveness, extra effort, and satisfaction in a community college classroom environment. Unpublished Dissertation. Nova Southeastern University, USA.

Peters, T. J. (1997). Transactional and transformational leadership: Predictors of employee satisfaction, commitment, and productivity. Unpublished Dissertation. Marquette University, USA.

Pillai, R., Schriesheim, C. A., & Williams, E. S. (1999). Fairness perceptions and trust as mediators for transformational and transactional leadership: a two-sample study. *Journal of Management, 25*, 897–933.

Russell, R. G. (1996). The relationship between transformational and transactional leadership styles and employee turnover intentions. Unpublished Dissertation. Nova Southeastern University, USA.

Sosik, J. J. (1997). Effects of Transformational Leadership and anonymity on idea generation in computer-mediated groups. *Group & Organization Management, 22*, 460–487.

Sosik, J. J., Avolio, B. J., & Kahai, S. S. (1998). Inspiring group creativity: Comparing anonymous and identified electronic brainstorming. *Small Group Research, 29*, 3–31.

Sosik, J. J., Avolio, B. J., Kahai, S. S., & Jung, D. I. (1998). Computer-supported work group potency and effectiveness: The role of transformational leadership, anonymity, and task interdependence. *Computers in Human Behavior, 14*, 491–511.

Sosik, J. J., Kahai, S. S., & Avolio, B. J. (1998). Transformational leadership and dimensions of creativity: Motivating idea generation in computer-mediated groups. *Creativity Research Journal, 11*, 111–121.

Sosik, J. J., Kahai, S. S., & Avolio, B. J. (1999). Leadership style, anonymity, and creativity in group decision support systems: The mediating role of optimal flow. *Journal of Creative Behavior, 33*, 227–256.

Sosik, J. J. (1995). The impact of leadership style and anonymity on performance, creative output, and satisfaction in GDSS-supported groups. Unpublished Dissertation. State University of New York, USA.

Srisilpsophon, P. (1999). Transformational leadership and performance outcomes of multinational corporations in Thailand. Unpublished Dissertation. Nova Southeastern University, USA.

Steeves, R. (1997). Why leaders are effective: An examination into leader developmental level and leader-follower developmental fit as predictors of effective leadership. Unpublished Dissertation. The Fielding Institute, USA.

Stepp, P. L. Cho, H., & Chung, S. (1998). Perceived differences in leadership styles of people of color: Transformational or transactional? Unpublished manuscript.

Tracey, J. B., & Hinkin, T. R. (1998). Transformational leadership or effective managerial practices? *Group & Organizational Management, 23*, 220–236.

Tucker, M. L., McCarthy, A. M., & Jones, M. C. (1999). Women and men politicians: Are some of the best leaders dissatisfied? *Leadership & Organization Development, 20*, 285–290.

VanDoren, E. (1998). The relationship between leadership/followership in staff nurses and employment setting. Unpublished Dissertation. Western Michigan University, USA.

Weierter, S. (1995). Transformational leadership and transactional substitutes: An exploratory analysis. Unpublished manuscript.

Wofford, J. C., Goodwin, V. L., & Whittington, J. L. (1998). A field study of a cognitive approach to understanding transformational and transactional leadership. *Leadership Quarterly, 9*, 1.

THE DUAL EFFECT OF TRANSFORMATIONAL LEADERSHIP: PRIMING RELATIONAL AND COLLECTIVE SELVES AND FURTHER EFFECTS ON FOLLOWERS

Ronit Kark and Boas Shamir

ABSTRACT

In this chapter, we integrate recent theories on followers' self-concept and transformational leadership theory in order to develop a conceptual framework for understanding the exceptional and diverse effects transformational leaders may have on their followers. We propose that transformational leaders may influence two levels of followers' self-concept: the relational and the collective self, thus fostering personal identification with the leader and social identification with the organizational unit. Specific leader behaviors that prime different aspects of followers' self-concepts are identified, and their possible effects on different aspects of followers' perceptions and behaviors are discussed.

In the last two decades there has been accumulating evidence to suggest that transformational leadership is an influential form of leadership that is associated with high levels of individual and organizational performance (e.g. Barling, Weber & Kelloway, 1996; Dvir, Eden, Avolio & Shamir, in press).

Transformational and Charismatic Leadership, Volume 2, pages 67–91.
ISBN: 0-7623-0962-8

However, research on transformational leadership has not fully explored the question of what are the underlying processes and mechanisms by which transformational leaders exert their influence on followers and ultimately on performance.

As Yukl (1998) concluded after reviewing research on this topic, "a variety of different influence processes may be involved in transformational leadership, and different transformational behaviors may involve different influence processes. Research on these processes is needed to gain better understanding of transformational leadership" (p. 328). Theorists generally agree that identification processes play a central role in the influence dynamics of leadership. In the present article, we suggest that transformational leaders can have a dual effect, exerting their influence on followers through the creation of personal identification with the leader and social identification with the work unit, and that these different forms of identification can lead to differential outcomes.

Recently, leaders' ability to influence different aspects of followers' self-concept has been suggested as one of the mechanisms for understanding the ability of leaders to influence followers' perceptions and behaviors. However, to date, there have been only limited attempts to understand leadership processes by focusing on followers' self-concepts. Among these attempts, are Eden's (1992) research on the Pygmalion effect, and the work of Shamir and colleagues on the self-concept based theory of charismatic leadership (e.g. Shamir, 1991; Shamir, House & Arthur, 1993; Shamir, Zakay, Breinin & Popper, 1998). Lord, Brown and Feiberg (1999) proposed a new theory focusing on the different levels of followers' self-concept in the leader-follower relationship, asserting that leaders can affect followers by priming different aspects of the self-concept and by changing the way followers perceive themselves. These theoretical developments may be helpful in the attempt to understand the ability of transformational leaders to influence followers by arousing different identification processes.

The goal of the current chapter is to draw from transformational leadership theory (Avolio, Bass & Jung, 1999; Bass & Avolio, 1994) and from Shamir et al.'s (1993) self-concept based motivational theory of charismatic leadership and Lord et al.'s (1999) self-concept based theory of leadership, in order to develop a conceptual framework to advance further studies on the underlying mechanisms that enable transformational leaders to influence followers' identifications, and ultimately their behaviors and organizational outcomes. In the following section, we define and review the identification processes by which transformational leaders can exert their influence on followers. We then present a framework for understanding followers' self-concept and leaders' possible effects on followers' self-concept, following the theory of Lord and his associates (1999), and use this framework to conceptualize the mechanisms that enable transformational leaders to affect followers' identities and identifications. We develop propositions that differentiate between transformational behaviors that prime different aspects of follower's self-concepts: relational and collective. Finally, we explore various possible outcomes of this dual effect of transformational leadership.

TRANSFORMATIONAL LEADERSHIP AND FOLLOWERS' IDENTIFICATION

Transformational leadership has been presented in the literature as different from transactional leadership. While transactional leadership was defined on the basis of the influence process underlying it, as an exchange of rewards for compliance, transformational leadership was defined on the basis of its effects, as transforming the values and priorities of followers and motivating them to perform beyond their expectations (Yukl, 1998). Bass and Avolio (1994) proposed that the behaviors transformational leaders exhibit include four components: inspirational motivation, idealized influence, individualized consideration and intellectual stimulation. Inspirational motivation includes the creation and presentation of an attractive vision of the future, the use of symbols and emotional arguments, and the demonstration of optimism and enthusiasm. Idealized influence includes behaviors such as sacrificing for the benefit of the group, setting a personal example, and demonstrating high ethical standards.

The third component, individualized consideration, includes providing support, encouragement and coaching to followers. The fourth component, intellectual stimulation, involves behaviors that increase awareness of problems and challenge followers to view problems from new perspectives. Previous research has shown that these transformational behaviors are related to leadership effectiveness (Lowe, Kroeck & Sivasubramaniam, 1996) and high employee performance (Barling et al., 1996, Dvir et al., in press).

A review of transformational and charismatic leadership theories suggests that such leadership may achieve its effects partly through the creation of followers' identification with the leader (personal identification) and with the work group (social identification) (Yukl, 1998). Engendering identifications can facilitate the followers' functioning and organizational outcomes (Pratt, 1998). As summed up by Cheney (1983): ". . . fostering identification is the 'intent' of many corporate policies, for with it comes greater assurance that

employees will decide with organizational interests uppermost in mind"
(p. 158). Cheney's words regarding corporate policies are likely to apply to
leaders and leadership practices as well.

Personal Identification with the Leader

Borrowing from Pratt's (1998) definition of organizational identification,
personal identification can be defined as the process whereby an individual's
belief about a person (a leader) becomes self-referential or self-defining.
Various theories of transformational and charismatic leadership highlight the
role of identification with the leader (for review see Yukl, 1998, Table 12-1,
p. 309). For example, the charismatic leadership theory of Conger and
Kanungo (1998) emphasizes personal identification as a central process
through which charismatic leaders influence their followers, suggesting that
such influence is based on referent power (French & Raven, 1959). Similarly,
Shamir, House and Arthur (1993) posit role modeling as one of the major
processes by which charismatic leaders influence followers. Role modeling
implies a process by which followers mold their beliefs, feelings, and behavior
according to those of the leader. Although the theme of personal identification
is more prominent in theories of charismatic leadership (Yukl, 1998),
transformational leadership includes charismatic components, and the theory
also stresses the role of followers' identification with the leader (Avolio,
1999).

In these theories, personal identification may be seen as representing one of
two modes of identification suggested by Pratt (1998):

(1) evoking follower's self concept in the recognition that they share similar
    values with the leader; and
(2) giving rise to followers' desire to change their self-concept so that their
    values and beliefs become more similar to those of the leader.

Both modes of identification are likely to contribute to the ability of a
transformational leader to influence his/her followers.

Social Identification with the Organization

Another underlying process that might account for the exceptional effects of
transformational leadership on followers' perceptions and behaviors is social
identification. Social identification has been defined as the process whereby an
individual's belief about a group (or an organization) becomes self-referential
or self-defining (Pratt, 1998). When individuals identify with a group, they base

their self-concept and self-esteem partly on their belonging to the group, and group successes and failures are experienced as personal successes and failures (Mael & Ashforth, 1992). Ashforth and Mael (1989) were among the first to suggest that transformational leadership might influence followers' social identification.

The influence of leaders on the social identification of followers is central to Shamir et al.'s (1993) motivational theory of charismatic leadership. They have suggested that the influence of charismatic/transformational leaders is based on their success in connecting followers' self-concept to the mission and the group, such that followers' behavior for the sake of the group becomes self-expressive. Recent findings support this assertion, showing that leaders who raise followers' identification with the group increase followers' willingness to contribute to group objectives (Shamir et al., 1998).

In sum, following the theoretical arguments presented above, we propose that transformational leadership is related to both personal and social identification of followers.

Proposition 1a: Transformational leadership positively affects followers' personal identification with the leader.

Proposition 1b: Transformational leadership positively affects followers' social identification with the group.

FOLLOWERS' LEVELS OF SELF-IDENTITY

Despite widespread reference to identification with the leader and the group as key processes in the influence of transformational and charismatic leadership on followers, little attention has been given to the question of what are the underlying mechanisms that enable transformational leaders to have this dual effect on followers and to arouse different types of identifications. Following Lord and his associates (1999), we maintain that the ability of leaders to activate or prime two different levels of social identities, relational and collective social identities, may account for the different forms of influence exerted by transformational leaders.

Social psychological theories of the self tend to see the individual's self-identity as comprising both personal and social identities (Banaji & Prentice, 1994; Brewer & Gardner, 1996). The individuated or personal-selves are those aspects of the self-concept that differentiate the self from all others and define a person's sense of uniqueness as an individual. The social-self comprises those aspects of the self-concept that reflect assimilation to others or to significant social groups (Brewer & Gardner, 1996; Lord et al., 1999).

Brewer and Gardner (1996) provided an elegant theory for classification of the self, suggesting a further distinction between two levels of the social selves – the relational (or interpersonal) and the collective identity. According to these authors, the self-concept is multifaceted, consisting of three fundamental loci of self: the self as an individual, as an interpersonal being, and as a group member. These three loci of self-definitions are of importance because they represent distinct orientations of identity, each with its own social motivation, sources of self-worth and types of significant self-knowledge (see Brewer & Gardner, 1996, p. 83). The relational and collective levels of self-identity, which link the individual to the leader and the organization and affect followers' motivations and behaviors, may be central to the understanding of the effect of transformational leadership on followers. Therefore, in this paper, we will focus on these social aspects of the self-identity.

The *relational self* is derived from interpersonal connections and role relationships with specific others (e.g. child-parent, subordinate-leader). At this level, individuals conceive of themselves predominantly in terms of their roles in relation to significant others, and self-worth is derived from appropriate role behavior (e.g. being a good follower), as conveyed through reflected appraisals of the other person involved in the relationship (Brewer & Gardner, 1996; Gabriel & Gardner, 1999). When a relational orientation is activated, the primary motivation of individuals is to enhance the relationship partner's well-being and derive mutual benefits (Brewer & Gardner, 1996; Gabriel & Gardner, 1999).

Collective social identities, however, do not require personal relationships among members; they are derived from membership in larger more impersonal collectives or social categories (e.g. particular work team or organization). At this level of identity, individuals use the group prototype as a basis for inter-group comparisons and self-definition, and evaluate their self-worth by comparing their group with an out-group (Brewer & Gardner, 1996).

TRANSFORMATIONAL LEADERSHIP AND FOLLOWERS' SELF-CONCEPT

This framework for understanding the self promotes a view of the self-concept as dynamic and multifaceted. According to this conception, all people identify themselves as individuals, relationship partners, and group members in some context. Yet forces at various levels of analysis (e.g. personality traits, quality of relationship, group norms) can influence the cognitive accessibility of a given self-concept, leading to the activation of a particular identity level at a given point in time (Brickson, 2000). This dynamic enables transformational leaders to play a major role in the activation of the various levels of the self.

Lord et al. (1999) were first to consider how this three-level system for understanding self-identity would function in an organizational context, and more specifically in the relationships between leaders and followers. According to the theory proposed by Lord and his associates (1999), leaders can profoundly influence subordinates self-concepts, and thereby influence follower behavior and other social processes. The theory asserts that leaders can achieve their effects on followers by priming the different aspects of followers' self-concepts and by making various identity levels more salient. Following Markus and Wurf (1987), Lord and his colleagues assert that the self-concept is malleable and suggest that leaders can influence self-structures temporarily through activities that influence the accessibly of various self-concepts. For example, by emphasizing similarities among workers, leaders can increase activation of collective identities while inhibiting individual-level identities. In addition, they maintain that leaders can also have more enduring effects if they are able to alter chronic self-schemas, beyond activating existing self-schemas and changing their relative salience.

This conceptualization can be most valuable in an attempt to understand the distinct ways in which transformational leadership achieves its influence on followers' personal and social identifications. Lord and his co-authors (1999) note that leadership theories and research can be organized in terms of level of self-identity that is most relevant to the theory and its assertions, suggesting that transformational leadership operates mostly at the collective level, emphasizing collective identities (see their table, p. 174). However, we believe that transformational leadership is a powerful form of influence owing to the ability of transformational leaders to exert a dual effect and activate both the relational and collective levels of the self.

Applying the perspective of followers' levels of self-concepts to the case of transformational leadership, we maintain that transformational leadership may be able to elicit personal identification with the leader by priming followers' relational aspects of the self-concept, as well as give rise to followers' social identification with the work unit, by activating aspects of the collective self.

Following the self-concept-based motivational theory of charismatic leadership (Shamir et al., 1993) and the followers' levels of self-concept theory (Lord et al., 1999), we propose that transformational leadership exerts its effects by strongly engaging two levels of follower's social-self concepts – the relational self and the collective self – leading to followers' identification with the leader and the organizational unit.

Transformational leadership, as conceptualized by Avolio et al. (1999) and Bass and Avolio (1994), comprises a variety of behaviors that are specified in the Full Range Model of Leadership and the Multifactor Leadership Questionnaire (MLQ). Yukl (1998) suggests that different transformational behaviors can account for different influence processes. Combining Yukl's suggestion with the self-concept theories reviewed above, we propose that different transformational behaviors activate different identity levels, thus accounting for distinct effects on followers' identifications.

Proposition 2a: Transformational leadership behaviors that prime the relational self will be evidenced in personal identification with the leader.

Proposition 2b: Transformational leadership behaviors that prime the collective self will be evidenced in social identification with the group.

Two qualifications should be added at this point: First, although we maintain that leaders can affect followers' levels of self-concepts and identification, we do not imply that leaders can always consciously control this influence. Affective and emotional processes such as identification may be particularly difficult to manage consciously and may occur without the leader's awareness.

Second, although we maintain that different leadership behaviors can prime different aspects of identity, it is of importance to note that some of these behaviors might influence both the relational and collective aspects of the self. Since leaders are important links between individuals and their organizations, the relationship with one's supervisor is a lens through which the entire work experience can be viewed (Gerstner & Day, 1997), and a leader is often consequently seen as a representative character who embodies a unit's identity and values (Shamir et al., 1998), certain behaviors of transformational leaders may simultaneously increase not only relational aspects of the self and identification with the leader, but also followers' collective identities and identification with the unit.

Furthermore, it is possible that identities are dynamic over time, whereas early in a subordinate's organizational tenure and in the initial stages of superior-subordinate relationship, affective and relational concerns can predominate, but later on, identities can move towards more collective levels (Lord, 1999). Thus, what affects relational self at some earlier point may affect collective self at some later point in time. The opposite is also possible. Leaders' initial behaviors may be directed toward the entire group of followers, and followers may respond at the collective identity level. In time, more differentiated behaviors may emerge, priming the relational self of followers.

However, because, as we will show later, different identifications might have different consequences, it is important to distinguish between the leadership behaviors that are more likely to prime the relational self and those that are more likely to prime the collective self. Therefore, at this stage, we highlight and specify different symbolic and verbal transformational behaviors that raise the salience of either the relational or the collective identities in followers' self-concept, possibly leading to divergent effects on followers' attachment to the leader and the group, and on followers' motivations, perceptions and performance.

Behaviors that Prime the Relational Self

A substantial body of work has emerged urging organizations to rethink traditional structures and practices in favor of a more relational approach (Fletcher & Jacques, 1999). This approach can be helpful in an attempt to understand leadership behaviors that are likely to prime the relational aspects of followers' self-concept. Among this work is the emerging construct of relational practice that has been suggested by Fletcher (1999) to refer to a way of working that is directed towards the welfare of others. The concept of relational practice is rooted in the relational theory of human development of "growth-in-connection", developed by Miller and colleagues (Miller, 1976; Miller & Stiver, 1997), which stresses that human growth occurs through a process of connections and relationships rather than a process of individuation and separation.

According to Fletcher (1999), engaging in relational practice and growth-fostering interactions in the organizational context, is a complex affair that requires a number of competencies and relational skills. These include empathy, an ability to acknowledge vulnerability, an ability to express and experience emotions, mutuality and the ability to nurture and participate in the development of others.

Following the theory presented above regarding different levels of followers' self-concept, it seems likely that leaders who behave according to standards of relational practice, will give salience to various aspects of relationships and will activate followers' relational aspect of the identity. This in turn should lead to followers' identification with the leader (see Table 1).

Transformational leaders are expected to build strong connections and emotional bonds with followers, and the effects of transformational leadership have been attributed, at least in part, to the creation of such emotional bonds. Considering transformational leadership theory, it would be expected that leaders who engage in transformational behaviors that are focused on the

Table 1. Leaders' Effects on Followers' Levels of Identity and Identifications.

Transformational Behaviors: MLQ Components	Examples of Leaders' Behaviors[1]	Level of Self-concept Primed	Mode of Identification	Levels of Leadership Effects	Basic Social Motivation	Possible Effects on Followers
Individualized consideration Intellectual stimulation	– Emphasis of leader-follower similarity – Mutuality in the relationship – Nurturing behaviors, participation in the development of followers – Interest in the individual as a whole – Disclosure and intimacy – Acknowledgement of leader and follower vulnerability – Encouragement of expression of a wide range of emotions – Empathy and compassion – Expression of positive affect toward followers – Emphasis on independent and critical thinking – Inclusion of followers in thinking, planning and decision process	Relational	Personal identification	Dyadic level (Little within-group consensus)	Mutual benefit: Followers' benefits Leaders' benefits	Follower-targeted outcomes: – Personal-efficacy – Self-esteem – Energy – Meaningfulness Leader-targeted outcomes: – Loyalty and commitment to the leader – Cooperation with the leader

Table 1. Continued.

Transformational Behaviors: MLQ Components	Examples of Leaders' Behaviors[1]	Level of Self-concept Primed	Mode of Identification	Levels of Leadership Effects	Basic Social Motivation	Possible Effects on Followers
Idealized influence Inspirational motivation	– Highlight organizational membership – Emphasize attractiveness and distinctiveness of organization – Use of organizational symbols – Reference to the group as a whole – Highlight group commonalities – Provide a common vision – Structure the work as group-based: measurement of performance and reward at the group level.	Collective	Social identification	Group level (High within-group agreement)	Collective welfare (Organizational welfare)	– Collective efficacy – Group potency – Unit cohesiveness – Motivation to contribute to the group – Group cooperation – OCB

[1] These represent a selection of leadership behaviors (some that are included in the current MLQ and some that are not).

individual follower, are affective, and consider the welfare of the follower will prime the interpersonal level of followers' self-identity.

Thus, individualized consideration behaviors, including developmental, supportive, and nurturing behaviors that focus on each individual follower's needs, concerns, and possible growth potential, are likely to convey the leader's concern about the welfare of the subordinates. Indeed, both the conceptualization of individualized consideration by the theory's authors (Bass & Avoilo, 1994) and its operationalization in the MLQ emphasize behaviors that recognize the distinctiveness of each individual follower. This may lead to the activation of followers' relational-self and is likely to be reciprocated by the subordinates, resulting in a high level of connection and personal identification with the leader.

Furthermore, there are other behaviors that may trigger the relational self, which are not as prominently specified in the current conceptualization of the "full range of transformational leadership" (Avolio, Bass & Jung, 1999), and should perhaps be included in a "fuller range" model of leadership. Included among these behaviors are displays of warmth, psychological support, compassion, development of close intimate relations, leaders enabling mutual disclosure and the ability to acknowledge vulnerability (Avolio, 1999), an ability to express and experience a wide range of emotions (e.g. providing affective role feedback and enabling the expression of followers' negative emotions), and leaders' treatment of the followers as whole human beings, including understanding of other aspects of their identity that are not related to the work context (e.g. their role in the family, the community, other personal interests).

These relational behaviors can enhance connections between the leader and followers, and form a basis for subordinates to identify with the leaders. Moreover, they highlight the similarity between the leader and followers, and this in turn can foster identification, which, according to different theories (e.g. Kohlberg, 1966; Tsui & O'Reilly, 1989; Turner, 1985), builds on recognition of similarity and a sense of unity with the target of identification.

The behaviors specified above assume direct contact between leaders and followers, and may therefore apply primarily to direct leader-follower relationships. According to Shamir (1995), there is a difference between close leadership, in which followers and leaders have daily face-to-face interactions, and leadership at a distance. In the former, followers do not idealize the leader, and are more influenced by the leader's observed behavior and how the leader treats them, than by the leader's vision, ideology, or rhetoric. Some of the transformational/charismatic behaviors considered to promote identification with the leader emphasize the latter aspects and, furthermore, may even emphasize the leader's superiority or the social distance between leader and followers. Such behaviors may not contribute to the development of identification with the leader in close leadership situations. Perhaps they would have a stronger impact on followers' identification with the leader in distant leadership situations, where idealization of the leader is more common.

In this regard, it is pertinent to note that in the age of globalization, a growing number of direct managers can be categorized as distant leaders, since they are physically distant from their followers (who work from home, or from another state or country) and they interact with them mostly through e-mail and voice mail. According to Hallowell (1999), distance can limit what he calls the "human moment" at work: an authentic psychological encounter that can occur only when people share the same physical space. Absence of "human moments" in technology-mediated leadership relations might make it more difficult for leaders to prime the relational self of followers, thus restricting them to the effects that can be mediated by priming the collective self.

This interpretation suggests that identification with close leaders and distant leaders may be very different processes. We suggest that in the case of close leadership in the organizational context (e.g. mid-level organizational leaders), where the managers maintain a relatively close daily relationship with the employees, the leaders' relational behaviors, which emphasize similarity and interest in the well-being of the subordinates, will be those behaviors that elicit personal identification. Two recent studies of close organizational leadership show support for our hypothesized relationship. The first study, carried out by Shamir and associates (1998) on leaders of field companies in the Israel Defence Forces (IDF), shows that of four different types of leadership behaviors (i.e. supportive behaviors, ideological emphasis, exemplary behaviors and emphasis on collective identity), supportive behaviors had the strongest relationship with followers' personal identification with the leader.

In the second study by Kark (2000), which focused on identification of bank branches' employees with their direct managers, personal and developmental transformational behaviors (i.e. individualized consideration and intellectual consideration) showed a higher correlation with personal identification with the leader than the charismatic components of transformational leadership (inspirational motivation and idealized influence).

Behaviors that Prime the Collective Self

The process of personal identification is viewed as a meaningful form of bonding between transformational leaders and their followers (Howell, 1988; Shamir, 1991), but has been suggested to be secondary in its importance in comparison with social identification (Lord et al., 1999; Shamir, 1991; Shamir et al., 1993). Social identification can be evoked by transformational behaviors that prime the collective aspects of followers' self-concept. Thus, behaviors of the leader that are focused on the group entity, linking the self-concept of individual followers to the shared values and key role identities of the group, can prime the collective aspect of followers' self-concept and foster individuals' perception of belonging to, and unity with, an organizational unit or organization (Shamir et al., 1993).

Transformational leaders can shift subordinates from an individual to a collective level of self-identity by engaging in various symbolic, verbal and performance acts. First, transformational leaders can increase the salience of the collective identity of followers by highlighting their membership in the organizational unit and simultaneously emphasize the identity of the unit or organization, by stressing its uniqueness and by distinguishing it from other units (Shamir et al., 1998). As suggested in Table 1, this can be achieved by a skillful use of slogans and symbols (e.g. flags, tags, logos), rituals (e.g. singing the organizational songs), labels, metaphors, and ceremonies (Ashforth & Mael, 1989; Shamir et al., 1998), and by the creation of attractive and desirable organizational images (Dutton, Dukerich & Harquail, 1994).

The sense of membership to the group can be influenced by a strategy called the "assumed or transcendent we" (Pratt, 1998). In this case, the leader simply refers to the followers as "we" in verbal communication and publications. Support for this comes from prior research manipulations, which have shown that the use of collective focused communication cues (we/us) in a text or in instructions to an experimental task (as opposed to the use of individually focused cues: I/me) can affect the outcomes of the study and the way in which individuals perceive and define themselves (Brewer & Gardner, 1996; Gardner & Gabriel, 1999). This suggests that even simple aspects of a leader's communication style may provide important cues to prime the collective self and shape followers' social identification.

Second, a leader may enhance the collective identity in followers' self-concepts by emphasizing common ground, stressing shared values and ideology, connecting followers' personal goals and aims with the groups' interests, and interpreting present and past experiences of followers in terms of group values and identity (Shamir, Arthur & House, 1994). Furthermore, emphasizing a shared goal and mission, and providing organizational members with an attractive common vision, can enable leaders to foster group-level identities (Lord et al., 1999; Shamir et al., 1998).

Leaders can also give rise to followers' collective self-concept by shaping the work context (e.g. work-group structure, task structure and reward structure). According to Brickson (2000), group boundaries can be reinforced and highlighted by the way in which work is performed and rewarded. A collective identity will be enhanced when work is performed by a distinct group of individuals (especially if membership is static) and when performance is measured and rewarded at the group level. Research suggests that because group-based task and reward structures lead to identifying oneself as a group member, they elicit the motivation to enhance one's group relative to other groups (e.g. Sherif, 1966), namely, collective identity orientation (Brickson, 2000).

Considering transformational leadership theory, it could be expected that leaders who engage in transformational behaviors targeted toward the whole group, highlighting group commonalties in terms of values and ideals and express a vision will prime the collective level of followers self-identity, leading to social identification with the work-unit. The behaviors specified above are mostly evident in the transformational components of idealized influence and inspirational motivation.

As with behaviors that prime the relational self-concept, most current versions of transformational leadership theory do not include all the above-mentioned behaviors, which can lead to a collective orientation. An example of a transformational leadership scale that includes some of these behavior is that developed by Podsakoff, MacKenzie and Bommer (1996). Their scale includes a component of "fostering the acceptance of group goals" which comprises items of leadership behavior such as: "fosters collaboration among work groups", "encourages employees to be 'team players'" and "develops a team attitude and spirit among his/her employees". Our discussion in this section suggests that transformational leadership theory may benefit from the addition of components that can contribute to extending the "Full Range" of transformational behaviors.

LEVELS OF TRANSFORMATIONAL LEADERSHIP

The conceptualization offered in this chapter also provides a potential way for linking transformational leadership theory to dyadic models of leadership and reconciling some of the controversy in this regard. Recent interest in levels of leadership and levels of analysis has raised the issue of whether transformational leadership is primarily a group level phenomenon or a dyadic phenomenon. The differences between transformational leadership theory and leader-member exchange theory (LMX) and the relationships between the two theories have also been questioned (Uhl-Bien & Arnaud, 2001). The conceptual framework offered in this paper suggests that transformational leadership operates at both levels.

Leader behaviors such as individualized consideration, which prime the relational self, emphasize the distinctiveness of each follower and the unique relationship between the leader and each follower. These behaviors are directed toward individual followers. Furthermore, each follower is likely to relate to the leader differently on the basis of the behaviors directed toward him or her as well as his or her personal dispositions and preferences. Therefore, these behaviors are likely to operate primarily at the dyadic level, and differences among followers of the same leaders can be expected in their relationships with the leader, the extent to which their relational self is being evoked, and further effects stemming from the evocation of the relational self. This aspect of transformational leadership is similar to the leadership processes emphasized by LMX theory (Graen & Uhl-Bien, 1995) and the recent Individualized Leadership theory offered by Dansereau and associates (1998).

In contrast, leader behaviors that prime the collective self are more 'ambient' behaviors directed toward the entire group of followers. These behaviors do not differentiate between followers portraying them as a larger collective or group. Furthermore, their whole purpose is to raise the prominence of the collective aspects of followers' self-concepts and downplay differences among followers in their relationships with the leader and the group. Therefore, these behaviors are likely to operate at the group or unit level. Dyadic theories of leadership do not account for the effects of such behaviors, which are likely to extend beyond the sum or combination of dyadic effects. We can therefore propose:

Proposition 3a: The effects of transformational leadership behaviors that prime the relational self are likely to be evident primarily at the dyadic level. No within-group consensus is expected with respect to personal identification with the leader and further effects of these behaviors.

Proposition 3b: The effects of transformational leadership behaviors that prime the collective self are likely to be evident primarily at the group level. Within-group agreement can be expected with respect to followers' description of these behaviors, social identification with the unit, and further effects on followers.

OUTCOMES OF PERSONAL AND SOCIAL IDENTIFICATION

Different levels of self-construal and different levels of identifications (with the leader and with the group) are important because they have perceptual, motivational and behavioral consequences (Brewer & Gardner, 1986; Pratt, 1998). As Brewer (1991) postulated, "when the definition of self changes, the meaning of self-interest and self-serving motivations also changes significantly" (p. 476). Transformational leadership theory suggests that such leadership is likely to result in a wide range of outcomes at the personal level (e.g. followers' empowerment, personal efficacy, extra effort) and group or organizational level (e.g. unit cohesiveness, organizational citizenship behavior, collective efficacy). In this section, we suggest that these outcomes are mediated by identity shifts and identifications.

Possible Outcomes of a Relational Orientation and Personal Identification

The effects of transformational leadership behaviors that prime the relational-self and increase followers' personal identification with the leader are likely to be evident primarily at the dyadic level, as suggested above. Transformational leadership theory suggests that some of the benefits for the followers can take the form of followers' growth and empowerment (Avolio, 1999; Bass, 1985; Dvir et al., in press). The impact of transformational leadership on followers' performance is often explained as stemming from followers' development and empowerment, which increase both their ability and their motivation. We suggest that transformational leaders produce these effects primarily by priming followers' relational self and identification with the leader.

According to Brewer and Gardner (1996), at the relational level of identity, self-representations and perceptions of self-worth are dependent on the reflected self, or the self as seen through the reactions of the other person involved in the relationship. These notions suggest that transformational leadership behaviors such as individualized consideration and intellectual stimulation, and perhaps also some aspects of inspirational motivation, will increase the follower's self-worth and self-efficacy because they transmit the message that the leader believes in the follower and has high confidence in the follower's integrity and ability. It further suggests that these effects will be stronger to the extent that the leader engages in other behaviors that prime the relational self and are not currently included in the full-range model of leadership. We have suggested several such behaviors in an earlier section of this chapter, for instance the leader's treatment of the follower as a whole person and his or her interest in the non-work aspects of the follower's life. Such behaviors are likely to increase the emotional connection between the leader and the follower, make the leader a more significant other for the follower, and thus increase the impact of the reflected-self on the follower's self-perceptions.

In a similar vein, Miller and Stiver (1997) argue that growth-fostering relational interactions between individuals (e.g. between a leader and a follower) will result in outcomes that they refer to as the "five good things": zest, empowered action, increased knowledge, increased self-worth, and a desire for more connection. Thus, leadership practices that prime the relational aspects of the self and elicit feelings of personal identification are likely to result in empowerment effects similar to those specified in the "five good things": followers' increased feelings of vitality, liveliness and energy, sense of self-worth, sense of meaningfulness, and their belief in their ability to act towards achieving their personal goals.

Furthermore, according to Brewer and Gardner (1996), when an individual's relational self is salient, his or her primary motivation is to enhance the relationship partner's well-being and benefits. Batson (1994) defined this concern for the outcomes of the other as the basis of altruistic motivation, which he stressed was not to be confused with self-sacrifice (which concerns costs to the self), but as the motivation to benefit the other. Following this, we would expect that followers of transformational leaders who are triggered to focus on their relational-self would be motivated to enhance the well-being and possible benefits of the leader. This, among other possible outcomes, can take the form of loyalty to the leader, commitment to the leader and willingness to cooperate with the leader.

It is commonly believed that follower growth and empowerment imply a greater follower independence, and therefore that transformational leadership that fosters follower growth and empowerment decreases follower dependence on the leader. However, strong emotional connections between followers and leaders and personal identification with the leader have also been suggested to lead to the dependency of followers on the leader (Howell, 1988). For instance, Conger and Kanungo (1998) claim that, "Dependence stems in large part from a strong identification with the leader" (p. 216). While this has commonly been associated with a negative form of leadership (e.g. the dark side of charisma), the theoretical rationale presented above suggests that any stress by the leader on the relational self may increase personal identification with the leader and dependence on the leader. It may be noted, in this regard, that relational perspectives (e.g. Fletcher, 1999; Miller & Stiver, 1997) challenge the commonly accepted distinction and opposition between dependence and empowerment, claiming that this distinction rests on traditional models of masculine development that view the development of independence, autonomy, and self-reliance as including disengagement from significant others, and as negating strong forms of relatedness, which include interdependence.

In contrast, these relational perspectives present a model of development and growth within a relationship, which emphasizes both independence and inter-dependence. Within such a model, a relationship may be characterized by both a sense of empowerment and at least some sense of interpersonal dependence. Thus, transformational behaviors that prime followers' relational aspects of the self-concept are likely to contribute to followers' empowerment and simultane-ously followers' inter-dependence. In support of this thesis, recent findings from a large-scale study of bank employees and their managers (Kark, 2000) showed that the developing aspects of transformational leadership (indi-vidualized consideration and intellectual stimulation) were positively related simultaneously to both followers' empowerment and dependence on the leader. Furthermore, followers' empowerment and dependence on the leader were not negatively correlated with each other.

On the basis of these considerations, we offer the following proposition:

Proposition 4: The more a leader engages in behaviors that give salience to the relational self-concept and elicit identification with the leader, the higher the level of:

(1) followers' personal-efficacy, self-esteem, energy, and sense of mean-ingfulness;
(2) followers' willingness to cooperate with the leader and their loyalty and commitment to the leader;
(3) followers' dependence on the leader.

Possible Outcomes of a Collective Orientation and Social Identification

Theoretically, the most significant effect of transformational leadership according to both Burns (1978) and Bass (1985) is getting followers to transcend their self-interests for the sake of the group, organization or movement. However, Burns and Bass have not specified the mechanism through which this effect is achieved. Shamir, House and Arthur (1993) suggested that this effect is achieved by engaging the follower's self-concepts, primarily those aspects of the self-concept (values and identities) that connect the individual with the groups to which he or she belongs. In terms of the identity levels model of Brewer and Gardner (1996) and the leadership theory based on this model (Lord et al., 1999), this suggests that transformational leaders achieve this effect by priming the collective-self of followers.

According to Brewer and Gardner (1996), at the collective level of identity, the basic social motivation of individuals is the collective welfare, and group welfare becomes an end in itself. Experimental research on individual choices in situations of social dilemmas has demonstrated the powerful effect of group identification on participants' willingness to restrict individual gain to preserve a collective good (e.g. Brewer & Kramer, 1986). This effect suggests that when transformational leaders behave in ways that prime followers' sense of collective-self and increase their social identification, the followers are prone to show an interest in the welfare of the organization or organizational unit. Therefore, organizational leaders who can raise followers' identification with the group (organization or organizational unit) are likely to increase followers' commitment and willingness to contribute to group objectives (Shamir et al., 1998). Such commitment and willingness to contribute to group objectives can be expressed by followers' exhibition of organizational citizenship behaviors. Additionally, identification with an in-group can elicit a cooperative orientation toward shared problems and result in cooperative behavior, even in the absence of interpersonal communication among group members (Brewer & Gardner, 1996).

Furthermore, followers' collective orientation and identification with the group are often associated with the attribution of positive qualities to the group (Tajfel, 1982). Hence, leader behaviors that increase the attractiveness of the group and foster social identification with it are likely to empower the group and increase followers' collective efficacy beliefs and their sense of group potency (Shamir et al., 1998). Collective efficacy refers to individuals' beliefs that their group, unit or organization can function effectively and perform its tasks successfully (Bandura, 1986). Group potency refers to the group members' shared beliefs that their group, unit or organization can function effectively (Guzzo, Yost, Campbell & Shea, 1993).

Proposition 5: The more a transformational leader engages in behaviors that give salience to the collective self-concept and elicit identification with the unit, the higher the levels of:

(1) collective efficacy and group potency perceptions;
(2) unit cohesiveness;
(3) followers' motivation to contribute to the group, cooperative behaviors, and other organizational citizenship behaviors.

CONCLUSIONS AND IMPLICATIONS FOR RESEARCH

The conception of transformational leadership presented here and summarized in Table 1 portrays transformational leadership as a multifaceted, complex, and dynamic form of influence. It suggests that leaders can affect followers by highlighting different aspects of followers' social self-concept, relational and collective aspects, and possibly change their focus from one level of their self-concept to the other. This suggestion is likely to influence whether followers see themselves primarily in terms of their relationship with the leader and their role in relation to him/her, or in terms of their organizational group membership. In other words, it influences followers' tendency to identify with the leader or with the group and possibly over time with both. Leaders come to symbolize what the organization stands for, and the relational can emerge at the collective, or a collective orientation can become more relational as the leader learns to differentiate between the followers and the personal bonds between the leader and certain followers become stronger.

We suggest that different leadership behaviors can account for priming these distinct aspects of followers' self-concept and followers' identification. Furthermore, these different forms of influence are important because they can lead to differential outcomes. Personal identification can result in dyadic level outcomes such as followers' empowerment coupled with dependence on the leader and loyalty to him/her. Social identification can result in followers' willingness to contribute to the groups' welfare and take the form of organizational citizenship behaviors, group cohesiveness and the group's sense of potency. The theoretical framework suggested in this chapter begins to shed light on the complex ways in which transformational leadership can affect multiple and diverse aspects of followers' perceptions and behaviors, resulting in organizational effectiveness and followers' well-being.

We have offered some propositions to guide further research on these influence processes. In addition, we have raised some issues that merit attention in future studies. Although transformational leadership theory specifies various leadership behaviors that can prime different aspects of followers' self-concepts and foster personal and social identifications, other behaviors mentioned in our discussion are not included in the current theory and measurements. Future research should not be limited to the existing transformational behaviors and can benefit from looking into a wider variety of behaviors, and possibly from the development of a more inclusive leadership behavior scale. Furthermore, the dynamic of followers shifting from one identity orientation to the other and the ways in which a leader can influence these shifts still need to be studied. Several questions may be raised in this regard. Can leaders simultaneously activate both the collective and relational self orientations, or are there negative and inhibitory relations among identity levels in that activating one level inhibits the other, as Lord and his co-authors (1999) suggested? Can leaders consciously manipulate these shifts of identity? Can leaders be trained to emphasize certain behaviors in order to prime a certain level of followers' self-concept? How does technology mediate the impact of leaders' effects on followers' self-concept?

This chapter has focused on leaders' behaviors and their effects on followers. However, the followers are also likely to contribute to the dynamics suggested in this chapter. According to Lord et al. (1999), leaders are most effective when there is a match between the values and identities they stress and the cognitive structures held by followers. A similar argument was made by Shamir et al. (1993). For instance, individuals, organizational cultures, and national cultures are known to differ on a dimension that ranges from a more individualistic orientation to a more collectivistic orientation (e.g. Markus & Kitayama, 1991). It is reasonable to suggest that followers with a more collectivistic orientation will be more likely than followers with an individualistic orientation to respond to leader behaviors that attempt to prime the collective self, to develop social identification with the work unit, and to manifest the attitudinal and behavioral outcomes associated with such an identification.

Another example of a follower's characteristic that might influence the dynamics discussed in this chapter is gender. It has recently been demonstrated by Gabriel and Gardner (1999) that women tend to focus more on the relational aspects of interdependence, whereas men tend to focus more on the collective aspects. This finding suggests that women might be more prone to respond to the relational aspects of transformational leadership, whereas men will be more prone to the collective aspects of transformational leadership. Future research should therefore examine not only the relationships between various transformational behaviors and various outcomes as they are mediated by personal and social identification, but also the moderating effects of various followers' characteristics and orientations on these relationships. We also need a more thorough understanding of how contextual forces elicit identity orientations and identifications. Future research needs to address whether different contextual factors, both those that can be shaped by the leader and those that are not within a leader's control (e.g. organizational structure, profession, rate of change) can foster different identities and moderate the leader's effects.

It should be acknowledged that we do not know the extent to which transformational leaders' influence on their followers is mediated by the self-concept dynamics discussed in this chapter. However, given the strong evidence for the effects of transformational leadership, on the one hand, and the lack of sufficient understanding of the mechanisms by which these effects are produced, on the other, theoretical frameworks such as that proposed in this chapter are needed at this stage of the development of transformational leadership theory. We believe that because the conceptual framework proposed here rests on a relatively strong theoretical rationale and is supported by initial empirical evidence, it deserves to be on the agenda of future research on transformational leadership.

REFERENCES

Ashforth, B. E., & Mael, F. (1989). Social identity theory and the organization. *Academy of Management Review, 14*, 20–39.

Avolio, B. J. (1999). *Full Leadership Development: Building the vital forces in organizations.* Thousand Oaks, CA: Sage Publications.

Avolio, B. J., Bass, B. M., & Jung, D. I. (1999). Reexamining the components of transformational and transactional leadership using the multifactor leadership questionnaire. *Journal of Occupational and Organizational Psychology, 72*, 441–462.

Banaji, M. R., & Prentice, D. A. (1994). The self in social contexts. *Annual Review of Psychology, 45*, 297–332.

Bandura, A. (1986). *Social foundations of thought and action: A social cognitive theory.* Englewood Cliffs, NJ: Prentice Hall.

Barling, J., Weber, T., & Kelloway, E. K. (1996). Effects of transformational leadership training on attitudinal and financial outcomes: A field experiment. *Journal of Applied Psychology, 81*, 827–832.

Bass, B. M. (1985). *Leadership and performance beyond expectation.* New York: The Free Press.

Bass, B. M., & Avolio, B. J. (1994). *Improving organizational effectiveness through transformational leadership.* Thousand Oaks, CA: Sage Publications.

Batson, C. D. (1994). Why act for the public good? Four answers. *Personality and Social Psychology Bulletin, 20*, 603–610.

Brewer, M. B. (1991). The social self: On being the same and different at the same time. *Personality and Social Psychology Bulletin, 17*, 475–482.

Brewer, M. B., & Gardner, W. (1996). Who is this "We"? Levels of collective identity and self representations. *Journal of Personality and Social Psychology, 71*(1), 83–93.

Brewer, M. B., & Kramer, R. M. (1986). Choice behavior in social dilemmas: Effects of social identity, group size, and decision framing. *Journal of Personality and Social Psychology, 50*, 543–549.

Brickson, S. (2000). The impact of identity orientation on individual and organizational outcomes in demographically diverse settings. *Academy of Management Review, 25*(1), 82–101.

Burns, J. M. (1978). *Leadership.* New York: Harper & Row.

Cheney, G. (1983). The rhetoric of identification and the study of organizational communication. *Quarterly Journal of Speech, 69*, 143–158.

Conger, J. A., & Kanungo, R. N. (1998). *Charismatic leadership in organizations.* Thousand Oaks, CA: Sage Publication.

Dansereau, F., Yammarino, F. J., Markham, S. E., Alutto, J. A., Newman, J., & Dumas, M. et al. (1998). Individualized leadership: A new multiple level approach. In: F. Dansereau & F. J. Yammarino (Eds), *Leadership: The Multiple Level Approaches* (Vol. 24, Part A, pp. 363–405). Stamford, CT: JAI Press.

Dutton, J. E., Dukerich, J. M., & Harquail, C. V. (1994). Organizational images and member identification. *Administrative Science Quarterly, 39*, 239–263.

Dvir, T., Eden, D., Avolio, B. J., & Shamir, B. (in press). Impact of transformational leadership on follower development and performance: A field study. *Academy of Management Journal*, 2002.

Eden, D. (1992). Leadership and expectations: Pygmalion effects and other self-fulfilling prophecies in organizations. *Leadership Quarterly, 3*, 271–305.

Fletcher, J. K. (1999). *Disappearing acts: Gender, power, and relational practice at work.* Cambridge, MA: MIT Press.

Fletcher, J. K., & Jacques, R. (1999). Relational practice: An emerging stream of theory and its significance for organizational studies (Working Paper 2). Boston: Center for Gender in Organizations, SIMMONS Graduate School of Management.

French, R. P., & Raven, B. H. (1959). The bases of social power. In: D. Cartwright (Ed.), *Studies in Social Power*. Ann Arbor: University of Michigan.

Gabriel, S., & Gardner, W. L. (1999). Are there "his" and "hers" types of interdependence? The implications of gender differences in collective vs. relational interdependence for affect, behavior, and cognition. *Journal of Personality and Social Psychology, 77*(3), 642–655.

Gerstner, R. C., & Day, D. V. (1997). Meta-analytic review of leader-member exchange theory: Correlates and construct issues. *Journal of Applied Psychology, 82*, 827–845.

Graen, G. B., & Uhl-Bien, M. (1995). Relationship based approach to leadership: Development of leader-member exchange (LMX) theory of leadership over 25 years: Applying a multi-level multi-domain perspective. *Leadership Quarterly, 6*, 219–247.

Guzzo, R. A., Yost, P. R., Campbell, R. J., & Shea, G. P. (1993). Potency in groups: Articulating a construct. *British Journal of Social Psychology, 32*, 87–106.

Hallowell, E. M. (1999). The human moment at work. *Harvard Business Review*, January–February.

Howell, J. M. (1988). Two faces of charisma: Socialized and personalized leadership in organizations. In: J. A. Conger & R. N. Kanungo (Eds), *Charismatic Leadership* (pp. 213–236). San Francisco: Jossey-Bass.

Kark, R. (2000). Gender differences in transformational leadership, followers' identifications, and effects on followers' perceptions. Unpublished Ph.D. Dissertation. Hebrew University of Jerusalem, Jerusalem.

Kohlberg, L. (1966). A cognitive-developmental analysis of children's sex-role concepts and attitudes. In: E. E. Maccoby (Ed.), *The development of sex differences*. Stanford, CA: Stanford University Press.

Lord, R. G., Brown, D. J., & Feiberg, S. J. (1999). Understanding the dynamics of leadership: The role of follower self-concepts in the leader/follower relationship. *Organizational Behavior and Human Decision Processes, 78*(3), 167–203.

Lowe, K. B., Kroeck, K. G., & Sivasubramaniam, N. (1996). Effectiveness of correlates of transformational and transactional leadership: A meta-analytic review of the MLQ literature. *Leadership Quarterly, 7*, 385–425.

Mael, F., & Ashforth, B. E. (1992). Alumni and their alma matter: a partial test of the reformulated model of organizational identification. *Journal of Organizational Behavior, 13*, 103–123.

Markus, H., & Kitayama, S. (1991). Culture and the self: Implications for cognitions, emotion and motivation. *Psychological Review, 98*, 224–252.

Markus, H., & Wurf, E. (1987). The dynamic self-concept: A social psychological perspective. *Annual Review of Psychology, 38*, 299–337.

Miller, J. B. (1976). *Towards a new psychology of women*. Boston, MA: Beacon Press.

Miller, J. B., & Stiver, I. P. (1997). *The healing connection: How women form relationships in therapy and in life*. Boston, MA: Beacon Press, Inc.

Podsakoff, P. M., MacKenzie, S. B., & Bommer, W. H. (1996). Transformational leader behaviors and substitutes for leadership as determinants of employee satisfaction, commitment, trust, and organizational citizenship behaviors. *Journal of Management, 22*(2) 259–298.

Pratt, M. G. (1998). To be or not to be: Central questions in organizational identification. In: D. A. Whetten & P. C. Godfrey (Eds), *Identity in organizations: Building theory through conversation* (pp. 171–207). Thousand Oaks, CA: Sage Publications.

Shamir, B. (1991). The charismatic relationship: Alternative explanations and predictions. *Leadership Quarterly, 2*, 81–104.

Shamir, B. (1995). Social distance and charisma: Theoretical notes and an exploratory study. *Leadership Quarterly, 6*, 19–47.

Shamir, B., Arthur, M. B., & House, R. J. (1994). The rhetoric of charismatic leadership: A theoretical extension, a case study, and implications for research. *Leadership Quarterly, 5*, 25–42.

Shamir, B., House, R. J., & Arthur, M. B. (1993). The motivational effects of charismatic leadership: A self concept based theory. *Organization Science, 4*, 577–593.

Shamir, B., Zakay, E. E. B., & Popper, M. (1998). Correlates of charismatic leader behavior in military units: Subordinates' attitudes, unit characteristics, and superiors' appraisals of leader performance. *Academy of Management Journal, 41*, 387–409.

Sherif, M. (1966). *In Common Predicament: Social psychology of intergroup conflict and cooperation*. Boston, MA: Houghton Mifflin.

Tajfel, H. (1982). *Social identity and intergroup relations*. Cambridge: University Press.

Tsui, A. S., & OŘeilly, C. A. (1989). Beyond simple demographic effects: The importance of relational demography in superior-subordinate dyads. *Academy of Management Journal, 32*, 402–423.

Turner, J. C. (1985). Social categorization and the self-concept: A social cognitive theory of group behavior. In: E. J. Lawler (Ed.), *Advances in Group Processes* (Vol. 2, pp. 77–122). Greenwich, CT: JAI Press.

Uhl-Bien, M., & Arnaud, A. (2001). Comparing and contrasting lmx with transformational & neo-charismatic leadership approaches: How might these literatures speak to one another? Paper presented at the Festschrift for Dr. Bernard M. Bass, Center for Leadership Studies, Binghamton, NY.

Yukl, G. (1998). *Leadership in organizations*. Englewood Cliff, NJ: Prentice-Hall.

PART II:
CHARISMATIC LEADERSHIP

DEAR PUBLIUS: REFLECTIONS ON THE FOUNDING FATHERS AND CHARISMATIC LEADERSHIP

Richard A. Couto

ABSTRACT

Charisma holds a central place in discussions about leadership. The Founding Fathers were opposed to some forms of charisma but endorsed some as well. They sought to entrust government to select-people, like themselves, who could be trusted to rule for the many – in Bass (1998) terms, "socialized" as opposed to "personalized" charismatic leaders. This chapter responds to Publius, the authors of the Federalist Papers, *to explain the problems the Founding Fathers' fears have caused us in presidential elections, including that of 2000.*

INTRODUCTION

Bernard M. Bass built his work about charismatic leadership on James MacGregor Burns and Robert House. Burns gave up on the word "charisma" and substituted "heroic" (Burns, 1978, pp. 243–244), but whatever its name, it remained the underpinning of Burns's transforming leadership as well as Bass's transformational leadership. From House's work on charismatic leadership (House, 1977; Shamir, House & Arthur, 1993), Bass borrowed characteristics of idealized influence, inspirational leadership, and intellectual stimulation. To these, he added individualized consideration (Bass, 1998, pp. 5–6, 23) and,

Transformational and Charismatic Leadership, Volume 2, pages 95–108.
Copyright © 2002 by Elsevier Science Ltd.
All rights of reproduction in any form reserved.
ISBN: 0-7623-0962-8

with Avolio (1999), fashioned these four "I's" into the core of transformational leadership and the surest means to achieve followers' performance beyond expectations (Bass, 1985). Bass broke charisma into measurable components but, with time, also came to agree with Burns that values distinguish genuine from pseudo forms of transformational leadership. The world views of the latter – Adolph Hitler, James Jones, Osama bin Laden – reside at some distance from the universal bonds of humanity extolled by Gandhi, Eleanor Roosevelt, or Martin Luther King, Jr.

Genuine transformational leadership is "socialized" and transcends self-interest for utilitarian or moral reasons. It seeks a convergence of values between leaders and followers and the internalization of values. ". . . [S]ocialized charismatic leaders are oriented to serving others. They develop shared goals with their followers and inspire the attainment of such goals" (Bass, 1981, p. 188). "Personalized" charismatic leadership depends on compliance – the use of transactional leadership – and identification – unquestioning obedience to the goals of the leader, even when ethnocentric or xenophobic (Bass, 1985, pp. 24–25).

As a set of charismatic leaders, the Founding Fathers were deeply suspicious of charismatic leadership. They feared popular government for the likelihood that a heroic figure, without leadership ability or sufficient respect for the propertied classes, could be swept into political power. As a result, they devised constitutional measures to keep such leaders from reaching public office, especially the presidency of the government they crafted. Over time and with increased efforts to find government of the people, by the people, and for the people, we have taken down some of their original electoral barriers.

In fact, no single aspect of the United States Constitution has had more amendments than its provisions for federal elections. Yet, in the presidential election of 2000 the remaining electoral barriers provided United States residents, and much of the rest of the world, a lesson on the complicated electoral system the Founding Fathers divined in their effort to obstruct charisma and popular government. Hidden in the reams of printed comments and the hours of broadcast commentary on the mechanics of the electoral system lies the willingness of the Founding Fathers to suffer occasional confusion over an electoral outcome. They much preferred this glitch to the risk that a wave of popular sentiment could carry a charismatic leader to the office of president. Buried deeper yet in the cumbersome procedures of presidential elections lies the aversion of the Founding Fathers for democratic practice.

What follows is a letter to Publius, the authors of the *Federalist Papers*, Alexander Hamilton, John Jay, and James Madison. It attempts to explain the conundrum of the presidential election of 2000 in constitutional, undemocratic, and anti-charismatic terms.

Dear PUBLIUS

Some trepidation goes along with my writing. More than 200 years after the drafting of the Constitution for the revised government of the United States, it still governs well. You know the provisions of that document. More than anyone else, you explained them to your contemporaries in *The Federalist Papers*, which are still read, studied, and cited today. You can imagine my nervousness then, as I write to tell you about one shortcoming in your work, the selection of the president (we no longer capitalize the term). Even more intimidating, you considered your devices for the selection of president, if "not perfect, . . . at least excellent." You were probably encouraged in your view because so few people commented or objected to it at the time (Rossiter, 1961, No. 68, p. 412).

Yet, I have to tell you that your system has worked best in landslide victories. In close elections, it has led to major problems time after time. First, we found that combining the selection of president and vice president led to serious conflicts. We decided early in our history to set aside the original system. As you probably recall, the election of 1800 provided the monumental achievement of a peaceful transfer of power from one party in power to a party out of power. However, it left us with incompatible men as president and vice president. The twelfth article of constitutional amendments calls for the election of a president and a vice president rather than the runner-up system that you devised. By the way, we are still befuddled by the office of vice president. We know how to elect one but it seems a lot of trouble for the few tasks the Constitution provides to the office. I take it that the selection procedure for the vice president was a vestige of your insistence on the separation of the executive and legislative branches. You considered having the Senate choose the vice president from its ranks, as some state legislatures chose and still choose their lieutenant governors, but decided against it because it would link one office of the executive branch with part of the legislative branch of government (Rossiter, 1961, No. 68).

A second problem persists despite the amended procedures. Several times, including the most recent presidential election of 2000, we have had one candidate win the popular vote nationally and another candidate win the electoral college vote. When such a difference in outcome occurs, we come close to a constitutional crisis. In 1876, political horse trading ended military reconstruction in the South for the electoral votes of South Carolina. In 2000, the U.S. Supreme Court intervened in the counting of ballots in Florida in a manner that assured a narrow victory in the state and an electoral college victory for the candidate with fewer votes nationally. Even the Supreme Court implicitly recognized the difficult problem it faced recently and asked that its decision not be taken as a precedent for other cases dealing with equal protection, a Constitutional provision of the Fourteenth article of amendments (Garrett, 2001, p. 44; Issacharoff, 2001, p. 70; Karlan, 2001, p. 91). Imagine, the Court asked that its decision not be taken as a precedent. The evolution of the Supreme Court is another issue, on the whole, less troublesome than presidential elections. In this particular case, however, the Court had a troublesome split along partisan lines. This division and a preceding pattern of partisanship raised anew the question of a distinction between law and politics (Pildes, 2001, p. 141; Sunstein, 2001, p. 2). The system you devised does not work well in close elections and requires extra-constitutional problem-solving.

We would have even more severe problems, but political practice and adaptation have helped us solve some of the problems inherent in the Constitution. Ironically, political parties, a form of the factions from which you sought to protect the federal government (Rossiter, 1961, No. 10), make the electoral college system work. The voters of each state still elect a slate of men and women to proceed to the Electoral College, but they go as delegates of a political party, pledged to its candidates for president and vice president. They are not the trustees you envisioned but members of a "faction", which you feared. In a manner you probably did not anticipate, our electoral winner-take-all arrangement provides great incentive for only two parties.

You correctly observed that factions could be curbed by "giving to every citizen the same opinions, the same passions, and the same interests" but protested the unwanted consequences of the draconian effort required to make all citizens adhere to one system of thought (Rossiter, 1961, No. 10, p. 78). You had read your Plato and knew that social order based on a hegemonic belief system required a totalitarian state. None the less, your system provides voters powerful incentives to line up in one or another of two parties. We don't have the same opinions on all issues, but we have an incentive to tailor our opinions to fit one or another faction. Winner-take-all elections provide little opportunity for minority views to gain elected representation within the system you left us. Thus, if voters disagree with candidates of both major parties, they still are likely to choose one or the other, because of the differences between them, and thereby increase the chances of effecting the victory of one over the other. Many residents in Florida, in this past election, chose to vote for a third-party candidate. Though apparently in disagreement with the declared winner in the state's election, they shaped his victory decisively. Your system did not reduce factions among people but it channeled factions into very few political parties. You still have your anti-factional and less democratic advocates. All five justices that voted to intervene in the Florida recount were also in the majority of six that overturned lower court findings and upheld state prohibitions on third parties to "fuse" with major parties by nominating the same candidate (Timmons vs. Twin Cities Area New Party). Your electoral system continues to work most of the time precisely because of some of the mechanisms, factions, that you opposed and because of extra-constitutional adaptations that we have made, although they do not and have not come easily.

But these two enduring problems are symptoms of a problem deeply rooted in your political philosophy. Again, I approach this with hesitation because I recognize the towering accomplishment of the Constitution given the context of the times. You and the other framers of the Constitution were asked to do more than most political theorists. You had to constitute a government and not merely speculate on its outline. You did well. Still you left us with major problems of which the 2000 election is symptomatic.

Politics express the moral philosophy of a society. You said this yourself when you asked rhetorically, ". . . [W]hat is government itself but the greatest of all reflections on human nature?" (Rossiter, 1961, No. 51, p. 322). Most political theorists, from ancient Greece and China to our own times, worked to balance order and justice in society. Clearly, your work on government power resembles the traditional task of devising order. Your work on individual liberty took precedence over justice, however. You were, of course, concerned with justice; in fact, you called it "the end of government . . . [and] . . . of civil government. It ever has been and ever will be pursued until it be obtained or until liberty be lost in the pursuit" (Rossiter, 1961, No. 51, p. 324). Your preamble explains the need to "establish justice" as the purpose of the Constitution and by extension, I infer, liberty. Midway between your time and ours, Max Weber explained the wisdom of not establishing absolute values, such as some particular form of justice, as the goal of politics (Weber, 1958). Since Weber's time, we learned of unprecedented human horrors carried out in the name of absolute values. On September 11, 2001, we were painfully reminded again of the horrors resulting from absolute values in politics.

So there may be some wisdom in your choice of individual liberty from government restraint, as a means to the pursuit of justice. I imagine that you were greatly influenced by the thoughts and discoveries of your time, as we are in our own time. In that vein, I see a parallel between Adam Smith's assertion that the pursuit of our own advantage will bring about the common good by the distribution of an invisible hand (Smith, 1976) and your efforts to make the protection of privilege, which arise from differences among people, a bond to hold the body politic together.

We have had to amend law and practice, but not the Constitution, to make liberty work on the side of justice. The liberty of some, we found, came *through* government and not *from* government (Burns, 1978, pp. 150–157) but we found ourselves boxed in by your protection of minorities, propertied people, from majorities, those without wealth. You barely left us with sufficient means to promote the equality heralded in the *Declaration of Independence*. President Abraham Lincoln's lasting contribution to American government placed the *Declaration's* assertion that "all men are created equal" at the center of the purpose of government (Wills, 1992). At least that is how he explained a Civil War. (Yes, we were divided in a terrible war that our Constitution and its provisions could not resolve. Four years of devastating violence imposed order and resolved the crudest of all political questions: who has the monopoly of legitimate violence and force of arms?) Still it has to be admitted that liberty has been the most frequently used means to promote justice *through* government. Occasionally, we have reversed your preference to protect the minority, relative powerless people, from exclusive and discriminatory measures of those in power. Women can vote because of the 19th article of the amendments of the Constitution and *through* their rights of assembly and freedom of speech guaranteed by the very first article of amendments.

The federal government also became an instrument of liberty *through* its actions. The New Deal acted to provide liberty to a third of a nation, which was ill-housed, ill-clothed, and ill-fed. Its modestly redistributive policies remained popular for almost four decades as the federal government took action to increase and preserve the liberties – civil rights and economic opportunities – of racial minorities, women, the disabled, gays and lesbians, the elderly, the poor, and other disadvantaged groups. We have pursued justice, in the sense of democratic equality, not only or even primarily by the liberties you gave us *from* government. We refashioned what you gave us formally, and other political traditions you may not have intended to leave behind such as civil disobedience, into liberties for subordinate groups within the United States society to pursue justice *through* government action.

The new forms of liberties might be hard for you to accept, and this takes us back to the electoral college. The government you devised premised severe distinctions among human beings. Women were excluded from political life in any meaningful way, and slaves were counted as three-fifths of a person. Even after setting these inequalities aside, including of course the constitutional continuation of human bondage, it seems clear that you saw important differences among male citizens. Truth be told, you seemed to fear the common people. You feared that they and their peers could be too easily manipulated to seize opportunities for increased economic opportunity through land redistribution or increased wealth through income redistribution. You took the lesson of Shays' Rebellion to heart and asserted the need for a standing army because that rebellion instructed you "how little the rights of a feeble government are likely to be respected, even by its own constituents" (Rossiter, 1961, No. 25, p. 167). You referred to Shays' Rebellion frequently to argue for the necessity of force against acts of rebellion (Rossiter, 1961, No. 6, pp. 28 and 75).

Your creation of the electoral college may best express your opinion of human nature in government arrangements most specifically your fear of the common person. You may or may not be surprised that your reflection on government and human nature has been quoted frequently. You remember that you wrote:

> If men were angels, no government would be necessary. If angels were to govern men, neither external nor internal controls on government would be necessary. In framing a government, which is to be administered by men over men, the great difficulty lies in this: you must first enable the government to control the governed; and in the next place oblige it to control itself. A dependence on the people is, no doubt, the primary control on the government; but experience has taught mankind the necessity of auxiliary precautions (Rossiter, 1961, No. 51, p. 322).

The Electoral College provided, in your estimation, an auxiliary precaution to protect liberty *from* government and *through* government, in the form of electoral processes, as well. It seems rooted in your fear of popular government. For example, you cite your critics approvingly that the election of the president is "pretty well guarded." You argue that the Electoral College provides people with a "sense" of choosing the person while withholding the immediate electoral participation to the most capable men. The Electoral College further separates the latter in a "detached and divided" situation – voting in each state separately – to lessen further the chances for "heats and ferments" spreading from one to another. Finally, you explained that a man with "talents for low intrigue, and the little arts of popularity" might win in a single state, but it would require more than these factors to win esteem and confidence in a sufficient number of states of the Union to win office (Rossiter, 1961, No. 68).

After two centuries and several troubled, close presidential elections what we have left of your design is a remnant of your fear of popular government and the risk of losing control of government to a charismatic leader. With the changes in technology, the average voter can be well informed about the candidates and their qualifications. You could not envision in 1787 that there would be so little difference between the electors and those voting for them in "the information and discernment requisite to so complicated an investigation" such as discerning the qualifications of candidates for the office of the presidency. Nor could you imagine how this same technology, the mass media in particular, plus the grueling tasks of primary election victories and raising campaign funds make it almost inevitable that only candidates with talents for the little arts of popularity, if not low intrigue – the very people you sought to block – can be elected president.

Consider the unforeseen consequences of your arrangements that have brought us to this sad state of affairs.

- Your focus of negative liberty, a liberty *from* government grew from a fear of popular government and expressed itself in a convoluted electoral system that can no longer be justified by its superiority of producing the most carefully reasoned judgment of each state's most capable men.
- Changes in education and technology have greatly changed the information that the electorate has as much as the democratic expansion of suffrage has changed the electorate itself.
- Electoral campaigns, primary and the general election, have evolved so that the electoral college no longer provides, "a moral certainty that the office of President will seldom fall to the lot of any man who is not in an eminent degree endowed with the requisite qualifications" (Rossiter, 1961, No. 68, p. 414).
- The lingering fear of popular government not only continues the electoral college but expresses itself
  - in limited access to the ballot for all voters,
  - in a large percentage of invalidated ballots,
  - in a disproportionate number of invalid ballots cast in precincts with low-income, minority voters,
  - in opposition to arrangements, such as fusion ballots, to strengthen third parties, and
  - in a proclivity to fend off democratic forms of liberty – which advance the rights of relatively powerless groups *through* government – and to defend its aristocratic forms.

Your fear of popular government and charismatic leadership still supports and undergirds the de facto and de jure disfranchisement of large portions of the electorate, most pointedly low-income minority groups.

This brings us to the place of order in your political thought and your concern to control government and to emphasize liberty *from* it rather than through it. In fact, you seemed to be preoccupied with stability of government. One has to hunt for mention of justice in your thoughts; the best one can do is infer your ideas about justice from your ideas on liberty. But there is no difficulty in finding your concern for order or stability.

Obviously, any systematic thought of political leadership has concern for order and stability. Your ideas on stability seem related to the new science of Isaac Newton. He found the laws that governed the paths and movements of the bodies of the heavenly firmament. You sought the laws that governed the benefits and conduct of the bodies of earthly republics. You searched history, certainly (Rossiter, 1961, No. 63), as Aristotle and Machiavelli did, and like them took great pride in the science you made of your historical studies. The friends of liberty, in your estimation, would have had to abandon the possibility of a successful republican government in which the few carry out rule for the many, at the very least, and for all people, at the very best. Fortunately, you had the great improvement of the "science of politics" that made the "efficacy of various principles . . . well understood." Then, like the elements of a Newtonian universe, you broke the world of republican government into parts – state and national government – and branches – judicial, legislative, and executive – separated but held together by a system of checks and balances comparable with Newton's gravitational force.

You held great confidence in your "wholly new discoveries" or familiar elements of republican government that "made their principal progress towards perfection in modern times" (Rossiter, 1961, No. 9, p. 72). You dared to imagine a new political universe, "the ENLARGEMENT of the ORBIT within which such systems are to revolve" (Rossiter, 1961, No. 9, p. 73). You set in motion a republican venture of unprecedented scale and scope. Your "scientific" work has certainly contributed to the representative democracy and democratic republic that continues to this day.

Yet your science has its limits. Our twentieth-century physics found Newton's laws inadequate to explain new discoveries that we were making. We discovered that at the speed of light, which scientists had calculated in your own time, time and space become a continuum. It is called relativity, and I am sorry that I cannot explain it. I can report that scientists have stopped light and then started it again. Presently, we are working out the theories of chaos and complexity and their relationship to leadership (Wheatley, 2001). These theories sound frightening but they apply to your work and the work we have done since yours. Chaos tells us that disorder, rather than order, characterizes systems, such as our federal government. Complexity tells us that before the tendency to disorder turns to complete disorder, systems have a self-organizing principle that restores some semblance of order like its original state.

Relativity, chaos, and complexity were all in the Newtonian universe and foremost in your thoughts as you crafted the Constitution (Rossiter, 1961,

No. 9) even if they had not yet been "discovered." It was your greatest achievement to foresee that liberty – freedom within the political system – would be needed to preserve the system of government that you provided us. Without our freedom, liberty *from* and *through* government, our political system could morph (another scientific term that I cannot explain) into a tyranny of the many ruling for their own benefit, your greatest fear, or a tyranny of the few ruling for their own benefit, the place that aristocracy becomes oligarchy. The political science of our own time frankly acknowledges these risks and uses the term *polyarchy* to describe the contrivance that we fashioned to prevent our democratic system, no matter how rudimentary, from devolving into chaos. Polyarchy suggests that representative democracy finds its expression in the capacity of citizens to form groups and gain representation and participation in government (Dahl, 1971). More recent "science" in politics suggests that civil society, for which you provided, is a necessary element for the preservation of democracy (Putnam, 2000), albeit not a sufficient one (Ehrenberg, 1999; Young, 1995).

In light of the last election, it may be time to exercise the liberty that you provided *through* the Constitution to bring our political system closer to a higher version of political equality, *from* which you sought to protect government and the Constitution. As confusing as that may sound, it aptly summarizes the two forms of liberty that you left us – a democratic liberty – which pursues human rights and political, social, and to a lesser extent economic equality – and an aristocratic liberty – which preserves privilege against the claims of its democratic version.

At times, the USA has championed democratic liberty. For example, Eleanor Roosevelt, the widow of the most frequently-elected president, had a direct role in developing the *Declaration of Human Rights of the United Nations*. However, I am not sure if you would approve of the UN. It contains some of the worst characteristics of the government of the Articles of Confederation. I am not sure what you would think of the *Declaration* itself. Certainly, many of our current leaders ignore it. Since its inception, we have invoked our aristocratic liberty, dragged our feet, and lost our moral leadership on human rights. As a nation, we seem incapable of ratifying international agreements on child labor, capital punishment, land mines, and environmental quality. We lost our place on the UN Commission on Human Rights as well as our informal leadership just before terrorist attacks on September 11, 2001 moved us to fashion a worldwide campaign against terrorism. As part of our response to that attack, we are considering tribunals that violate the protection of human rights expressed in the *Declaration*.

However, it might be that you would find the *Declaration of Human Rights* a bold extension of the *Declaration of Independence* that you issued. We don't seem to have the same boldness that you had. Some of us even point out the contradictions in your words and deeds: slave owners declaring that all men are created equal and a Constitution that preserves the inequalities you assumed about race, gender, and wealth. These contradictions encourage some of us to slink to cynicism and assume that you never meant what you said. Others of us, however, assume that your enterprise, like all human endeavor, combined the moral ambiguity of sincerity and shortcomings. You gave us bold directions but modest means of government to pursue them. We have had to amend what you gave us to keep going in the direction of democratic liberty that you provided and to overcome some of the prejudices that you built into the Constitution. It may be time to deal with your fears of popular government and your preference for aristocratic control. They have brought us to the brink of oligarchy that jeopardizes the federal republic and its democratic potential.

Our last election brought us closer to preserving order at the cost of democracy and justice. By a single vote, the federal Supreme Court chose law over justice if we use your terms. You acknowledged different opinions in the formal and technical distinction between LAW and EQUITY (Rossiter, 1961, No. 80, p. 480 your emphasis) and recognized that the courts would have to deal with cases of both. You even explained contracts "in which, though there may have been no direct fraud or deceit sufficient to invalidate them in a court of law, yet there may have been some undue and unconscionable advantage taken of the necessities or misfortune of one of the parties which a court of equity would not tolerate." You made the case even stronger, "it would be impossible for the federal judicatories to do *justice* without an equitable as well as a legal jurisdiction" (Rossiter, 1961, No. 80, p. 480 my emphasis).

This is not to say that you would have objected to the action of the court's majority in this case. They did, after all, place order and stablity, including the appearance of legitimacy (Garrett, 2001, p. 47), before all else and manifested a preference for authoritative expertise to the messy process of democratic politics (Pildes, 2001, p. 162). Its majority expressed a concern to protect government from broader claims of democratic liberty. Certainly, there are legal arguments to justify the Court's majority opinion (Posner, 2001). In larger terms, however, the majority of the Court invoke legal jurisdiction to renege on the contract within the Constitution for equity and democratic liberty. The conduct of the Supreme Court enacts the most current scene of the long-running democratic drama in the USA in which law and order and equity and justice have leading roles.

It remains our task and indeed our obligation to you to work to restore equity to the conduct of law and justice to the pursuit of order. One step in this work is to discard the founding fear of democracy. For example, we need to continue the enfranchisement of all Americans, voting schedules that permit greater participation, and mechanisms that assure the validity of each ballot. Naturally, our work must not stop there, nor will it because we will not achieve these changes without direct action, a foundation of democracy more fundamental than the ballot. Fortunately, you have left us a system of freedom *from* a government that now prefers law above justice or equity. That freedom permits us to pursue new and more complete forms of justice *through* government. It is in that effort that we find justice, equity, and a renewal of your commitment to democratic liberty.

Your admiring and humble servant,

DEMOCRATUS

CONCLUSION

Ironically, creating new and more democratic practices in elections and other facets of American life has required charismatic, heroic, or transforming leadership to counter the sacrosanct aura of the Founding Fathers and their work. They did not fear charismatic leadership itself, but only its more popular forms that worked against hierarchical arrangements watched over by a benevolent aristocracy, albeit a natural one. In classic Aristotelian terms, the Founding Fathers distrusted democracy, the rule of the many for the benefit of the many, and favored an aristocratic constitution in which the few, men like themselves, would rule for the benefit of all. They preferred what Bass has called "socialized" charismatic leadership but despaired of the possibility of internalizing the values of a propertied aristocracy into the hearts and minds of other men and women.

Alternatives to aristocratic political arrangements existed. Aristotle envisioned an alternative form of constitution, the polis, whereby the many ruled for all. The Founding Fathers ruled this out because the republic they fashioned had a geographic expanse far beyond the city-state scale with which Aristotle worked. However unfeasible the polis seemed in 1787, communication now binds the nation and indeed the world, and makes possible a level of information about public affairs that the Founding Fathers thought possible only for a few of the most intelligent and economically successful men of their time.

They underestimated the power of their own ideals especially expressed in the *Declaration of Independence* and in their actions to establish liberty *from* government imposed restrictions through direct action. Fortunately, they preserved sufficient liberty in their constitutional arrangements, especially the first 10 amendments, for the pursuit of increased forms of democratic equality, including political participation, *through* government action. They also underestimated how the power of their ideas of liberty, justice, and equality would bind people together. Gunnar Myrdal found a deep belief in American ideals even among the very people most denied their equitable practice, African Americans (Myrdal, 1944). Every effort to extend democratic liberty to some excluded group has been an effort to express American political ideals better, even though initially opposed.

It takes socialized charismatic leadership to extend the democratic form of liberty in face of the inertia and resistance of aristocratic liberty. Fortunately, Bass enables us to understand the more and less genuine forms of charismatic leadership. He and his colleagues have demystified some aspects of charismatic leadership with the four "I's" and other analysis (Bass, 1981, pp. 188–192). This work inspires his confidence that political leadership, charismatic and transformational, can increase American democratic performance beyond expectations.

Fortunately, the Founding Fathers provided a flexible document that evolved with demands for more inclusive democratic practices, if the people use it. The question remains if a majority of Americans have come to trust the people more than some of the Founding Fathers to use the liberty provided us by them. Idealized influence, inspirational leadership, intellectual stimulation, and individualized consideration serve as very reasonable starting points for that leadership and liberty with the last I, acting appropriately, as a check and balance on the first. Through them, perhaps, we may instill the American polity with the confidence that democratic practice, including the selection of the president, is the best safeguard that charismatic leadership will remain within Lincoln's democratic trinity, "of the people, by the people, and for the people."

ACKNOWLEDGMENTS

This chapter grew from work conducted in a seminar on political leadership in Spring 2001 at the Jepson School of Leadership Studies. I am delighted to acknowledge the contributions which its participants – Bethany Cooper, Matt Devine, Logan Dunn, Mariel Rodak, Beth Anne Newman, Jonathan Nichols, Ahern Schneider, Joshua Schreier, Bethany Smocer, Tim Sullivan, and Ben Tengwall – made to this chapter.

REFERENCES

Avolio, B. J. (1999). *Full leadership development: Building the vital forces in organizations.* Thousand Oaks, CA: Sage.

Bass, B. M. (1981). Charismatic, charismalike, and inspirational leadership. In: B. M. Bass & R. M. Stogdill (Eds), *Handbook of leadership: Theory, research, & managerial applications* (3rd ed., pp. 184–221). New York: The Free Press.

Bass, B. M. (1985). *Leadership and performance beyond expectations.* New York: Free Press.

Bass, B. M. (1998). *Transformational leadership: Industrial, military, and educational impact.* Mahwah, NJ: Lawrence Erlbaum Associates.

Dahl, R. A. (1971). *Polyarchy: Participation and opposition.* New Haven: Yale University Press.

Ehrenberg, J. (1999). *Civil society: The critical history of an idea.* New York: New York University Press.

Garrett, E. (2001). Leaving the decision to Congress. In: C. R. Sunstein & R. A. Epstein (Eds), *The Vote: Bush, Gore, and the Supreme Court* (pp. 38–54). Chicago: University of Chicago Press.

Issacharoff, S. (2001). Political judgments. In: C. R. Sunstein & R. A. Epstein (Eds), *The vote: Bush, Gore, and the Supreme Court* (pp. 55–76). Chicago: University of Chicago Press.

Karlan, P. (2001). The newest equal protection: Regressive doctrine on a changeable court. In: C. R. Sunstein & R. A. Epstein (Eds), *The Vote: Bush, Gore, and the Supreme Court* (pp. 77–97). Chicago: University of Chicago Press.

Michelman, F. I. (2001). Suspicion, or the new prince. In: C. R. Sunstein & R. A. Epstein (Eds), *The Vote: Bush, Gore, and the Supreme Court* (pp. 123–139). Chicago: University of Chicago Press.

Myrdal, G. (1944). *An American dilemma: The negro problem and modern democracy.* New York: Harper & Row Publishers.

Pildes, R. H. (2001). In: C. R. Sunstein & R. A. Epstein (Eds), *The Vote: Bush, Gore, and the Supreme Court* (pp. 140–164). Chicago: University of Chicago Press.

Posner, R. A. (2001). *Breaking the deadlock: The 2000 election, the constitution, and the courts.* Princeton, NJ: Princeton University Press.

Putnam, R. D. (2000). *Bowling alone: The collapse and revival of American community.* New York: Simon & Schuster.

Rossiter, C. (Ed.) (1961). In: A. Hamilton, J. Madison & J. Jay (Eds), *The Federalist Papers.* New York: New American Library.

Smith, A. (1976). *The moral sentiments.* New York: Oxford University Press.

Sunstein, C. R. (2001). Introduction: Of law and politics. In: C. R. Sunstein & R. A. Epstein (Eds), *The Vote: Bush, Gore, and the Supreme Court* (pp. 1–12). Chicago: University of Chicago Press.

Timmons, M. L. vs. Twin Cities Area New Part (1977). 520 U.S. 351; 117 S. Ct. 1364 (April 28).

Weber, M. (1958). Politics as a vocation. In: C. Wright Mills & H. H. Gerth (Eds), *From Max Weber: Essays in sociology* (pp. 77–128). New York: Oxford University Press.

Wheatley, M. (2001). *Leadership and the new science: Discovering order in a chaotic world revised.* Emeryville, CA: Berrett-Koehler Publishers.

Wills, G. (1992). *Lincoln at Gettysburg: The words that remade America.* New York: Simon & Schuster.

Young, I. M. (1995). Social groups in associative democracy. In: E. O. Wright (Ed.), *Associations and Democracy: The real utopias project* (pp. 207–213). London: Verso.

VISION AND MENTAL MODELS: THE CASE OF CHARISMATIC AND IDEOLOGICAL LEADERSHIP

Michael D. Mumford and Jill M. Strange

ABSTRACT

Articulation of a vision is commonly held to be a critical component of theories of outstanding leadership – both transformational and charismatic leadership. Although there is reason to suspect that vision contributes to leader performance, less is known about the nature and origin of viable visions. In the present chapter, we argue that leaders' visions can be viewed as a prescriptive mental model reflecting beliefs about the optimal functioning of an organization. To test this proposition, outstanding leaders possessing two contrasting types of prescriptive mental models were identified: ideologues whose models stress the maintenance of extant standards and charismatics whose models stress adaptive change. These two types of prescriptive mental models were associated with distinct patterns of leader behavior in a sample of notable historic leaders. The implications of these findings are discussed with respect to current theories of outstanding leadership.

For many Americans, George Washington is the embodiment of outstanding leadership. Not only did he lead the Continental Army through a prolonged struggle, his presidency, the first presidency in the United States, defined a standard that has guided the actions of many subsequent presidents. As is the

Transformational and Charismatic Leadership, Volume 2, pages 109–142.
ISBN: 0-7623-0962-8

case for transformational and charismatic leaders (Bass, 1985; Bass & Avolio, 1996; Conger & Kanungo, 1987; House, 1995), Washington's leadership was linked to a striking vision. This vision is perhaps best articulated in a letter – a letter commonly referred to as his farewell address. In this letter, Washington made two points he hoped his "countrymen" would bear in mind as he left office:

(1) remain united; and
(2) avoid "foreign" entanglements

(Ellis, 2001).

These statements are remarkable not just because of their ongoing influence over the politics and government of the United States, but also for what they tell us about the nature and origin of the vision characteristic of outstanding leaders. The principles articulated in the farewell address were a direct reflection of Washington's experience (Ellis, 2001). His belief in the need to remain united can be attributed to the fact that success in the Revolutionary War was due more to holding the Continental Army together than military prowess. His belief that we must avoid "foreign" entanglements can be attributed to both:

(1) a suspicion about the ideas of the French Revolution; and
(2) a belief that pragmatic day-to-day work has more influence on building a nation, and an army, than lofty ideals.

It was these two key principles, his vision, that guided Washington's actions during his term as America's first president.

This principle-based knowledge structure, where principles are abstracted from past experience in a complex social system, have been referred to as mental models (e.g. Daniels, Chernatony & Johnson, 1995; Rouse, Cannon-Bowers & Salas, 1992). In this chapter, we will argue that the formation of a viable prescriptive mental model provides the cognitive foundation for the vision that lies at the heart of outstanding leadership. Subsequently, we will examine the findings obtained in a study intended to illustrate the impact of different prescriptive mental models on the behavior of outstanding, histor-ically notable leaders. More specifically, we will contrast ideological and charismatic leaders who differ with respect to the substantive, and normative, orientation of the models being applied. Finally, we will consider some of the other characteristics of these mental models that might contribute to leader performance.

VISION AND MENTAL MODELS

Charismatic and Transformational Leadership

Beginning with the work of Weber (1947) and Burns (1975), students of leadership, including Bass (1985) and House (1995), have sought to understand the factors that distinguish truly outstanding leaders (e.g. Washington, Churchill, or Ghandi) from their less outstanding counterparts. The concepts of charismatic and transformational leadership represent an attempt, a truly successful attempt, to identify the characteristics of outstanding leaders. Traditional models of leadership were based on transactional principles or an exchange of support for rewards (Bass, 1997). Although transactional leadership appears useful in accounting for routine incidents of institutional leadership, these transactional models cannot account for the disproportionate impact of some leaders: especially, their impact with respect to follower motivation and performance (Bass, 1985; Mumford & Van Doorn, 2001).

One answer to the question posed by the limited impact of transactional leadership may be found in Bass's (1985, 1997) notion of transformational leadership. In Bass's view, transformational leadership is a multidimensional phenomenon. Specifically, transformational leadership is held to involve idealized influence (charisma), inspirational motivation, intellectual stimulation, and individualized consideration. Embedded in the notion of idealized influence is the concept that the leader creates and articulates a vision, or image of the future, which not only motivates followers but provides a structure around which meaning can be defined and action initiated.

Over the course of the last decade, a number of studies have provided evidence for the plausibility of this model as one system that might be used to account for incidents of outstanding leadership. For example, Howell and Avolio (1993) found that transformational leadership, as assessed by Bass and Avolio's (1996) MLQ Measure, was related to improved unit performance. Sosik, Avolio and Kahai (1997) have shown that transformational leadership may spur innovation and creativity through intervening motivational mechanisms. Perhaps the most compelling evidence for the validity of this model may be found in a meta-analysis conducted by Lowe, Kroeck and Sivasubramaniam (1996). They found that the MLQ dimensions, in particular idealized influence, intellectual stimulation, and individualized consideration were positive influences on leader performance across more than 30 studies.

The notion of transformational leadership, of course, represents only one model that might be used to account for incidents of outstanding leadership (Mumford & Van Doorn, 2001). An alternative view of outstanding leadership may be found in the theories of charismatic leadership proposed by Conger and Kanungo (1987, 1997, 1998) and House and his colleagues (House, 1977; House & Shamir, 1993; Shamir, House & Arthur, 1993). Although these theories display some notable differences with regard to the specific behaviors characterizing charismatic leaders (e.g. House & Podsakoff, 1994), these theories all stress the importance of presenting an appealing, motivating vision that resolves conflict and provides followers with meaning and direction.

The potential impact of the vision articulated by charismatic leaders has been illustrated in a study conducted by O'Connor, Mumford, Clifton, Gessner and Connelly (1995). Using a distinction drawn by House, Spangler and Woycke (1993), they obtained a sample of 80 notable historic leaders, half of whom were socialized and half personalized. Socialized charismatics evidence prosocial visions whereas personalized charismatics evidence visions bound up in their own individual concerns. Using a content coding of leaders' biographies, they found that charismatic leaders generally had a large impact on society. However, socialized charismatics had a large positive impact whereas personalized charismatics had a large negative impact. Other studies by Hunt, Boal and Dodge (1999), Kirkpatrick and Locke (1996), and Yorges, Weiss and Strickland (1999) also indicate that charismatic leaders, and the accompanying visions, may exert a marked impact on leader performance and prove capable of accounting for outstanding leadership.

These observations about our two dominant models of outstanding leaders point to a rather straightforward conclusion – outstanding leadership appears to involve vision. The apparently straightforward conclusion, however, begs a number of questions (Beyer, 1999; Yukl, 1999). One question that might be asked, a question broached by Mumford and Van Doorn (2001), is, does outstanding leadership always require vision? Another question, broached by Bass and Steidlmeier (1999) and House and Howell (1992), is, does the prosocial orientation of a vision influence the effects of outstanding leadership? Still a third question is, does the content and structure of this vision have an impact on how people go about leading? It is this third, and final, question that we will address in the remainder of this chapter.

Vision and Mental Models

On the whole, the literature on organizational leadership has focused on the social consequences of the vision articulated by notable leaders. We have examined the impact of articulation of a vision with respect to follower motivation, social achievement, and creativity. As important as it is to know the consequences of articulating a vision, we must also know exactly what we mean by the term "vision". Vision has been defined as, an idealized goal that the leader wants the organization to achieve in the future (Conger, 1999). Alternatively, vision has been defined as an image of the future that articulates the values, purposes, and meanings of followers (Boal & Bryson, 1980). Still another definition of vision holds that it reflects both goals and strategies for attaining these goals (Yukl, 1998).

Although these definitions of the term vision differ in some notable ways, they are bound together by a common thread. A vision may be seen as a set of beliefs about how people should act in a social setting. These prescriptive beliefs about idealized actions imply that outstanding leadership involves belief structures indicating the goals that should be pursued by a group and how the group should go about attaining these goals. These integrated belief structures describing interactions within a social system may, in turn, be viewed as an idealized mental model, or image, of *optimal* system operations (Albert, 1998; Williams, 2001).

The term mental models is a notion derived from cognitive psychology (e.g. Johnson & Laird, 1983). Within this cognitive framework, a mental model is seen as a conceptual representation of complex system interactions that may be used to both understand the actions of a system and guide action (Sein & Bostrom, 1989). These conceptual representations identify key causal concepts that engender action and bring about goal attainment within a system articulating associations, or causal linkages, among these causal concepts along with the variables that impinge on their operation (Holyoak & Thagard, 1997; Largan-Fox & Code, 2000). These models are, in turn, used to describe, explain, and predict the actions occurring in a system (Rouse, Cannon-Bowers & Salas, 1992) thereby providing a framework to both guide and direct subsequent actions intended to optimize system operations. In fact, at least three lines of evidence suggest that the availability of these mental models might prove useful in understanding performance, in general, and leadership performance, in particular.

One line of research has examined the impact of mental models on team performance (Cannon-Bowers & Salas, 1990; Entin & Sefarty, 2000; Orasanu, 1990). Broadly speaking, the results obtained in these studies indicate that when team members share common mental models, coordination and adaptation improve. A second line of research indicates that the availability of shared mental models results in improved communication within the group (Mumford, Feldman, Hein & Nago, 2001; Volpe, Cannon-Bowers, Salas & Spector, 1996). The third line of research indicates that the availability of shared mental models results in improved planning performance (Stout,

Cannon-Bowers, Salas & Milanovich, 1999; Zaccaro, Guiltieri & Minionis, 1995).

These observations about the impact of mental models on group perform-ance, led Mumford, Schultz and Osburn (in press) to argue that one way leaders exert influence on group performance is through the definition, articulation, and communication of viable mental models. A viable mental model, however, should not be arbitrarily equated with the vision characteristic of outstanding leaders. A mental model describes the system as it is – a normative model. A vision, however, describes the system as it ought to be – a prescriptive model. Thus, people's mental models provide a basis for creation of a vision, but the vision may represent something more or something different.

Although mental models and vision should not be arbitrarily equated, it also seems plausible to argue that mental models provide the cognitive foundation for development of a vision. Figure 1 illustrates how this process might occur. Initially, individual history, experience in a system, and social feedback lead to formation of a descriptive mental model articulating goals and causes of goal attainment. With application of this model and, more centrally, reflection on past experience in relation to personal values and perceived social needs, it becomes possible for people to abstract the key goals they, or others, should act on, and the key causes and restrictions impinging on goal attainment. The abstraction of key goals and key causes leads, in conjunction with the individual's perception of the standards that must be maintained and the events that must be changed, to a prescriptive model. If application of this prescriptive model provides personal meaning for the leader and interpersonal meaning for followers (recognizing that the meaning may differ for leaders and followers), a vision may emerge along with an attribution of outstanding leadership.

Of course, the question that arises at this juncture is whether there is any reason to assume that this theory provides a plausible basis accounting for origin of the visions that are a hallmark of outstanding leadership. Although this theory is complex, it does hold that two key processes are likely to underlie the development of visionary leadership:

(1) reflection on experience in relation to personal values and perceived social needs; and
(2) abstraction of key goals and key causes applicable to the social system at hand.

Prior studies of leader performance have, in fact, provided some support for both these propositions.

Jacobs and Jaques (1987, 1990, 1991) have argued that reflection and integration of personal and social experiences may represent a key component

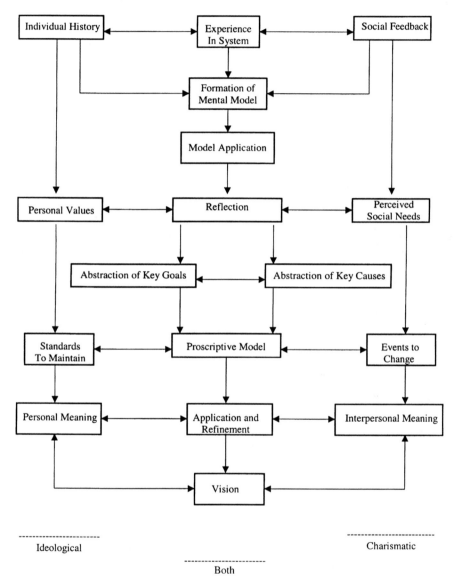

Fig. 1.   Process Underlying the Development of Vision.

of leader performance. In accordance with this proposition, Zaccaro, Mumford, Connelly, Marks and Gilbert (2000) developed a measure of wisdom that used ratings of managerial dilemmas to assess:

(1) reflection;
(2) objectivity;
(3) judgment;
(4) systems perception;
(5) systems commitment; and
(6) solution fit.

Subsequently, this measure was administered to 1818 Army officers ranging in grade from Second Lieutenant to Full Colonel. It was found that leaders evidenced growth in these skills as they moved from junior to more senior positions with reflection, objectivity, judgment, and solution fit being particularly important for movement into senior, as opposed to mid-level, leadership roles (Mumford, Marks, Connelly, Zaccaro & Reiter-Palmon, 2000). Moreover, these skills, including reflection, were found to predict indices of leader performance accounting for variance in performance above and beyond that accounted for by more basic abilities and motivation (Connelly, Gilbert, Zaccaro, Threlfall, Marks & Mumford, 2000).

Evidence for the importance of abstracting key goals and key causes has been provided by Eisenhardt (1989), Thomas, Clark and Gioia (1993), and Thomas and McDaniel (1990). In one study, Thomas and McDaniel (1990) examined the strategic planning strategies used by hospital chief executive officers. Using survey questions examining the attributes considered in planning, they found that chief executives focused on a limited number of key controllable causes in formulating plans. In fact, Isenberg (1986), in a study contrasting experienced managers with MBA students, found, using a "think aloud" procedure, that experienced managers, in contrast with students, applied more general models that stressed a limited number of key causes and contingencies.

Ideological and Charismatic Leadership

If it is granted that there is some reason to suspect that the model of vision creation presented earlier is plausible, one might pose still another question. More specifically, do differences in the material used to construct the prescriptive models underlying a vision lead to different styles of outstanding leadership? The model presented in Fig. 1 suggests that a prescriptive model, in part, emerges from the leaders' personal values, their beliefs about the importance of maintaining certain standards, and the personal meaning the leader derives from adherence to these standards. Following the observations of Gerring (1997), Huer (1978), and Rejai (1991), we would argue that leaders emphasizing this approach to the construction of prescriptive models will display a distinctly ideological bent stressing adherence to a prori defined standards. In contrast, leaders who construct prescriptive models based on perceived social needs, necessary changes, and interpersonal meaning may, in accordance with the observations of Bass (1985), Conger and Kanungo (1987), and House (1995), be viewed as purely charismatic, or transformational leaders.

These differences in the weights given to various inputs in the formation of prescriptive mental models and the generation of a vision are noteworthy, in part, because they suggest that ideological and charismatic leaders will display rather different patterns of behavior and potentially rather different styles of outstanding leadership. The focus of ideological leaders on values, standards, and personal meaning implies that leaders will focus on value maintenance, with less consideration being given to followers or the need for change. The ideological leader, moreover, will justify actions based on a limited number of relatively inflexible core beliefs and values. Appeal to others will be based, not on the leader per se, but rather the truth embedded in these beliefs and values (Gerring, 1997; Mills, 1967). In contrast, the charismatic leader will appeal to followers based on the image of a better future embodied in the leader as a role model with appeal to followers being based on the image of a better future as articulated in the leader's actions (House & Podsakoff, 1994; Hunt, Boal & Dodge, 1999).

In considering the distinction between the ideological and charismatic forms of visionary leadership, three points should be borne in mind. First, both ideological and charismatic leaders may differ with respect to the orientation towards a social, as opposed to a personalized, pattern of interaction (House & Howell, 1992; O'Connor, Mumford, Clifton, Gessner & Connelly, 1995). Thus, ideological leaders might base their prescriptive models on prosocial beliefs and values, as is evident in the case of Woodrow Wilson, or they might base their prescriptive models on self-serving beliefs and values, as is evident in the case of Joseph McCarthy. Second, as implied by our foregoing observations, ideological and charismatic leaders may evidence a range of beliefs and values but share a common orientation with respect to the kind of beliefs and values being stressed. Third, these styles represent a matter of emphasis rather than qualitatively different types. As a result, outstanding leaders may evidence some ideological and some charismatic, or transformational, elements in their behavior.

Our intent in the study to be described in the following sections of this chapter was to assess the distinction drawn above between the ideological and charismatic forms of outstanding, visionary, leadership. To conduct this evaluation, we used a psycho-historical approach (O'Connor, Mumford, Clifton, Gessner & Connelly, 1995; Simonton, 1991) identifying notable twentieth century leaders who evidenced an ideological, charismatic, or mixed approach, and then contrasting these leaders with respect to charismatic and ideological behaviors. By showing the expected behavioral differences between ideological and charismatic leaders, we hoped to provide some further evidence for the model of vision formation presented earlier while illustrating the "real-world" consequences of differences among leaders with respect to the prescriptive mental models held to underlie the construction of a vision.

COMPARING IDEOLOGICAL AND CHARISMATIC LEADERS

Method

Sample

The sample used to test these hypotheses consisted of 60 historically notable leaders. General history texts and biographical web sites were used to identify an initial pool of 132 leaders for whom academic biographies were available. Within this pool, available documentary material was reviewed to identify whether leaders appeared to exhibit ideological, charismatic, or a mixed style, and whether the leader was socialized or personalized. Socialized and personalized leaders were identified using the definition proposed by O'Connor, Mumford, Clifton, Gessner and Connelly (1995). Ideological leaders were identified, in accordance with our foregoing propositions, based on the leaders' consistent expression of strongly held beliefs and values, whereas charismatic leaders were identified based on their expression of a future-oriented vision. Leaders who exhibited both these characteristics were classified as mixed cases.

Based on this material, 60 leaders were selected for use in the present study, evenly distributed across the three styles of outstanding leadership, to include both personalized and socialized leaders. Thus, value content was reflected in the personalized vs. socialized classification (leader orientation), whereas the emphasis placed on certain kinds of content (leader style) was reflected in the ideological, charismatic, or mixed classification. In selecting this final sample of leaders, an attempt was made to insure that a variety of distinct leadership roles were represented with leaders being drawn from the business, political, military, and religious areas. Only twentieth century leaders were included in their sample owing to the need for high-quality, factually oriented academic biographies. Table 1 provides a listing of the leaders included in this sample and the a priori style and orientation classifications.

Biographies and Content Coding
Academic biographies were obtained for each of the leaders selected for inclusion in the present study. Biographies were selected for each leader who met the following criteria:

(1) the biography must report factual, historically verified behaviors and actions;
(2) it must include a "rise to power chapter" and a chapter examining the leaders' behaviors and actions during the period they were at the "pinnacle of power"; and

Table 1. Sample of Ideological, Charismatic, and Mixed Style Leaders.

	Ideological	Charismatic	Mixed
SOCIALIZED	Charles de Gaulle	Edward R. Murrow	Abdel G. Nasser
	George Marshall	F. D. Roosevelt	Douglas MacArthur
	John L. Lewis	Fiorello H. LaGuardia	Emma Goldman
	Margaret Thatcher	Henry Ford	General Tito
	Michael Collins	John F. Kennedy	Harry S Truman
	Eleanor Roosevelt	Jomo Kenyatta	Indira Gandhi
	Mohandas Gandhi	Sam Rayburn	Jwame Nkrumah
	Ronald Reagan	Samuel Gompers	Martin Luther King, Jr.
	W. E. B. Du Bois	Winston Churchill	Susan B. Anthony
	Woodrow Wilson	J. P. Morgan	T. Roosevelt
PERSONALIZED	Che Guevera	Benito Mussolini	Ho Chi Minh
	Deng Xiaoping	Idi Amin	Adolph Hitler
	Francisco Franco	J. Edgar Hoover	Ferdinand Foch
	J. D. Rockefeller	Jim Bakker	Fidel Castro
	Joseph McCarthy	Francois Duvalier (Doc)	Georges Clemenceau
	Vladimir Lenin	Manuel Noriega	Juan Peron
	Leon Trotsky	W. C. Westmoreland	Malcom X
	Mao Tse Tung	Neville Chamberlain	Kaiser Wilhelm II
	Warren Harding	Huey Long	William Jennings Bryan
	Joseph Stalin	Nicholae Ceauşescu	William Randolph Hearst

(3) it must include a prologue, or epilogue, chapter summarizing the leader's accomplishments.

Academic biographies meeting all three of these criteria were obtained for each of the 60 leaders included in the sample.

Content coding of the biographies was based on a behavioral "observation" approach. Implementation of this approach began by having a psychologist read through the "rise-to-power" and "in-power" chapters. This psychologist was then asked to mark the passages describing each discrete behavior exhibited by the leader in relation to followers and each behavior exhibited by followers in relation to the leader. It is of note that editorial opinions, evaluations, and event context were not considered behavior. Instead, behavior was reflected only in actions, or communications, among leaders and followers. A reliability check indicated 80% agreement, across two psychologists, in the behaviors identified in a sample of 10 chapters. Typically, 30 to 100 behaviors were identified in a given chapter.

After these behaviors had been identified, the "rise-to-power" and "in-power" chapters were presented to three judges. In evaluating the behaviors appearing in each chapter, judges were to apply the coding sheets presented in Tables 2 and 3. In this coding scheme, judges were presented a list of hypothesized ideological and charismatic behaviors. The list of ideological behaviors (Gerring, 1997; Huer, 1978; Rejai, 1991) and the list of charismatic behaviors (Conger & Kannungo, 1987; House & Howell, 1992; House & Podsakoff, 1994) were developed based on a review of the relevant literature. Each list was expressly designed to include both socialized and personalized behaviors relevant to each style (ideological and charismatic). In all, 29 ideological and 30 charismatic behaviors were included in the two lists.

In making their evaluations, judges were to examine the behavior underlined in the chapter, taking into account the broader contextual material provided in the chapter being read. They were then to review the behaviors provided in a given list, and determine whether the underlined behavior was similar to any one of the behaviors appearing on the list – indicating identification of a similar behavior with a check mark. The average number of check marks assigned to a behavior across judges resulted in the initial score obtained for each behavior on a given chapter. To control for cross-chapter differences in length and specificity, the average number of behavioral manifestations identified by the judges was divided by the total number of behaviors occurring in the chapter.

A total of nine judges took part in this rating process. Prior to making their ratings, judges took part in a 3-week training program. In this training program, judges were familiarized with the nature of the task and were provided with

Table 2.   List of Ideological Behaviors.

---

1. The leader has a limited set of extreme, consistent, strongly held beliefs and values.
2. The leader is inflexible about his or her beliefs/values and will stay committed to them throughout his or her leadership.
3. The leader's beliefs and values determine the goals defined for the organization.
4. Evaluation of others' situations, business opportunities, etc. is defined in relation to their leader's beliefs and values.
5. Leadership occurs through articulation and action in the leader's beliefs and values as opposed to charisma, intellectual stimulation, and vision construction.
6. In the leader's mind, everything has a clearly differentiated space – some things are good, some things are bad (black and white – no gray).
7. The leader will communicate in such a way that the attention is not placed on himself or herself, but on his or her ideas.
8. Followers are attracted to and influenced by the leader's ideas, not necessarily the leader.
9. People will have an extreme reaction to the beliefs and values of the leader.
10. The leader will be willing to sacrifice himself or herself for his or her ideas.
11. In order for the leader to be effective, there must be some catalyst to make the followers open to the beliefs and values of the leader.
12. The leader will tell people directly what to do. There is little room for autonomy because the leader wants things carried out in accordance to his or her beliefs and values.
13. The leader will back up orders with justification based on his or her beliefs and values.
14. The leader will push his or her beliefs/values on those around him.
15. The leader will not be persuaded away from his or her beliefs/values, no matter how good the argument.
16. The leader will derive his or her power from his or her beliefs/values and the organization's confidence that he or she can accomplish a lot with regard to these beliefs/values.
17. The leader will gain power by discrediting those currently in power.
18. The leader will not care if he or she is liked by others as long as they agree with his or her beliefs/values.
19. The leader will take no personal interest in a follower unless they are of use to him.
20. The leader will manipulate followers to achieve his or her goals.
21. The leader will excel in persuading people to agree with his or her beliefs/values.
22. The leader will not negotiate when it comes to his or her ideas.
23. The leader is motivated by the idea of having everyone share his or her beliefs/values.
24. The leader will disregard the needs of the organization in order to achieve the goals based on his or her beliefs/values.
25. The leader will only appeal to those people who have the same beliefs/values.
26. The leader will use punishment for those who do not adhere to his or her beliefs/values.
27. The leader will not tolerate those who do not agree with his or her beliefs/values, and they will be viewed as traitors.
28. The leader will trust only a few people to help him carry out his or her ideas.
29. The leader will expect his or her followers to sacrifice themselves for his or her beliefs/values.

Table 3.   List of Charismatic Behaviors.

1. The leader will act accordingly to a certain "vision" that specifies a better future state.
2. The leader will strive toward distal, rather than proximate, goals.
3. The leader will communicate messages that contain references to his or her overall vision.
4. The leader will behaviorally role model the values implied by the vision by personal example.
5. The leader will express high performance expectations of followers.
6. The leader will communicate a high degree of confidence in followers' ability to meet expectations.
7. The leader will demonstrate behaviors that selectively arouse unconscious achievement, power, and affiliative motives of followers when these motives are specifically relevant to the attainment of the vision.
8. Leadership occurs through articulation of the vision and accomplishments that pertain to vision attainment.
9. Followers are attracted to the leader himself or herself.
10. People will have an extreme reaction to the leader.
11. Followers will sacrifice themselves for the leader and/or the leader's vision.
12. In order for the leader to be effective, there must be some catalyst to make the followers open to the leader and his or her vision.
13. The leader will allow followers the autonomy to make their own decisions, but will influence them to make decisions in line with his or her vision.
14. The leader will back up orders with justification based on the goodness of his or her vision.
15. Followers are directly influenced by the leader and their personal relationship with him or her.
16. The leader cares about his or her image and plays to the desires of followers.
17. The leader will take an interest in all current and potential followers.
18. The leader will excel in persuading people to agree with him or her.
19. The leader is motivated by the accomplishment of his or her vision.
20. The leader will negotiate his or her ideas when it benefits his or her image or his or her vision.
21. The leader will take into account the needs of the organization in his or her decision-making.
22. The leader will use positive rewards and reinforcement with his or her followers.
23. The leader will try to persuade those who disagree with his or her vision to agree with it.
24. The leader will delegate authority for the attainment of his or her vision.
25. The leader may change his or her vision to meet the needs and wants of the followers and the organization.
26. The leader will exude confidence, dominance, and a sense of purpose.
27. Followers are devoted and unquestioning to the leader.
28. The leader will motivate the followers to act upon ideas already in place in society.
29. The leader will be narcissistic and wish to bring power and attention to himself or herself.
30. The leader will interact with followers – social distance is low.

illustrations of behaviors falling into the various categories. Subsequently, they were asked to make practice ratings using the behaviors identified in two training chapters. After making their initial ratings, the panel was reconvened to compare results and discuss observed discrepancies. At this time, additional feedback was provided concerning the nature of the checklists.

Neither in the training process, nor in making their ratings, were judges provided with any information about the initial classification of leaders. Different groups of three judges rated the ideological and charismatic behaviors appearing in the two chapters identified for a given leader. The interrater agreement coefficients obtained for these behavioral evaluations ranged between 0.54 and 0.94 across the behaviors included in the two checklists. The median interrater agreement coefficient obtained for the three judges across behaviors was in excess of 0.70 for both checklists. The average of the judges' ratings, divided by the number of behaviors appearing in the chapter, provided the score used in subsequent analyses.

To help ensure the adequacy of these ratings, four covariate control measures were obtained using the information provided in the prologue and epilogue chapters. The first control measure was a five-point rating of how favorably the author viewed the leader. The second control measure, again a five-point rating, assessed the degree of factual orientation in the chapter. The third control, intended to take into account historic shifts and temporal distance, was a simple coding of whether the leader was in power pre- or post-World War II. The fourth, and final, control measure, intended to consider the volume of available historic data, was derived from a count of Library of Congress citations.

Analyses
Initially, to assess potential archival biases, the four control measures were correlated with behavioral counts, divided by the total number of behaviors, obtained for the "rise-to-power" and "in-power" chapters. The results obtained in these analyses indicated that neither the ideological nor the charismatic behaviors were correlated with the controls. Thus, the data obtained for this study do not appear unduly influenced by archival biases.

Having completed these preliminary analyses, attention turned to the primary analyses of concern in the present study. In the analyses, a multivariate analysis of variance was conducted where leader style (ideological, charismatic, and mixed), career point ("rise-to-power" vs. "in-power"), and leader orientation (socialized vs. personalized) were treated as independent variables, and the behaviors included in each checklist were treated as dependent variables. It is of note that separate analyses were conducted for the ideological and charismatic behaviors. In the case of the multivariate analyses, a standard ($p < 0.05$) significance level was applied, whereas in the univariate analyses,

Table 4. Summary Manova Tables for Ideological and Charismatic
Behaviors.

	F	Sig
Ideological Behaviors		
Repeated Measure	8.73	0.001
Leader Style	1.65	0.024
Leader Orientation	1.73	0.059
Career Point	1.47	0.138
Style by Orientation	1.53	0.043
Style by Career Point	0.28	0.772
Orientation by Career Point	0.88	0.629
Style by Orientation by Career Point	0.66	0.946
Charismatic Behaviors		
Repeated Measure	10.97	0.001
Leader Style	1.67	0.021
Leader Orientation	2.44	0.007
Career Point	2.83	0.002
Style by Orientation	1.84	0.009
Style by Career Point	1.80	0.011
Orientation by Career Point	1.19	0.307
Styles by Orientation by Career Point	0.88	0.681

Notes: *F* ratio and significance levels based on Wilks Lambda.
Based on a subsample of leaders.

where repeated measures error control could not be applied, a more liberal
($p < 0.15$) significance level was applied to take into account a type two error.

Results

Table 4 presents the results obtained in the multivariate analysis of variance. As
may be seen, the leader style variable produced significant effects ($p < 0.05$) in
both analyses. Comparison of the specific ideological and charismatic leaders
indicated that nine of the 29 ideological behaviors, and 12 of the 30 charismatic
behaviors, yielded significant ($p < 0.15$) differences in comparing leaders
exhibiting different styles. These behaviors are presented in Table 5.

The ideological behaviors yielding significant differences all focused on
leadership expressed through a fixed set of beliefs and values with ideological
and mixed style leaders displaying these behaviors more frequently than

Table 5. Leader Style Differences with Respect to Ideological and Charismatic Behaviors.

	Ideological		Charismatic		Both		F	P
	$\bar{x}$	SD	$\bar{x}$	SD	$\bar{x}$	SD		
Ideological Behaviors								
(1) Leader has limited set of extreme, consistent strongly held beliefs	0.22	0.02	0.08	0.03	0.17	0.03	4.59	0.014
(2) Leader is inflexible about beliefs/value	0.08	0.01	0.03	0.02	0.12	0.02	5.98	0.004
(3) Leaders' beliefs and values determine goals defined for the organization	0.11	0.01	0.04	0.02	0.11	0.02	4.17	0.020
(5) Leadership occurs through articulation of beliefs and values	0.06	0.01	0.02	0.02	0.11	0.02	7.47	0.001
(10) Leader will not be persuaded to go against his or her beliefs and values	0.03	0.01	0.02	0.01	0.06	0.01	5.12	0.009
(15) The leader will not be persuaded to go against his or her beliefs and values	0.03	0.01	0.02	0.01	0.05	0.01	4.90	0.010
(19) The leader takes no personal interest in followers	0.03	0.01	0.01	0.01	0.02	0.01	3.31	0.043
(23) The leader is motivated by having everyone share his or her beliefs and values	0.03	0.01	0.01	0.01	0.05	0.01	4.90	0.010
(25) The leader will appeal to those people who have the same beliefs and values	0.02	0.01	0.00	0.01	0.01	0.01	3.00	0.098

Table 5. Continued.

	Ideological		Charismatic		Both		F	P
	$\bar{x}$	SD	$\bar{x}$	SD	$\bar{x}$	SD		
Charismatic Behaviors								
(3) The leader communicates messages that reverence overall vision	0.11	0.02	0.09	0.03	0.16	0.02	2.71	0.074
(7) The leader arouses follower motives through vision	0.09	0.01	0.06	0.01	0.04	0.01	8.15	0.001
(9) Followers are personally attracted to leader	0.04	0.01	0.09	0.01	0.08	0.02	3.53	0.041
(10) People will have an extreme reaction to leader	0.03	0.01	0.08	0.01	0.04	0.01	6.42	0.003
(12) Catalyst exists that makes followers open to leader and his or her vision	0.03	0.01	0.08	0.01	0.06	0.01	9.71	0.001
(15) Followers are directly influenced by the leader and their personal relationship	0.03	0.01	0.05	0.01	0.06	0.01	3.16	0.049
(16) The leader cares about his or her image and plays to the desires of followers	0.05	0.01	0.10	0.02	0.05	0.01	5.51	0.006
(17) The leader will take an interest in all current and potential followers	0.03	0.01	0.03	0.01	0.06	0.01	5.59	0.006
(21) The leader will take into account the needs of the organization in his or her decision-making	0.02	0.01	0.08	0.01	0.04	0.01	7.48	0.001
(27) Followers are devoted to, and unquestioning of, the leader	0.02	0.01	0.06	0.01	0.02	0.01	2.89	0.063
(28) The leader will motivate followers to act on the ideas already in place in society	0.001	0.01	0.01	0.01	0.02	0.01	6.41	0.003
(30) The leaders will react with followers – social distance low	0.02	0.01	0.03	0.01	0.04	0.01	2.53	0.088

charismatic leaders. Thus, it was found the ideological and mixed style leaders, as opposed to charismatics, were inflexible in their beliefs and values, used these beliefs and values to determine goals for the organization, expressed extreme beliefs and values, and were willing to sacrifice themselves for their beliefs and values.

In keeping with the proposition that both ideological and charismatic leaders rely on vision, it was found, in examining the charismatic behaviors, that ideological leaders expressed a strong consistent vision. In fact, marginally significant differences ($p < 0.10$) were found in favor of ideological as opposed to charismatic leaders, with respect to the use of vision referenced communication and motivation of followers through a clear vision. One explanation of this pattern of findings, of course, is that articulation of a persuasive vision is a more powerful influence tool when common extant beliefs and values are appealed to rather than an idealized future. The remaining 10 behaviors yielding significant ($p < 0.05$) differences favored charismatic, and mixed style, leaders over ideological leaders.

Broadly speaking, these differences indicated that charismatic and mixed style leaders evidenced a closer, more affect-laden relationship with followers such that followers evidenced more extreme reactions, the leader took an interest in followers, the leader changed vision to satisfy needs of followers or organizations, and the leader maintained a low social distance. This pattern of findings suggests that ideological leaders are more concerned with abstract ideas, whereas charismatic and mixed style leaders are more concerned with people and their needs.

One question that might be broached with regard to these observations is whether changes in the expression of the ideological and charismatic behaviors occurred across leaders' careers. As may be seen, career point, as reflected in the "rise-to-power" and "in-power" chapters, did produce significant effects for the charismatic behaviors ($p < 0.05$) and marginally significant effects for the ideological behaviors ($p < 0.15$). Table 6 presents the five charismatic and three ideological behaviors showing significant ($p < 0.15$) differences in this regard. These behaviors indicate that the presence of catalysts was more important earlier in leaders careers along with a willingness of followers to sacrifice for the leader and his beliefs or vision. More extreme reactions and emotional attachment became evident as leaders moved into positions of greater power later in their careers.

In appraising these developmental changes, however, the significant ($p < 0.05$) interaction between career point and leader style with respect to the charismatic behaviors should be noted. As may be seen in Table 7, the presence of catalysts, in accordance with the observations of Conger and Kanungo

Table 6. Career Point, Rise to Power vs. in Power, with Respect to Ideological and Charismatic Behaviors.

	Rise to Power		In Power		F	P
	$\bar{x}$	SD	$\bar{x}$	SD		
Ideological Behaviors						
(8) Followers attracted to and influenced by leader's ideas but not necessarily the leader	0.06	0.01	0.03	0.01	5.53	0.022
(11) Some catalyst must make followers open to the beliefs and values of the leader	0.09	0.01	0.03	0.01	12.81	0.001
(24) The leader will expect followers to sacrifice themselves for his or her beliefs and values	0.03	0.01	0.01	0.01	2.11	0.151
Charismatic Behaviors						
(10) People will have an extreme reaction to the leader	0.04	0.01	0.06	0.01	2.99	0.089
(11) Followers will sacrifice themselves for the leader and/or the leader's vision	0.01	0.005	0.007	0.005	2.80	0.099
(12) Some catalyst makes followers open to the leader and his or her vision	0.10	0.01	0.02	0.01	5.13	0.001
(25) The leader may change his or her vision to meet the needs of followers or the organization	0.10	0.005	0.02	0.005	5.12	0.027
(27) Followers are devoted to, and unquestioning of, the leader	0.02	0.01	0.05	0.01	3.99	0.050

Table 7. Leader Style and Career Point Interactions for Charismatic Behaviors.

	Rise to Power						In Power							
	Ideological		Charismatic		Both		Ideological		Charismatic		Both		F	P
	$\bar{x}$	SD	$\bar{x}$	SD	$\bar{x}$	SD	$\bar{x}$	SD	$\bar{x}$	SD	$\bar{x}$	SD		
Charismatic Behaviors														
(12) A catalyst must exist to make followers open to the leader and his or her vision	0.05	0.01	0.14	0.02	0.10	0.01	0.01	0.01	0.03	0.02	0.02	0.01	4.62	0.007
(16) The leader will take an interest in all current and potential followers	0.03	0.01	0.03	0.01	0.04	0.01	0.02	0.01	0.02	0.01	0.07	0.01	2.32	0.091
(20) The leader will negotiate when it benefits his or her vision	0.02	0.005	0.02	0.01	0.008	0.007	0.02	0.005	0.01	0.01	0.04	0.007	2.63	0.072
(25) The leader may change his or her vision to meet the needs of followers or the organization	0.01	0.004	0.02	0.01	0.004	0.006	0.01	0.004	0.02	0.007	0.03	0.006	3.47	0.033
(27) Followers are devoted to, or unquestioning of, the leader	0.02	0.01	0.02	0.02	0.03	0.02	0.03	0.01	0.10	0.02	0.02	0.01	3.52	0.028

(1987), and Hunt, Boal and Dodge (1999), was more important for charismatic and mixed style leaders than for ideological leaders during "rise-to-power" periods, whereas follower devotion was particularly important for charismatic leaders during the "in-power" period. In contrast, mixed style leaders evidenced greater flexibility during the "in-power" period than charismatic and ideological leaders as indicated by negotiation, change of vision, and interest in followers. Thus, adaptation of a mixed style may reflect greater flexibility on the part of the leader or, alternatively, allow the leader greater flexibility once they have attained power.

Of course, these findings suggest that ideological, charismatic, and mixed style leaders may move into, and maintain, power using somewhat different tactics. The impact of these styles on leader behavior, however, also appeared to vary as a function of the leaders' personal orientation – socialized or personalized. The leader orientation variable yielded significant ($p < 0.05$) main effects with respect to both the charismatic and ideological behaviors. The five ideological and 13 charismatic behaviors yielding significant ($p < 0.15$) differences in this regard are presented in Table 8. With respect to the ideological behaviors, personalized leaders seem more authoritarian allowing limited autonomy and punishing those who do not adhere to the beliefs and values articulated by the leader. Socialized leaders, however, were more clear about their beliefs and values, showing a willingness to sacrifice for their attainment. These findings are, of course, consistent with the earlier observations of House and Howell (1992) and O'Connor, Mumford, Clifton, Gessner and Connelly (1995).

In keeping with these observations, along with the comments of Bass and Steidlmeier (1999) concerning the role of prosocial behavior on outstanding leadership, socialized, as opposed to personalized, leaders were more likely to articulate a vision pointing to a better future and delegate authority for attaining this vision. Along similar lines, the charismatic behaviors indicated that socialized leaders evidenced less distance and more interest in followers, whereas personalized leaders were more narcissistic and concerned with their image – changing this image to maximize its impact on followers and capitalize on catalysts. Thus, personalized leaders appear more manipulative than socialized leaders – a pattern of findings that may account for their emphasis on follower accomplishments.

However, the impact of a personalized or socialized orientation on ideological and charismatic behaviors appears to vary as a function of leader style. In both these analyses, a significant ($p < 0.05$) interaction was obtained. The nine ideological and seven charismatic behaviors producing significant ($p < 0.15$) differences in this analysis are presented in Table 9. The most clear-

Table 8. Leader Orientation, Socialized vs. Personalized, with Respect to Ideological and Charismatic Behaviors.

	Socialized		Personalized			
	$\bar{x}$	SD	$\bar{x}$	SD	F	P
Ideological Behaviors						
(5) Leadership occurs through articulation of beliefs and values	0.09	0.01	0.04	0.01	6.19	0.015
(6) Everything occurs in a clearly differentiated evaluative space	0.06	0.01	0.03	0.01	4.11	0.047
(10) Leader will be willing to sacrifice himself or herself for his ideas	0.04	0.01	0.02	0.01	2.95	0.091
(12) Leader tells people what to do – little room for autonomy	0.03	0.01	0.05	0.01	3.06	0.085
(26) Leader will punish those who do not adhere to ideas and values	0.02	0.01	0.04	0.01	3.13	0.090
Charismatic Behaviors						
(1) The leader will act according to a vision that specifies a better future state	0.13	0.01	0.07	0.02	5.63	0.020
(6) The leader will communicate confidence in followers' ability to meet expectation	0.02	0.001	0.06	0.001	6.26	0.015
(8) Leadership occurs through articulation of a vision and accomplishments that pertain to vision	0.04	0.01	0.05	0.01	2.10	0.152
(10) People will have an extreme reaction to the leader	0.03	0.01	0.07	0.01	10.15	0.002
(12) Catalyst exists that makes followers open to the leader and his or her vision	0.05	0.01	0.07	0.01	2.66	0.108
(16) The leader cares about his or her image and plays to the desires of followers	0.04	0.01	0.09	0.01	9.97	0.002
(17) The leader will take an interest in all current and potential followers	0.05	0.01	0.02	0.01	4.36	0.041
(21) The leader will take into account the needs of the organization in his or her decision-making	0.03	0.01	0.06	0.01	3.08	0.084

Table 8. Continued.

	Socialized		Personalized			
	$\bar{x}$	SD	$\bar{x}$	SD	F	P
Charismatic Behaviors – Continued						
(24) The leader will delegate authority for attainment of his or her vision	0.19	0.01	0.05	0.01	4.98	0.029
(27) Followers are devoted to, and unquestioning of, the leader	0.02	0.01	0.05	0.01	5.00	0.029
(28) The leader will motivate followers to act upon ideas already in place in society	0.02	0.005	0.01	0.005	3.92	0.052
(29) The leader will be narcissistic and attempt to bring power and attention to himself or herself	0.02	0.01	0.05	0.01	5.10	0.027
(30) The leader will interact with followers – when social distance is low	0.04	0.01	0.02	0.01	6.07	0.017

Table 9. Leader Style and Leader Orientation Interactions for Ideological and Charismatic Behaviors.

| | Socialized | | | | | | Personalized | | | | | | | |
| | Ideological | | Charismatic | | Both | | Ideological | | Charismatic | | Both | | | |
	$\bar{x}$	SD	$\bar{x}$	SD	$\bar{x}$	SD	$\bar{x}$	SD	$\bar{x}$	SD	$\bar{x}$	SD	F	P
Ideological Behaviors														
(3) The leaders beliefs and values determine the goals of the organization	0.08	0.02	0.05	0.02	0.15	0.02	0.12	0.02	0.03	0.04	0.08	0.03	4.23	0.023
(5) Leadership occurs through articulation of beliefs and values	0.06	0.02	0.03	0.02	0.16	0.02	0.05	0.02	0.01	0.01	0.06	0.02	3.06	0.040
(11) Catalyst exits that makes people open to the beliefs and values of the leader	0.05	0.02	0.04	0.02	0.07	0.02	0.67	0.01	0.08	0.03	0.02	0.02	3.08	0.041
(12) The leader tells people what to do – little room for autonomy	0.03	0.01	0.02	0.01	0.05	0.01	0.05	0.01	0.05	0.02	0.03	0.01	3.43	0.048
(15) The leader will not be persuaded to go against his or her beliefs and values	0.02	0.01	0.02	0.01	0.07	0.01	0.03	0.01	0.02	0.02	0.03	0.01	1.95	0.441
(20) The leader will manipulate followers to achieve his or her goals	0.03	0.01	0.03	0.01	0.04	0.02	0.10	0.02	0.02	0.03	0.06	0.02	2.30	0.091
(26) The leader will punish those who do not adhere to his or her beliefs and values	0.02	0.01	0.09	0.01	0.02	0.01	0.07	0.01	0.03	0.02	0.01	0.01	2.76	0.061
(27) The leader will not tolerate people who do not agree with his or her beliefs and values	0.005	0.01	0.008	0.01	0.03	0.02	0.05	0.01	0.002	0.02	0.02	0.01	3.06	0.040
(29) The leader will expect followers to sacrifice themselves for his or her beliefs and values	0.02	0.01	0.007	0.01	0.01	0.01	0.02	0.01	0.02	0.01	0.05	0.01	2.46	0.086

Table 9. Continued.

	Socialized						Personalized							
	Ideological		Charismatic		Both		Ideological		Charismatic		Both		F	P
	$\bar{x}$	SD	$\bar{x}$	SD	$\bar{x}$	SD	$\bar{x}$	SD	$\bar{x}$	SD	$\bar{x}$	SD		
Charismatic Behaviors														
(3) The leader communicates messages that reference overall vision	0.14	0.02	0.11	0.02	0.13	0.03	0.07	0.02	0.06	0.01	0.02	0.002	2.41	0.080
(7) The leader activates follower motives through vision	0.01	0.01	0.03	0.01	0.06	0.02	0.07	0.01	0.10	0.02	0.03	0.001	5.88	0.004
(10) People will have an extreme reaction to the leader	0.04	0.01	0.02	0.01	0.04	0.01	0.02	0.01	0.14	0.02	0.04	0.01	11.52	0.001
(12) Catalyst exists that makes followers open to the leader and his or her vision	0.03	0.01	0.04	0.01	0.08	0.02	0.02	0.01	0.13	0.02	0.05	0.01	8.27	0.001
(21) The leader will take into account the needs of the organization in his or her decision-making	0.02	0.01	0.04	0.01	0.05	0.01	0.03	0.01	0.12	0.02	0.02	0.01	6.06	0.003
(27) Followers are devoted to, and unquestioning of, the leader	0.03	0.01	0.02	0.01	0.02	0.02	0.02	0.01	0.11	0.02	0.04	0.001	5.53	0.007
(28) The leader will motivate followers to act on ideas already in place in society	0.01	0.005	0.01	0.005	0.03	0.005	0.005	0.004	0.01	0.01	0.01	0.006	2.31	0.098

cut trend to emerge in this interaction was evident in contrasting personalized charismatics with all other groups. Personalized charismatics were more likely to induce extreme reactions and devotion, activate motives through a vision, and capitalize on available catalysts. Mixed style socialized leaders tended to communicate through vision and rely on existing ideals in generating a vision. What is of note here, however, is that personalized charismatics, as opposed to personalized ideologues, were more likely to rely on intense affective reactions – a finding consistent with the more abstract value based nature of ideological leadership.

Personalized ideologues, however, seemed more likely to express destructive tendencies through beliefs and values. Thus, personalized ideologues were more likely to manipulate followers to attain their goals, display intolerance of norm violations, and punish those who violated their beliefs and values. In contrast, socialized charismatics expected less sacrifice from followers, whereas socialized ideologues and socialized charismatics relied less on catalysts to attain and maintain power. Finally, mixed style leaders relied more on their beliefs and values to influence people, particularly when they could not appeal to positive, prosocial values. Given the greater flexibility of mixed style leaders, it seems likely that charisma is used to amplify or reinforce value-laden messages just as the prosocial messages are used to build support for the better future envisioned by the leader.

CONCLUSIONS

Empirical Findings

Before turning to the broader conclusions flowing from the present study, certain limitations of the approach applied herein should be noted. To begin, the present study has focused on historically notable twentieth century leaders. Thus, some caution is called for in generalizing our findings to leaders identified in earlier historic periods (Simonton, 1991). In this regard, however, it should be noted that given the limited differences observed in comparing pre- and post-World War II leaders, some generalization over historic periods may be justified. Moreover, although we drew leaders from different occupational domains and cultures, the sample was weighted more heavily towards western political leaders than any other single group – due primarily to the availability of adequate academic biographies. Accordingly, replication in a larger, more comprehensive sample seems indicated.

In addition to these limitations, an inherent limitation of the coding procedures being applied in the present study should be considered. Clearly, neither the list of ideological behaviors nor the list of charismatic behaviors examined herein was exhaustive. Instead, an attempt was made to develop a manageable checklist of ideological and charismatic behaviors capturing key socialized and personalized behaviors identified in prior studies examining these two styles of outstanding leadership (e.g. Gerring, 1997; House & Podsakoff, 1994). Although this approach helped ensure a reliable coding of biographical material obtained for the leaders, it also ensures that not all dimensions of ideological and charismatic leadership were examined in the present study.

Even bearing this caveat in mind, however, the results obtained in this effort do suggest that the coding scheme applied in the present study evidenced some construct validity as a framework for examining the nature of outstanding leadership (Messick, 1999; Mumford & Threlfall, 1992). More specifically, prior theoretical work by House and Howell (1992), and O'Connor, Mumford, Clifton, Gessner and Connelly (1995), would lead one to expect differences in the behaviors evidenced by personalized and socialized leaders. In accordance with the conclusions emerging from these studies, we found that personalized leaders exhibited narcissistic manipulative behaviors, whereas socialized leaders exhibited more willingness to sacrifice for others or their beliefs and values. Along similar lines, in comparing career periods, "rise-to-power" vs. "in-power", we found that emerging outstanding leaders capitalized on social catalysts, or crises, building a band of committed followers.

Although these findings are noteworthy from a methodological and substantive perspective, our primary concern in the study at hand was accruing evidence for the notion that there might be at least two alternative styles of outstanding leadership. Overall, the results obtained in the present effort appear to provide some compelling support for this proposition. Visioning appeared to play a noteworthy role in outstanding leadership for all leader types with ideological, and mixed style leaders evidencing more articulate expression of a vision than even the charismatic leaders. Otherwise, these leaders displayed the expected differences based on the model of vision formation presented earlier. Thus, ideological and mixed style leaders were more likely to evidence ideological behaviors than charismatic leaders, whereas charismatic and mixed style leaders were more likely to evidence charismatic behaviors than ideological leaders.

More centrally, the nature of the observed differences between ideological and charismatic leaders seemed consistent with the model of vision formation underlying this study. Earlier, we noted that ideological leaders create their vision based on personal values, the need to maintain standards, and the personal meaning accorded to adherence to these standards. In keeping with these propositions, we found that the ideological behaviors that distinguished ideological, and mixed style leaders from charismatic leaders involved articulation of, and adherence to, a limited set of beliefs and values that were used to define organizational goals.

In contrast, charismatic leaders were hypothesized to create their vision based on perceived social needs, identifying things that needed to be changed, and deriving meaning from interpersonal reactions to these changes. In accordance with these hypotheses, charismatic and mixed style leaders were more likely than ideological leaders to take into account the needs of the organization in generating a vision, adjust their vision to the needs of followers, and maintain a close relationship with followers whose interpersonal reactions provided a basis for establishing the meaningfulness of their vision.

The finding that there may be two distinct styles of outstanding, vision-based leadership is noteworthy for three reasons. First, studies of outstanding leadership have tended to emphasize charismatic and transformational leadership (Bass, 1997; Mumford & Van Doorn, 2001). Although the available evidence indicates the impact of these styles on leader performance (Lowe, Koreck & Sivasubramaniam, 1996), it is possible that, at least under certain conditions, ideological leadership may be an equally powerful influence on people's behavior and their performance. Put more directly, we need to know how articulation of values and standards shapes leader performance and in what settings this kind of vision proves an especially powerful influence over people's behavior.

Second, the results obtained in the present effort indicate that a more careful consideration of these stylistic differences may prove critical in articulating the theoretical implications of vision-based outstanding leadership. The need for research along these lines was nicely illustrated in the interactions observed between the leader style and the personal orientation variable. For example, personalized ideological leaders did not exhibit the narcissism characteristic of charismatic leaders (House & Howell, 1992; O'Connor, Mumford, Clifton, Gessner & Connelly, 1995). Instead, they seemed to evidence a highly punitive orientation toward transgression of vision relevant beliefs and values. Along similar lines, socialized charismatics seemed to rely on any interpersonally evocative motivational style, whereas ideological leaders emphasized abstractions.

Third, the results obtained in the present study, aside from stressing the need to consider the moderating influence of visionary style, suggest that there may be a third style that merits some attention. The mixed style examined in the present study did not simply represent a gray, in-between, case. Instead, mixed style leaders appeared capable of flexibly applying elements of both the charismatic and ideological approaches. Thus, in the mixed style, beliefs and values were emphasized along with the need for change and interpersonal meaning. It is possible, given the observations of Bass and Steidlmeier (1999), that this integration of values and change requirements may represent a unique and particularly powerful form of visionary-based outstanding leadership.

Model Implications

Of course, the finding that ideological and charismatic leaders display the behavioral differences provides some further support for the model of vision formation presented earlier. When this evidence is considered along with the available data indicating the importance of reflection (e.g. Mumford, Marks, Connelly, Zaccaro & Reiter-Palmon, 2000) and the data indicating that leadership requires abstracting key causes operating within a complex social system (e.g. Thomas, Clark & Gioia, 1993), there does seem to be some reason to believe that the conceptual model presented earlier may provide at least a plausible description of the vision creation process. The development of an initial conceptual model capable of describing vision creation process is noteworthy because, although theories of outstanding leadership stress the role of vision, they have not told us where this vision comes from (Hunt, Boal & Dodge, 1999). Hopefully, the present study has provided at least an initial model capable of answering this question.

Answers to this question are significant for both practical and theoretical reasons. Research on outstanding leadership is of interest, in part because it provides guidelines for the development of more effective leaders (Barling, Weber & Kelloway, 1996). Unless, however, we know the mechanisms people use to generate viable visions, it becomes difficult to develop sound recommendations in this regard. The model developed and tested in the present effort, however, does provide some concrete recommendations in this regard.

For example, the model under consideration indicates that, if we want outstanding leadership, we must encourage reflection. This reflection, however, is not simply an analysis of one's strengths and weaknesses. Instead, it is a reflection on system issues: what causes system success and failure? What goals should be pursued by the system? What actions can be taken to change things? How do I relate these goals and actions to what I personally believe? How do I organize these considerations to construct a prescriptive model that will provide a basis for a vision? How do I use others' reactions to adjust this prescriptive model in developing a viable vision?

It seems likely that training programs can be formulated that will help leaders answer these questions and that such programs will prove useful in developing outstanding leadership. In this regard, however, it is important to bear in mind that a broader point might be made by this effort. The success of such efforts depends ultimately on the viability, complexity, and richness of the mental models the leader has abstracted from past interactions within a social system. Thus, developmental efforts along the lines outlined above are built upon experience and expertise (Mumford, Marks, Connelly, Zaccaro & Reiter-Palmon, 2000). Moreover, one might plausibly argue that by providing the breadth and depth of experience needed to construct viable mental models, through training or job assignments, we may do much to make outstanding leadership possible.

Work along these lines, however, is most likely to prove fruitful if it expressly seeks to understand how leaders create initial, descriptive, mental models and the prescriptive mental models that proved the basis for formulating a viable vision. For example, is it better for leaders to identify a cause clearly linked to a limited number of goals or whether they should work with causes influencing the attainment of multiple goals? Is it better to apply externally validated goals and causes, or internal experientially based goals and causes, in the formation of prescriptive models? What kind of feedback should leaders seek in shaping prescriptive models into a true vision for a social system?

Answers to these questions are critical if we are truly to understand the implications of visionary-based leadership. Over the last 20 years, the work of Bass (1985) and his colleagues (e.g. Bass, 1985; Bass & Avolio, 1996; House & Shamir, 1993; House, Spangler & Woycke, 1993; Howell & Avolio, 1993) has clearly demonstrated the importance of vision for outstanding leadership. To fully appreciate the significance of this work, however, we must now begin to ask a new series of questions – one of which is where did visions, such as the unique vision of George Washington, come from? Our ability to ask these questions, however, ultimately derives from the contribution of Bass (1985) and House (1995), who, in their theories of charismatic and transformational leadership, have called our attention to the fundamental importance of vision in providing a foundation for outstanding leadership.

ACKNOWLEDGMENTS

We would like to thank Shane Connelly, Gina Marie Scott, Blaine Gaddis, Judy Van Doorn, and Whitney Helton for their contributions to the present effort. Parts of this work were sponsored by a series of grants from the United States Department of Defense, Michael D. Mumford and Mary Shane Connelly, Principal Investigators.

REFERENCES

Albert, M. A. (1998). Shaping a learning organization through the linkage of action research interventions. *Organization Development Journal, 16,* 29–39.

Barling, J., Weber, T., & Kelloway, E. K. (1996). Effects of transformational leadership training on attitudinal and financial outcomes: A field experiment. *Journal of Applied Psychology, 81,* 827–832.

Bass, B. M. (1985). *Leadership and performance beyond expectation.* New York: Harper.

Bass, B. M. (1996). *Multifactor Leadership Questioner manual.* Palo Alto, CA: Mindgarden.

Bass, B. M. (1997). Does the transactional-transformational leadership paradigm transcend organizational and national boundaries? *American Psychologist, 52,* 130–139.

Bass, B M., & Steidlmeier, P. (1999). Ethics, character, and authentic transformational leadership. *Leadership Quarterly, 10,* 181–218.

Beyer, B. M. (1999). Taming and promoting charisma to change organizations. *Leadership Quarterly, 10,* 307–330.

Boal, K. B., & Bryson, J. M. (1988). Charismatic leadership: A phenomenological and structural approach. In: J. G. Hunt, B. R. Baligia, H. P. Dachler & C. A. Schriesheim (Eds), *Emerging leadership vistas* (pp. 11–28). Lexington, MA: Lexington Books.

Burns, J. M. (1978). *Leadership.* New York: Harper and Row.

Cannon-Bowers, J. A., & Salas, E. (1990). Cognitive psychology and team training: Shared mental models in complex systems. Paper presented at the 5th Annual Meeting of The Society for Industrial and Organizational Psychology, Miami, FL.

Conger, J. A., & Kanungo, R. S. (1987). Toward a behavioral theory of charismatic leadership in organizations. *Academy of Management Review, 12,* 637–647.

Conger, J. A., & Kanungo, R. S. (1994). Charismatic leadership in organizations: Perceived behavioral attributes and their measurement. *Journal of Organizational Behavior, 15,* 439–452.

Conger, J. A., & Kanungo, R. S. (1998). *Charismatic leadership in organizations.* Thousand Oaks, CA: Sage.

Connelly, M. S., Gilbert, J. A., Zaccaro, S. J., Threlfall, K. V., Marks, M. A., & Mumford, M. D. (2000). Exploring the relationship of leader skills and knowledge to leader performance. *Leadership Quarterly, 11,* 65–86.

Daniels, K., Chernatony, L., & Johnson, L. (1995). Validating a method for mapping managers' mental models of competitive industry structures. *Human Relations, 48,* 975–991.

Eisenhardt, K. M. (1989). Making fast strategic decisions in high-velocity environments. *Academy of Management Journal, 32,* 543–576.

Ellis, J. J. (2001). *Founding brother: The revolutionary generation.* New York: Alfred Knopf.

Entin, E. E., & Serfaty, D. (2000). Adaptive team coordination. *Human Factors, 41,* 312–325.

Gerring, J. (1997). Ideology: A definitional analysis. *Political Research Quarterly, 50,* 957–994.

Holyoak, K. J., & Thagard, P. (1997). The analogical mind. *American Psychologist, 52,* 35–44.

House, R. J. (1971). A path goal theory of leader effectiveness. *Administrative Science Quarterly, 16,* 321–338.

House, R. J. (1995). Leadership in the 21st Century: A speculative inquiry. In: A. Howard (Ed.), *The changing nature of work* (pp. 411–450). San Francisco, CA: Josey-Bass.

House, R. J., & Howell, J. M. (1992). Personality and charismatic leadership. *Leadership Quarterly, 3,* 81–108.

House, R. J., & Podsakoff, P. M. (1994). Leadership and effectiveness: Past perspectives and future directions for research. In: J. Greenberg (Ed.), *Organizational behavior: The state of science* (pp. 45–82). Hillsdale, NJ: Erlbaum.

House, R. J., & Shamir, B. (1993). Toward the integration of charismatic, visionary, and transformational leadership theories. In: M. Chemmens & R. Ryman (Eds), *Leadership theory and research: Perspectives and directions* (pp. 81–107). San Diego, CA: Academic Press.

House, R. J., & Spangler, W. D., & Woycke, J. (1993). Personality and charisma in the U.S. Presidency: A psychological theory of leader effectiveness. *Administrative Sciences Quarterly, 36*, 374–396.

Howell, J. M., & Avolio, B. J. (1993). Transformational leadership, transactional leadership, loss of control, and support for innovation. *Journal of Applied Psychology, 78*, 891–902.

Huer, J. H. (1978). *Ideology and social character*. Washington, D.C.: University Press of America.

Hunt, J. G., Boal, K. B., & Dodge, G. E. (1999). The effects of visionary and crisis-responsive charisma on followers: An experimental examination of two kinds of charismatic leadership. *Leadership Quarterly, 10*, 423–448.

Isenberg, D. J. (1986). Thinking and managing: A verbal protocol analysis of managerial problem-solving. *Academy of Management Journal, 29*, 775–788.

Jacobs, T. O., & Jaques, E. (1987). Leadership in complex systems. In: J. Zeidner (Ed.), *Human productivity enhancement: Organizations, personnel, and decision making* (Vol. 2, pp. 201–245). New York: Praeger.

Jacobs, T. O. & Jaques, E. (1990). Military executive leadership. In: K. E. Clark & M. B. Clark (Eds), *Measure of leadership* (pp. 281–295). West Orange, NJ: Leadership Library of America.

Jacobs, T. O., & Jaques, E. (1991). Executive Leadership. In: R. Gael & A. O. Mangelsdorff (Eds), *Handbook of military psychology* (pp. 12–462). Chichester, UK: Wiley.

Johnson-Laird, P. (1983). *Mental models*. Cambridge, MA: Harvard University Press.

Kirkpatrick, S., & Locke, E. A. (1996). Direct and indirect effects of three core charismatic leadership components on performance and attitudes. *Journal of Applied Psychology, 81*, 36–51.

Largan-Fox, J., & Code, S. (2000). Team mental models: Technique, methods, and analytical approaches. *Human Factors, 42*, 242–271.

Lowe, K. B., Koreck, K. G., & Sivasubramaniam, N. (1996). Effectiveness correlates of transformational and transactional leadership: A meta-analytic review of the MLQ literature. *Leadership Quarterly, 7*, 385–425.

Messick, S. (1998). Alternative modes of assessment, uniform standards of validity. In: M. D. Hakel (Ed.), *Beyond multiple choice: Evaluating alternatives to standardized tests* (pp. 59–76). Hillsdale, NJ: Erlbaum.

Mills, C. W. (1967). *The Marxists*. New York: Dell.

Mumford, M. D., Feldman, J. M., Hein, M. B., & Nago, D. J. (2001). Tradeoffs between ideas and structure: Individual vs. group performance in creative problem solving. *Journal of Creative Behavior, 35*, 1–24.

Mumford, M. D., Marks, M. A., Connelly, M. S., Zaccaro, S. J., & Reiter-Palmon, R. (2000). Development of leadership skills: Experience and timing. *Leadership Quarterly, 11*, 87–114.

Mumford, M. D., & Threlfall, K. V. (1992). Quantifying genius. *Contemporary Psychology, 37*, 216–218.

Mumford, M. D., & Van Doorn, J. (2001). The leadership of pragmatism: Reconsidering Franklin in the Age of Charisma. *Leadership Quarterly, 12*, 313–346.

O'Connor, J. A., Mumford, M. D., Clifton, T. C., Gessner, T. E., & Connelly, M. S. (1995). Charismatic leaders and destructiveness: A historiometric study. *Leadership Quarterly, 6*, 529–555.

Orasanu, J. M. (1990). *Shared mental models and crew decision making*. Princeton, NJ: Princeton University.

Rejai, M. (1991). *Political ideologies: A comparative approach*. Armonk, NY: M. E. Sharpe.

Rouse, R. B., Cannon-Bowers, J. A., & Salas, E. (1992). The role of mental models in team performance in complex systems. *IEEE Transactions on Systems, Man, and Cybernetics, 22*, 1290–1308.

Sein, M. K., & Bostrom, R. P. (1989). Individual differences and conceptual models in training novice users. *Human-Computer Interaction, 4*, 197–229.

Shamir, B., House, R. J., & Arthur, M. B. (1993). The motivational effects of charismatic leadership: A self-concept based theory. *Organizational Science, 4*, 577–594.

Simonton, D. K. (1991). *Psychology, science, and history: An introduction to historiometry*. New Haven, CN: Yale University Press.

Sosik, J. J., Avolio, B. J., & Kahai, S. S. (1997). Effects of leadership style and anonymity on group potency and effectiveness in a group decision support system environment. *Journal of Applied Psychology, 82*, 89–103.

Stout, R. J., Cannon-Bowers, J. A., Salas, E., & Milanovich, D. M. (1999). Planning, shared mental models, and coordinated performance: An empirical link is established. *Human Factors, 41*, 61–71.

Thomas, J. B., Clark, S. M., & Goia, D. A. (1993). Strategic sensemaking and organizational performance: Linkages among scanning, interpretation, action, and outcomes. *Academy of Management Journal, 36*, 239–270.

Thomas, J. B., & McDaniel, R. R. (1990). Interpreting strategic issues: Effects of strategy and the information processing structure of top management teams. *Academy of Management Journal, 32*, 286–306.

Volpe, C. E., Cannon-Bowers, J. A., Salas, E., & Spector, P. (1996). The impact of cross-training on team functioning. *Human Factors, 38*, 87–100.

Weber, M. (1947). In: A. M. Henderson & T. Parsons (Ed.), *Max Weber: The theory of social and economic organization*. New York: Oxford University Press.

Williams, A. P. O. (2001). A belief-focused process model of organizational learning. *Journal of Management Studies, 38*, 67–85.

Yorges, S. C., Weiss, H. M., & Stickland, O. J. (1999). The effect of leader outcomes on influence, attributions, and perceptions of charisma. *Journal of Applied Psychology, 84*, 428–436.

Yukl, G. (1999). An evaluation of conceptual weaknesses in transformational and charismatic theories. *Leadership Quarterly, 10*, 285–305.

Yukl, G. J. (1998). *Leadership in organizations*. Englewood Cliffs, NJ: Prentice-Hall.

Zaccaro, S. J., Gualatieri, J., & Minionis, D. (1995). Task cohesion as a facilitator of team decision making under temporal urgency. *Military Psychology, 7*, 77–93.

Zaccaro, S. J., Mumford, M. D., Connelly, M. S., Marks, M. A., & Gilbert, J. A. (2000). Assessments of leader problem solving capabilities. *Leadership Quarterly, 11*, 37–64.

EXTENDING THE CONCEPT OF CHARISMATIC LEADERSHIP: AN ILLUSTRATION USING BASS'S (1990) CATEGORIES

Kyoungsu Kim, Fred Dansereau and Insook Kim

ABSTRACT

Using five categories summarized by Bass (1990), this chapter attempts to address three key questions about charismatic leadership:

(1) What are the key behavioral dimensions of charismatic leadership?
(2) How does charismatic leadership differ from other forms of leadership?
(3) Who may become followers of charismatic leaders and when do they become followers?

By focusing on Weber's original view of charisma, we suggest that his three dimensions of charismatic leader behaviors underlie most contemporary approaches. By considering these three dimensions in more detail, we demonstrate how this view allows for different views of leadership and is distinguishable from management. Finally, by extending Weber's view and by identifying two types of charismatic leaders who differ in their power motives, we suggest how the characteristics of followers and the

---

Transformational and Charismatic Leadership, Volume 2, pages 143–172.
ISBN: 0-7623-0962-8

context influence followers' acceptance of charismatic leaders as legitimate. Some implications for leadership effectiveness are discussed.

Bass (1990) has integrated leadership theories and research into five categories and five sections in his widely cited handbook of leadership. The categories are:

(1) leader traits and behaviors;
(2) leadership vs. management;
(3) leadership and followership;
(4) legitimacy and power; and
(5) context as a moderator.

In this paper, we focus on the topic of charismatic leadership by focusing on Bass' five categories. First, in line with the issues that arise regarding leadership behaviors, we attempt to identify some key behaviors that seem to define charismatic leadership using Weber' perspective. Second, we use the definition to distinguish charismatic leadership from other views of leadership as well as management. Third, we focus on how to understand charismatic leadership from the perspective of followership. Fourth, we consider the question of how followers come to view individuals as legitimate charismatic leaders, and then generate propositions about followership. Fifth, we focus on how the situation may moderate the degree and way charismatic leaders bring about followership.

Our purpose in this chapter is not to attempt to provide "the" final word about charismatic leadership. Rather, we are interested in investigating the consequences of working through systematically the various categories suggested by Bass's integration for only charismatic leadership. What we believe that we have discovered using this approach is that it enhanced and clarified our thinking about charismatic leadership. We hope that others will find the perspective on charismatic leadership presented in this chapter and the approach to developing the perspective based on Bass' five categories useful. By using these categories, we came to agree with Bass that the five categories will be very useful in future research.

Although various theorists (Conger & Kanungo, 1988, 1998; House, 1977; Howell, 1988; Klein & House, 1995; Meindl, 1990; Shamir, House & Arthur, 1993; Shamir & Howell, 1999; Weber, 1947, 1968) shed light on identifying leaders' qualities or behaviors and the influence process of charismatic leadership, they seem to disagree about the core behavioral dimensions comprising charismatic leadership (Yukl, 1999). They also seem to ignore the question of how charismatic leadership differs from other types of leadership and the question of what types of people become followers of charismatic leaders and when (Beyer 1999a, b; Conger, 1999; Yukl, 1999).

The romanticized approach to leadership (Meindl, 1990) is perhaps an exception to this claim. However, the romanticized approach focuses mainly on contextual factors such as crisis, collectivism, and arousal states (e.g. Pillai & Meindl, 1998). It does not pay much attention to the characteristics of leaders and followers (Meindl, 1995). Thus, it fails to answer the question of what are the key behavioral dimensions of charismatic leadership, how does charismatic leadership differ from other types of leadership, and who becomes followers of charismatic leaders. Bass and his colleagues (Avolio & Bass, 1998; Bass, 1985, 1996), who distinguished transformational/charismatic leadership from transactional leadership, suggest that four behavioral components make up the dimension of transformational leadership and that the effectiveness of these two types of leadership differ under different contexts. However, they leave open the question of what types of people become followers of charismatic leaders.

Although Weierter (1997) argues that charismatic relationships are determined by followers' characteristics, he does not consider the issue of how charismatic leadership differs from other views of leadership and when the charisma occurs. Therefore, previous approaches still leave open the question of how charismatic leadership differs from other types of leadership and under what conditions different types of people become followers of charismatic leaders. However, these issues seem critical to charismatic leadership, because charisma may depend on people's characteristics as well as the situation (Conger, 1999; Conger & Kanungo, 1998; Klein & House, 1995; Yukl, 1999).

In this paper, we suggest an approach to address the questions of:

(1) What are the key behavioral dimensions of charismatic leadership?
(2) How does charismatic leadership differ from other types of leadership?
(3) What types of people become followers of charismatic leaders and when?

This attempt is first implemented by focusing on charismatic leadership, and then by identifying key behavioral dimensions of charismatic leaders. Second, based on the key dimensions, we distinguish charismatic leadership from other types of leadership. Third, by considering two types of charismatic leaders and by identifying the characteristics of followers and the environment, we derive testable propositions for examining charismatic followership – i.e. who become followers of charismatic leaders and when. The chapter ends by discussing leadership effectiveness and by suggesting implications for future research.

CHARISMATIC LEADERSHIP

Three Dimensions of Charismatic Leadership

Although there may appear to be many dimensions of charismatic leadership reported in the literature, Weber's approach to charismatic leadership still seems to underlie contemporary approaches to the topic. We believe that it is important to try and identify a parsimonious definition of charismatic leadership and believe that Weber's original definition serves that purpose well. The following three key dimensions described by Weber capture much of the contemporary approaches to charismatic leadership: vision-related behaviors, personal behaviors, and empowering behaviors. We selected these three dimensions on the basis of Weber's (1968) definition of charisma and a literature review of behavioral theories of charismatic leadership.

Our approach is in line with Weber (1968), who suggested that the concept of charisma includes:

(1) vision or mission;
(2) extraordinary or exceptional qualities; and
(3) recognition.

These three concepts match our three behavioral dimensions. That is, first, vision or mission is one of the most critical elements in defining charisma. Bryman (1992) extends Weber's notion of vision, goal or mission as follows:

> Goal or mission should not be excluded from defining charisma, since a leader with extraordinary qualities but without a mission or vision is not regarded as a charismatic leader (p. 41).

Second, a leader with exceptional or extraordinary qualities displays behaviors such as demonstrating extremely high levels of self-confidence, taking personal risk, showing self-sacrifice and a strong conviction in the moral righteousness of his or her beliefs (Bass, 1988; House, 1977; House & Howell, 1992). Third, as Weber recognized, a leader cannot be said to be charismatic unless followers have validated his or her claim to charisma. To be charismatic, a leader must have the followers' support and their preparedness to submit to his or her will. As Conger (1989) noted, followers recognize their leader as a charismatic leader and devote themselves to their leader, when they feel empowered. Therefore, empowerment may be at the essence of followers' recognition of a charismatic leader.

Our review of theories about charismatic leadership suggests that contemporary approaches to leader behaviors may be classified into these three general dimensions. For example, among the five behaviors suggested by House

(1977), goal articulation belongs to the vision-related dimension, role modeling and image building belong to leader's personal behavior dimension, whereas exhibiting high expectations and showing confidence belong to the empowering behavioral dimension.

Among the five behaviors suggested by Conger and Kanungo (1998), first, environmental sensitivity and articulating a strategic vision belong to the vision-related dimension. Second, personal risk and unconventional behavior belong to leader's personal behavioral dimension. Third, confidence in followers belongs to the empowering behavioral dimension. Therefore, these three behavioral dimensions include most previous work. We will return to this classification again in the summary section, but first, we need to define each key dimension in relation to contemporary models of charismatic leadership.

Vision-related Behaviors
Theories of charismatic leadership include vision or mission as being the most critical variable in defining charismatic leadership. For example, Weber (1968) viewed vision or mission as the most essential factor in the concept of charisma. Berlew (1974) also stated "the first requirement for (. . .) charismatic leadership is a common or shared vision for what the future could be" (p. 269). Charismatic leadership is sometimes called visionary leadership (Sashkin, 1988). Similarly, charismatic leaders are often characterized by a sense of strategic vision (Bass, 1985; Conger & Kanungo, 1988; Dow, 1969; House, 1977; Willner, 1984). Conger and Kanungo (1988) also argue that vision is the most important factor to distinguish charismatic leaders from non-charismatic leaders. Most recently, Awamleh and Gardner (1999) found that a leader's speech characterized by visionary content elicited higher levels of charisma.

Vision has been defined as "a picture both of the future and of the present, appealing simultaneously to logic and to feeling" (Snyder, Dowd & Houghton, 1994, p. 74). Tichy and Devanna (1986) described vision in terms of future-oriented goals that are highly meaningful to followers. Similarly, Conger and Kanungo (1998) defined vision as "a set of idealized future goals established by the leader that represent a perspective shared by followers" (p. 156). A vision then includes the nature of the status quo and its strengths and weaknesses, a future goal to meet follower needs, and a plan of action for realizing the vision. Howell (1988) viewed a vision as a leader's ability to be sensitive to the environment and follower needs, to formulate and articulate a future goal and to make a plan for achieving the goal.

Thus, we define vision-related behaviors in terms of behaviors that are related to formulating and articulating a future goal. To formulate a future goal, a leader has to attend to environmental constraints and resources (Conger &

Kanungo, 1988, 1998). If a leader fails to assess the status quo, he or she has no idea about the future of an organization, community or society. For a vision to be shared by followers, the vision has to reflect follower needs and to be articulated in a way that followers will embrace (Conger & Kanungo, 1988, 1998; House, 1977; Tichy & Devanna, 1986). If a vision does not include follower needs, followers will not accept the vision. Similarly, for a vision to be accepted, a leader has to articulate the nature of the status quo and its shortcomings, a future goal, how the future goal will fulfill follower needs, and the leader's plan of action (Conger & Kanungo, 1998, p. 55).

Therefore, vision-related behaviors include displaying sensitivity to the environment (Castro & Schriesheim, 1999; Conger & Kanungo, 1998), demonstrating that the vision meets followers' needs (Conger & Kanungo, 1988), formulating and articulating a future goal (Bennis & Nanus, 1985; House, 1977, 1998; Sashkin, 1988), envisioning (Bass, 1997; Nadler & Tushman, 1990), emphasizing ideology (House, 1977; Shamir et al., 1993), and demonstrating a plan for achieving the future goal (Conger & Kanungo, 1998). These behaviors are critical to distinguishing charismatic leaders from non-charismatic leaders. Displaying visionary leadership is necessary but not sufficient to be considered a charismatic leader.

Leader's Personal Behaviors
In addition to vision-related behaviors, we add a leader's personal behaviors as behaviors that reflect the leader's own motivation. These behaviors include displaying dedication to the vision, self-confidence, self-sacrifice or personal risk, as well as behavior that is exemplary or should be used to role model. Authors writing about charismatic leadership are in agreement that vision itself is not enough to achieve the vision or create charismatic effects. To achieve a vision, as Sashkin (1988) points out, "leaders must communicate their visions in ways that reach out to organizational members, gripping them and making them want to get involved in carrying out the vision" (p. 142). Sashkin (1988) and Sashkin and Fulmer (1985) suggest five types of personal behavior: focusing attention on important aspects of a vision, communicating a vision personally, demonstrating consistency and trustworthiness, displaying respect, and taking risks.

Similarly, Conger and Kanungo (1988, 1998) argued that to achieve a vision, charismatic leaders must articulate their own motivation by displaying:

(1) their convictions of their beliefs;
(2) self-confidence; and
(3) dedication to bring about what they advocate for leading their followers.

If a leader does not have confidence in his or her ability to achieve the vision, he or she cannot dedicate full effort to the vision and engage in behaviors that demonstrate personal risk or self-sacrificing behavior. This lack of self-confidence results in failing to view the leader as an extraordinary person. Conger and Kanungo (1998) and Friedland (1964) also argue that charismatic leaders have to create strong perceptions that they are highly trustworthy through actions that are seen by followers as involving great personal risks, costs, and energies.

Gandhi is an outstanding role model who engaged in "self-sacrificing behaviors, such as giving up his lucrative law practice to live the life of a peasant, engaging in civil disobedience, fasting, and refusing to accept the ordinary convenience offered to him by others" (House, 1977, pp. 194–195). Conger and Kanungo (1988) also point out leaders who demonstrate that they are indefatigable workers prepared to take on high personal risks or incur high personal costs, and who come to reflect charisma in the sense of being worthy of complete trust. Most recently, Choi and Mai-Dalton (1999) suggest that a leader's personal risk or self-sacrificing behavior is an important factor for followers to make attributions of charisma to the leader. Therefore, we define a leader's personal behaviors in terms of behaviors that articulate a leader's own motivation.

These behaviors include taking personal risk (Bennis & Nanus, 1985; Conger & Kanungo, 1998; Sashkin, 1988), showing self-confidence (Castro & Schriesheim, 1999; House, 1977, 1998), displaying exemplary and innovative behavior (House, 1977, 1998; Shamir et al., 1998), role modeling (Conger, 1999) and image building (Castro & Schriesheim, 1999). Nevertheless, if a leader develops a vision and has the appropriate personal characteristics, he or she will be a charismatic leader only in part because a third factor comes into play. The third factor contributing to charismatic leadership has to do with empowering followers.

Leader's Empowering Behaviors

According to House (1977), leaders who communicate high performance expectations for followers and exhibit confidence in their ability to meet such expectations are hypothesized to enhance followers' self-esteem and to affect the goals they accept or set for themselves. A charismatic leader is able to receive trust from followers or be accepted by followers through empowerment. Empowerment refers to "a process whereby an individual's belief in his or her self-efficacy is enhanced" (Conger & Kanungo, 1988, p. 474).

Thus, as Conger and Kanungo (1998) state, a leader could make followers feel empowered by providing beliefs in their own self-efficacy. Similarly,

Kouzes and Posner (1995) argue that followers feel empowered when a leader ensures self-leadership, believes in followers' abilities, develops their competence, assigns critical tasks, offers visible support, etc. A leader's empowering behavior influences whether he or she is accepted as a charismatic leader. If a leader is arrogant or has a conceited attitude, followers will not be accepted by him or her as a leader and will not follow him or her. Therefore, we define leaders' empowering behaviors in terms of behaviors that enhance followers' beliefs in their self-efficacy.

These behaviors include demonstrating confidence in followers' ability to implement a vision (Castro & Schriesheim, 1999; Conger & Kanungo, 1998; House, 1977, 1998), providing self-efficacy and self-worth information (Conger & Kanungo, 1988), and communicating high performance expectations (Castro & Schriesheim, 1999; Conger & Kanungo, 1998; House, 1977, 1998).

Summary
We have suggested that these three dimensions of charismatic behaviors from Weber underlie contemporary approaches to charismatic leadership. In other words, we have classified the charismatic behaviors presented by theorists of charismatic leadership that fall into this classification scheme. Table 1 shows our classification of charismatic behaviors from previous works into Weber's three categories.

DISTINGUISHING CHARISMATIC LEADERSHIP FROM OTHER VIEWS OF LEADERSHIP

Putting the three behavioral dimensions together provides an answer to the question of how charismatic leadership differs from other types of leadership. Theorists of charismatic leadership agree that the constellation of some common behavioral components is a critical factor in making an attribution of charisma to a leader (Conger & Kanungo, 1988, 1998). From this perspective, we will now show that if a person does not demonstrate all three dimensions of charismatic leadership, the person may be a leader but not a charismatic one.

First, if a leader displays vision-related behaviors and personal behaviors, but fails to show empowering behaviors, he or she may still be a leader after the fashion of what Maccoby (1976) calls *an entrepreneurial jungle fighter.* According to Maccoby, a jungle fighter is the first to break away from the traditional practices and has an individual vision or goals such as profit and power. To achieve a goal, he or she sacrifices self and takes a risk. However, he or she distrusts the people he or she controls and views followers as objects to

Table 1. Summary of Charismatic Behaviors Classified into Three Dimensions.

Three Dimensions	House (1977, 1998)	Bennis and Nanus (1985), Sashkin (1988)	Nadler and Tushman (1990)	Shamir et al. (1998)	Conger and Kanungo (1998)	Conger (1999)	Castro and Schriesheim (1999)
Vision-related behaviors	Goal articulation Emphasizing ideological aspects	Articulating vision	Envisioning	Emphasizing ideology	Sensitivity to environment Strategic vision	Vision Inspiration	Environmental sensitivity Articulating vision Frame alignment Innovating behaviors
Leader's personal behaviors	Role modeling Image building Showing confidence Exemplary behaviors Fairness Integrity	Demonstrating trustworthiness Taking risk	Energizing	Displaying exemplary behavior	Personal risk Unconventional behavior	Role modeling	Self-sacrifice Confidence Image building Acceptance goal External representatives
Leader's empowering behaviors	Exhibiting high expectations Showing confidence Arousing motivation	Displaying respect	Enabling	Emphasizing collective identity	Confidence in followers	Intellectual stimulating Meaning making Empowerment Setting high expectation	Arousal motivation Individualized support Exhibiting high expectation Confidence in followers Intellectual stimulation

be utilized and keeps them as dependent as possible. According to Mintzberg (1973), entrepreneurs search the organization and its environments for opportunities and initiate projects to bring about change. In addition, in an entrepreneurial organization, the power is centralized with the entrepreneur (Minzberg, 1983), and therefore members are not empowered.

Second, if a leader displays vision-related and empowering behaviors without personal behaviors, he or she would not sacrifice him- or herself and take personal risk. We can call such a person an *intellectual leader* (Burns, 1978). According to Burns, an intellectual leader is one who is concerned critically with values, purposes, and ends that transcend immediate practical needs. An intellectual leader discerns the evolving needs of followers and is able to analyze the environment. He or she also has the capacity to conceive values or purposes in such a way that ends and means are linked analytically and creatively. Such leaders seek to change society or an organization, set new direction and empower followers. They also fail to take personal risks or act self-sacrificially and thus are not charismatic.

Third, if a leader displays only vision-related behaviors, the person is not charismatic but rather a strategic leader. Strategic leadership has been defined as a person's ability to anticipate, envision, maintain flexibility, think strategically, and work with others to initiate changes that will create a viable future for the organization (Christensen, 1997; Ireland & Hitt, 1999). Similarly, according to Hitt, Ireland and Hoskisson (1995), strategic leadership includes six critical components:

(1) determining strategic direction;
(2) exploiting and maintaining core competencies;
(3) developing human capital;
(4) sustaining an effective corporate culture;
(5) emphasizing ethical practices; and
(6) establishing strategic controls.

Strategic leaders, armed with substantial decision-making responsibilities, have the ability to influence significantly the direction of the firm and how it is to be managed in the pursuit of a strategic goal. However, strategic leaders are usually top managers of firms and thus tend to influence followers through position power rather than personal power. Personal powers are based on the leader's personal behaviors such as personal risk, self-sacrificing, and exemplary behaviors. However, strategic leaders do not use these personal behaviors. Lee Iacocca and Ross Perot would have been strategic leaders rather than charismatic leaders, if they had not shown self-sacrificing behaviors as they did (e.g. giving up privileges, reducing their salary, etc.). Therefore, if a leader displays only vision-related behaviors, we can call him or her a *strategic leader.* This concept of a strategic leader differs from the concept of strategic transformationally oriented leadership (Bass, 1990; Hunt, 1991; Pawar & Eastman, 1997) in which charisma is a key component (Waldman & Yammarino, 1999).

Fourth, if a leader displays personal behaviors and empowering behaviors without vision-related behaviors, he or she still may be a leader as Greenleaf (1977) calls such a person *a servant leader.* According to Greenleaf, a servant leader is a servant first to make sure that other people's – i.e. followers' – highest-priority needs are being served. He or she initiates risks and takes the risk of failure along with the chance of success, and then trusts others. In other words, a servant leader sacrifices his or her personal interest to the other party or his or her work. Such a leader also trusts the other party and provides a feeling of being empowered. He or she does not show a direction for the future and long-range planning for the future and thus is not charismatic. Although Graham (1991) argues that servant leadership goes beyond transformational leadership because of the concept of social responsibilities and moral agent, servant leaders' behaviors differ from transformational leader behaviors. Graham notes, "their actual behavior will include sensitivity to the needs and interests of all organizational stakeholders . . . and provision of opportunities for wide participation in discussions about policies and practices" (1991, p. 112).

Fifth, if a leader shows only personal behaviors without vision-related and empowering behaviors, we can call him or her a *self-sacrificing leader* (Choi & Mai-Dalton, 1998, 1999; Goode, 1978), selfless leader (Tead, 1935), or self-humbling leader (Klapp, 1968). According to Choi and Mai-Dalton, a self-sacrificing leader abandons his or her personal interests, privileges or welfare in division of labor, distribution of rewards, and exercise of power. In their example of truck drivers, Choi and Mai-Dalton (1999) argue that the driver who allows the other to take the lighter items displays self-sacrificing behaviors. Then, is the driver a charismatic leader? If a person other than Iacocca decides to take a cut in salary, is he or she a charismatic leader?

Sixth, if a leader provides only empowering behaviors without vision-related and personal behaviors, followers will feel a sense of self-efficacy, and they will return a benefit to the leader as an exchange. Dansereau et al. (1995) calls such a person an *individualized leader.* According to individualized leadership theory, a follower provides satisfying performance with a superior, depending on the degree to which the superior provides a sense of self-worth and support to the subordinate. This sense of self-worth support includes a superior's:

(1) confidence in the follower's motivation, integrity, and ability;
(2) attention to the follower's needs and feelings; and
(3) support for the follower's ideas.

These behaviors are consistent with empowering behaviors.

Seventh, if a leader fails to show the three dimensions of charismatic leadership behaviors, he or she may be *another type of leader* – e.g. a manager who rewards effective performance. The eighth type of leadership is *charismatic*. Table 2 shows eight different types of leaders. In the next section, we focus only on charismatic leadership to address the question of who becomes followers of charismatic leaders and when.

CHARISMATIC FOLLOWERSHIP

House (1977) and Graham (1988) argue that one approach to charismatic leadership is to study followers or the effects of charisma on followers. Charismatic effects on followers may take various forms such as trust in the correctness of the leader's beliefs, unquestioning acceptance of the leader, affection for the leader, willing obedience to the leader, identification with the leader, and emotional involvement in the mission (Conger & Kanungo, 1988, 1998; House, 1977). Among them, we view follower acceptance of the charismatic leader as a key factor in defining charismatic followership. Two different types of acceptance have been suggested in the literature. Followers respond to charismatic leaders by unquestioning acceptance (House, 1977) or by voluntary acceptance (Graham, 1988). Therefore, we view charismatic

Table 2.   Eight Different Types of Leaders.

Dimensions of Leader Behavior			
Vision-related Behaviors	Personal Behaviors	Empowering Behaviors	Type of Leadership
Yes	Yes	Yes	Charismatic leader
Yes	Yes	No	Entrepreneurial jungle fighter
Yes	No	Yes	Intellectual leader
Yes	No	No	Strategic leader
No	Yes	Yes	Servant leader
No	Yes	No	Self-sacrificing leader
No	No	Yes	Individualized leader
No	No	No	Other types

followership as a process in which people come to follow charismatic leaders via voluntary acceptance or unquestioning acceptance. This view of charismatic followership may help to answer the questions of who voluntarily or unquestioningly follows charismatic leaders and when do they do so.

To begin to address the question of what types of people become followers of charismatic leaders and when do they do so, we consider two different types of charismatic leaders – i.e. socialized and personalized (Howell, 1988). According to Howell (1988, pp. 223–224), personalized leaders articulate goals that are leader-driven and recognize followers' needs only to the degree necessary to achieve their goals. They objectify their followers, viewing them as objects to be manipulated. Adolf Hitler provides a representative example of this type of leader. However, socialized leaders articulate goals that are follower-driven, recognize followers' needs, and help them develop in their own right. These two types of leaders are similar to pseudo- and authentic transformational leaders (Bass & Steidlmeier, 1999), respectively.

We view the two types of power motive – i.e. personalized and socialized – as different dimensions rather than as one dimension, because they qualitatively differ in the expression of power (McClelland, 1975). Socialized power motive is characterized by the degree of expression of power for the benefit of others. However, personalized power motive is characterized by the degree of expression of power for the benefits of the leader, oftentimes at the expense of their followers. Leaders with a socialized power motive also differ from leaders with a personalized power motive in their approach to social influence and behaviors. Therefore, the two types of leaders may appeal to followers who have different personality characteristics. In other words, these two types of charismatic leaders are a part of trying to understand who may become charismatic leaders and when. So, we now consider followers' characteristics in examining charismatic leadership.

Followers' Characteristics

Theorists of charismatic leadership have suggested a variety of followers' characteristics that can influence followers' perceptions of charisma. These characteristics include high or low self-esteem, self-confidence, independence or dependence (Conger, 1989, 1993; Conger & Kanungo, 1988, 1998; Gardner & Avolio, 1998), self-concept clarity and self-monitoring (Weierter, 1997), expressive or instrumental orientation, pragmatic or principled, and values and identity (Klein & House, 1995; Shamir et al., 1993). These characteristics relate to the evaluative aspect of the self-concept – e.g. self-esteem (Gecas, 1982; Harter, 1986; Marsh, 1986) processes – i.e. self-esteem.

Accordingly, we view self-esteem, which refers to general feelings of self-worth, self-regard, or self-acceptance (Rosenberg, 1979), as a characteristic that may influence followers' acceptance of charismatic leaders. However, there is some disagreement about what types of followers are susceptible to charismatic leaders. For example, according to Conger and Kanungo (1998), charismatic leaders have followers who tend to be submissive and dependent. Similarly, psychoanalytic views of charismatic leadership (Kets de Vries, 1988; Lindholm, 1990) argue that a charismatic leader is more likely to emerge among followers who lack self-confidence and convictions or who fail to develop maturity.

However, some argue that followers in charismatic relationships may have high self-confidence (Conger & Kanungo, 1988, 1994). For example, Conger (1993, p. 206) found that followers in entrepreneurial companies founded by charismatic leaders are more seekers of risk and uncertainty, and of the great wealth associated with a new venture. Based on these two opposite perspectives, we believe that two types of followers – i.e. followers with high and low self-esteem that may influence their acceptance of charismatic leaders – may be important components of trying to understand who becomes a follower of a charismatic leader.

Environmental (Contextual) Characteristics

In addition to follower characteristics, theorists of charismatic leadership agree that environmental crisis is a key element that produces charisma in addition to other elements (Beyer, 1999a; Conger & Kanungo, 1998; Klein & House, 1995; Shamir et al., 1993; Trice & Beyer, 1986). There are two different views on the role of crisis in the emergence of charismatic leaders – i.e. it is a causal factor or a moderator (Bass, 1999; Beyer, 1999a, b; House, 1999; Shamir & Howell, 1999). However, we view crisis as a factor facilitating the emergence of charisma (i.e. as a moderator), because it has been argued that charismatic leaders can also emerge in non-crisis or opportunistic situations (Conger, 1989; Conger & Kanungo, 1998; Shamir et al., 1993; Yukl, 1999).

The concept of crisis, which originated in the medical field (e.g. Shrivastava, 1993) has been defined in terms of the interaction between a subjective state and an objective environmental situation (Caplan, 1964; Schulberg & Sheldon, 1968) or cognitive perspectives (Taplin, 1971; Viney, 1973; Williams, 1957). For example, Williams (1957) defines crisis as a situation in which the actor faces the necessity of making appropriate choices of action. In a similar way, Pearson and Clair (1998) define organization crisis as "a low probability, high-impact event that threatens the viability of the organization and is characterized by ambiguity of cause, effect, and means of resolution, as well as by a belief that decisions must be made swiftly" (p. 60).

Milburn, Schuler and Watman (1983) also define organization crisis as a threat to the organization that either prevents the organization from attaining its goal or actually reduces an organization's ability to attain its goals. This concept of crisis may apply to individuals, groups, or societies. Accordingly, we define crisis as a situation that increases the threat for the individual, group, organization, or even society to being able attain its goals. These definitions of crisis across levels of analysis imply that charismatic phenomena may occur at the dyad, group, organization, and society level. Nevertheless, we view crisis as a critical condition describing when people become followers of charismatic leaders.

A MODEL OF CHARISMATIC FOLLOWERSHIP

We present a model of charismatic followership in Fig. 1. Charismatic followership differs from charismatic leadership in its emphasis on followers rather than leaders. As noted previously, charismatic followership addresses the question of what types of people become followers of charismatic leaders and when do they do so. Charismatic followership can take on two different forms – i.e.:

(1) unquestioning acceptance or willing obedience to the leader; and
(2) voluntary or autonomous acceptance (Graham, 1988; House, 1977).

It has also been argued that the positive side of charismatic leadership is associated with voluntary acceptance, whereas the negative or dark side of leadership is associated with unquestioning acceptance or obedience (Bass & Steidlmeier, 1999; Bryman, 1992; Howell, 1988: Klein & House, 1998; Waldman & Yammarino, 1999). Therefore, we view unquestioning acceptance or obedience and autonomous or voluntary acceptance of a charismatic leader as the two different outcomes of charismatic followership.

Propositions for the Types of People Who Become Followers and When

Theorists of charismatic leadership have disagreed about whether crisis is a causal factor for the emergence of charismatic leaders (Bass, 1999; Beyer, 1999a, b; House, 1999; Shamir, 1999). Previous authors have also disagreed about whether high or low self-esteem individuals are susceptible to charismatic leaders (Conger & Kanungo, 1988, 1998; Klein & House, 1995). One way to resolve such disagreements is to consider the characteristics of

A. Followers' Voluntary Acceptance of Charismatic Leaders

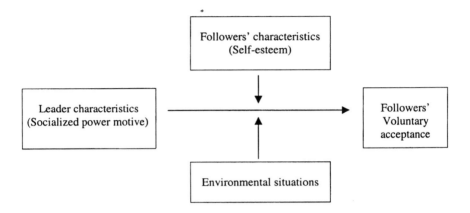

B. Followers' Unquestioning Acceptance of Charismatic Leaders

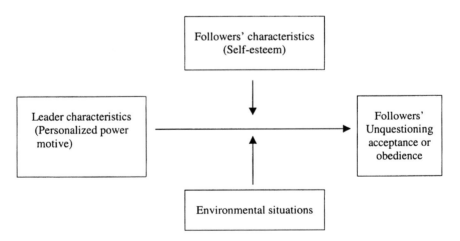

Fig. 1.   A Model of Charismatic Followership.

followers and the environment together in defining charismatic followership. Based on these characteristics, we differentiate four different situations – i.e.:

(1) crisis situation and low self-esteem followers;
(2) crisis situation and high self-esteem followers;
(3) non-crisis or opportunistic situation and low self-esteem followers; and
(4) non-crisis or opportunistic situation and high self-esteem followers.

We believe that followers may or may not unquestioningly accept or voluntarily accept a charismatic leader in each of the four situations. We develop propositions for each situation.

Crisis and Low Self-esteem
It has been argued that high and low self-esteem individuals differ in their patterns of attitudes and behaviors under crisis situations (Brockner, 1988; Brockner et al., 1993; Cohen, 1959; Hui & Lee, 2000; Jackson, 1978; Leventhal & Perloe, 1962; Silverman, 1964a, b). Low self-esteem individuals are more responsive to stimuli that lead to the perception of threats, because they lack confidence in their ability to meet challenges posed by stressful circumstances (e.g. Baumeister, 1993; Brockner, 1984, 1988; Campbell & Lavallee, 1993). Fitts (1972) found that low self-esteem individuals are more likely to exhibit anxiety and neurotic behaviors under stress and failure. Under crisis situations, low self-esteem individuals' breadth of perspective is reduced, and their cognitive focus is exclusively oriented toward the problem resulting from the crisis situations (e.g. Bord, 1975).

Brockner et al. (1993) suggest that low self-esteem individuals have greater worries during the threat of future layoffs and work harder to have a chance to avoid losing their jobs in future layoffs. Brockner (1988) also suggests that low self-esteem individuals are more behaviorally plastic – i.e. the individuals are more affected by external factors – than high self-esteem individuals under stressful circumstances. These findings indicate that under crisis situations, low self-esteem individuals should tend to focus on coping with the threat from the crisis situations. Under such situations, the leader who helps them to cope with the threat should be viewed as valuable.

Under a crisis situation, personalized charismatic leaders may appeal to followers with low self-esteem, because they have abilities to handle crises. Personalized leaders recognize followers' wants and needs under a crisis situation (i.e. coping with the threat from the crisis), displace their private motives on to followers and exploit those motives for their own benefits rather than followers' benefits (Howell, 1988). Although personalized leaders articulate a goal or vision for their own benefits, followers with low self-esteem tend to show obedience and loyal submission, because the goal and vision are related to coping with crisis, and their focus is mainly on coping with the threat from the crisis.

Where a leader helps low self-esteem individuals to cope with the threat generated by a crisis, they would be more likely to submit to, or obey, the leader. Personalized charismatic leaders may not appeal to followers with high self-esteem, because their exercise of power for their own benefits threatens the self-esteem of individuals and because high self-esteem individuals are likely to avoid threatening events or situations (e.g. Baumeister, 1993; Boney-McCoy, Gibbons & Gerrard, 1999) and repudiate this power situation. Thus, high self-esteem individuals are less vulnerable to influence from the personalized leaders. We will discuss this point in the next section.

Socialized leaders, however, may not appeal to followers with low self-esteem, although they also have the ability to handle the crisis. Howell notes, "the socialized face of power is in theory characterized by efforts to assist organizational members in formulating higher-order, transcendent goals and by instilling in them a sense of power to pursue such goals" (1988, p. 217). However, low self-esteem individuals would not formulate such goals, because they are more likely to be uncertain about the correctness of their thought and judgments (e.g. Campbell & Lavallee, 1993). They do not want to get empowered either, because of their expectations of failure (e.g. Campbell & Lavallee, 1993; Cohen, 1959). Accordingly, low self-esteem individuals should tend to avoid or ignore this situation. Thus, socialized leaders are less likely to appeal to followers with low self-esteem.

Proposition 1. Under crisis situations, followers with low self-esteem are more likely to unquestioningly accept or obey charismatic leaders with a personalized power motive (i.e. personalized leaders).

Crisis and High Self-esteem

However, high self-esteem individuals are less responsive to the threat from crisis situations, because they feel confident that they have ability to cope with the threat (e.g. Asford, 1988; Jackson, 1978). High self-esteem individuals possess confidence in their own judgments and expectations of being successful and are more self-directed (Campbell & Lavallee, 1993). They also have a feeling of value and equality with respect to others, maintain relationships characterized by mutual feelings of respect, dignity, value, and worth, and thus are less likely to be susceptible to others' attempts to influence them (Brockner et al., 1993; Spencer, Josephs & Steele, 1993). Brockner et al. (1993) suggest that high self-esteem individuals tend not to be scared under the threat of layoffs and tend not to work harder to keep their jobs in such situations. Dodgson and Wood (1998) suggest that high self-esteem individuals did not focus on negative thoughts after failure, but focused on their strengths. Silvermann (1964b) also suggests that high self-esteem individuals are less likely to be persuaded in the threat of performance-failure. These findings imply that high self-esteem individuals may be less likely to be influenced under crisis situations. Therefore, personalized leaders and socialized leaders may not appeal to followers with high self-esteem.

Under crisis situations, high self-esteem individuals may display various alternative behaviors, because their breadth of perspective won't be reduced (Bord, 1975). Under crisis situations, high self-esteem individuals may not be worried about the threat from the crisis (e.g. Baumeister, 1993; Hui & Lee, 2000). For example, Hui and Lee suggest that employees with high organizational based self-esteem were less responsive to organizational uncertainty. Therefore, they may not submit to or obey the leader, although the leader is capable of coping with the threat. High self-esteem individuals seem more likely to avoid such situations and may leave those situations where the self is devalued by the threat associated with the crisis.

As noted previously, personalized leaders exploit their motives for their own benefits. Although personalized leaders are capable of handling the crisis, personal confidence may lead them to repudiate the power exercised by personalized leaders and are less vulnerable to influence from the personalized leaders. On the other hand, socialized leaders may handle the crisis by articulating a shared vision and displaying personal and empowering behaviors. They also express power for the benefits of others. Nevertheless, the socialized leaders may not appeal to high self-esteem individuals, because high self-esteem individuals have enough confidence to handle the crisis themselves. Their cognitive focus is not mainly on coping with the crisis, but on maintaining and enhancing self-esteem.

Socialized leaders may enhance the self-esteem of followers by articulating a follower-driven goal. However, under crisis situations, the leader's first goal may be to cope with the crisis that may differ from a follower-driven goal. In this situation, high self-esteem individuals are less likely to be influenced by the socialized leaders. Thus, the following proposition is derived.

Proposition 2. Under crisis situations, followers with high vs. low self-esteem are less likely to accept leaders with a personalized power motive (i.e. personalized leaders) and leaders with socialized power (i.e. socialized leaders).

Non-crisis and High Self-esteem

High self-esteem individuals are more responsive to stimuli that are self-enhancing than to stimuli that devalue the self (e.g. Baumeister, 1993; Bobey-McCoy et al., 1999; Silverman, 1964a). According to Conger (1993), followers in entrepreneurial companies founded by charismatic leaders "may be seekers of risk, uncertainty, and the potential for great wealth associated with a new venture" (p. 206). Similarly, Conger (1999) notes that, "followers are attracted to the charismatic or transformational leader because of a constructive identification with the leader's abilities, a desire to learn from them, a quest for personal challenge and growth, and the attractiveness and rewards of the mission" (p. 162). Shamir et al. (1993) also point out that the values and identities of followers within charismatic relationships should be congruent with their leader's vision.

High self-esteem individuals tend to get involved in entrepreneurial organizations, because they have confidence in their own ability to meet the challenges posed by such organizations, and there is a high probability of self-enhancement or self-actualization. It has been suggested that high self-esteem individuals are more readily influenced by optimistic, gratifying, potentially self-enhancing communications than by pessimistic threatening ones (Baumeister, 1993; Leventhal & Perloe, 1962). Socialized leaders link followers' needs to important values, purposes, and meanings through articulation of a shared vision (Howell, 1988). Therefore, socialized leaders are more likely to appeal to followers with high self-esteem under non-crisis or opportunistic situations.

According to Conger (1989), charismatic leaders are sometimes emerged in entrepreneurial environments of great opportunity, munificence, and optimism. In entrepreneurial environments:

(1) high self-esteem individuals rather than low self-esteem individuals tend to get involved;
(2) leaders tend to formulate and articulate a vision that is congruent with their followers' vision; and
(3) followers tend to take some risks to attain their goals, actualize their potentials, and fulfill their needs.

Therefore, Conger's findings suggest that socialized leaders are more likely to influence individuals with high self-esteem under non-crisis or opportunistic situations. Individuals with high self-esteem are more likely to voluntarily follow socialized leaders.

However, personalized leaders are less likely to appeal to individuals with high self-esteem, because of their exercise of power for their own benefits.

Personalized leaders exploit their motives for their own benefits, and high self-esteem individuals have confidence in handling non-crisis or opportunistic situations. High self-esteem individuals can be successful without submission to personalized leaders or without being manipulated by the personalized leaders.

Proposition 3. Under non-crisis or opportunistic situations, followers with high self-esteem are more likely to voluntarily accept charismatic leaders with a socialized power motive.

Non-crisis and Low Self-esteem

Under non-crisis or opportunistic situations, low self-esteem individuals attempt to enhance their feelings of personal worth (Brown, Collins & Schmidt, 1988). Unfortunately, personalized leaders are not able to enhance the followers' self-worth, because they tend to exploit followers for their own benefits and tend to evoke feelings of obedience or submission in followers (Howell, 1988). Under non-crisis or opportunistic situations, individuals with low self-esteem tend not to have limited breadth of perspective. Bord argues, "during periods of relative stability people occupy various statuses demanding different investments of time, energy, and loyalties. This means that people ordinarily have multiple identities . . . The presence of multiple perspectives limits any potential leader's influences" (1975, p. 488). His argument indicates that individuals' multiple breadth of perspective is determined by crisis or non-crisis situations rather than by individuals' self-esteem.

Therefore, under non-crisis situations, personalized leaders are less likely to appeal to followers with low self-esteem, because followers would perceive there to be more opportunities to pursue. Socialized leaders may not appeal to individuals with low self-esteem, either. As Howell (1988) noted, socialized leaders tend to assist followers in formulating higher-order goals and empower followers to purse such goals. However, low self-esteem individuals tend not to have confidence in formulating goals and do not want to get empowered, either. The situation is opportunistic, and thus low self-esteem individuals do not need to submit to the leaders. Therefore, low self-esteem individuals would not accept the socialized leaders.

Proposition 4. Under non-crisis or opportunistic situations, followers with low self-esteem are less likely to accept leaders with a personalized power motive and leaders with a socialized power motive.

CONCLUSIONS AND RESEARCH IMPLICATIONS

In this chapter, we have proposed propositions for charismatic followership – i.e. followers with different characteristics (i.e. high and low self-esteem) voluntarily or unquestioningly accept charismatic leaders with different characteristics under different environmental situations. These propositions are a first attempt to begin to resolve current disagreements and ambiguities about charisma and charismatic relationships. First, theorists of charismatic leadership have emphasized the need for propositions concerning the interaction of leader, follower, and environment in charisma (Beyer, 1999a; House, 1999; Shamir & Howell, 1999). For example, as Beyer notes, theorists of charismatic leadership ignore "the possibility that different contexts or situations may make different personal qualities and behaviors in leaders more or less attractive, persuasive, and effective because potential followers may be more or less receptive to that type of leader" (1999a, p. 310). Propositions 1 to 4 indicate that different types of followers are attracted to different types of leaders under different situations. As House notes (1999), these kinds of propositions are not found in the current literature, but they did arise from considering the categories described by Bass (1990).

Second, theorists of charismatic leadership disagree about the role of crisis in defining charisma (Beyer, 1999a, b; Conger, 1999; Shamir, 1999; Shamir & Howell, 1999; Yukl, 1999). Propositions 1, 2 and 3 suggest one solution to the question about whether crisis is a necessary factor in defining charisma. First, according to Proposition 1, in a crisis situation, low self-esteem individuals tend to unquestioningly accept the personalized leaders. Therefore, it seems likely that crisis is a causal factor for charisma. However, according to Propositions 2 and 3, in a crisis situation, high self-esteem individuals tend not to be influenced by charismatic leaders, and in a non-crisis or opportunistic situation, high self-esteem individuals are willing to voluntarily follow the socialized leaders. Therefore, crisis is not a causal factor for charisma, but a moderator for charisma.

Our view is consistent with Shamir and Howell's (1999), who point out that crisis facilitates the emergence of charismatic leader, but is not a necessary factor in defining charisma. Again, we see the use of contextual factor described by Bass (1990) as offering a potential avenue to resolve.

We proposed a three-dimensional model of charismatic leadership behavior that is based on Weber's concept of charisma. This model may be an alternative to previous models – e.g. six-dimensional model (Conger & Kanungo, 1994), five-dimensional model (Conger & Kanungo, 1998) or another three-dimensional (Bass, 1985) or four-dimensional model (Bass & Avolio, 1993) of transformational leadership. These previous models have clearly shed light on explaining charismatic leadership. These previous models are based on Burns' (1978) and Tichy and Devanna's (1986) concept of transformational leadership rather than Weber's concept of charisma (see also Beyer, 1999b). For example, Conger and Kanungo's (1988, 1998) three-stage model is based on Tichy and Devanna's (1986) concept of transformation. Also, we did not follow Beyer's (1999a, b) definition of charismatic leadership. According to Trice and Beyer (1986), charisma includes five elements (i.e. an extraordinary person, crisis, radical solution, followers, and validation by repeated successes), and all of them must be present to some degree for charisma to occur. However, as Bass (1990, 1999) noted, some founders or leaders can be seen as charismatic in the absence of crisis and success. We propose that charismatic leaders must display the three behaviors (i.e. vision-related, personal, and empowering behaviors) to some degree in order to be perceived as charismatic. However, we also propose that it depends on the characteristics of followers (high and low self-esteem) and the environment (crisis and non-crisis) whether individuals become followers of charismatic leaders.

Research Implications

One set of additional implications has to do with conducting research. To do research, first, hypotheses about the charismatic behavioral dimensions should be multivariate or multi-dimensional. Unfortunately, few studies have tested the multi-dimensional nature of charismatic leader behaviors. Conger and Kanungo (1994) conducted a confirmatory factor analysis and found that a six-dimensional model provides an adequate model fit. Conger and Kanungo (1998) changed the model to a five-dimensional model on the basis of the issues of dimensionality, parsimony, and brevity. They found that a five-dimensional model provided a significant fit with the data. However, in conceptualizing charismatic leadership, we suggest that there are three key behavioral dimensions of charismatic leadership. Our three-dimensional model that is based on Weber's concept of charisma may be an alternative to previous ones. Accordingly, the first statement we can make is that research is needed to examine the dimensionality of charismatic leader behavior. We need to collect data from leaders and followers and test the dimensionality of charismatic leader behaviors through a confirmatory and exploratory factor analyses.

Second, hypotheses about how charismatic leadership differs from other forms of leadership, need to be derived and tested. Most studies of charismatic leadership have focused on examining the relationship between charismatic leader behaviors and non-charismatic leader behaviors such as task-oriented, people-oriented, etc. (Conger et al., 1997; Conger & Kanungo, 1998). However, the comparison of charismatic behaviors with non-charismatic behaviors fails to show the differences among eight types of leadership in Table 2. Accordingly, research is needed to examine the difference between charismatic leadership and other approaches to leadership.

Third, testable hypotheses about crisis should be derived from the propositions presented in this chapter. Although leader and follower types have been conceptually and empirically developed, the concept of crisis has not been developed as extensively. Theorists of charismatic leadership differ in their conceptualizations of crisis. For example, Beyer (1999a) views crisis as a macro variable and a rare phenomenon. However, others view crisis as a more micro-level variable and a common phenomenon in organizations, communities and societies (Conger, 1999; Shamir, 1999). Consequently, it is hard to select a specific crisis variable. However, as we noted, the concept of crisis can be extended from person to society. Therefore, the selection of a specific crisis variable depends on the level of crisis – e.g. person, group or organization. For example, when a researcher focuses on a personal crisis, followers' perceptions of helplessness, distress, or anxiety or a more objective variable – e.g. job loss – might be used as a crisis variable. In the case of organization crisis, a more objective variable might be selected. Severe change in technology, market shares and profit might be used as a specific crisis variable.

Fourth, to do research on charismatic followership, leadership effectiveness needs to be assessed. Followers' acceptance of charismatic leaders may lead to various outcomes such as higher motivation (Shamir et al., 1993), trust in, commitment to, and satisfaction with the leader (Conger & Kanungo, 1988, 1998; Shamir et al., 1993), higher performance (Conger & Kanungo, 1988, 1998), and/or organizational citizenship behavior (Conger & Kanungo, 1988, 1998). Specific hypotheses on leadership effectiveness follow from the propositions. For example, based on propositions 1 to 4, it can be hypothesized that dyads (groups or organizations) led by socialized leaders should be more effective when followers have high self-esteem, and situations represent non-crisis or opportunistic situations. We may also hypothesize that dyads (groups or organizations) led by personalized leaders should be more effective when followers have low self-esteem, and the situation is a crisis.

In conclusion, we have addressed the questions of what types of people become followers of charismatic leaders and when do they do so. We hope that our attempt shows that Bass's (1990) argument about focusing on the five categories in future research is applicable. We also hope that by considering the characteristics of leader, follower, and situation, future research will test whether the propositions in this chapter hold. If not, we hope that this is a first step in attempting to develop an approach that includes leaders, followers, and the situation simultaneously and as indicated in Bass's (1990) work.

ACKNOWLEDGMENTS

This paper was supported by research funding provided by the Korea Research Foundation, Support for Faculty Research Abroad.

REFERENCES

Ashford, S. J. (1988). Individual strategies for coping with stress during organizational transitions. *Journal of Applied Behavioral Science, 24*, 19–36.
Avolio, B. J., & Bass, B. M. (1998). Individual consideration viewed at multiple levels of analysis, A multi-level framework for examining the diffusion of transformational leadership. In: F. Dansereau & F. J. Yammarino (Eds), *Leadership: The multiple-level approaches* (Part A, pp. 53–74). Stamford, CT: JAI Press.
Awamleh, R., & Gardner, W. L. (1999). Perceptions of leader charisma and effectiveness: The effects of vision content, delivery, and organizational performance. *Leadership Quarterly, 10*, 345–373.
Bass, B. M. (1985). *Leadership and performance beyond expectations*. New York: Free Press.
Bass, B. M. (1988). Evolving perspectives on charismatic leadership. In: J. A. Conger & R. N. Kanungo (Eds), *Charismatic leadership* (pp. 40–77). San Francisco: Jossey-Bass.
Bass, B. M. (1990). *Bass and Stogdill's handbook of leadership: Theory, research and managerial expectation* (3rd ed.). New York: Free Press.
Bass, B. M. (1996). A new paradigm of leadership: An inquiry into transformational leadership. Unpublished manuscript.
Bass, B. M. (1997). Does the transactional-transformational paradigm transcend organizational and national boundaries? *American Psychologist, 52*, 130–139.
Bass, B. M. (1999). On the taming of charisma: A reply to Janice Beyer. *Leadership Quarterly, 10*, 541–553.
Bass, B. M., & Avolio, B. J. (1993). Transformational leadership: A response to critiques. In: M. M. Chemers & R. Ayman (Eds), *Leadership theory and research: Perspectives and directions* (pp. 49–80). New York: Free Press.
Bass, B. M., & Steidlmeier, P. (1999). Ethics, character, and authentic transformational leadership behavior. *Leadership Quarterly, 10*, 181–217.
Baumeister, R. F. (1993). Understanding the inner nature of low self-esteem: Uncertain, fragile, protective, and conflicted. In: R. F. Baumeister (Ed.), *Self-esteem: The puzzle of low self-regard* (pp. 201–218). New York: Plenum.
Bennis, W., & Nanus, B. (1985). *Leaders: The strategies for taking charge*. New York: Harper & Row.
Berlew, D. E. (1974). Leadership and organizational excitement. *California Management Review, 17*, 21–30.
Beyer, J. M. (1999a). Taming and promoting charisma to change organizations. *Leadership Quarterly, 10*, 307–330.
Beyer, J. M. (1999b). Two approaches to studying charismatic leadership: Competing or complementary? *Leadership Quarterly, 10*, 575–588.

Boney-McCoy, S., Gibbbons, F. X., & Gerrard, M. (1999). Self-esteem, compensatory self-enhancement, and the consideration of health risk. *Personality and Social Psychological Bulletin, 25*, 954–965.

Bord, R. J. (1975). Toward a social-psychological theory of charismatic social influence processes. *Social Forces, 53*, 485–497.

Brockner, J. (1984). Low self-esteem and behavioral plasticity: Some implications for personality and social psychology. In: L. Wheeler (Ed.), *Review of personality and social psychology* (pp. 237–271). Berverly Hills, CA: Sage.

Brockner, J. (1988). *Self-esteem at work: Research, theory, and practice.* Lexington Books, Lexington, MA.

Brockner, J., Grover, S., O'Malley, M. N., Reed, T. F., & Glynn, M. A. (1993). Threat of future layoffs, self-esteem, and supervisor's reactions: Evidence from the laboratory and the field. *Strategic Management Journal, 14*, 153–166.

Brown, J. D., Collins, R. L., & Schmidt, G. W. (1988). Self-esteem and direct vs. indirect forms of self-enhancement. *Journal of Personality and Social Psychology, 55*, 445–453.

Bryman, A. (1992). *Charisma and leadership in organizations.* London: Sage.

Burns, J. M. (1978). *Leadership.* New York: Harper & Row.

Campbell, J. D. (1990). Self-esteem and clarity of the self-concept. *Journal of Personality and Social Psychology, 59*, 538–549.

Campbell, J. D., & Lavallee, L. F. (1993). Who am I? The role of self-concept confusion in understanding the behavior of people with low self-esteem. In: R. F. Baumeister (Ed.), *Self-esteem: The puzzle of low self-regard* (pp. 3–20). New York: Plenum.

Caplan,, G. (1964). *Principles of preventative psychiatry.* New York: Basic Books.

Castro, S. L., & Schriesheim, C. A. (1999). Transformational leadership: A summary of behavioral dimensions of the construct and an assessment of the validity of new scales measuring each dimension. Paper presented at the Research Methods Division of the annual meeting of the Academy of Management, Chicago, IL.

Choi, Y., & Mai-Dalton, R. R. (1998). On the leadership function of self-sacrifice. *Leadership Quarterly, 9*, 475–501.

Choi, Y., & Mai-Dalton, R. R. (1999). The model of followers' responses to self-sacrificial leadership: An empirical test. *Leadership Quarterly, 10*, 397–421.

Christensen, C. M. (1997). Making strategy: Learning by doing. *Harvard Business Review, 75*(6), 141–156.

Cohen, A. (1959). Some implications of self-esteem for social influence. In: C. Hovland & I. Janis (Eds), *Personality and persuasibility* (pp. 102–120). New Haven: Yale University Press.

Conger, J. A. (1989). *The charismatic leader: Behind the mystique of exceptional leadership.* San Francisco: Jossey-Bass.

Conger, J. A. (1993). Max Weber's conceptualization of charismatic authority: Its influence on organizational research. *Leadership Quarterly, 4*, 277–288.

Conger, J. A. (1999). Charismatic and transformational leadership in organizations: An insider's perspective on these developing streams of research. *Leadership Quarterly, 10*, 145–179.

Conger, J. A., & Kanungo, R. N. (1988). Behavioral dimensions of charismatic leadership. In: J. A. Conger & R. N. Kanungo (Eds), *Charismatic leadership* (pp. 40–77). San Francisco: Jossey-Bass.

Conger, J. A., & Kanungo, R. N. (1994). Charismatic leadership in organizations: Perceived behavioral attributes and their measurement. *Journal of Organizational Behavior, 15*, 439–452.

Conger, J. A., & Kanungo, R. N. (1998). *Charismatic leadership in organizations.* Thousand Oaks: CA. Sage.

Conger, J. A., Kanungo, R. N., Menon, S. T., & Mathur, P. (1997). Measuring charisma: Dimensionality and validity of the Conger-Kanungo scale of charismatic leadership. *Canadian Journal of Administrative Sciences, 14,* 290–302.

Dansereau. F., Yammarino, F. J., Markham, S. E., Alutto, J. A., Newman, J., Dumas, M., Nachman, S. A., Naughton, T. J., Kim, K., Al-Kelabi, S. A., Lee, S., & Keller, T. (1995). Individualized leadership: A new multiple-level approach. *Leadership Quarterly, 6,* 413–450.

Dodgson, P. G., & Wood, J. V. (1998). Self-esteem and the cognitive accessibility of strengths and weaknesses after failure. *Journal of Personality and Social Psychology, 75,* 178–197.

Dow, T. E. (1969). A theory of charisma. *Social Quarterly, 10,* 306–318.

Fitts, W. (1972). *The self-concept and psychopathology.* Nashville, TN: Counselor Recordings and Tests.

Friedland, W. H. (1964). For a sociological concept of charisma. *Social Forces, 43,* 18–26.

Gardner, W. L., & Avolio, B. J. (1998). The charismatic relationship: A dramaturgical perspective. *Academy of Management Review, 23,* 32–58.

Gecas, V. (1982). The self-concept. *Annual Review of Sociology, 8,* 1–33.

Goode, W. J. (1978). *The celebration of heroes: Prestige as a social control system.* Berkley, CA: University of California Press.

Graham, J. W. (1988). Chapter 3 commentary: Transformational leadership: Fostering follower autonomy, not automatic followership. In: J. G. Hunt, B. R. Baliga, H. P. Dachler & C. A. Schriesheim (Eds), *Emerging leadership vistas* (pp. 73–79). Lexington, MA: Lexington Books.

Graham, J. W. (1991). Servant leadership in organizations: Inspirational and moral. *Leadership Quarterly, 2,* 105–119.

Greenleaf, R. K. (1977). *Servant leadership: A journey into the nature of legitimate power and greatness.* New York: Paulist Press.

Harter, S. (1986). Processes underlying the construction, maintenance and enhancement of self-concept in children. In: J. Suls & A. Greenwald (Eds), *Psychological perspective on the self* (pp. 136–182). Hillsdale, NJ: Lawrence Erlbaum Associates.

Hitt, M. A., Ireland, R. D., & Hoskisson, R. E. (1995). *Strategic management: Competitiveness and globalization* (3rd ed.). Cincinnati: South-Western College Publishing Company.

House, R. J. (1977). A 1976 theory of charismatic leadership. In: J. G. Hunt & L. L. Larson (Eds), *Leadership: The cutting edge* (pp. 189–207). Carbondale: Southern Illinois University Press.

House, R. J. (1998). Measures and assessments for the charismatic leadership approach: Scales, latent constructs, loadings, Cronbach alphas, and interclass correlations. In: F. Dansereau & F. Yammarino (Eds), *Leadership: The multiple-level approaches contemporary and alternatives* (pp. 23–29). Stamford, CT: JAI Press.

House, R. J. (1999). Weber and the neo-charismatic leadership paradigm: A response to Beyer. *Leadership Quarterly, 10,* 563–574.

House, R. J., & Howell, J. M. (1992). Personality and charismatic leadership. *Leadership Quarterly, 3,* 81–108.

House, R. J., Spangler, W. D., & Woycke, J. (1991). Personality and charisma in the U.S. Presidency: A psychological theory of leader effectiveness. *Administrative Science Quarterly, 36,* 364–396.

Howell, J. M. (1988). Two faces of charisma: Socialized and personalized leadership in organizations. In: J. A. Conger & R. N. Kanungo (Eds), *Charismatic leadership: The elusive factor in organizational effectiveness* (pp. 213–236). San Francisco: Jossey-Bass.

Hui, C., & Lee, C. (2000). Moderating effects of organization-based self-esteem on organizational uncertainty: Employee response relationships. *Journal of Management, 26,* 215–232.

Hunt, J. G. (1991). *Leadership: A new synthesis.* Newbury Park, CA: Sage.

Ireland, R D., & Hitt, M. A. (1999). Achieving and maintaining strategic competitiveness in the 21st century: The role of strategic leadership. *Academy of Management Executive, 13,* 43–57.

Jackson, D. N. (1978). Interpreter's guide to the Jackson Personality Inventory. In: P. McReynolds (Ed.), *Advances in psychological assessment.* San Francisco: Jossey-Bass.

Kets de Vries, M. (1988). Origins of charisma: Ties that bind the leader and the led. In: J. A. Conger & R. N. Kanungo (Eds), *Charismatic leadership* (pp. 237–252). San Francisco: Jossey-Bass.

Klapp, O. E. (1968). *Symbolic leaders: Public dramas and public men.* Chicago: Minerva Press.

Klein, K. J., & House, R. J. (1995). On fire: Charismatic Leadership and levels of analysis. *Leadership Quarterly, 6,* 163–198.

Klein, K. J., & House, R. J. (1998). Further thoughts on fire: Charismatic leadership and levels of analysis. In: F. Dansereau & F. J. Yammarino (Eds), *Leadership: The multiple-level approaches* (Part B, pp. 45–52). Stamford, CT: JAI Press.

Kouzes, J. M., & Posner, B. Z. (1995). *The leadership challenge: How to keep getting extraordinary things done in organizations.* San Francisco: Jossey-Bass.

Leventhal, H., & Perloe, S. I. (1962). A relationship between self-esteem and persuasibility. *Journal of Abnormal and Social Psychology, 64,* 385–388.

Lindholm, C. (1990). *Charisma.* Cambridge, MA: Basil Blackwell Ltd.

McClelland, D. C. (1975). *Power: The inner experience.* New York: Irvington.

Maccoby, M. (1976). *The gamesman.* New York: Simon & Schuster.

Marsh, H. W. (1986). Global self-esteem: Its relation to specific facets of self-concept and their importance. *Journal of Personality and Social Psychology, 51,* 1224–1236.

Meindl, J. R. (1990). On leadership: An alternative to the conventional wisdom. In: B. M. Staw & L. L. Cummings (Eds), *Research in Organizational Behavior* (pp. 159–203). Greenwich, CT: JAI Press.

Meindl, J. R. (1995). The romance of leadership as a follower-centric theory: A social constructionist approach. *Leadership Quarterly, 6,* 329–341.

Milburn, T. W., Schuler, R. S., & Watman, K. H. (1983). Organizational crisis. Part I: Definition and conceptualization. *Human Relations, 36,* 1141–1160.

Minzberg, H. (1973). *The nature of managerial work.* New York: Harper & Row.

Minzberg, H. (1983). *Structure in fives: Designing effective organizations.* Englewood Cliffs, NJ: Prentice Hall.

Nadler, D. A., & Tushman, M. L. (1990). Beyond the charismatic leader: Leadership and organizational change. *California Management Review, 32,* 77–97.

Pawar, B. S., & Eastman, K. K. (1997). The nature and implications of contextual influences on transformational leadership: A conceptual examination. *Academy of Management Review, 22,* 80–109.

Pearson, C. M., & Clair, J. A. (1998). Reframing crisis management. *Academy of Management Review, 23,* 59–76.

Pillai, R., & Meindl, J. R. (1998). Context and charisma: A meso level examination of the relationship of organic structure, collectivism, and crisis to charismatic leadership. *Journal of Management, 24,* 643–671.

Rosenberg, M. (1979). *Conceiving the self.* New York: Basic Books.

Sashkin, M. (1988). The visionary leader. In: J. A. Conger & R. N. Kanungo (Eds), *Charismatic leadership: The elusive factor in organizational effectiveness* (pp. 122–160). San Francisco: Jossey-Bass.

Sashkin, M., & Fulmer, R. M. (1985). A new framework for leadership: Vision, charisma, and culture creation. Paper presented at the Biennial International Leadership Symposium, Texas Tech University.

Schulberg, H. C., & Sheldon, A. (1968). The probability of crisis and strategies for preventative intervention. *Archieves of General Psychology, 18,* 553–558.

Shamir, B. (1999). Taming charisma for better understanding and greater usefulness: A response to Beyer. *Leadership Quarterly, 10,* 555–562.

Shamir, B., House, R. J., & Arthur, M. B. (1993). The motivational effects of charismatic leadership: A self-concept based theory. *Organization Science, 4,* 577–594.

Shamir, B., & Howell, J. M. (1999). Organizational and contextual influences on the emergence and effectiveness of charismatic leadership. *Leadership Quarterly, 10,* 257–283.

Shamir, B., Zakay, E., & Popper, M. (1998). Correlates of charismatic leader behavior in military units: Subordinates' attitudes, unit characteristics, and superiors' appraisals of leader performance. *Academy of Management Journal, 41,* 387–409.

Shrivastava, P. (1993). Crisis theory and practice: Towards a sustainable future. *Industrial and Environmental Crisis Quarterly, 7,* 23–42.

Silverman, I. (1964a). Self-esteem and differential responsiveness to success and failure. *Journal of Abnormal and Social Psychology, 69,* 115–119.

Silverman, I. (1964b). Differential effects of ego threat upon persuasibility for high and low self-esteem subjects. *Journal of Abnormal and Social Psychology, 69,* 567–572.

Smith, M., Wethington, E., & Zhanm G. (1996). Self-concept clarity and preferred coping styles. *Journal of Personality, 62,* 407–434.

Snyder, N. H., Dowd, J. J. Jr., & Houghton D. M. (1994). *Vision values, and courage: Leadership for quality management.* New York: Free Press.

Spencer, S. J., Josephs, T., & Steele, C. M. (1993). Low self-esteem: The uphill struggle for self-integrity. In: R. F. Baumeister (Ed.), *Self-esteem: The Puzzle of Low Self-regard* (pp. 21–36). New York: Plenum.

Taplin, J. R. (1971). Crisis theory: Critique and reformulation. *Community Mental Health Journal, 7,* 13–23.

Tead, O. (1935). *The art of leadership.* New York: Whittlesey House.

Tichy, N. M., & Devanna, M. A. (1986). *The transformational leader.* New York: Wiley.

Trice, H. M., & Beyer, J. M. (1986). Charisma and its routinization in two social movement organizations. *Research in Organizational Behavior, 8,* 113–164.

Viney, L. L. (1973). Coping with crisis and he transition from school to university. Paper read at the 25th World Mental Health Conference, Sydney, Australia.

Waldman, D. A., & Yammarino, F. J. (1999). CEO charismatic leadership: Levels-of-management and levels-of-analysis effects. *Academy of Management Review, 24,* 266–285.

Weber, M. (1947). *The theory of social and economic organizations* (A. M. Henderson & T. Parsons, Eds). New York: Free Press.

Weber, M. (1968). *Economy and society* (R. Guenther & C. Wittich, Eds). New York: Bedminster. (Original work published 1925).

Weierter, S. J. M. (1997). Who wants to play follow the leader? A theory of charismatic relationships based on routinized charisma and follower characteristics. *Leadership Quarterly, 8,* 171–193.

Williams, H. B. (1957). Some functions of communication in crisis beavior. *Human Organization,*
    16, 15–19.
Willner, A. R. (1984). *The spellbinders: Charismatic political leadership.* New Haven, CT: Yale
    University Press.
Yukl, G. (1999). An evaluation of conceptual weaknesses in transformational and charismatic
    leadership theories. *Leadership Quarterly, 10,* 285–305.

CHARISMATIC LEADERSHIP AT THE STRATEGIC LEVEL: TAKING A NEW LOOK AT UPPER ECHELONS THEORY

David A. Waldman and Mansour Javidan

ABSTRACT

The primary purpose of this chapter is to examine some old truths about leadership at the CEO level, and to summarize a new perspective based on charismatic leadership theory that could help cast light on this important area of strategic management. In so doing, we attempt to move charismatic leadership theory in some new directions by bridging micro- and macro-level conceptualizations. The upper echelons perspective from the strategic management literature is first summarized. We then identify problems in conceptualization and measurement that have served to limit the usefulness of this theoretical approach with regard to understanding the leadership role and effects of CEOs. We present two alternative new models that incorporate the constructs of strategic change, CEO charisma, and perceived environmental uncertainty. Data are also presented, suggesting mixed support for the models. Suggestions are made with regard to future quantitative and qualitative research.

INTRODUCTION

Do chief executive officers (CEOs) have a substantive effect on the overall performance of the firms they lead? Leadership on the part of CEOs has been

Transformational and Charismatic Leadership, Volume 2, pages 173–199.
ISBN: 0-7623-0962-8

recognized as an essential ingredient for the continual revitalization of organizations (Peters, 1987; Tichy & Devanna, 1986) and as critically important to the top management of large organizations (Katz & Kahn, 1978). However, proponents of external control and population ecology theories assert that CEO leadership is simply a perceptual or attributional phenomenon and relatively inconsequential to organizational performance (Hannan & Freeman, 1984; Meindl & Ehrlich 1987). Despite the claims of those representing various perspectives, little empirical evidence exists regarding the performance-stimulating potential of CEOs. The primary purpose of the present chapter is to examine some old truths about leadership at the CEO level and to summarize a new perspective that could help cast light on this important area of strategic management.

Another purpose of this chapter is to move charismatic leadership theory in some new directions by bridging micro- and macro-level conceptualizations. A number of authors have recently proclaimed the importance of cross-level research in the advancement of organizational theories (e.g. Heath & Sitkin, 2001; Kozlowski & Klein, 2000). Much of the current work on charismatic leadership theory and research deals specifically with individual, dyadic, and group-level phenomena. However, this theory can be readily applied to top-level executives and their effects across levels; indeed, some examples can be found in the literature (cf. Bass, 1985; Tichy & Devanna, 1986). A logical next step is to bridge charismatic leadership theory with relevant perspectives in the strategic management literature.

Leadership at the Strategic Level

Over the past 20 years, the field of strategic management has become increasingly concerned with top-level managers and their effects on strategy formulation and firm performance. For example, upper echelons theory rejects the purely deterministic view taken by external control proponents mentioned above and suggests that specific characteristics and leadership of top managers do indeed make a difference in strategy formulation and organizational performance (Hambrick & Mason, 1984; Staw & Sutton, 1993).

Upper echelons theory was first put forth in the work of Hambrick and Mason (1984), and since then, it has been widely cited and expanded somewhat under the rubric of strategic leadership (Canella & Monroe, 1997; Finkelstein & Hambrick, 1996). The essence of this theory is that strategic choices and change are determinants of firm performance. Further, strategic decisions clearly represent what Mischel (1977) referred to as a "weak situation" in that available stimuli are complex and ambiguous. In such situations, the choices of decision-makers can vary widely, thus allowing them to insert aspects of themselves (e.g. leadership qualities) into such choices (Finkelstein & Hambrick, 1996; House & Aditya, 1997).

In its earlier development, Hambrick and Mason (1984) focused on background and demographic characteristics of CEOs. These included such variables as age, functional track, formal education, and socioeconomic background. As an example, executive tenure is a potentially important driver of strategic choice and, ultimately, firm performance. While the literature on this topic is limited and fragmented, there seem to be a few general conclusions. Finkelstein and Hambrick (1990) found that the longer the executive tenure, the more the company's strategy was similar to industry norms. Others have shown that executives tend to make larger or more far-reaching strategic decisions earlier in their tenure (Gabarro, 1987), while becoming more committed to the status quo and risk-averse later in their tenure (Miller, 1991). Norburn and Birley (1988) showed that executive tenure is positively associated with company performance in stable industries but negatively associated in turbulent industries.

An executive's functional background is another potentially relevant variable. There is very little information on the impact of functional background, and the few studies available tend to be inconclusive. As Finkelstein and Hambrick stated:

> As yet, we know of no evidence of a generally advantageous functional profile for top executives. Instead, the external environment and the company's chosen strategy create a context in which certain functional orientations may have distinct but conditional benefits (1996, p. 99).

Findings concerning the effects of executive succession on firm performance are relevant to upper echelons theory. Based on a sample of 167 firms in 13 industries, Lieberson and O'Connor (1972) reported that executive succession (new presidents or board chairpersons) accounted for only 7.5% of the variance in concurrent net income. However, after controlling for the effect of economic variation among the industries and organizational size, succession accounted for 32% of net income variance when lagged over three years. Thomas (1988) reported that executive successions in 12 retailing companies over a 20-year period explained 51% of the variance in profit margins after controlling for industry effects. Bowman and Helfat (2001) recently summarized the results of prior executive succession research and concluded that succession does indeed affect firm profitability. However, they mistakenly refer to these results as "leadership effects" (Bowman & Helfat, 2001, p. 11). We contend that it is more accurate to attribute such findings to a change of individuals in the role of CEO – not leadership per se.

Finkelstein's (1992) research moved the upper echelons perspective closer to understanding the actual role of CEO leadership. He suggested that the upper echelons perspective should be expanded to take into account how managerial power affects the association between top managers and organizational outcomes. He pointed out how "power may emanate from a manager's personality" (1992, p. 510). This argument is in line with others who have claimed that simple demographic or background factors (e.g. age and functional track), or executive succession, do not go far enough in assessing relevant upper management characteristics. A consideration of personal or leadership characteristics is necessary for a more complete test of upper echelons theory (Hambrick & Mason, 1984; Hitt & Tyler, 1991).

It is interesting to note some common parallels of thinking in the literature. For example, a panel of financial experts concluded a few years ago that CEO ego was the primary force driving mergers and acquisitions in the USA (Marks & Mirvis, 1998). Hayward and Hambrick (1997) defined CEO ego in terms of four measures:

(1) recent performance of the acquiring firm;
(2) recent media praise of the acquiring firm's CEO;
(3) the ratio between the CEO's and other firm executives' pay; and
(4) a composite of the above three.

The authors reported that the larger the acquiring company's CEO's ego, the higher the premium paid for the target company. Given the fact that over $1.5 trillion were spent on mergers in this USA (Hamel, 2000), the "ego effect" can amount to billions of dollars.

Hage and Dewar (1973) reported that top management values influenced the degree of innovation taking place in their organizations. They showed that those CEOs who valued change spearheaded high levels of program change in their organizations. Miller and Droge (1986) showed that the CEO's personality affected the type of structure adopted by the organization. The greater the CEO's need for achievement, the greater the organization's structural centralization and the higher the level of formalization.

Bennis and O'Toole (2000, p. 171) recently warned boards of directors to not "hire the wrong CEO." Bennis and O'Toole criticized the self-defeating manner in which boards often select CEOs. Specifically, they often focus on such "hard" or factual information as experience, track record of increasing a firm's stock price or market share, and technical skills or functional background. However, Bennis and O'Toole also suggest that boards are missing the boat by dwelling on such variables, and their actions have lead to an increasing number of CEO failures and resulting turnover in recent years. Bennis and O'Toole recommend that boards focus more on:

(1) the demonstration of integrity;
(2) providing meaning;
(3) generating trust;
(4) communicating values;
(5) pushing people to meet challenging business goals; and
(6) galvanizing an organization (at all levels) toward a vision and change.

Perhaps it is not surprising that such variables are very much in line with charismatic leadership qualities and behaviors, as described below.

OLD PROBLEMS AND NEW POSSIBILITIES

At the outset, Hambrick and Mason (1984, p. 196) recognized the limitations of demographic and background variables in that they "may contain more noise than purer psychological measures." That is, psychological measures were seen as potentially more direct in terms of revealing the types of CEO values, beliefs, and behavioral inclinations relevant to strategy formation and performance, i.e. to fill in the "black box" created by an exclusive focus on demographic and background variables (Finkelstein & Hambrick, 1996, p. 46). As an example, a person's educational or functional background may only serve as indirect (and even "muddied") indicators of a leader's cognitive style or propensity for risk. For example, one could propose that marketers may have a somewhat greater propensity for risk as compared to people with a background in accounting. However, the validity of such extrapolations based on background data can only go so far. Indeed, Priem, Lyon and Dess (1999) were critical about the use of such data in strategic leadership research, raising questions about their meaning and construct validity. Boal and Hooijberg (2001, p. 523) went so far as to "call a moratorium on the use of demographic variables as surrogates for psychosocial constructs."

While potentially advantageous, Hambrick and Mason (1984) and Finkelstein and Hambrick (1996) viewed psychological measures as also problematic because of:

(1) lack of conceptual or theoretical clarity regarding the nature of appropriate psychological constructs;
(2) lack of observable measures; and
(3) reluctance on the part of top executives to participate in the assessment of such measures.

Table 1.   Upper Echelons Theory: Old Problems and New Possibilities.

Old Problems	New Possibilities
• Lack of clarity regarding psychological constructs and their usefulness	• Meso paradigms • Better understanding of the role of leadership in strategy implementation • Charismatic leadership theory • Better understanding of the potential role of such moderators as environmental uncertainty
• Lack of observable measures	• MLQ and other related measures
• CEO reluctance to participate in research	• Data elicited from lower-level managers or others • Qualitative research

Table 1 depicts the primary problems identified early on by upper echelon theorists, along with new possibilities and solutions that have developed over the past few decades that can address these problems.

Conceptual or Theoretical Clarity

First, we feel that emerging leadership theory may provide new possibilities for the upper echelons perspective. In the past, leadership theory has been seen as the domain of organizational behavior and micro-oriented perspectives. Indeed, a quick perusal of most organizational behavior textbooks shows how leadership processes are typically cast at the dyadic and small group levels. For example, leader-member-exchange (LMX) theory focuses on the role-making processes of followers and the resulting low- vs. high-quality relationships that can develop between a leader and respective followers (Graen & Uhl-Bien, 1995).

Newer frameworks that can be applied to leadership theory include meso-level paradigms that attempt to provide an integration of micro- and macro-organizational behavior (House, Rousseau & Thomas-Hunt, 1995). Concurrent with the development of meso-level paradigms, the field of leadership has witnessed an infusion of theory dealing with charismatic and inspirational leadership. Our definition of charismatic leadership is based largely on the work of House and colleagues (e.g. House & Shamir, 1993). Specifically, we define charisma as a *relationship* between an individual (leader) and one or more followers based on leader behaviors combined with favorable attributions on the part of followers. Key behaviors on the part of the leader include providing a sense of mission, articulating an inspirational vision based on powerful imagery and values, showing determination when accomplishing goals, and communicating high performance expectations. These characteristics also correspond to those described by Bass (1985) as being associated with charismatic leadership.

Favorable attributional effects on the part of followers include the generation of confidence in the leader, making followers feel good in his/her presence, and strong admiration or respect. It is very difficult to define charisma without simultaneously considering some of the consequences likely to result from the charismatic relationship. Indeed, numerous effects of charisma have been proposed in theory. For example, members identify with a charismatic leader's vision and with the organization to which that vision pertains, and thus, a high level of collective cohesion is likely to develop (Waldman & Yammarino, 1999).

Charisma represents another potentially key construct relevant to strategic leadership (Pawar & Eastman, 1997). Indeed, some recent theoretical perspectives have begun to link charisma to strategic leadership. For example, Finkelstein and Hambrick (1996) acknowledged that charismatic leadership could affect firm performance in one of several ways. First, the values of such leaders could influence strategic choices through their impact on their field of vision, their perception and interpretation of information, and their strategic decision-making. Furthermore, the day-to-day actions and behaviors on the part of charismatic executives could also affect organizational functioning and performance. Unfortunately, Finkelstein and Hambrick (1996) did not make potential linkages between charisma and performance especially clear, and indeed devoted little attention to such linkages in their consideration of strategic leadership.

Cannella and Monroe (1997) proposed that charisma and inspirational leadership are relevant not so much because of their effect on choice of strategies, but rather because of their effect on the implementation of the strategic decisions and change that top managers make. Hence, the work of Cannella and Monroe would extend the upper echelons perspective to take into account relationships with followers and how charismatic leadership can help develop such relationships to ensure the effective implementation of strategic decisions. Other related theory and some anecdotal evidence would suggest that followers support changes in technology, strategies, and structure introduced by top-level charismatic leaders, and may even sacrifice their self-interests in the interests of the organization (Lord & Maher, 1991; Tichy & Devanna, 1986).

In line with the meso-level paradigm, recent theoretical development by Waldman and Yammarino (1999) provides a cross-levels analysis to show how CEO charismatic leadership may work to stimulate cohesion in an organization by simultaneously affecting:

(1) close relationships (i.e. with the top management team); as well as
(2) more distant relationships (i.e. at levels further removed from the CEO).

Their thinking is in line with Finkelstein and Hambrick (1996), who proposed that CEO dominance or power would foster more homogeneity within a top management team. Although not specifically considered by Hambrick and Finkelstein, charisma is a likely source of CEO power and influence that might affect the selection of top management executives, as well as help to ultimately form a cohesive team.

The effect on more distant relationships is likely to be fostered by a cascading process whereby role modeling on the part of the CEO inspires followers across organizational levels, stimulates the display of leadership at lower levels, and gains commitment on the part of followers at all levels to implement strategic change. For example, the founding CEO of Disney, Walt Disney, has been recognized as an innovator and risk-taker. He encouraged others at Disney at all levels to follow his lead by experimenting with new and different ideas themselves. His enthusiasm for creativity proved to be contagious, inspiring commitment and cohesion among his followers (Hughes, Ginnett & Curphy, 1996).

Jack Welch of General Electric provides another example of a CEO who has attempted to reach out as a role model to employees at much lower organizational levels. Employees who do not directly witness such leadership can still be affected by the "social contagion" processes that are likely to ensue (Gardner & Avolio, 1998, p. 52). As noted by Klein and House (1995, p. 189), "cinder" subordinates can foster social contagion by igniting passion for a group or organization's identity and mission in fellow subordinates.

Of course, cohesion can be fostered by the power of a CEO to select and retain top management team members who fit the cultural values and strategies that the CEO seeks to attain. The attraction, selection, and attrition cycle described by Schneider (1987) provides an appropriate heuristic for considering how homogeneous charisma may develop. This cycle suggests that homogeneity is created when followers are attracted to the CEO, are selected specifically by the CEO, could have been released or fired by the CEO but were not, and had the option of leaving the organization but chose not to do so.

Environmental uncertainty is another construct that may help to add conceptual clarity to how charisma may be relevant at the strategic level.

Finkelstein (1992) argued that the ability of top managers to overcome constraints and to exercise power stems from the existence of environmental uncertainty, a condition similar to the notion of weak situation described earlier (Mischel, 1977). He listed several sources from the task environment that can create uncertainty for an organization, such as its customers, suppliers, and competitors. Finkelstein (1992) proposed that various sources of executive power, e.g. expert power, may be especially important in relation to organizational outcomes when a firm is confronted with a high degree of uncertainty from its environment. Waldman and Yammarino (1999) took this thinking one step further and proposed that *perceived* environmental uncertainty on the part of organizational members would serve as a moderator between CEO charisma and performance.

The concept of environmental uncertainty was discussed by Javidan (1984) and Milliken (1987). Although both authors considered how uncertainty has been used as an objective characterization of an environment, they argued for its use as a perceptual phenomenon. According to Javidan (1984) and Milliken (1987), uncertainty can be defined in terms of an individual's perceived inability to understand the direction in which an environment might be changing, the potential impact of those changes on that individual's organization, and whether or not particular responses to the environment might be successful.

Environments perceived as highly uncertain will likely be viewed as very risky, whereby a few erroneous decisions could result in severe trouble, and possibly risk the survival of the organization. Obviously, an environment perceived in such a manner would tend to generate a high degree of concern, stress, and lack of assuredness on the part of an organization's managers and employees. Under such conditions, CEOs are likely to have more latitude of discretion and are expected to make decisions and take actions to reduce the perceived environmental risks for the organization and its members. As a weak situation, such conditions engender receptivity to change efforts (Mischel, 1977; Pawar & Eastman, 1997). Consequently, CEOs will most likely feel less inhibited by existing bureaucratic structures or political circumstances in their organizations.

A charismatic relationship between the CEO and followers will theoretically allay follower concerns and generate confidence. The assuredness, confidence, and vision of the leader are a source of psychological comfort for the followers, thus reducing their stress by showing how uncertainty can be turned into a vision of opportunity and success (Bass, 1985). We should note that the importance of perceived environmental uncertainty in the creation of charismatic effects is in line with sociological perspectives that emphasize the relevance of crisis situations in the manifestation of charisma and its effects (Beyer & Browning, 1999).

In sum, these arguments begin to provide conceptual and theoretical clarity regarding the nature of psychological constructs that could help to expand the upper echelons perspective. Specifically, we have identified charisma and perceived environmental uncertainty as relevant constructs. We now turn our attention to growing empirical evidence in an attempt to address other potential problems mentioned above.

Empirical Evidence

The meta-analytic work of Lowe, Kroeck, and Sivasubramaniam (1996) provides support for the performance-stimulating potential of charisma at lower management levels. However, their findings cannot be readily generalized to the performance of CEOs of large firms. Nevertheless, there is growing evidence that charismatic leadership may indeed be relevant at upper echelons. For example, Javidan and Datmalchian (1995) showed the importance of charismatic leadership in senior ranks from the perspective of their direct reports. Agle and Sonnenfeld (1994) reported positive relationships between CEO charisma and objective (e.g. stock returns) organizational performance. In a comprehensive study of U.S. presidents, House, Spangler and Woycke (1991) reported that charismatic leadership was positively associated with five measures of presidential performance related to economic, social, and international arenas.

More recently, Waldman, Ramirez, House and Puranam (2001) used a sample of Fortune 500 firms across a number of industries to demonstrate the moderating effect of perceived environmental uncertainty (as described above) on the relationship between CEO charisma and firm net profit margin. Their research provides a demonstration of how the lack of observable measures problem originally identified by Hambrick and Mason (1984) may now be overcome. For example, they showed how charisma could be observed and measured using the Multifactor Leadership Questionnaire (Bass, 1985; Bass & Avolio, 1990).

Further, the issue of the reluctance of CEOs to participate became somewhat irrelevant since Waldman et al. (2001) used senior managers immediately below the level of CEO as their survey respondents. Indeed, self-perceptions of charisma on the part of CEOs themselves are likely to be biased or over-inflated. In contrast, senior managers can provide a more objective view, especially when assured of anonymity. Moreover, they are the most relevant recipients of a CEO's leadership since a CEO's ability to effectively implement a strategic vision could be affected by the degree to which senior managers agree with, and provide support for, that vision (Robbins & Duncan, 1988). For research purposes, senior managers can be readily identified and contacted through the use of such directories as *Disclosure*.

A Missing Link: Strategic Change

Early on in the development of transformational and charismatic leadership theories, the idea of introducing change seemed to run hand in hand with the display of such leadership (Bass, 1985; House, 1977). However, as noted by House and Aditya (1997), little empirical evidence exists with regard to the connection between charismatic leadership and the introduction of change. Yet strategic change is an obviously important element of any theory of strategic leadership, although its precise role remains unclear. As we will demonstrate later, we agree with upper echelon theorists that strategic change is best considered as an independent or mediator variable (Finkelstein & Hambrick, 1996; Hambrick & Mason, 1984). However, we also acknowledge more recent conceptualizations of strategic change as a dependent variable in its own right (Boal & Hooijberg, 2001).

Firms are different in the strategies that they pursue. Contrary to the premises of neoclassical theory, firms are not mathematical abstractions (Hunt, 2000). Some firms are very small, catering to a limited market. Others are so large that their total revenues are larger than some countries' GDP. Some firms sell hundreds of products; some are highly integrated, whereas others are more like networks of alliances. Some firms are extremely profitable, whereas others suffer through regular losses.

Companies are different largely because they pursue different strategies. Strategy is the pursuit of a sustainable competitive advantage that would ensure superior financial performance and long-term survival (Hunt, 2000). Corporations are often engaged in a dynamic competitive market (Markides, 2000). They are in a continuing struggle to recruit and exploit heterogeneous resources to capture advantageous market positions (Barney, 1991; Hunt, 2000). Strategy can also be defined as a continuous process of taking advantage of opportunities and avoiding threats created by an uncertain business environment (Cravens, LaForge & Ingram, 1990), and as a set of behaviors put forth by an organization to establish a transient niche in its environment (Mintzberg, 1978). But firms do not just react passively to their respective industries. They anticipate potential market segments, envision new offerings to new market segments, and plan for developing the required resources to succeed in new arenas (Hunt, 2000), i.e. they plan for strategic change.

The competition facing firms is dynamic in nature. Firms possessing heterogeneous and inimitable resources make strategic choices and changes that can impact their respective industries and may enhance their own financial performance (Barney, 1991; Hunt, 2000). Success in a dynamic competitive system requires organizational ability to learn, adapt, and change (Jick, 1993). It requires strategic decisions and change that help navigate the firm in increasingly turbulent environments.

An organization's CEO is the most visible and pertinent strategic manager, responsible for guiding both the formulation and implementation of strategies (Thompson & Strickland, 1992). Typically, strategic decisions or actions cannot be accomplished without the CEO's endorsement. An organization's CEO may also spearhead strategic initiatives or changes. Hambrick and Finkelstein (1987) maintained that top-level executives have a substantial effect on the formation of organizational strategies and on strategic changes, which, in turn, affect subsequent organizational performance.

Case studies of General Electric illustrate how CEO Jack Welch was able to substantially alter the product lines and markets of the firm through persistent strategies of divestiture, investment, acquisition, and internal corporate renewal efforts (Aguilar & Hamermesh, 1981; Aguilar, Hamermesh & Brainard, 1985). These studies show that Welch's effects on the performance of General Electric were due largely to the strategic changes that he introduced.

More rigorous large-scale studies have focused on the drivers of firm profitability. As stated earlier, organizations are in pursuit of superior financial performance. If, as claimed by proponents of the neoclassical theory and population ecology, management has little impact, and industry is the determining factor (Bain, 1956; Hannan & Freeman, 1984), one would expect industry to have the largest predictive power in firm performance and firm effect to be minimal. But the evidence seems to contradict this assertion. Rumelt (1991) showed that business unit effects explained 44% of the variance in return on assets, compared to 8% by industry effects. Roquebert, Phillips, and Westfall (1996) found business unit effects to be 37% vs. 10% for industry effect. Other more recent studies show the business unit effect to approximate 30% (Mauri & Michaels, 1998; McGahan & Porter, 1997).

These findings lead to the conclusion that firms are not helpless prisoners in their industries (Di Maggio & Powell, 1983). They are capable of learning, adapting, and changing to ensure a continuing, advantageous market position. Further, CEOs and senior executives are the key decision-makers in corporations. They are entrusted by shareholders with the authority to make the types of strategic choices that would ensure the firm's long-term success (Finkelstein & Hambrick, 1996). Thus, the above evidence for firm and business unit effect can be interpreted as evidence that organizational outcomes may be due to strategic changes introduced by senior leadership. Or, as argued recently by Bowman and Helfat (2001), corporate strategy does matter. Next we will describe a recent study that attempts to delineate linkages between strategic change, CEO charismatic leadership, and firm performance.

Some Recent Research

We conducted a study involving a total of 112 U.S. and Canadian firms. The primary purpose of the study was to replicate and go beyond the work of Waldman et al. (2001) by incorporating the extent of strategic change throughout the tenure of a CEO. This would allow for a consideration of strategic change, a construct that, as noted above, has had an important presence in the strategic management literature.

In order to be considered for inclusion in the sample, a firm had to conform to three criteria:

(1) net sales greater than one billion dollars;
(2) the CEO had at least two years of tenure; and
(3) at least six individuals per firm at the VP, senior VP, or general manager level who could be identified in a corporate directory.

The first criterion was based on the notion that it would be easier to obtain performance data for larger firms. The CEO tenure criterion was used in order to allow the CEO time to implement strategic change and demonstrate charismatic leadership. The third criterion was necessary in an attempt to obtain input from multiple managers per firm allowing for non-response to the survey.

Subsequently, after meeting the above criteria, firms were randomly chosen from a potential pool of 929 U.S. and 188 Canadian firms available on *Disclosure* (a database that can be used to obtain information about large firms). This resulted in a total of 95 U.S. and 55 Canadian firms targeted for participation. These firms represented a wide range of industries such as telecommunications, retailing, utilities, food processing, banking, and manufacturing (e.g. automotive). Nearly twice as many American firms were solicited because there was a greater proportion of American firms that met the aforementioned criteria. The names and addresses of 900 managers from these firms were obtained from corporate directories including *Disclosure*, the *Financial Post Directory of Directors*, and the *Million Dollar Directory: America's Leading Public & Private Companies*. These managers represented a broad spectrum of areas including general management, marketing, finance, accounting, human resources, strategic planning, engineering, and legal.

Survey administration occurred at the end of 1992. After a second mailing, usable surveys were obtained from a total of 234 respondents. Non-respondents included 52 individuals who had either retired, were away on business, no longer were with the firm, or were unable to be located. They also included those who returned their surveys but had tampered with ID numbers (to identify respective firms), thus making their surveys not usable for analytic purposes. Without including such individuals in the original targeted sample, the effective response rate is approximately 28%. Given the high level of these managers in their respective organizations, such a response rate can be considered appropriate and acceptable.

The 234 respondents represented a total of 112 firms. Despite attempts to obtain at least two managers per firm, 41 of the 234 respondents were the sole representatives of their firms. The other respondents represented 71 firms (between two and six respondents per firm). Forty-two of these firms were U.S.-based, and 29 were Canadian. For the analyses reported below, we chose to use only these 71 firms because of the enhanced validity of using multiple respondent firms (cf. Waldman et al., 2001). In addition, for analyses involving our dependent variable, net profit margin, the sample was further reduced to 51 because of missing data.

Measures
Three primary variables were tapped in the survey process. First, we assessed perceptions of the extent of strategic change since the firm's current CEO had been in office. Specifically, we asked respondents "since the current CEO has been in office, to what extent has your firm introduced changes in the following areas?" Seven areas were chosen to be representative of common targets of strategic change (cf. Fry & Killing, 1986; Kryzanowski, Gandhi & Gitman, 1982; Mintzberg, 1978; Pitts & Hopkins, 1982). The seven areas included:

(1) product focus;
(2) organizational structure;
(3) financial structure;
(4) internal organizational processes/programs;
(5) executive personnel;
(6) divestments; and
(7) acquisitions.

Ratings were on a five-point scale with anchors ranging from "very small extent" to "very large extent". The seven areas were summed and averaged to form a composite measure of strategic change displaying an alpha of 0.73.

Second, we assessed charismatic leadership of the firm's CEO using nine items from the Multifactor Leadership Questionnaire (Bass & Avolio, 1990). Sample items included: "provides a vision of what lies ahead" and "I am ready to trust him/her to overcome any obstacle". Each participant was asked to think about the CEO of his/her respective firm, and then to rate that individual on each item on a five-point scale with anchors ranging from "not at all" to "frequently, if not always". Each respondent was asked to provide the name of the CEO of that person's firm to ensure that respondents from a respective firm rated the same individual. This precaution was necessary because of the possibility of CEO turnover at or about the time of the survey. The nine items were summed and averaged to form an overall measure of charismatic leadership. The alpha coefficient for this measure was 0.90.

We also included a four-item measure of intellectual stimulation. Sample items included "his/her ideas have made me reconsider some of my own ideas which I had never questioned before" and "suggests ways to get at the heart of complex problems". Intellectual stimulation represents a factor of the greater construct of transformational leadership that includes charismatic leadership at its core (Bass, 1985). Although Lowe et al. (1996) have shown charisma to account for the lion's share of variance in outcomes, we felt it appropriate to include intellectual stimulation as a point of comparison since, in addition to charisma, Boal and Hooijberg (2001) emphasized the intellectual or cognitive aspects of strategic leadership. We summed and averaged the four items to form an overall measure of intellectual stimulation with an alpha coefficient of 0.86.

Third, we assessed perceived environmental uncertainty using 10 items based on the work of Khandwalla (1976, pp. 641–643) and Miles and Snow (1978). The Khandwalla portion of the measure (five items) is similar to that used by Singh (1986), which he labeled environmental turbulence. Respondents were asked to characterize the general external environment within which their respective firms operate, taking into account economic, social, political, and technological factors. A sample item was "very risky, one false step can mean the firm's undoing." The latter five items of the measure were adapted from Miles and Snow (1978) with each item more specific to either market, governmental, or geographic political considerations. A sample item is "your concern for customers' demands for existing and/or new products has become more stable and predictable (reverse-coded)". Ratings were on a 5-point scale with anchors ranging from "strongly disagree" to "strongly agree". The 10 items were summed and averaged to form a composite measure with an alpha of 0.69.

Tests were conducted to determine the appropriateness of aggregating strategic change, charisma, intellectual stimulation, and perceived environmental uncertainty scores provided by respondents of respective firms. First, between-firm differences were significant for strategic change ($F = 1.84$, $p < 0.01$) and charisma ($F = 1.83$, $p < 0.01$), but were not significant for either intellectual stimulation ($F = 1.17$, $p > 0.05$) or perceived environmental uncertainty ($F = 1.16$, $p > 0.05$). Second, we computed inter-rater reliability coefficients (rwg) to determine the extent to which rater perceptions converged in a given firm for the items composing each measure (James, Demaree & Wolf, 1984). The average rwg across firms for strategic change, charisma, intellectual stimulation, and perceived environmental uncertainty were 0.86, 0.95, 0.80, and 0.93, respectively, suggesting adequate within-firm agreement on each of these variables. In total, these tests provide support for combining respondents' perceptions of strategic change and charisma to produce averaged, aggregated scores for respective firms. However, the evidence was more mixed for intellectual stimulation and perceived environmental uncertainty because of the lack of significant between-firm differences. Despite this evidence, we proceeded to combine respondents' scores on intellectual stimulation and perceived environmental uncertainty to produce averaged, aggregated scores. Nevertheless, as noted below, caution may need to be taken in interpreting results based on these two variables.

In line with the work of Waldman et al. (2001), we chose to measure firm performance using net profit margin (NPM). Data were obtained from *Research Insights*. NPM is an accounting-based measure of performance that was also used by Waldman et al. (2001). It is derived by dividing net income by net sales. As such, it represents a measure of performance based upon current data, as opposed to more historically based measures such as return on equity.

Measures of firm performance are known to vary by industry. This is due partly to higher rates of return in certain industries, and because of different industry-specific accounting practices (Venkatraman & Ramanujam, 1986). Therefore, we adjusted NPM for industry averages.

We also measured adjusted NPM across the five years following survey administration, i.e. 1993–1997. As explained by Youndt, Snell, Dean, and Lepak (1996), averaging a performance measure across time periods helps guard against random fluctuations and anomalies in the data. Thus, our 5-year time frame helped to provide a reliable assessment of performance, subsequent to the measurement of strategic change, leadership, and environmental uncertainty. In addition, Lord and Maher (1991) proposed that at least with regard to charismatic leadership, performance linkages should be viewed on a long-term basis. In other words, the results of strategic change and charismatic leadership may not be felt immediately and indeed, may take some years to develop. Theoretically, long-term effects should be expected since the charismatic CEO leader emphasizes an optimistic vision of what lies ahead for an organization, rather than simply focusing on the status quo.

Alternative Models
We used the two alternative models that are depicted in Fig. 1 as a basis for our analyses. Model A represents the strategic leadership theory articulated above. Specifically, in line with the work of Cannella and Monroe (1997), we suggest in Model A that strategic change will interact with charismatic leadership in the prediction of firm performance. In short, charismatic leadership is necessary to ensure the effective implementation of strategic decisions, especially those involving large-scale changes. Model A is also in line with the recent work of Waldman and colleagues (Waldman et al., 2001; Waldman & Yammarino,

Model A:

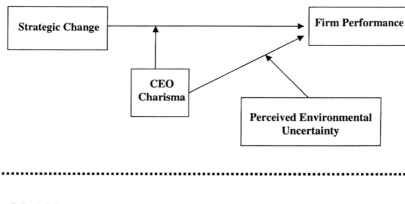

Model B:

Fig. 1. Alternative Models of Charismatic Leadership at the Strategic Level.

1999) suggesting that charisma will interact with perceived environmental uncertainty in the prediction of firm performance. Specifically, charisma will be most highly associated with performance when the environment is viewed as highly uncertain.

Model B represents an alternative explanation. This explanation follows in part from the work of Meindl and Ehrlich (1987), who suggest that leadership is simply a perceptual or attributional phenomenon and relatively inconsequential to organizational performance. That is, there is a perceptual tendency to attribute good (or poor) organizational performance to the actions of top-level leaders when, in reality, such performance is more likely due to a myriad of technological or environmental factors. Meindl and Ehrlich (1987) referred to this perceptual tendency as romanticized leadership in that leadership is more illusionary than real. Taking the attributional process one step further, as shown in Model B, we expect that the accomplishment of large-scale strategic change during the tenure of a CEO may cause perceptions or attributions on the part of followers that the leader is charismatic. In other words, accomplishment of strategic change will foster strong admiration and other perceptions indicative of active, charismatic leadership.

In contrast to the conclusions of Meindl and Ehrlich (1987), we further suggest in Model B that the attribution of charisma may actually, in turn, give a leader more subsequent, potential influence over organizational performance. In other words, CEO leadership really does matter and is not merely a romanticized illusion. Stated another way, charismatic attributions and behaviors may cause followers to collectively pursue the vision and accompanying performance goals and strategies generated by a CEO leader. This thinking is also in line with the work of Bowman and Helfat (2001), who proposed that corporate strategy may have more of an indirect, rather than direct, influence over firm profitability. We further note that the lack of interaction with environmental uncertainty depicted in Model B follows from psychologically oriented theories that treat crisis (and its accompanying uncertainty) as a facilitating but not necessary condition of charismatic effects (Conger & Kanungo, 1988; Shamir, House & Arthur, 1993).

Results and Discussion
Means, standard deviations, and correlations among study variables are shown in Table 2. Several findings are of interest. First, as was the case in the Waldman et al. (2001) study, the mean value for charisma is high (i.e. 4.36 on a five-point scale) suggesting leniency in charismatic leadership items, although the mean score for intellectual stimulation is somewhat lower (i.e. 3.28 on a five-point scale).

Table 2. Descriptive Statistics and Correlations.

Variables	M	SD	1	2	3	4	5	6	7	8	9
1. Country	1.59	0.50	–								
2. Total assets	18.9	34.7	-0.08	–							
3. CEO tenure (prior to survey)	6.82	5.34	0.28*	-0.12	–						
4. CEO tenure (performance period)	3.70	1.66	0.16	-0.21	0.07	–					
5. Strategic change	3.29	0.56	0.06	-0.23$^+$	0.14	0.06	–				
6. CEO charisma	4.36	0.45	0.12	0.08	-0.14	0.21	0.38**	–			
7. Intellectual stimulation	3.28	0.56	-0.12	0.04	-0.04	0.04	0.15	0.44**	–		
8. Environmental uncertainty	3.48	0.34	0.02	0.04	-0.07	0.00	0.42**	0.25*	0.22$^+$	–	
9. Net profit margin	0.05	0.03	0.29*	0.19	-0.04	0.23$^+$	-0.20	0.43**	0.22$^+$	0.02	–

$^+$ $p < 0.10$; * $p < 0.05$; ** $p < 0.01$

Note: Country is coded as 1 = Canada, and 2 = USA. Total assets is in billions of dollars. CEO tenure (prior to survey) reflects the number of years an individual had been CEO at his/her respective firm in 1992, the time of the survey. CEO tenure during the performance period reflects the number of years that the CEO remained in the firm as CEO during the 5-year performance period following survey administration. Net profit margin is corrected for industry averages. $n = 71$ firms for all variables with the exception of net profit margin, for which data were available for 51 firms.

Second, several control variables are shown in Table 2 including country (i.e. Canada vs. the U.S.), total assets of the firm, CEO tenure prior to the survey, and CEO tenure during the 5-year performance period following survey administration. Regarding the last variable, it can be argued that despite our proposed long-term effects of charismatic leadership measured at a point in time (e.g. at the time of the survey), it is necessary to control for CEO tenure during the actual performance period. Table 2 reveals significant relationships between country and CEO tenure during the performance period and corrected NPM.

Third, charisma is significantly correlated with NPM ($r = 0.43$, $p < 0.01$), intellectual stimulation is only marginally correlated with NPM ($r = 0.22$, $p < 0.1$), and strategic change is not significantly correlated with NPM ($r = -0.20$, $p > 0.05$). Fourth, strategic change is significantly correlated with charisma ($r = 0.38$, $p < 0.01$). While it could be argued that this finding is due largely to common-source bias, it is interesting to note the contrast with the lack of relationship between strategic change and intellectual stimulation ($r = 0.15$, $p > 0.05$). In short, as shown in Model B, strategic change appears to be associated uniquely with charisma, rather than intellectual stimulation. However, we must caution that such findings may represent an artifact of the lack of between-firm differences with regard to intellectual stimulation.

We also conducted three moderator regression analyses. In each of these analyses, the four control variables mentioned above were entered in the initial regression step. In the first analysis, we found no main effect of strategic change, and no interaction of strategic change and charisma, in the prediction of NPM. In a second analysis, the results of which are shown in Table 3, charisma added significant variance to the prediction of NPM in the second regression step. Environmental uncertainty and the interaction of charisma and uncertainty failed to add additional significant variance in subsequent regression steps. In a final regression analysis, intellectual stimulation was substituted for charisma. The results revealed no additional variance accounted for by intellectual stimulation beyond the control variables in the prediction of NPM, and there was no additional variance added by the interaction of intellectual stimulation and environmental uncertainty. Again, the lack of between-firm differences for intellectual stimulation may be coming into play.

In sum, the results of the correlational and regression analyses showed no support for the interactional predictions of Model A of Fig. 1. Cannella and Monroe (1997) suggested that charismatic relationships with followers could help ensure the effective implementation of strategic decisions initiated by top executives. In other words, charisma should interact with strategic change in the prediction of firm performance. However, we found no such interaction.

Table 3. Hierarchical Regression Analysis with CEO Charisma in the Prediction of Corrected Net Profit Margin.

Predictor Variables	Step 1	Step 2	Step 3	Step 4
Country[1]	0.29*	0.25+	0.27+	0.24
Total Assets	0.18	0.15	0.15	0.18
Overall CEO tenure	−0.11	−0.04	−0.04	0.01
CEO tenure during the study	0.24	0.17	0.14	0.13
		0.31*	0.38*	−1.42
Environmental Uncertainty			−0.17	−1.87
Charisma × Uncertainty				2.94
ΔR^2		0.09	0.02	0.03
Total R^2	0.19+	0.28*	0.30*	0.33*
ΔF		4.53*	1.26	1.40

[1] Standardized regression coefficients are shown.
+ $p < 0.10$; * $p < 0.05$; ** $p < 0.01$.
Note: $n = 51$ firms.

Perhaps future research will need to examine the precise nature of strategic change, rather than a more global measure of degree of change.

More favorable evidence was found in support of Model B. Specifically, strategic change appears to be predictive of charisma, which is in turn predictive of firm performance. We should note that the main effect of charisma is in line with the results of Agle and Sonnenfeld (1994), but it runs counter to the results of Waldman et al. (2001), who found an interaction between charisma and environmental uncertainty.

In attempting to make sense of these discrepant results, the recent insights of Rousseau and Fried (2001) may be helpful. Specifically, they point to the need to contextualize organizational research to better understand potential differences in the findings between studies. Two issues raised by Rousseau and Fried (2001) may be particularly relevant to understanding why the present findings differ from those of Waldman et al. (2001). First, range restriction is a likely reason for inconsistencies across studies. As shown in Table 2, the standard deviation of perceived environmental uncertainty is quite low (i.e, 0.34 on a five-point scale) and certainly lower than the comparable variable in the Waldman et al. (2001) study (i.e. 0.53 on a five-point scale). Indeed, this restriction of range is a likely contributor to the lack of between-firm differences noted above.

Second, because of alternative interpretations of a study's constructs, the differing nature of respondents can affect results. Survey respondents in the Waldman et al. study largely had financial backgrounds. However, only 17% of the present respondents (as revealed on return surveys) had such functional backgrounds. In sum, these contextual differences could have contributed to the present findings and should certainly be carefully considered in future research.

Research Recommendations and Conclusions

Our discussion and research findings suggest that upper echelons theory can and should be extended beyond simple demographic characteristics to encompass such personal qualities as charismatic leadership. The connection between top executives and firm outcomes may depend to a large extent on the executives' charismatic leadership.

With regard to future quantitative research, we have three recommendations. First, as noted above, perceived uncertainty has received mixed support to date as a moderator of charisma and firm performance. Uncertainty may serve as just one proxy for the larger construct of managerial discretion. Based on ratings by industry analysts, Finkelstein and Hambrick (1996) classified a number of industries in terms of the potential discretion that might be shown by CEOs regarding the initiation of change and display of strategic leadership. It might be interesting to determine whether CEO charismatic leadership affects performance outcomes most positively in industries classified as high in terms of discretion. Second, we recommend that survey measures used in strategic leadership research be redesigned or administered in such a way as to maximize between-firm variance and reduce leniency. Third, we recommend a broader array of performance outcome measures. NPM is based on current sales and, thus, can be considered a measure focused on present operational activities. Other accounting measures such as return on equity, which emphasizes the return on a firm's historical buildup of equity, might also be incorporated into strategic leadership research. Moreover, we recommend the use of market-based measures of shareholder return (e.g. Jensen & Murphy, 1990).

In addition to quantitative research, perhaps qualitative efforts could take a closer look at some of the complexities surrounding the formation of charisma and environmental uncertainty perceptions at the strategic level, as well as their potential interaction in the prediction of performance. Specifically, such research might examine why senior managers may view an environment as uncertain, and how CEO charismatic leadership is linked to the implementation of strategic change. It could be that a reinforcing process occurs whereby charismatic tendencies foster the pursuit of strategic change on the part of a CEO that, in turn, leads to greater attributions of charisma on the part of followers. Research directed toward these issues could help explain the results obtained in quantitative studies. It is interesting to note how systematic, qualitative studies of top management teams and CEOs have grown in number over the past 15 years. For example, Eisenhardt (1989) performed a multiple case study of the microcomputer industry and showed how decision-making and leadership styles of CEOs could be readily identified.

In sum, through a combination of quantitative and qualitative research, we believe that the field is now in a position to explore more fully the upper echelons perspective. Such research will have the added benefit of bringing together micro- and macro-perspectives in an attempt to better understand the antecedents and effects of charismatic leadership on organizations. We also believe that the time has come for multidisciplinary research and theory development in the field of leadership. This chapter is an attempt to move in that direction by providing specific theoretical linkages with regard to charismatic leadership as applied in the organizational behavior and strategic management domains.

REFERENCES

Agle, B. R., & Sonnenfeld, J. A. (1994). Charismatic chief executive officers: Are they more effective? An empirical test of charismatic leadership theory. In: D. P. Moore (Ed.), *Academy of Management Best Papers Proceedings* (pp. 2–6).

Aguilar, F. J., & Hammermesh, R. G. (1981). *General Electric: Strategic position – 1981*. Cambridge, MA: Publishing Division, Harvard Business School.

Aguilar, F. J., Hammermesh, R. G., & Brainard, C. (1985). *General Electric – 1984*. Cambridge, MA: Publishing Division, Harvard Business School.

Bain, J. S. (1956). *Barriers to new competition*. Cambridge: Harvard University Press.

Barney, J. (1991). Firm resources and sustained competitive advantage. *Journal of Management, 17*, 99–120

Bass, B. M. (1985). *Leadership and performance beyond expectations*. New York: Free Press.

Bass, B. M., & Avolio, B. J. (1990). *The Multifactor Leadership Questionnaire*. Palo Alto, CA: Consulting Psychologists Press.

Bennis, W., & O'Toole, J. (2000, May-June). Don't hire the wrong CEO. *Harvard Business Review, 78*, 171–176.

Beyer, J. M., & Browning, L. D. (1999). Transforming an industry in crisis: Charisma, routinization, and supportive cultural leadership. *Leadership Quarterly, 10*, 483–520.

Boal, K. B., & Hooijberg, R. (2001). Strategic leadership research: Moving on. *Leadership Quarterly, 11*, 515–549.

Bowman, E. H., & Helfat, C. E. (2001). Does corporate strategy matter? *Strategic Management Journal, 22*, 1–23.

Canella, A. A. Jr., & Monroe, M. J. (1997). Contrasting perspectives on strategic leaders: Toward a more realistic view of top managers. *Journal of Management, 23*, 213–237.

Conger, J. A., & Kanungo, R. (1988). *Charismatic leadership in organizations*. Thousand Oaks, CA: Sage Publications.

Cravens, D. W., LaForge, R. W., & Ingram, T. N. (1990). Sales strategy: Charting a new course in turbulent markets. *Business, 40*, 3–9.

Dimaggio, P. & Powell, W. W. (1983). The iron cage revisited: Institutional isomorphism and collective rationality in organizational fields. *American Sociological Review, 48*, 147–160.

Eisenhardt, K. M. (1989). Making fast strategic decisions in high-velocity environments. *Academy of Management Journal, 32*, 543–576.

Finkelstein, S. (1992). Power in top management teams: Dimensions, measurement, and validation. *Academy of Management Journal, 35*, 505–538.

Finkelstein, S., & Hambrick, D. C. (1990). Top management team tenure and organizational outcomes: The moderating role of managerial discretion. *Administrative Science Quarterly, 35*, 484–503.

Finkelstein, S., & Hambrick, D. C. (1996). *Strategic leadership: Top executives and their effects*. Minneapolis/St. Paul: West Publishing Company.

Fry, J. N., & Killing, J. P. (1986). *Strategic analysis and action*. Scarborough, Ontario: Prentice-Hall Canada.

Gabarro, J. J. (1987). *The dynamics of taking charge*. Boston: Harvard Business School Press.

Gardner, W. L., & Avolio, B. J. (1998). The charismatic relationship: A dramaturgical perspective. *Academy of Management Review, 23*, 32–58.

Graen, G. B, & Uhl-Bien, M. (1995). Relationship-based approach to leadership: Development of leader-member-exchange (LMX) theory over 25 years: Applying a multi-level multi-domain perspective. *Leadership Quarterly, 6*, 219–247.

Hage, J., & Dewar, R. (1973). Elite values vs. organization structure in predicting innovations. *Administrative Science Quarterly, 18*, 279–290.

Hambrick, D. C., & Finkelstein, S. (1987). Managerial discretion: A bridge between polar views of organizational discretion. *Research in Organizational Behavior, 9*, 369–406.

Hambrick, D. C., & Mason, P. A. (1984). Upper echelons: The organization as a reflection of its top managers. *Academy of Management Review, 9*, 193–206.

Hamel, G. (2000). *Leading the revolution*. Boston: Harvard Business School Press.

Hannan, M., & Freeman, J. (1984). Structural inertia and organizational change. *American Sociological Review, 49*, 149–164.

Hayward, L. A., & Hambrick, D. C. (1997). Explaining the premiums paid for large acquisitions: Evidence of CEO hubris. *Administrative Science Quarterly, 42*, 103–127.

Heath, C., & Sitkin, S. B. (2001). Big-B vs. big-O: What is organizational about organizational behavior? *Journal of Organizational Behavior, 22*, 43–58.

Hitt, M. A., & Tyler, B. B. (1991). Strategic decision models: Integrating different perspectives. *Strategic Management Journal, 12*, 327–351.

House, R. J. (1977). A 1976 theory of charismatic leadership. In: J. G. Hunt & L. Larson (Eds), *Leadership: The Cutting Edge* (pp. 189–207). Carbondale, IL: Southern Illinois University Press.

House, R. J., & Aditya, R. (1997). The social scientific study of leadership: Quo vadis? *Journal of Management, 23*, 409–474.

House, R. J., Rousseau, D. M., & Thomas-Hunt, M. (1995). The meso paradigm: A framework for the integration of micro and macro organizational behavior. *Research in Organizational Behavior, 17*, 71–114.

House, R. J., & Shamir, B. (1993). Toward an integration of transformational, charismatic and visionary theories of leadership. In: M. Chemmers & R. Ayman (Eds), *Leadership: Perspectives and research directions* (pp. 81–107). New York: Academic Press.

House, R. J., Spangler, W. D., & Woycke, J. (1991). Personality and charisma in the U.S. presidency: A psychological theory of leader effectiveness. *Administrative Science Quarterly, 36*, 364–396.

Hughes, R. L., Ginnett, R. C., & Curphy, G. J. (1996). *Leadership: Enhancing the lessons of experience*. Boston: Irwin/McGraw-Hill.

Hunt, S. (2000). *A general theory of competition*. Thousand Oaks, CA: Sage.

James, L. R., Demaree, R. G., & Wolf, G. (1984). Estimating within-group interrater reliability with and without response bias. *Journal of Applied Psychology, 69*, 85–98.

Javidan. M. (1984). The impact of environment uncertainty on long-range planning practices of the U.S. savings and loan industry. *Strategic Management Journal, 5*, 381–393.

Javidan, M., & Dastmalchian, A. (1993). Assessing senior executives: A study of the impact of context on their roles. *The Journal of Applied Behavioral Science, 29*, 328–342.

Jensen, M. C., & Murphy, K. J. (1990). Performance, pay and top management incentives. *Journal of Political Economy, 98*, 225–264.

Jick, T. D. (1993). *Managing change*. Homewood, IL: Irwin.

Katz, D., & Kahn, R. L. (1978). *The social psychology of organizations* (2nd ed.). New York: John Wiley & Sons.

Khandwalla, P. N. (1976). *The design of organizations*. New York: Harcourt Brace Jovanovich.

Klein, K. J., & House, R. J. (1995). On fire: Charismatic leadership and levels of analysis. *Leadership Quarterly, 6*, 183–198.

Kozlowski, S. W. J., & Klein, K. J. (2000). A multilevel approach to theory and research in organizations: Contextual, temporal, and emergent processes. In: K. J. Klein & S. W. J. Kozlowski (Eds), *Multilevel theory, research, and methods in organizations: Foundations, extensions, and new directions* (pp. 3–90). San Francisco: Jossey-Bass.

Kryzanowski, L., Gandhi, D. K., & Gitman, L. J. (1982). *Principles of managerial finance*. New York: Harper & Row Publishers.

Lieberson, S., & O'Connor, J. F. (1972). Leadership and organizational performance: A study of large corporations. *American Sociological Review, 37*, 117–130.

Lord, R. G., & Maher, K. J. (1991). *Leadership and information processing: Linking perceptions and performance*. Boston, MA: Unwin Hyman.

Lowe, K. B., Kroeck, K. G., & Sivasubramaniam, N. (1996). Effectiveness correlates of transformational and transactional leadership: A meta-analytic review of the MLQ literature. *Leadership Quarterly, 7*, 385–425.

McGahan, A. M., & Porter, M. (1997). How much does industry matter, really? *Strategic Management Journal, 18*, 15–30.

Markides, C. C. (2000). *All the right moves*. Boston: Harvard Business School Press.

Marks, M. L., & Mirvis, P. H. (1998). *Joining forces*. San Francisco: Jossey-Bass.

Maurie, A., & Michaels, M. P. (1998). Firm and industry effect within strategic management. *Strategic Management Journal, 19*, 211–221.

Meindl, J. R., & Ehrlich, S. B. (1987). The romance of leadership and the evaluation of organizational performance. *Academy of Management Journal, 30*, 91–109.

Miles, R. E., & Snow, C. C. (1978). *Organizational strategy, structure, and process*. New York: McGraw-Hill.

Miller, D. (1991). Stale in the saddle: CEO tenure and the match between organization and environment. *Management Science, 37*, 34–52.

Miller, D., & Droge, C. (1986). Psychological and traditional determinants of structure. *Administrative Science Quarterly, 31*, 539–560.

Milliken, F. J. (1987). Three types of perceived uncertainty about the environment: State, effect, and response uncertainty. *Academy of Management Review, 12*, 133–143.

Mintzberg, H. (1978). Patterns in strategy formulation. *Management Science, 24*, 934–978.

Mischel, W. (1977). The interaction of person and situation. In: D. Magnusson & N. S. Ender (Eds), *Personality at the crossraods: Current issues in interactional psychology*. Hillsdale, NJ: Erlbaum.

Norburn, D., & Birley, S. (1988). The top management team and corporate performance. *Strategic Management Journal, 9*, 225–237.

Pawar, B. S., & Eastman, K. K. (1997). The nature and implications of contextual influences on transformational leadership: A conceptual examination. *Academy of Management Review, 22*, 80–109.

Peters, T. (1987). *Thriving on chaos*. New York: Alfred A. Knopf.

Pitts, R. A., & Hopkins, H. D. (1982). Firm diversity: Conceptualization and measurement. *Academy of Management Review, 7*, 620–629.

Priem, R. L., Lyon, D. W., & Dess, G. G. (1999). Limitations of demographic proxies in top management team heterogeneity research. *Journal of Management, 6*, 935–953.

Robbins, S. R., & Duncan, R. B. (1988). The role of the CEO and top management in the creation and implementation of strategic vision. In: D. C. Hambrick (Ed.), *The Executive Effect: Concepts and Methods for Studying Top Managers* (vol. 2, pp. 205–233). Greenwich, CT: JAI Press.

Roquebert, J. A., Phillips, R. L., & Westfall, P. A. (1996). Markets vs. management: What drives profitability? *Strategic Management Journal, 17*, 653–664.

Rousseau, D. M., & Fried, Y. (2001). Location, location, location: Contextualizing organizational research. *Journal of Organizational Behavior, 22*, 1–13.

Rumelt, R. P. (1991). How much does industry matter? *Strategic Management Journal, 12*, 167–185.

Schneider, B. (1987). The people make the place. *Personnel Psychology, 40*, 437–453.

Shamir, B., House, R. J., & Arthur, M. B. (1993). The motivational effects of charismatic leadership: A self-concept theory. *Organization Science, 4*, 1–17.

Singh, J. V. (1986). Performance, slack, and risk taking in organizational decision making. *Academy of Management Journal, 29*, 562–585.

Staw, B. M., & Sutton, R. I. (1993). Macro organizational psychology. In: J. K. Murnighan (Ed.), *Social psychology in organizations: Advances in theory and research* (pp. 350–384). Englewood Cliffs, NJ: Prentice-Hall.

Thomas, A. (1988). Does leadership make a difference to organizational performance? *Administrative Science Quarterly, 33*, 388–400.

Thompson, A. A., & Strickland, A. J. (1992). *Strategy formulation and implementation* (3rd ed.). Boston, MA: Irwin.

Tichy, N. M., & Devanna, M. A. (1986). *The transformational leader*. New York: Wiley.

Venkatraman, N., & Ramanujam, V. (1986). Measurement of business performance in strategy research: A comparison of approaches. *Academy of Management Review, 11*, 801–814.

Waldman, D. A., Ramirez, G. G., House, R. J., & Puranam, P. (2001). Does leadership matter?: CEO leadership attributes under conditions of perceived environmental uncertainty. *Academy of Management Journal, 44*, 134–143.

Waldman, D. A., & Yammarino, F. J. (1999). CEO charismatic leadership: Levels-of-management and levels-of-analysis effects. *Academy of Management Review, 24*, 266–285.

Youndt, M. A., Snell, S. A., Dean, J. W. Jr., & Lepak, D. P. (1996). Human resource management, manufacturing strategy, and firm performance. *Academy of Management Journal, 39,* 836–866.

PART III:
PSYCHOLOGICAL PERSPECTIVES

INTERNAL WORLD OF TRANSFORMATIONAL LEADERS

Micha Popper and Ofra Mayseless

ABSTRACT

We know a great deal today about the impact of transformational leaders, their actions, typical behaviors and their ways of influencing others (Bass, 1985, 1999a, b; Bass & Avolio, 1990). However, we know relatively little about the psychological substructure, the internal world of these leaders, namely who they are and how they developed this way. These aspects were raised earlier in Bass's early work (Bass, 1985) but have received little attention so far (Bass, 1998; Judge & Bono, 2000). We argue that the internal world of a transformational leader is characterized by a motivation to lead, leadership self-efficacy, motivation and capacity to relate to others in a pro-social way, optimism and openness to new experiences and viewpoints of others. We further argue that the origins of the ability and motivation to be a transformational leader lie in childhood experiences, and that the development of this ability and motivation can be understood and conceptualized by means of major developmental theories such as attachment theory (Bowlby, 1969, 1973, 1977, 1988). On the basis of these theories, we suggest a researchable conceptual framework for characterization of the internal world and the development of transformational leaders.

Transformational and Charismatic Leadership, Volume 2, pages 203–229.
Copyright © 2002 by Elsevier Science Ltd.
All rights of reproduction in any form reserved.
ISBN: 0-7623-0962-8

INTRODUCTION

In the last two decades, there has been a growing discussion in the leadership literature on the dynamics of leader-follower relationships (Klein & House, 1995; Meindl, 1995; Shamir, 1995), particularly on the emotional relationship labeled by different titles of which the most common are "charismatic" (House, 1977; Lindholm, 1988; Shamir, 1991) and "transformational" (Burns, 1978; Bass, 1985). Emotional bonding with a leader can cause the followers to lose their autonomous judgment and merge with the leader's wishes and aspirations, at times even to the point of "self loss" (Kets de Vries, 1989; Lindholm, 1988; Popper, 2001). However, relationships with a leader can be highly positive, bestowing meaning and ideals, empowering the followers and helping them to become autonomous and competent individuals who reach self actualization and high levels of morality (e.g. Bass, 1985; Burns, 1978). In this chapter we focus on "transformational leadership", which exemplifies the latter type of emotional bonding between leaders and followers, the bond that is highly benevolent in nature.

Since its inception, the study of transformational leadership has flourished, and we now have a clear picture of what transformational leaders do and how they behave. Transformational leaders' relationships with their followers were found to be characterized by four factors (Bass, 1999b; Bass & Avolio, 1990): idealized influence, inspirational motivation, intellectual stimulation, and individualized consideration. Idealized influence and inspirational motivation are revealed by a leader who envisions a desirable future, articulates how it can be reached, sets an example to be followed, determines high standards of performance, and shows determination and confidence. Followers want to identify with such leadership, and such identification does not restrict their upward growth potential. Intellectual stimulation finds expression when the leader helps followers to become more innovative and creative. Individualized consideration is manifested by leaders who pay attention to their followers' developmental needs, and support and coach them in their personal development.

We now also have a clearer picture of the kinds of outcomes transformational leaders bring about in their followers, or in their organizations. A large body of research compared transformational and transactional leadership on various outcome variables such as the leader's perceived effectiveness, satisfaction with the leader, and the followers' sense of self-efficacy, and found these variables to be higher among followers whose leaders were transformational (see, for example, Bycio, Hackett & Allen, 1995; Yammarino & Bass, 1990). Similar findings were reported with regard to measures of behavior and performance (Bass & Avolio, 1993).

In sum, we know a great deal today about the actions, behavior, and influence of transformational leaders (Bass, 1985, 1999a, b; Bass & Avolio, 1990). However, we know very little about the psychological substructure, the internal world of these leaders, namely what "makes them tick", and how they developed this way. This point has been indicated by some prominent scholars of leadership (e.g., Bass, 1998; House & Howell, 1992) and has been highlighted recently by Judge and Bono (2000) claiming that: "Even if one considers transformational leadership to be a behavioral theory, the origins of the behaviors are unclear" (p. 752).

The link between psychological experiences in childhood and manifestations of leadership in adulthood has often been highlighted in leaders' own descriptions of themselves (e.g. Churchill in Gardner, 1995; Franklin Delano Roosevelt in Burns, 1956; Gandhi in Chadha, 1997; Woodrow Wilson in George & George, 1956). The literature addressing this issue includes mostly biographies written by historians (e.g. Bullock, 1991), a few well-known psycho-biographies (e.g. Erikson on Gandhi, 1969), and a few historiometric studies (Mumford et al., 1993; Mumford & Mowry, this volume) that are mainly descriptive. Thus, despite the recognition of the importance of childhood in shaping the character of the adult in general (Freud, 1920; Storr, 1972) and of leaders in particular (Avolio & Gibbons, 1988; Kets de Vries, 1989), we do not possess sufficient systematic knowledge on what was referred to by Kets de Vries (1989) as "leaders' internal theater", that is to say, the intra-psychic factors that shape leaders' internal world, their approach, and their outlook. This fact is not fortuitous: it stems from the absence of models and empirically testable conceptualizations (for a similar argument, see Avolio & Gibbons, 1988; Mayseless & Popper, 2001; Popper, 2000).

The purpose of this chapter is to present a conceptual framework for the description and understanding of the internal world of transformational leaders and its developmental roots. Specifically, we intend:

(1) to present a conceptualization regarding transformational leaders' internal world, their approach and outlook, their emotions and their basic attitudes towards themselves, towards others, and towards the world around them;
(2) to describe possible developmental precursors of these characteristics; and
(3) to demonstrate how these concepts may be translated into empirical research.

For this purpose, we will draw on the vast literature in personality and developmental psychology. Our arguments are presented as a set of propositions, which together form a testable conceptual framework.

THE PSYCHOLOGICAL INFRASTRUCTURE

In order for individuals to express themselves and excel in any field (music, sport, art, science), they have to be both able and willing to engage in that field. This seemingly commonplace statement also applies to the issue of leadership. We propose that in order to reach a position of leadership, an individual must have the desire to influence others, as well as specific abilities. The fact that leaders want to be dominant and influential is self-evident. However, the leadership literature has barely dealt with the psychological antecedents of the desire to lead (Burns, 1987; Popper, 2000). Our argument is that the desire to lead has its roots (like many psychological phenomena) in the conditions of growth and development in early childhood.

Motivation

Several explanations have been offered for the desire to be in a position of leadership most of them ascribe central importance to events in childhood as shaping the development of the motivation to lead (e.g. Avolio & Gibbons, 1988; Burns, 1978; Popper, 2000; Zaleznik, 1992). For example, in the case of negative leaders (those described in the literature as personalized charismatic leaders; see the discussion in House & Howell, 1992; Howell, 1988), the motivation to lead is generally explained by narcissistic deprivations in early childhood.

The assumption of these theories is that parents' demonstration of their adoration for their growing baby is central to the child's developmental process. According to these explanations, the leader's status provides opportunities for admiration and adoration that were lacking in early childhood. See Kohut (1971) for a general discussion of this narcissistic need, and Post (1986), Deluga (1997), as well as Streyrer (this volume) for a discussion and examination of this aspect with regard to leaders. Indeed, historical and psychological analyses conducted with regard to distinctly personalized charismatic leaders such as Adolf Hitler (Bullock, 1991), Jim Jones (Lindholm, 1990), and Joseph Stalin (Bullock, 1991) point to narcissistic deprivation as a dominant theme in the persistent desire to acquire leadership position so as to win admiration.

In other conceptualizations, the motivation of socialized charismatic leaders (of which transformational leaders are the most distinct manifestation) is also explained as a way of dealing and coping with feelings aroused and experiences shaped in childhood. Zaleznik (1992), for example, argues that the motivation of many leaders is related to the absence of a significant father figure in the child's consciousness. These children, according to Zaleznik, attempt to turn themselves into fantasized father figures in a compensatory effort. In other words, leadership according to this conceptualization is seen as a type of psychological reparation rooted in the longing for an ideal father.

Burns (1956, 1976, 1978) identified a similar pattern and added an Oedipal interpretation to Zaleznik's explanation while focusing on male leaders. Lacking the clearly felt, supportive presence of a father, the developing child, says Burns, lacks a focus for identification. Namely, the psychological element needed to resolve the Oedipal conflict is missing, hence, according to the psychoanalytical argumentation, the child's motivation to be a "big father" grows increasingly powerful. This kind of motivation can, of course, be especially strong when there is also a deep emotional attachment to the mother. Then, the desire to be the "strong father" who protects the beloved mother, is intensified.

Although these explanations (especially the psychoanalytical ones) are frequently criticized as speculative, there are biographies and statistical evidence that support these directions with a consistency and degree that cannot be dismissed. For instance, while collecting material for biographies of 24 British Prime ministers, from Spencer Percival in 1809 to Chamberlain in 1937, a British researcher, Lucille Iremonger, found that 15 of them (66%) had lost a father in childhood. Examining the population register in the wake of these findings, Iremonger discovered that only about 2% of the general population had been orphaned in childhood. According to Iremonger, these figures may indicate some kind of link between the loss of a father and the longing to be a leader (Iremonger, 1970), and in fact, this motif appears in the biographies of some of the most outstanding leaders in history (e.g. Burns, 1978; Gardner, 1995).

Another explanation is related to the mother's expectations. This explanation, as the one involving the Oedipal conflict, has been applied mostly to sons and not daughters. In the absence of a father, the mother may (even unconsciously) convey expectations that lead the child to perceive himself as a father substitute, and with this come the feelings that are usually related to the father's roles.

The explanations based on expectations can be extended to other situations, not necessarily related to the absence of a father, in which case they are equally relevant to men and women. For example, children who receive messages that they are expected to take responsibility, to be role models, for example first-born children (e.g. Steinberg, 2001), or children perceived by their parents as more gifted than their siblings (Raz, 2001), may internalize these expectations and grow up with the feeling that taking responsibility and exerting influence are natural roles for them, which then become part of their identity.

These roles are internalized as possible selves (e.g. Markus & Nurius, 1986) – ideas regarding what they might become and what they want to become, provide a link between parental expectation, self cognition and motivation and guide their future behavor. For example, in some cases, childhood role reversal when successful and appreciated may be internalized as a disposition to take responsibility, care for others and lead them (Mayseless, 1996, 1998). Similarly, cultural expectations of people in certain social classes or cultural and familial expectations of children who are heirs of leaders may also operate to socialize children to leadership positions. Aspiring to leadership positions is thus a natural continuation of the socialization these children experienced (Gibbons, 1986).

Notwithstanding the centrality of childhood experiences, the importance of temperament should not be overlooked. For example, shy and inhibited children (Arcus, 2001; Rubin, Hastings, Stewart & Henderson, 1997) would probably be less inclined to develop a motivation to influence others even in a context of familial expectations or narcissistic deprivation.

Capacity

The fact that certain children develop the wish to influence others and lead them is not, as stated, sufficient in itself. These children have to feel they are capable of doing that and succeeding. This point was mentioned by Bass (1985), arguing that leaders are characterized by self-confidence, attributed to successful resolution of internal conflicts (p. 47). This argument was not developed conceptually, and has never been a central theme in the psycho-logical research on leadership (Popper, 2000).

The concept of "self-efficacy", introduced and studied by Bandura (1977, 1986, 1995), provides a theoretical framework that can link the wish to lead with the sense that one is capable of being a leader. Self-efficacy is described as a self-perception that is formed in the context of behavior in specific areas (Bandura, 1977, 1986). This perception develops in a gradual learning process whereby the individual receives information from various sources regarding his/her abilities in a specific area of functioning. This accumulation of feedback indicating success or failure in the given area naturally affects the perception of one's ability, creating a high level of self-efficacy in the case of positive messages, and an opposite effect in the case of messages of failure (Bandura, 1977). The self perception formed as a result of these experiences influences aspects such as stability and persistence in certain behaviors, patterns of thinking and emotional response, decisions concerning course of action, and occupational choices (for a comprehensive discussion, see Bandura, 1986, 1995).

There are scholars who see self-efficacy as a generalized characteristic involving the individual's general belief in his/her ability in a broad range of achievement situations (Hacket & Betz, 1995). Our contention as well as others' (e.g. Maddux, 1995) is that besides a generalized level of self-efficacy, people have particular self-efficacy beliefs in specific domains depending on the general experiences in these areas. Thus, people also develop specific self-efficacy beliefs with regard to their ability to lead whose sources lie in experiences of success (or failure) in influencing people. We suggest that in order to become a leader, one must have developed a high level of self-efficacy as a leader, which may be defined as a generalized self-perception in the domain of leadership.

In support of this line of argumentation, Smith and Foti (1998) reported that the most important variable affecting group members' preferences of leaders was the degree of self-efficacy the followers attributed to the leader. Similarly, Chemers, Watson, and May (2000) reported that self-rated leadership efficacy was associated with leadership potential of military cadets as rated by their military science professors.

Interestingly, this self-rated specific sense of efficacy (leadership efficacy) was even more strongly related with the cadets' performance evaluations (reported by objective observers of a leadership simulation), and with leadership ratings by peers and supervisors during a summer leadership training program. Finally, examining Chinese high-school students in Hong Kong, Chan (2000) reported that the students who were identified as leaders based on observed behavioral characteristics were characterized by higher aspirations to leadership and achievement and by higher levels of energy and leadership self-efficacy. Together, these findings present some preliminary support for our proposition.

It should be noted that the experiences (successes or failures) may originate in various contexts such as the family, the peer group, and the community, and we propose that the more consistent these experiences are across contexts, the more coherent and strong the sense of efficacy (high or low) with regard to leadership. Similarly, Avolio and Gibbons (1988) highlight the accumulative effects of life experiences in different leadership positions. Though these two characteristics (capacity and motivation) are to some extent independent, in some cases outstanding capacity may also motivate a person to use it. This may also be due to the cues they receive from others, as noted above, that they have the capacity to make a difference. Similarly, high motivation may drive a person to invest a lot in this area and not to withdraw when meeting obstacles, hence eventually leading to more successes and a higher perceived level of efficacy.

Although the wish to exert influence along with the belief in one's ability to be a leader are important variables, they are not conceived as a sufficient condition for a person to become a transformational leader. These aspects are conceptualized as a necessary condition (Burns, 1978). Metaphorically, these variables may be seen as the foundations of a building; without them the building cannot be constructed. In most cases, these foundations are laid down in early childhood, and constitute the infrastructure for the possible leadership position and, of course, for the individual's typical behaviors as a leader.

The arguments thus far can be summarized in the following proposition:

Proposition 1. The wish to be influential, and self-efficacy with regard to leadership, are essential characteristics for becoming any kind of leader (including a transformational one).

On Becoming a Transformational Leader

In the previous paragraphs, we discussed the basic and necessary psychological prerequisites needed to become a leader. However, we contend that to become a transformational leader, additional characteristics must be developed. In what follows, we discuss three characteristics that we consider as fundamental to become a transformational leader.

Care for Others

One of the salient differences, if not the most salient, between charismatic leaders such as Jim Jones or Hitler and transformational leaders such as Gandhi or Nelson Mandela are in the way they treat others. The former are characterized by an attitude towards others that springs from narcissism (House & Howell, 1992; Popper, 2000, 2001). That is to say, they use others as a source of self-aggrandizement. In contrast, those who are classified as transformational leaders are characterized by the way they treat others, which is oriented by moral values such as justice or integrity (see Burns, 1978; Kohlberg, 1963) and which encourages personal development of their followers. Already, in 1985, Bass had suggested that for the transformational bond to endure, the leader must be empathic, in many respects is also a mentor, and must take a developmental orientation toward the followers.

In many aspects, transformational leadership can be metaphorically compared with good parenthood. Indeed, Popper and Mayseless (2001) reviewed studies dealing with parenting, and compared them with studies on transformational leadership. This comparison reveals a strong similarity between the developmental effects of good parents and those of transformational leaders. The resemblance between transformational leaders and good parents is expressed in the following main aspects:

(1) Both are sensitive and responsive, showing individual consideration to their "protégée" (Bass, 1985; De-Wolff & van IJzendoorn, 1997; Howell, 1988);
(2) both reinforce the protegee's autonomy (Bass, 1985; George & Solomon, 1989; Maccoby & Martin, 1983);
(3) in a supportive, non-judgmental way (Bass, 1985; Baumrind, 1978; Shamir, House & Arthur, 1993; Sroufe, 1983);
(4) and by actively providing opportunities, promoting relevant experiences, giving explanations, etc. (Bass, 1985; Baumrind, 1978; Howell, 1988; Matas, Arend & Sroufe, 1978);
(5) and both are positive examples to identify with and look up to (Conger & Kanungo, 1987; Howell, 1988; Main, 1983).

Some recent studies do point to characteristics of nurturing parents that were found to a greater extent in transformational leaders as compared with others. For example, a study by Clover (1990) reported transformational leaders to be higher than other types of leaders in measures such as nurturance, and lower in measures such as aggression and criticism. Ross and Offerman (1997) reported negative correlations between measures of critical parenting, aggression and criticism and transformational leadership. Roush and Atwater (1992) reported that transformational leaders ranked higher as sensing and feeling types than as thinking types, that is, they ranked high as people who place more emphasis on human relations, on the importance of others' attitudes, on concern for their welfare, and on promoting an atmosphere of openness compared with those who emphasize logical, analytical, and impersonal thinking. Recently, Judge and Bono (2000) reported that among the Big Five traits, agreeableness defined as being kind, gentle, trusting, altruistic, and warm was found as the strongest and most consistent predictor of transformational leadership.

We argue that transformational leaders who are both role models and oriented towards the development and encouragement of their followers have a strong motivation to give (a pro-social orientation) and are capable of giving in an emphatic and sensitive way similar to that of good parents (Popper & Mayseless, 2001). Research in the domain of developmental psychology has examined for quite some time the precursors of such altruistic and pro-social orientations with children and adolescents (Van-Lange, De-Bruin, Otten & Joireman, 1997; Zahn-Waxler, Cummings, & Iannotti, 1986). Generally, the capacity to give is based on many aspects, some genetic (Zahn-Waxler et al., 2001) and some environmental.

In general, parents who are warm, sensitive, and attentive to their children's needs, who employ positive internal attributions to pro-social deeds, are not coercive in their disciplinary actions, and who themselves model emphatic and pro-social behavior towards their offspring and towards others raise children who are more emphatic, concerned with others' welfare, and have both the motivation and the capacity to help others (see a review by Grusec & Dix, 1986).

In sum, among the environmental factors, a significant weight is ascribed to the internalization of good parental models in early childhood (Cassidy, 1999). In particular, internalization of a secure attachment pattern described below, was found to be the basis for the development of social motivation and skills (Eberly & Montmayor, 1998; Thompson, 1999). The arguments and findings discussed in this part can be summarized in the following proposition:

Proposition 2. Transformational leaders are individuals with a wish and a capacity to give.

Optimism

One of the major characteristics attributed to transformational leaders is their ability to present a vision, a future goal, or a new direction, to demonstrate their enthusiasm about their vision and to inspire others to share the vision (see a discussion of various types of vision by Mumford & Mowry, this volume). This has been described at length in most of the biographies and studies on outstanding leaders (e.g. Burns, 1978; Chadha, 1997; Gardner, 1995; Simonton, 1986) and also measured, using the Multifactor Leadership Questionnaire (MLQ), by the factors: "inspirational motivation" and "idealized influence" (Bass & Avolio, 1996).

In order to demonstrate a consistent future orientation and formulate it in terms of a vision that people can pursue with faith and enthusiasm, a person must be optimistic in terms of positive expectations for the self, for others, and for society at large. In other words, the leader must have a positive outlook on life. Hence, studies on optimism are relevant to understanding the approach taken and behavior of transformational leaders. Dispositional optimism was construed as a generalized inclination to expect favorable life outcomes and hold positive expectations for the future (Scheier & Carver, 1985). A large body of research pertains to the association between an optimistic outlook and the capacity to present a vision and to be enthusiastic about it (see two major edited books by Chang, 2001 and by Gillham, 2000).

For example, a comparative study of optimists and pessimists conducted by Scheier and Carver (1985), which examined their approach and behavior in connection with the achievement of desired aims, reported that optimists make much greater efforts to achieve their aims than do pessimists, who tend to display a higher degree of relinquishment and avoidance. Moreover, optimists reported a higher degree of interest in life, of satisfaction with their fields of occupation, and of well-being (Scheier & Carver, 1993). In particular Chemers, Watson and May (2000) reported a positive association between optimism and leadership potential of cadets as rated by their military science professors.

With regard to the antecedents of optimism as a personality trait, there are several indications that it is related both to a genetic origin and to experiences in childhood (e.g. Chang, 2001). For example Plomin et al. (1992) provided evidence that individual differences in dispositional optimism are partly inherited. They examined a sample of some 500 same-sex identical and fraternal middle-aged twins, half of whom were reared together and half adopted and raised separately early in life. Their analyses yielded significant heritability estimates of about 25%, as well as a significant shared rearing effect owing to environmental influences with respect to optimistic tendencies. Similar findings were also presented by Zuckerman (2001). In terms of the specific rearing environment that promotes optimism, little is as yet known with regard to longitudinal research. However, several studies have addressed this question with samples of adults.

For example, Peterson and Bossio (1991) present several studies that show that optimists are more likely than pessimists to recall their parents as happy, as being socially active, as having a positive self-image, and encouraging them to hope for the best. In addition, optimists described their parents as granting them autonomy, conveying trust, and stressing the importance of exploring the social world. Similarly, Hjelle, Busch, and Warren (1996) showed that dispositional optimism in adults was positively correlated with reported maternal and paternal warmth/acceptance and negatively associated with parental hostility, neglect, or rejection. Thus, again, a secure parenting style seems to be one of the precursors of an optimistic outlook in adulthood. These arguments and findings can be summarized in the following proposition:

Proposition 3. Transformational leaders are optimistic individuals.

Openness

One of the characteristics of transformational leaders is their ability to help their followers "think differently" and be creative and original. As mentioned above, "intellectual stimulation" is one of the factors of transformational leadership (Bass, 1985). Underlying the ability to promote intellectual stimulation is the assumption that the transformational leader is a person who is himself/herself creative or, perhaps more likely, is open and encourages others to express their creativity and originality. Transformational leaders are also confident in their abilities and willingness to explore the unknown. In either case, such a leader must be a person who is curious, cognitively flexible, and open. In line with this contention, adolescent Chinese students in Hong Kong, who were identified as leaders based on observed behavioral characteristics, were characterized by higher ratings of openness to novel experiences and different perspectives, which the author identified as a major aspect and termed leadership flexibility (Chan, 2000).

Openness to new experiences has been identified within the personality psychology literature as one of the Big Five dimensions of personality (Costa, & McCrae, 1992). Openness to Experience is strongly correlated with divergent thinking (McCrae, 1987), with personality-based measures of creativity (McCrae & Costa, 1997), as well as with behavioral measures of creativity (Feist, 1998). As summarized in a review by McCrae and Costa (1997), open people actively seek out experience and are apt to be particularly reflective and thoughtful about ideas they encounter. They are not only able to grasp new ideas, but enjoy doing so. Need for variety, tolerance of ambiguity, and preference for complexity all represent motivational aspects of open people. In addition, open people can be characterized by their non-traditional attitudes, their rich and complex emotional lives, and their behavioral flexibility. Indeed, Judge and Bono (2000) have recently found an association between transformational leadership and openness to experiences, as measured using the NEO personality inventory as part of the Big Five personality constructs (Costa & McCrae, 1992).

What might be the antecedents of this openness and curiosity in the leader's personality? Most of the writing on this subject, particularly in the literature on parenthood, indicates that proper stimulation and encouragement of curiosity and exploration in early childhood are the basis for developing this tendency (Baumrind, 1996). Specifically more positive, stimulating, autonomy- and communication-enhancing child-rearing environments contribute to the development of curious children who show an open and more flexible cognitive style (e.g. McCrae & Costa, 1988). In particular, the formation of a secure attachment pattern was distinguished as an antecedent to a sense of psychological freedom to explore and cognitive openness (Thompson, 1999).

Several studies conducted with adults point to the association between secure attachment and openness. For example, Mikulincer and Arad (1999) reported that secure attachment was related to higher cognitive openness and better recall of expectation-congruent information. Similarly, Green-Hennessy and Reis (1998) reported that secure individuals were more open to new information and showed a higher differentiation of their representations of others than individuals who were avoidant, one of two categories of insecure attachment described later on in this chapter. Finally, Mikulincer (1997) found that secure persons described themselves as more open and curious compared with avoidant people. In addition, they reported less preference for cognitive closure and were more likely to rely on new information in making social judgments than the two insecure categories.

Besides experiences in childhood, genetic contribution was also highlighted in the development of openness to experience. Employing a large sample of identical and fraternal twins reared apart and together, Bergeman, Chipuer, Plomin and Pedersen (1993) reported substantial genetic effects for this trait with about 40% of the variance explained by additive genetic contribution.

This section can be summarized in the following proposition:

Proposition 4. Transformational leaders are characterized by a high level of curiosity and openness.

DEVELOPMENTAL CONCEPTUALIZATION

To summarize, we argue that the internal world of transformational leaders involves:

(1) a disposition for social dominance;
(2) a belief in the ability to influence others;
(3) a motivation and a capacity to treat others in a positive and encouraging way while serving as role models;
(4) optimistic orientation towards the self, and others; and
(5) intellectual openness, curiosity and flexibility.

How and when are these tendencies and abilities formed in life?

For some of these attributes, a genetic origin might be assumed (i.e. optimism), and its magnitude is not negligible. In addition, we argue that the roots of these attributes lie in childhood experiences and that therefore their formation can be understood and conceptualized by employing major developmental theories and research. As highlighted throughout our discussion, one of the most relevant of these theories is attachment theory (Bowlby, 1969, 1973, 1977, 1988), which in recent years has become a very influential theory in explaining emotional development (Ainsworth, 1992; Rutter, 1996). (Just to illustrate the centrality of attachment theory: 662 entries appear only in 1999 psycINFO search.) In what follows, we will present how attachment theory can be relevant to understanding leadership development. However, this application does not necessarily mean that we see attachment theory as the only psychological theory relevant to the development of transformational leadership.

Overview of Attachment Theory

Based on ethnological, evolutionary, and control systems concepts, attachment theory postulates an innate, bio-social behavioral system in the infant, the purpose of which is to maintain proximity between the infant and his or her primary caregiver. The evolutionary purpose of this behavioral system is to promote the child's survival by receiving protection from a "stronger and wiser" figure, given that the newborn infant cannot survive on its own. Thus, in the course of evolution, only those infants who were motivationally and behaviorally equipped to obtain proximity to, and protection from, a stronger and wiser figure survived. The infant is assumed to be motivated to remain close to the caregiver and has numerous ways, some inborn and some learned (e.g. following, talking), of securing the desired proximity and protection.

These behaviors, termed attachment behaviors, arouse complementary behavior in the caregiver. According to attachment theory, adults have a complementary behavioral system whose main function is the protection of the infant (or the person whose well-being is sought), which is activated when there are signs of threat to that person's well-being. Both the infant and the caregiver maintain a certain desired range of proximity to each other, a range that may change depending on circumstances. If there is no perceived danger or threat, the infant may be content and feel secure even at a large distance from the caregiver. But when danger or a threat is perceived (e.g. hunger, loud noise), the infant will actively seek proximity and protection and will only terminate attachment behaviors when the desired protection has been achieved, and the feeling of security has been restored.

Thus, attachment behaviors may only be witnessed when the infant perceives some threat, and their intensity reflects the intensity of the threat. In safe circumstances, the level of activation of the attachment behavioral system can remain low for long periods of time while other behavioral systems, such as exploration, may come into play. The child uses the caregiver as a "secure base" from which to explore and only periodically checks for availability of the attachment figure. However, when threat arises, the attachment system is activated, and the child will seek protection from the caregiver, which then serves as a haven of safety. Hence, the person maintains a balance between attachment and exploration. When experiencing a sense of security, the person is free to pursue other desires and to explore the environment and other relationships. However, when threatened or anxious, attachment behavior is activated, and exploration is halted.

Differences in the ability to signal the need and desire for closeness, and especially differences in the caregiver's responsiveness, generate variations in a baby's attachment styles. It is assumed that from infancy onward, children form an internal working model, which includes internalization and representations of major aspects of their attachment relationships with their caregivers (Bowlby, 1969, 1973, 1977, 1988; Bretherton, 1985). These aspects include perception of the self as (un)worthy of love and attention, and perception of the attachment figure as (un)willing and (un)able to attend to the attachment needs when they arise. The internal working model guides the interpretation and planning of interpersonal transactions with the caregiver and later with other important figures. At first, it involves a representation of the specific relationship with a specific caregiver. Later, following repeated experiences, the model increasingly becomes a part of the child's developing personality and turns into a more abstract, generalized representation of the self and others (Bretherton, 1985; Collins & Read, 1994).

On the basis of Bowlby's theory, Ainsworth, Blehar, Wates and Wall (1978) identified three styles of infant attachment, one secure and two insecure: ambivalent and avoidant. These styles were later also identified in childhood and adulthood (see reviews by Solomon & George, 1999). As summarized in a review chapter by Cassidy (1999), the internal working model of secure individuals includes a basic trust in their caregiver and confidence that their caregiver will be available, responsive, and helpful when needed. With this assurance, they are bold in their explorations of the world and able both to rely on themselves and to turn to others when in need. This pattern is promoted by a caregiver, usually a parent, who is readily available, sensitive to the child's signals, and lovingly responsive when the child seeks protection and/or comfort.

The internal working model of the anxious/ambivalent pattern is characterized by uncertainty as to whether the parent or caregiver will be available, responsive, or helpful when called upon. Because of this uncertainty, the ambivalent individual is always prone to separation anxiety and tends to be clinging even while manifesting unresolved anger directed at the caregiver. This behavior is seen as an attempt to coerce an otherwise unresponsive caregiver to pay attention. This pattern, in which conflict is evident, is promoted by such conditions as a parent being available and helpful on some occasions but not on others (Cassidy & Berlin, 1994).

Avoidant attachment is a pattern in which individuals have no confidence they will receive care when they seek it. On the contrary, they expect to be rebuffed. In the extreme, these individuals attempt to become emotionally self-sufficient and live their life without the support of others. They tend to devalue the importance of attachment for their lives, using a strategy of minimizing attachment behavior and feelings (Cassidy, 1999; Main, 1990). They may, however, exhibit hostility and anti-social behavior toward others (Kobak & Sceery, 1988). This pattern is the result of the caregivers constantly rebuffing the child when he/she approaches them for comfort or protection (Cassidy, 1994).

As stated, adult attachment research is based on the premise that internal working models shape the self-image and the image of the other, and consequently affect feelings and cognition that govern behavior in relationships. Over the past decade, many studies have been conducted to examine the impact of the internal working models in various domains, such as: parenting (Main, Kaplan & Cassidy, 1985), romantic relationships (Hazan & Shaver, 1987), marital satisfaction and stability (Feeney, 1999), work-related behavior and affect (Hazan & Shaver, 1990), and friendship (Mayseless, Sharabany & Sagi 1997), and currently has also been applied to understand leadership relationships (Popper, Mayseless & Castelnovo, 2000).

We argue that attachment theory can be used not only in the analysis of relational processes, but also in analyzing intra-psychic processes. In fact, some studies have already been conducted in this field, for example, a study on self-schema and social cognition (Mikulincer & Orbach, 1995), studies on emotion regulation (Cassidy, 1999), and a study on mental health (Cicchetti, Toth & Lynch, 1995). In particular, attachment theory can also be useful in examining the internal emotional world of leaders in general, and of transformational leaders in particular. Examination of the processes that generate the various attachment patterns, together with an understanding of the psychological significance of each of these patterns, gives rise to the argument that the secure pattern – and the conditions that promoted it – are partly the basis of the internal world of transformational leaders and are at the root of the behaviors that characterize these leaders.

Attachment and Transformational Leadership

Recall our argument that besides the wish to influence others, a necessary (though not sufficient) condition to become a leader is the degree of the individual's confidence in his/her ability to lead. In other words, a person characterized by a high level of anxiety and feelings of incompetence would probably not seek out leadership roles (Judge & Bono, 2000; Kirkpatrick & Locke, 1991).

We argue that secure individuals and, to some extent, avoidant individuals (in the case of personalized charismatic leaders) have the ego resources required for taking on a leadership role, whereas anxious/ambivalent personality types lack such a base; hence, they will not tend to seek out leadership positions. Empirical support for this claim was presented by Mikulincer and Florian (1995) who reported that those who were "anxious ambivalent" were not perceived by their peers as leaders in an army basic training course. Similarly Englund, Levy, Hyson and Sroufe (2000) reported a noteworthy association between secure attachment as assessed in infancy and leadership ratings given by observers in a weekend camp organized in adolescence, some 15 years later.

Internalization of the secure pattern means, among other things, internalization of supportive parental models (Popper & Mayseless, 2001) and hence internalization of the ability to be a role model, which is the basis for the idealized influence exhibited by transformational leaders. In line with this contention, a recent study (Shields, Ryan & Cicchetti, 2001) reported that 8- to 12-year-old children who were nominated as leaders by their peers were characterized by a positive representation of their parents, as depicted in a narrative the children constructed following a presentation of story stems. The positive representation was conspicuous in the perception of their parents as responsive and as providing and supporting autonomy.

Thus, an internalization of a benevolent and secure parental model (or even a secure model of other significant caregivers) may serve as an antecedent of becoming a leader. Furthermore, the basic trust and sense of general confidence that a secure person internalizes contribute as well to a general sense of optimism and positive expectations, which, as argued above, are part of the internal theater of transformational leaders.

One of the most conspicuous outcomes of growing up as a secure child is the capacity to regulate one's emotion and hence to be capable of taking more risks with regard to new experiences. A person who is secure can afford to explore the environment and new experiences because of the general sense of a secure base, a haven of safety, and a high sense of efficacy (Cassidy, 1999). This was mostly described within attachment theory as the capacity to explore (Ainsworth, 1992), an aspect that contributes to the development of inherent curiosity, which is the basis necessary for intellectual stimulation, one of the characteristics of transformational leaders (Bass, 1985).

Finally, people with a secure attachment pattern see themselves and others in a positive and optimistic manner. They trust others, trust the world, and internalize a parental role model of a sensitive and considerate parent. This might be the basis of the ability – both of good parents and of transformational leaders – to give and care for others (Popper, Mayseless & Castelnovo, 2000), and this is a unique behavioral manifestation of transformational leaders (Bass, 1985; Burns, 1978; Howell & Avolio, 1992; Popper, Mayseless & Castelnovo, 2000).

In sum, attachment security seems to be associated with many aspects, which we described above as characterizing the transformational leader. In fact, besides the motivation to lead, which may not be directly related to attachment security, all other components of the hypothesized internal world of transformational leaders – self-efficacy, capacity and motivation to give in a pro-social way, optimism, and openness – might have developmental roots in secure attachment. Thus, it appears that attachment theory can provide a conceptual framework for describing intra-psychic processes relevant to the characterization of transformational leaders. The advantages of this theory are not only in the conceptual domain, but also in terms of helping to define and measure psycho-dynamic variables that could not hitherto be examined empirically (e.g. Cassidy, 1999; Solomon & George, 1999).

Theoretical, Empirical, and Practical Implications
We indicated at the beginning of this article that most of the efforts in leadership research have focused on examining relations between leaders' behaviors (i.e. leadership styles) and outcome variables such as performance and satisfaction (Bass, 1990). We pointed out that there is less systematic and empirical work in so far as the understanding of the inner world and development of leaders is concerned, particularly with regard to those leaders who are not historical leaders, but leaders at different levels of the hierarchy in organizations, individuals who might be labeled "leaders in everyday life."

It is only recently that we see indications of a growing interest in tackling issues of capacity and motivation to lead. For instance, Schneider et al. (1999) described the first stage of a longitudinal research program concerned with the prediction, understanding, and durability of early displays of leadership behavior. This research is being conducted at high schools and is based on the predictability of teachers' ratings of leadership behavior with respect to predictors such as interests, motivation, and academic ability.

Our analysis and the propositions presented in this chapter together form a conceptualization, which is research oriented and can be empirically tested. Most of the concepts we discussed have valid and reliable measures that can be used in future research projects on the developmental antecedents to transformational leadership. For example, optimism has been measured using paper and pencil questionnaires, which are widely used (Scheier & Carver, 1985). Similarly, the openness to new experiences construct may be assessed with the NEO Inventory (Costa & McCrae, 1992). As for attachment security, Hazan and Shaver's conceptual work and the attachment questionnaire they constructed (1987, 1990) indicate that the internal model formed in the course of attachment processes in infancy has ramifications for the development of the individual's adult personality. Indeed, as mentioned earlier, the notions of attachment theory, which have been applied to examine a wide range of developmental processes, can now be applied to investigating the development of leadership (for such an application, see Mikulincer & Florian, 1995; Popper, Mayseless & Castlenovo, 2000).

In addition to Hazan and Shaver's measurements of attachment styles, there is another instrument developed by Main, Kaplan and Cassidy (1985), known as the Adult Attachment Interview, which has also been used to identify adult internal working models. Both instruments have shown strong concurrent and predictive validity (Crowell, Fraley & Shaver, 1999) and can be used in research designed to examine leaders' internal working models, namely the provision and existence of a secure base and its effects. Thus, our conceptualization provides an opportunity for an empirical examination of the internal world of transformational leaders and their developmental roots.

The directions discussed here, if validated in research also have practical implications, particularly with regard to methodical selection and development of leaders – issues that are of special concern to large organizations. For example, the ability to assess and measure attachment patterns and motivation to lead may mean the ability to improve the assessment of the probability of a person's being a transformational leader. Characterization of individuals in terms of their capacity to become transformational leaders may be of significance also in leadership training and development. Investing in those who have high capacity and high motivation to lead seems to be the most beneficial approach in terms of instrumental cost-benefit considerations. This assumption does not necessarily mean that those individuals who do not have high capacity (e.g. do not have a secure pattern or are not open to experiences) cannot be transformational leaders. Although Bowlby (1969, 1973, 1988) believed that there is a tendency for continuity in attachment patterns, certain changes may occur in the course of life.

At any point in time, the individual may be vulnerable to negative experiences or derive benefit from positive experiences (Bowlby, 1988). Insecure models of self and others may be revised or replaced when the individual has a corrective experience such as a supportive and sensitive relationship, be it with a significant other, a friend, or a psychotherapist (Bowlby, 1988; Lieberman, Weston & Pawl, 1991; van Izendoorn, Juffer & Duyvesteyn, 1995). Internal models may also undergo revision because of a supportive manager at the workplace or when the individual is able to utilize his or her ability for reflection to examine contradictions in internal models, or to initiate and experience new relationships (Ainsworth, 1989).

For a large part of this chapter, we have focused on attachment theory and applied its notions to highlight various attributes of transformational leadership. As mentioned, the presentation of attachment theory was used here as an example using early developmental theories to explain the development of leaders at later points in life. Obviously, there are other developmental conceptualizations, such as that dealing with the development of "theory of mind" and self-reflection, or the conceptualization offered by Vygotsky's theory of cognitive development that may be highly relevant as well.

Similarly, throughout most of our discussion, we referred to developmental processes in childhood, and in particular in one's family of origin. However, we have noted in our discussion that many of the attributes of the internal world of the transformational leader have genetic origins, some quite high in magnitude. The study of leadership may therefore benefit from the investigation of these effects as well. It should also be noted that the focus on childhood and on the family of origin in the present discussion should not lead researchers to overlook other major arenas, such as the peer group in which important developmental processes occur as well as what occurs in other significant periods of development, such as adolescence. For example, in adolescence as compared with childhood, more spontaneous groups of youngsters (unsupervised by adults) are formed, where adolescents can practice their leadership skills and develop leadership self-efficacy. Exploring how these experiences shape development is essential to building a life-span theory of leadership development.

In sum, this chapter is an attempt to address questions already raised in Bass's early work (Bass, 1985), namely: who are the transformational leaders, and how do they develop? Although there is a remarkable progress in understanding transformational leaders' impact, the internal world of these leaders remained to a great extent unstudied. The suggested directions and concepts discussed here and their expansion can broaden our perspective on the less visible and less observed aspects underlying many of the behaviors and outcome variables so frequently investigated, measured, and discussed in leadership literature. By borrowing from developmental and personality psychology research, as exemplified in the case of attachment theory, the leadership domain may gain a better understanding of psychodynamic processes that have not been the focus of research so far. These angles might also add practical contribution relevant to the selection of leaders, placement in leadership roles, and the development of transformational leaders.

REFERENCES

Ainsworth, M. D. S. (1989). Attachment beyond infancy. *American Psychologist, 44*, 709–716.

Ainsworth, M. D. S. (1992). John Bowlby (1907–1990). *American Psychologist, 47*, 668.

Ainsworth, M. D. S., Blehar, M., Wates, E., & Wall, S. (1978). *Patterns of attachment: A psychological study of strange situations.* Hillsdale, NJ: Erlbaum.

Arcus. D. (2001). Inhibited and uninhibited children: biology in the social context. In: T. D. Wachs & G. A. Kohnstamm (Eds), *Temperament in context* (pp. 43–60). Mahwah, NJ: Lawrence Erlbaum.

Avolio, B. J., & Gibbons, T. C. (1988). Developing transformational leaders: A life span approach. In: J. A. Conger & R. N. Kanungo (Eds), *Charismatic leadership: The elusive factor in organizational effectiveness* (pp. 276–308). San Francisco, CA: Jossey-Bass.

Bandura, A. (1977). Self-efficacy: Toward a unifying theory of behavioral change. *Psychological Review, 2*, 191–215.

Bandura, A. (1986). *Social foundation of thought and action: A social cognitive view.* Englewood Cliffs, NJ: Prentice-Hall.

Bandura, A. (Ed.) (1995). *Self-efficacy in changing societies.* New York: Cambridge University Press.

Bass, B. M. (1985). *Leadership and performance beyond expectations.* New York: Free Press.

Bass, B. M. (1990). *Bass & Stogdill's handbook of leadership: Theory, research and management applications.* New York: Free Press.

Bass, B. M. (1998). *Transformational leadership: Industry, military and educational impact.* Mahwah, NJ: Erlbaum.

Bass, B. M. (1999a). Two decades of research and development in transformational leadership. *European Journal of Work and Organizational Psychology, 8*, 9–32.

Bass, B. M. (1999b). Current developments in transformational leadership: Research and applications. *Psychologist Manager Journal, 3*, 5–21.

Bass, B. M., & Avolio, B. J. (1990). The implications of transactional and transformational leadership for individual, team and organizational development. In: R. W. Woodman & W. A. Passmore (Eds), *Research in organizational change and development.* Greenwich, CT: JAI Press.

Bass, B. M., & Avolio, B. J. (1993). Transformational leadership: a response to critiques. In: N. M. Chemers & R. Agmarl (Eds), *Leadership theory and research: Perspectives and directions*. San Diego, CA: Academic Press.

Bass, B. M., & Avolio, B. J. (1996). *Manual for the Multifactor Leadership Questionnaire*. Palo Alto, CA: Mind Garden.

Baumrind, D. (1978). Parental disciplinary patterns and social competence in children. *Youth and Society, 9*, 239–275.

Baumrind, D. (1996). The discipline controversy revisited. *Family relations: Journal of Applied Family and Child Studies, 45*, 405–414.

Bergeman, C. S., Chipuer, H. M., Plomin, R., & Pedersen, N. L. (1993). Genetic and environmental effects on openness to experience, agreeableness, and conscientiousness: An adoption/twin study. *Journal of Personality, 61*, 159–179.

Bowlby, J. (1969). *Attachment and loss* (Vol. 1). *Attachment*. New York: Basic Books.

Bowlby, J. (1973). *Attachment and loss* (Vol. 2). *Separation*. New York: Basic Books.

Bowlby, J. (1977). The making and breaking of affectional bonds. *British Journal of Psychiatry, 130*, 201–210.

Bowlby, J. (1988). *A secure base: Clinical applications of attachment theory*. London: Routledge.

Bretherton, I. (1985). Attachment theory: Retrospect and prospect. In: I. Bretherton & E. Waters (Eds), *Growing points of attachment theory and research* (pp. 3–37).

Bullock, A. (1991). *Hitler and Stalin. Parallel lives*. London: Harper & Collins.

Burns, J. M. (1956). *Roosevelt*. New York: Harcourt Brace.

Burns, J. M. (1978). *Leadership*. New York: Harper & Row.

Bycio, P., Hackett, R. D., & Allen, J. S. (1995). Further assessments of Bass's (1985) conceptualization of transactional and transformational leadership. *Journal of Applied Psychology, 80*, 468–478.

Cassidy, J. (1999). The nature of the child's ties. In: J. Cassidy & P. R. Shaver (Eds), *Handbook of attachment: Theory, research and clinical implications* (pp. 3–20). New York: Guilford Press.

Cassidy, J., & Berlin, L. J. (1994). The insecure/ambivalent pattern of attachment: Theory and research. *Child Development, 65*, 971–991.

Chadha, Y. (1997). *Gandhi: A life*. New York: John Wiley & Sons.

Chang, E. C. (Ed.) (2001). *Optimism and pessimism: Implications for theory, research and practice*. Washington, D.C.: American Psychological Association.

Chemers, M. M., Watson, C. B., & May, S. T. (2000). Dispositional affect and leadership effectiveness: A comparison of self-esteem, optimism, and efficacy. *Personality and Social Psychology Bulletin, 26*, 267–277.

Cicchetti, D., Toth, S. L., & Lynch, M. (1995). Bowlby's dream comes full circle: The application of attachment theory to risk and psychopathology. In: T. H. Ollendick & R. J. Prinz (Eds), *Advances in clinical child psychology* (Vol. 17, pp. 1–75). New York: Plenum Press.

Clover, W. H. (1990). Transformational leaders: Team performance, leadership ratings, and first hand impressions. In: K. E. Clark & M. B. Clark (Eds), *Measures of leadership* (pp. 171–184). West Orange, NJ: Leadership Library of America.

Collins, N. L., & Read, S. J. (1994). Cognitive representations of attachment: The structure and function of working models. In: K. Bartholomew & D. Perlman (Eds), *Attachment processes in adulthood, advances in personal relationships* (Vol. 5, pp. 53–91). London, PA: Jessica Kingsley.

Conger, J. A., & Kanungo, R. N. (1988). The empowerment process: Integration and practice. *Academy of Management Review, 13*, 471–482.

Costa, P. T. Jr., & McCrae, R. R. (1992). *Revised NEO personality inventory (NEO-PI-R) and NEO Five-factor Inventory (NEO-FFI) professional manual.* Odessa, FL: Psychological Assessment Resources.

Crowell, J. A., Fraley, R. C., & Shaver, P. R. (1999). In: J. Cassidy & P. R. Shaver (Eds), *Handbook of attachment: Theory, research, and clinical applications* (pp. 434–468). New York: The Guilford Press.

De-Wolf, M., & Van IJzendoorn, M. H. (1997). Sensitivity and attachment: A meta-analysis on parental antecedents of infant attachment. *Child Development, 68*, 571–591.

Deluga, R. J. (1997). Relationship among American presidential charismatic leadership, narcissism, and rated performance. *The Leadership Quarterly, 9*, 265–291.

Digman, J. M. (1989). Five robust trait dimensions: Development, stability and utility. *Journal of Personality, 57*, 195–214.

Eberly, M. B., & Montemayor, R. (1998). Doing good deeds: An examination of adolescent prosocial behavior in the context of parent-adolescent relationships. *Journal of Adolescent Research, 13*, 403–432.

Englund, M. M., Levy, A. K., Hyson, D. M., & Sroufe, L. A. (2000). Adolescent social competence: Effectiveness in a group setting. *Child Development, 71*, 1049–1060.

Erikson, E. H. (1969). *Gandhi's truth: On the origins of militant non-violence.* New York: Norton.

Feeney, J. A. (1999). Adult romantic attachment and couple relationships. In: J. Cassidy & P. R. Shaver (Eds), *Handbook of attachment: Theory, research, and clinical implications* (pp. 355–377). New York: The Guilford Press.

Fiest, G. J. (1998) A meta-analysis of personality in scientific and artistic creativity. *Personality and Social Psychology Bulletin, 2*, 290–309.

Freud, S. (1920). *A general introduction to psychoanalysis* (American Edition, pp. 363–365). Garden City, NY.

Gardner, J. (1995). *Leading minds: An anatomy of leadership.* New York: Basic Books.

George, A. L., & George, G. L. (1956). *Woodrow Wilson and Colonel House: A personality study.* New York: Macmillan.

George, C., & Solomon, J. (1989). Internal working models of caregiving and security of attachment at age six. *Infant Mental Health Journal, 10*, 227–237.

Gibbons, T. C. (1986). Revisiting the question of born vs. made: Toward a theory of development of transformational leaders. Unpublished doctoral dissertation, Fielding Institute.

Gillham, J. E. (Ed.) (2000). *The science of optimism and hope: Research essays in honor of Martin E. P. Seligman. Laws of life symposia series.* Philadelphia, PA: Templeton Foundation Press.

Green-Hennessy, S., & Reis, H. T. (1998). Openness in processing social information among attachment types. *Personal Relationships, 5*, 449–466.

Grusec, J. E., & Dix, T. (1986). The socialization of prosocial behavior: Theory and reality. In: C. Zahn-Waxler, E. M. Cummings & R. Iannotti (Eds), *Altruism and aggression, biological and social origins* (pp. 218–237). Cambridge: Cambridge University Press.

Hackett, G., & Betz, N. E. (1995). Self-efficacy and career choice and development. In: J. E. Maddux (Ed.), *Self-efficacy, adaptation and adjustment: Theory, research and application.* New York: Plenum.

Hazan, C., & Shaver, P. (1987). Romantic love conceptualized as an attachment process. *Journal of Personality and Social Psychology, 52*, 511–524.

Hazan, C., & Shaver, P. (1990). Love and work: An attachment theoretical perspective. *Journal of Personality and Social Psychology, 59*, 270–280.

Hjelle, L. A., Busch, E. A., & Warren, J. E. (1996). Explanatory style, dispositional optimism, and reported parental behavior. *Journal of Genetic Psychology, 157*, 489–499.

House, R. J..(1977). A 1976 theory of charismatic leadership. In: J. G. Hunt & L. L. Larson (Eds), *Leadership: The cutting edge* (pp. 189–207). Carbondale, IL: Southern Illinois University Press.

House, R. J., & Howell, J. M. (1992). Personality and charismatic leadership. *Leadership Quarterly, 3*, 81–108.

Howell, J. M. (1988). Two faces of charisma: socialized and personalized leadership in organizations. In: J. A. Conger & K. N. Kanungo (Eds), *Charismatic leadership and the elusive factor in organizational effectiveness*. San Francisco, CA: Jossey Bass.

Howell, J. M., & Avolio, B. J. (1992). The ethics of charismatic leadership: Submission or liberation? *Academy of Management Executive, 6*, 43–54.

Iremonger, L. (1970). *The fiery chariot*. London: Secker & Warburg.

Judge, A., & Bono, J. E. (2000). Five factor model of personality and transformational leadership. *Journal of Applied Psychology, 85*, 751–765.

Kets de Vries, M. F. R. (1989). *Prisoners of leadership*. New York: Norton.

Kirkpatrick, S. A., & Locke, E. A. (1991). Leadership: Do traits matter? *Academy of Management Executive*, 48–60.

Klein, K., & House, R. (1995). On fire: Charismatic leadership and level of analysis. *Leadership Quarterly, 6*, 183–198.

Kobak, R. R., & Sceery, A. (1988). Attachment in late adolescence: Working models, affect regulation of self and others. *Child Development, 59*, 135–146.

Kohlberg, L. (1963). Moral development and identification. In: H. W. Stevenson (Ed.), *Child psychology* (pp. 277–232). Chicago: Chicago University Press.

Kohut, H. (1971). *The analysis of the self*. New York: International Universities Press.

Lieberman, A. F., Weston, D. R., & Pawl, J. (1991). Preventing intervention and ouctome with anxiously attached dyads. *Child Development, 62*, 199–209.

Lindholm, C. (1988). Lovers and leaders. *Social Science Information, 16*, 227–246.

Lindholm, C. (1990). *Charisma*. London: Blackwell.

Maccoby, E. E., & Martin, J. A. (1983). Socialization in the context of the family. In: P. H. Mussen (Ed.), *Handbook of child psychology* (4th ed., Vol. 4, pp. 1–101). New York: Wiley.

McCrae, R. R. (1987). Creativity, divergent thinking, and openness to experience. *Journal of Personality and Social Psychology, 52*, 1258–1265.

McCrae, R. R., & Costa, P. T. Jr. (1997). Conceptions and correlates of openness to experience. In: R. Hogan & J. A. Johnson (Eds), *Handbook of Personality Psychology* (pp. 825–847). San Diego, CA: Academic Press.

McCrae, R. R., & Costa, P. T. Jr. (1988). Recalled parent-child relations and adult personality. *Journal of Personality, 56*, 417–434.

McCrae, R. R., & John, O. P. (1992). An introduction to the five-factor model and its applications. *Journal of Personality, 2*, 175–215.

Maddux, J. E. (Ed.) (1995). *Self-efficacy, adaptation, and adjustment: Theory, research, and application. The Plenum Series in social/clinical psychology*. New York: Plenum Press.

Main, M. (1983). Exploration, play and level of cognitive functioning as related to security of infant -mother attachment. *Infant Behavior Development, 6*, 167–174.

Main, M. (1990). Cross-cultural studies of attachment organization: Recent studies, changing methodologies, and the concept of conditional strategies. *Human Development, 33,* 48–61.

Main, M., Kaplan, N., & Cassidy, J. (1985). Security in infancy, childhood, and adulthood: A move to the level of representation. In: I. Bretherton & E. Waters (Eds), *Growing points in attachment theory and research. Monographs of the Society for Research in Child Development* (Vol. 50, pp. 66–106).

Markus, H., & Nurius, P. (1986). Possible selves. *American Psychologist, 41,* 954–969.

Maslow, A. (1970). *Motivation and personality.* New York: Harper & Row.

Matas, L, Arend, R. A., & Sroufe, L. A. (1978). Continuity of adaptation in the second year: The relationship between quality of attachment and later competence. *Child Development, 49,* 547–556.

Mayseless, O. (1996). Attachment patterns and their outcomes. *Human Development, 39,* 206–223.

Mayseless, O. (1998). Characteristics of the controlling attachment pattern in adulthood – further validation. Paper presented at the 9th International Conference on Personal Relationships, Skidmore College, Saratoga Springs, New York.

Mayseless, O., Sharabany, R., & Sagi, A. (1997). Attachment concerns of others as manifested in parental, spousal and friendship relationships. *Personal Relationships, 4,* 255–269.

Mayseless, O., & Popper, M. (2001). *Leadership and followership: An attachment perspective.* Haifa: University of Haifa.

Meindl, J.,R. (1995). The romance of leadership as follower-centric theory: a social construction approach. *Leadership Quarterly, 6,* 329–341.

Mikulincer, M., & Orbach, I. (1995). Attachment styles and repressive defensiveness: The accessibility and architecture of affective memories. *Journal of Personality and Social Psychology, 68,* 917–925.

Mikulincer, M. (1997). Attachment style and information processing: Individual differences in curiosity and cognitive closure. *Journal of Personality and Social Psychology, 72,* 1217–1230.

Mikulincer, M., & Florian, V. (1995). Appraisal of and coping with a real-life stressful situation: The contribution of attachment styles. *Journal of Personality and Social Psychology, 21,* 406–414.

Mikulincer, M., & Arad, D. (1999). Attachment working models and cognitive openness in close relationships: A test of chronic and temporary accessibility effects. *Journal of Personality and Social Psychology, 77,* 710–725.

Mumford, M. D., Gessner, T. E., Connely, M. S., O'Connor, J. A., & Clifton, T. C. (1993). Leadership and destructive acts: Individual and situational influences. *Leadership Quarterly, 4,* 115–147.

Mumford, M. D., & Mowry, J. M. (this volume). Vision and mental models: The case of charismatic and ideological leadership.

Peterson, C., & Bossio, L. (1991). *Health and optimism.* New York: Free Press.

Plomin, R., Scheier, M. F., Bergeman, C. S., Pedersen, N. L., Nesselroade, J., & McClearn, G. (1992). Optimism, pessimism and mental health: A twin/adoption analysis. *Personality and Individual Differences, 13,* 921–930.

Popper, M. (1999). The sources of motivation of personalized and socialized charismatic leaders. *Psychoanalysis and Contemporary Thought, 22,* 231–246.

Popper, M (2000). The development of charismatic leaders. *Political Psychology, 21*(4), 729–744.

Popper, M. (2001). *Hypnotic leadership: Leaders, followers, and the loss of self.* Westport, CT: Praeger.

Popper, M., & Mayseless, O. (2001). Back to basics: Transformational leadership as good parenthood. Unpublished manuscript.

Popper, M., Mayseless, O., & Castelnovo, O. (2000). Transformational leadership and attachment. *Leadership Quarterly, 11*, 267–289.

Post, J. M. (1986). Narcissism and the charismatic leader-follower relationship. *Political Psychology, 7*, 675–687.

Raz, G. (2001). Socialization for leadership. Doctoral dissertation (in preparation). Haifa: Department of Psychology, University of Haifa, Israel.

Ross, S. M., & Offerman, L.. R. (1997). Transformational leaders: measures of personality attributes and work group performance. *Personality and Social Psychology Bulletin, 23*, 1078–1086.

Roush, P. E., & Atwater, L. (1992). Using the MBTI to understand transformational leadership and self-perception accuracy. *Military Psychology, 4*, 17–34.

Rubin, K. H., Hastings, P. D., Stewart, S. L., & Henderson, H. A. (1997). The consistency and concomitants of inhibition: Some of the children, all of the time. *Child Development, 68*, 467–483.

Rutter, M. (1996). Clinical implications of attachment concepts: Retrospect and prospect. In: M. E. Hertzig & E. A. Farber (Eds), *Annual Progress in Child Psychiatry and Child Development.* New York: Brunner/ Mazel.

Scheier, M. F., & Carver, C. S. (1985). Optimism, coping and health: Assessment and implications of generalized outcome expectations. *Health Psychology, 4*, 219–247.

Scheier, M. F., & Carver, C. S. (1993). On the power of positive thinking: The benefits of being optimistic. *Current Directions in Psychological Science*, 26–30.

Schneider, B., Paul, M. C., White, S. S., & Holcombe, K. M. (1999). Understanding high school student leaders. 1: Predicting teacher ratings of leader behavior. *Leadership Quarterly, 10*, 609–636.

Shamir B. (1991). The charismatic relationship: Alternative explanations and predictions. *Leadership Quarterly, 2*, 81–104.

Shamir, B. (1995). Social distance and charisma. Theoretical notes and explanatory study. *Leadership Quarterly, 1*, 19–48.

Shamir, B., House, R. J., & Arthur, M. B. (1993).The motivational effects of charismatic leadership: a self concept based theory. *Organization Science, 4*, 577–593.

Shields, A., Ryan, R. M., & Cicchetti, D. (2001). Narrative representations of caregivers and emotion dysregulation as predictors of maltreated children's rejection by peers. *Developmental Psychology, 37*, 321–337.

Simonton, D. K. (1986). Presidential style: Personality, biography, and performance. *Journal of Personal and Social Relationships, 55*, 928–936.

Smith, J. A., & Foti, R. J. (1998). A pattern approach to the study of leader emergence. *Leadership Quarterly, 9*, 503–526.

Solomon, J., & George, C. (1999). The measurement of attachment security in infancy and childhood. In: J. Cassidy & P. R. Shaver, (Eds), *Handbook of attachment: Theory, research, and clinical applications* (pp. 287–318). New York: The Guilford Press.

Sroufe, L. A. (1983). Infant-caregiver attachment and patterns of adaptation in preschool: The roots of maladaptation and competence. In: M. Perlmutter (Ed.), *Minnesota Symposium in Child Psychology* (Vol. 16). Hillsdale, NJ: Erlbaum.

Steinberg, B. S. (2001). The making of female presidents and prime ministers. The impact of borth order, sex of siblings and father-daughter dynamics. *Political Psychology, 22*, 89–114.

Stoppard, M. (1991). *Test your child.* London: Dorling Kindersley.

Storr, A. (1972). *The dynamics of creation.* London: Secker & Warburg.

Streyrer, J. (this volume). Stigma and charisma and the narcissistic personality.

Taylor, S. E., & Brown, J. D.(1988). Illusion and well-being: A social psychological perspective on mental health. *Psychological Bulletin, 103*, 193–210.

Thompson, R. A. (1999). Early attachment and later development. In: J. Cassidy, & P. R. Shaver (Eds), *Handbook of attachment, Theory research and clinical applications* (pp. 265–286). New York: Guilford Press.

Van Izendoorn, M. H., Juffer, F., & Duyvesteyn, M. G. C. (1995). Breaking the intergenerational cycle of insecure attachment: A review of the effects of attachment-based interventions on maternal sensitivity and infant security. *Journal of Child Psychology and Psychiatry, 36*, 225–248.

Van-Lange, P. A. M., De-Bruin, E. M. N., Otten, W., & Joireman, J. A. (1997). Development of prosocial, individualistic, and competitive orientations: Theory and preliminary evidence. *Journal of Personality and Social Psychology, 73*, 733–746.

Wiggins, J. S. (Ed.) (1996). *The five factor model of personality: Theoretical perspectives.* New York: Guilford Press.

Yammarino, F. J., & Bass, B. M. (1990). Transformational leadership and multiple levels of analysis. *Human Relations, 43*, 975–995.

Zahn-Waxler, C., Cummings, E. M., & Iannotti, R. (Eds) (1986). *Altruism and aggression, biological and social origins.* Cambridge: Cambridge University Press.

Zahn-Waxler, C., Schiro, K., Robinson, J. L., Emde, R. N., & Schmitz, S. (2001). Empathy and prosocial patterns in young MZ and DZ twins. Development and genetic and environmental influences. In: R. N. Emde & J. K. Hewitt (Eds), *Infancy to early childhood: Genetic and environmental influences on developmental change* (pp. 141–162). New York: Oxford University Press.

Zaleznik, A. (1992). Managers and leaders: are they different? *Harvard Business Review*, (March-April), 126–133.

Zuckerman, M. (2001). Optimism and pessimism: Biological foundations. In: E. C. Chang (Ed.), *Optimism and pessimism: Implications for theory research and practice* (pp. 169–188). Washington, D.C.: American Psychological Association.

STIGMA AND CHARISMA AND THE NARCISSISTIC PERSONALITY

Johannes Steyrer

ABSTRACT

In the 1990s, scientists succeeded in demonstrating the highly positive effects of transformational and charismatic leadership on performance effectiveness, based on a large number of empirical findings. Bass (1985) predicted that this type of leadership would be related to "performance beyond expectations". This has proved to be true to a very large extent. The so-called "new leadership approach", however, has not yet succeeded in a close analysis of the interaction and influencing processes between charismatic leaders and their followers. This paper provides such an analysis. After pointing out the main problems with prior theoretical work, we offer an alternative model to help explain the emergence of charisma using social-cognitive and psycho-dynamic theories. Basically, we start from the premise that a focal person may be categorized as a charismatic leader on the basis of evaluative borderline attributes assigned to him or her, which are closely related to characteristics stigmatized by society. These attributes are exhibited consciously or unconsciously by the leader, either by means of social dramatization or by means of social reversion. We then propose a model of charismatic leadership relationships, which deal with both intra-personal and inter-personal feedback processes, based on recent theories of narcissistic behavior. Our overall intent is to help explain and clarify the processes between leadership behavior and the attribution of charisma.

Transformational and Charismatic Leadership, Volume 2, pages 231–254.
ISBN: 0-7623-0962-8

INTRODUCTION

Within this chapter, there is no need to go into the history of how the so-called "new leadership approaches" (Bryman, 1992) or the "neocharismatic school" (House & Aditya, 1997) have been accepted in the literature, as there are already some excellent reviews of this literature to refer to in this volume and previous publications (e.g. Bass, 1995, 1998; Conger, 1999; Conger & Hunt, 1999; Jermier, 1993). Prior reviews indicate that the new leadership approach has introduced a paradigm shift that has provided important new insights into the nature of highly effective leadership practices. In this context, Bass (1985, 1998) and his colleagues (e.g. Avolio, 1999; Bass & Avolio, 1996) have worked towards making charismatic leadership measurable by means of their Multifactor Leadership Questionnaires and analyzing its positive effects in various areas. Placing charisma within the broader construct of transformational leadership has provided a wide range of opportunities for more in-depth work on construct validation of charisma. However, as one critic points out, there are some weaknesses, since these concepts, "do not describe the underlying influence processes clearly, nor do they specify how the leadership behaviors" associated with charismatic and transformational leadership "are related to these processes" (Yukl, 1999, p. 301).

In this chapter, we will try to counter this criticism and provide starting points for a reply to the questions it poses. For this purpose, it is necessary, as a first step, to prepare a short overview and critique of prior models of charismatic leadership. After pointing out the problems with prior models, we offer a new model to help explain charisma-based leadership using social-cognitive and psycho-dynamic theories.

DEFICITS OF CHARISMA RESEARCH

If we try to set up a conceptual system of charismatic concepts developed so far in the literature, we can distinguish in principle between four different approaches:

(1) leader-centered;
(2) follower-centered;
(3) interdependency-oriented; and
(4) context-centered approaches

(Steyrer, 1995). Since the last approach refers to concepts that deal with the phenomenon on a macro-level, and since the following model is based on micro-theory, we deal only with the first three approaches below.

Leader-centered approaches are based on the assumption that charisma is a phenomenon where followers respond to exceptional/exemplary characteristics of behavior exhibited by the leader by attributing charisma to him/her. The explanation pattern has the following form: exceptional/exemplary individual person + vision + contextual crisis as a moderator variable→followers under stress→attribution of charisma (e. g. Conger & Kanungo, 1987, 1998; House et al., 1991; Howell & Frost, 1989; Howell & Higgins, 1990; Puffer, 1990; Shamir et al., 1994; Willner, 1984; Yagil, 1998). Thus, the basic assumption is that no one specific context (e.g. a context of crisis) plays the determining role in the appearance or presence of a charismatic leader, but that specific characteristics of the leader cause an attribution of charisma. The question therefore is this: "If the follower's attribution of charisma depends on the observed behavior of the leader, then what are the behavioral components responsible for such attributions?" (Conger & Kanungo, 1987, p. 640).

Although researchers have succeeded in formulating relatively detailed indications regarding the specific types of behavior and characteristics exhibited by charismatic leaders, one central point of criticism remains: This approach is based on a "naive" interpretation of the charisma attribution process. With this behavioral model, followers are expected to respond to the perception of specific modes of behavior/characteristics on the part of the leader by mechanistically attributing charisma to him/her. The active part solely lies with the leader, whereas the followers react passively. Their position in the relationship system can therefore be compared to a mirror that reflects a "real" picture of the leader.

Conversely, in follower-centered theories, the question is: what makes followers project exceptional/exemplary qualities on to a leader, where the main emphasis is on the illusionary character of perception (e.g. Downton, 1973; Meindl, 1990, 1995; Miyahara, 1983)? The explanation pattern here has the following form: (contextual crisis)→followers under stress→appearance of leader + vision→attribution of charisma. The charismatic phenomenon emerges within the context of lateral relations that develop among followers themselves and has been referred to as the "social contagion effect". "These are, to a large degree, functionally autonomous from whatever forces are emanating from the traits and behaviors of the leaders per se" (Meindl, 1990, p. 197).

Thus, compared to the leader-centered perspective, relations are reversed. The active part in the relationship is ascribed to the followers, who, as a consequence of group-dynamic processes and psychic conflicts, project charisma on to a focal person if that person proves to be able to provide an answer to critical situations or crises being experienced by followers.

Interdependency models, which deal with the interactive relation between leaders and followers, have the following form: exceptional/exemplary leader + followers under stress→charismatic relationship. The decisive factor here is the idea that charisma cannot be analyzed from either a follower or a leader perspective, but only by considering the interactive relationship that takes place (e.g. House & Shamir, 1993; Lindholm, 1990; Pauchant, 1991; Schweitzer, 1984; Shamir et al., 1993, 1998).

Lindholm describes the research perspective on which this third approach is based as follows: "Charisma is, above all, a relationship, a mutual mingling of the inner selves of leader and follower. Therefore, it follows that if the charismatic is able to compel, the follower has a matching capacity for being compelled, we then need to consider what makes up the personality configuration of the follower, as well as that of the leader, if we are to understand charisma" (Lindholm, 1990, p. 7).

The charisma concept of House and Shamir (1993) and Shamir et al. (1993) appears to be promising in this connection. Their focus is to supplement current theories of charismatic leadership with a motivational theory that is able to better explain the relationship between leader behavior and its effects on followers. However, in a recent empirical study, Shamir et al. (1998) found that the ego-concept theory did not receive substantial support.

The main point of criticism against research carried out so far is that social-cognitive processes have not been taken into consideration in terms of explaining perceptions of charismatic leadership. The resulting ontological polarization of charisma is to be criticized using a social-cognitive framework of relations. Either a mechanistic allocation of charisma is implied, where the leader is what he/she appears to be in the eyes of his/her followers, or the phenomenon is "diluted" exclusively down to "projective" attributions, where the leader becomes a carrier of charisma without any efforts on his/her part.

LEADERSHIP AND INFORMATION PROCESSING

Cognitive processing research attempts to explain how people acquire, store, retrieve, or use information in their perception of leadership. The individual is defined here as an active information processor who, by means of "subjective" perception and processing of "objective" stimuli, creates his/her own image of reality (Lord & Maher, 1989, 1990, 1991; Offermann et al., 1994). Since social interaction often makes high processing demands on perceivers, efficiencies are created by having perceivers revert to pre-existing knowledge structures to interpret whether a behavior or action is charismatic leadership. Such knowledge has been referred to as "implicit leadership theories" or "cognitive categories" (Binning et al., 1986; Hartog et al., 1999; Lord, 1985; Lord & Foti, 1986; Lord et al., 1984; Phillips & Lord, 1982).

Through general day-to-day experiences as well as through experience in a particular organizational context, people develop detailed knowledge structures pertinent to perceiving and interpreting leadership. Empirical research shows that classifying an individual as a leader involves matching certain stimulus properties to a leader prototype held in memory. The "prototype" here is defined as, "an abstraction of features common to leaders that is developed through experience" (Lord & Maher, 1991, p. 54), with the whole perceptual process (selective attention, encoding, storage/retention and retrieval) being selectively influenced by these prototypical attributes.

The GLOBE project, which is an intercultural study involving 170 scientists from 64 countries (Hartog et al., 1999), had as one of its central objectives to study which attributes constituted prototypical attributes of outstanding leadership across, within, and between cultures. Our chapter builds on earlier work of Lord et al. (1984), since their initial research was based on determining the prototypical attributes associated with average everyday leadership. The most important of these attributes are: dedicated, goal oriented, informed, charismatic, decisive, responsible, intelligent, secure, organized, verbal skills, believable, directing, good administrator, honest, concerned, disciplined, trustworthy, just, strong character, open-minded, persuasive, interested, insightful, understanding, competitive, co-operative, loyal, educated, industrious, and caring.

Our goal is to extract from these attributes when and how a leader is perceived as being outstanding or exceptional/exemplary, or, in other words, as charismatic. Our goal is based on the theory that the attribution of charisma to a leader does not have its origin in the prototypical attributes contained in a follower's head. If leaders want to be perceived as outstanding or exceptional/exemplary, they have to go beyond what is expected. Our model is based on the thesis that the categorization of a stimulus person as a charismatic leader emerges from the allocation of evaluative *borderline attributes*. These borderline attributes are closely related to socially stigmatized characteristics and are either consciously or unconsciously intended on the part of the leader. They are realized either by means of *social dramatization* or by means of *social reversion* of prototypical attributes. The expressive quality of leaders and the cognitive impressive quality that they have on their followers are only partly congruent, depending upon cognitive information processing.

The basic concept of this model is the assumption that stigma and charisma mutually refer to each other and emerge from each other. This idea goes back to a sociological study by Lipp (1985). To make this thesis comprehensible, it is necessary, first of all, to discuss the concept of stigma. Then, Lipp's theory is explained, as necessary. Finally, we discuss our own model.

DIALECTICS BETWEEN STIGMA AND CHARISMA

The concept of stigma is related to the word sting, originally meaning a tattoo, and in a broader sense, a brand for a slave, criminal or traitor. In a sociological context, stigma refers to attributes that serve as signals within a group or society to treat carriers of these attributes in a way deviant from the usual. Goffman (1963, 1967) uses this concept in connection with a person who, "has a quality that distinguishes him/her from others in this category of people" (Goffman, 1967, p. 19), a stigma being a quality that "is deeply discrediting" (Goffman, 1967, p. 11). He differentiates between three different kinds of stigmata: disfigurements of the body, consisting of various types of physical deformation, individual character defects, as well as phylogenetic stigmata based on race, nationality, or religion. Carrying a stigma therefore means that somebody is, "other than anticipated in some undesired way" (Goffman, 1967, p. 13). Stigma in this sense is the dialectic counterpart of charisma, so to speak, where a person is different from what is generally expected in a *desired* way.

Lipp (1985) was the first to work out the dialectic relation between stigma and charisma. Lipp departs from the assumption that processes that lead to the formation of charismatic qualities are originally rooted in stigmatization: "Charismatic characteristics are closely related to stigmatic characteristics, the latter defining their carriers as primarily 'miserable', i.e. socio-morally deficient; ... making connections visible that are of a fundamental character" (Lipp, 1985, pp. 11–12).

Lipp regards deviant behavior, which he calls "borderline behavior", as essential for both the stigma and the charisma phenomena. Borderline behavior is experienced as being deviant because it pushes its carrier towards the edge or out of the group. Borderline behavior could, however, also make a group begin to doubt the validity of the practice it assumes to be normal. Consciously applied, borderline behavior could therefore create the possibility of initiating social changes and of making oneself the center of events, or even of occupying a morally highly valued position.

In this connection, Lipp also talks about self-stigmatization. Through the process of self-stigmatization, people would be capable of giving the situation of the establishment a negative connotation and the situation of the oppressed a positive connotation by re-evaluating the latter's afflictions cognitively and normatively, and by requiring potential addressees to make a virtue of necessity. That is, people would actively and consciously identify with the situation of the underprivileged members of society.

Lipp illustrated his hypothesis on the connection between stigma and charisma among others by referring to Jesus of Nazareth, "Jesus was not a 'victim of justice' in this sense, but he was his own victim; it was he himself who allowed the wounds and stabs, the stigma of death, to be inflicted on himself; by dying, he 'criminalized' not himself, but the judiciary, the powers of this world. The cross which he took upon himself should deliver the world eventually from evil in general – this is where self-stigmatization reaches its peak" (Lipp, 1985, p. 43). Christ therefore most obviously discloses the dialectics between sin and salvation, the sacrificial lamb and the scapegoat, martyrdom and grace, and stigma and charisma.

Lipp thus discusses the mutual interplay between stigma and charisma within the framework of the sociology of deviant behavior where banditry, sectarianism, and messianism play a decisive role, among other things. Charisma emerges from stigma or is rooted in self-stigmatization. This theoretical concept leads to the question of what has to be concluded from analyses of socially deviant behavior of members of social fringe groups – such as religious founders, provokers, ascetics, and so forth – for an analysis of leaders in organizations who are part of the core of the establishment in a society, so to speak, and whose charisma certainly does not result from expressly deviant behavior.

THE IMPRESSION CONTINUUM OF LEADERSHIP

The following model is based on the assumption that evaluative borderline attributes can be derived from the prototypical attributes connected with the concept of a leader. This represents a key extension of Lord and his colleagues' earlier work. These evaluative borderline attributes can hold their ground in the light of normative expectations of organizations, and thus do not make their carriers members of social fringe groups. They are, however, in a dialectic relation with prototypical attributes, and they determine the dialectics between stigma and charisma according to their specific expressiveness/impressiveness.

The dialectic relation can be based on a gradual increase in intensity of attributes and behaviors associated with those that are prototypical. This relation can be exemplified by means of the characteristic "dedicated" as follows: dedicated – passionate – fanatic. Observers, therefore, have available a *semantic continuum* of attributes at their disposal by means of which they are able to evaluate the leader regarding the leader's individual attributes.

Passionate as an impressive attribute (charisma) borders on fanatic, which is a discrediting attribute.

We depart from the assumption that these evaluations are not completely separated from the actual characteristics of the leader and that – depending on regularities of interpersonal perception – leadership expressiveness and impressiveness partly correspond to each other. Furthermore, we assume that there are psycho-dynamically justifiable needs that prompt a leader to advance towards becoming a carrier of charisma consciously/unconsciously, or to function as a focal person in charismatic relationships. A means to achieve this end are actions of impression management or self-presentation, where the prototypical elements of leadership are stylized and exaggerated.

We refer below to such behavior-related accentuation and intensification of prototypical leadership qualities as "social dramatization". On the part of the followers, these expressive qualities are connected with symbolic codes (encoding) at the cognitive information-processing level. These qualities are comparisons of prototypical attributes and mark hyper-representativity in the semantic sense. The dialectic between stigma and charisma lies in the fact that overdrawn action from a certain moment on becomes or appears to become, exaggeration.

The dialectic relation between these diametrical opposites can furthermore lie in a gradual reversion of the prototypical in a way where the leader represents a positively evaluated distinctness. This can be exemplified by means of the characteristic dedicated as follows: dedicated – poised, tolerant composure/tranquil – indifferent, impassive.

The prototypical leadership characteristics can therefore also be contrasted with attributes, which, in their first degree of intensity, signal that somebody is different, with a positive connotation. The carrier of these attributes appears to be raised beyond everyday life and is characterized by exceptionality. The stigmatic aspect lies in the fact that over-exaggeration of this expressive quality can easily turn it into its negative opposite, since it is diametrically opposed to what is expected from exemplary leaders: tolerant composure/tranquility, a crediting attribute (charisma), borders on being impassive/indifferent, which is a discrediting attribute (stigma). We refer to these inverse behavior-related accentuations and intensifications of prototypical leadership characteristics as *social reversion*. On the part of the followers, these expressive qualities are connected with symbolic codes on a cognitive level, which are also comparisons of prototypical attributes in a semantic sense, but marking *anti-representativity*.

Somebody who judges a leader using leadership-related representativity heuristics has a continuum of evaluative attributes at his/her disposal.

Table 1. Impression Continuum of Leadership.

stigma	charisma		charisma	stigma
anti-representativity		prototypicality		hyper-representativity

indifferent, impassive	poised, tolerant	dedicated	passionate	fanatic
hesitant	circumspect, cautious	decisive	resolute	reckless
insecure	humble	secure	self-assured, potent	presumptuous, conceited
aimless, without purpose	flexible, spontaneous	goal-oriented	visionary	dogmatic, totalitarian
expressionless	profound, knowing	verbally skilled	eloquent, expressive	demagogic
badly informed	has a good general idea of the whole	informed	knows every detail	tunnel-visioned
chaotic	improvising	organized	has a thorough grasp of everything	meticulous, obsessive
withholding guidance, not helpful	allowing, encouraging	caring	protecting, guiding	mothering, restrictive

Departing from prototypical assumptions, intensifications in the one direction and reversions in the other are located on this continuum. Intensifications appear as *hyper-representativity*, and reversions appear as *anti-representativity*. Placing a stimulus person on this continuum outside the area showing prototypical features is at the same time an occasion for classifying him/her as a charismatic leader. The symbolic codes (cognitive impressive qualities) can be plotted on a continuum that we later term *impression continuum of leadership*.

Based on the findings from Lord and his colleagues (1984), there is a prototypical attribute at the center of each impression continuum. Therefore, the continuum needs to be read from the center. The columns at the very left and right-hand side, respectively, contain the opposites of leadership with the maximum negative connotation. The columns left and right of the center show the positive opposites. Table 1 lists some selected prototypical attributes along such an impression continuum to illustrate this framework.

Dramatization and social reversion are acts of self-presentation of a leader. Processes of self-presentation are discussed in the socio-psychological literature under headings such as *impression management, image control*, or *self-presentation* (Mummendey, 1990). The core of this theory goes back to Goffman (1963), according to whom individuals in social interaction try to control the impression they make on their interaction partners as far as possible. Therefore not only are individuals passively exposed to social impressions, but they control the anticipated influence that is exerted upon them by conveying a certain expressive quality of themselves. Thus, within the scope of self-presentation, leaders show a behavior that they hope will trigger the desired reactions and attributions regarding their personal qualities (hyper/anti-representativity) with their target audience. Gardner and Avolio (1998) have shown how leaders use impression management strategies to shape their image by means of framing, scripting, staging, and performing. Related to our model, these are strategies that can be reflected as acts of social dramatization or reversion.

This model was supported by an empirical study (Steyrer, 2000) with 200 participants, who had to describe a charismatic and a non-charismatic leader each with the impression continuum of leadership. By means of factor analysis, a total of seven impression dimensions of leadership could be extracted (ego-strength and commitment; capacity for enthusiasm and ambition; predominance and rigidity; subtlety and independence; extraversion and effect calculation; organization and control; loving care and sympathy), which significantly distinguished the charisma group from the non-charisma group. Hyper-representative and anti-representative impression dimensions of leader-ship could also be demonstrated, e.g. extraversion and effect calculation (e.g. outgoing; extrovert life and soul of the party) vs. introversion and authenticity (e.g. profound, a deep person; allows himself to be himself, relaxed) or predominance and rigidity (e.g. dog-eat-dog mentality; reckless; would sell his own grandmother) versus readiness to cooperate and empathy (e.g. under-standing; just; co-operative). Furthermore, the study showed that in 80% of the cases, charismatic leaders were described by means of hyper-representativity attributes.

DIGRESSION: ARCHETYPES OF LEADERSHIP AND CHARISMA

Steyrer (1995, 1998, 2000) has also demonstrated that there is a polymorphous phenotype of charisma in principle. This position can be traced back directly to Weber's fundamental concept, which distinguishes between 17 different types of charisma (Hummel, 1972). For differentiating between possible phenotypes, he refers to a concept going back to Neuberger (1990). Neuberger assumes that behind the category of leadership, there is another and more basic dimension, namely archetypes of leadership that are structured according to the images of fathers, heroes, and saviors (Neuberger, 1990). Under the concept of archetypes, Neuberger subsumes "those mighty archetypes of the mind" that "embody the manifold phenotypes of one area of reality in a fundamental and typical way, thus representing the original" (Neuberger, 1990, p. 42). In addition to "father", "hero", and "savior", Steyrer (1995) defines a fourth archetype of leadership, namely the king. Subsequently, we can neither go into the complex mythological roots of the individual types nor describe the phenotypes in detail (Steyrer, 1998). The following characterization in broad outline will, however, give the reader some idea of these types.

Within the framework of a society dominated by patriarchy, the father (*paternalistic charisma*) represents the "archetype of the creator, generator and absolute lord". He appears as someone superior, strong, knowing, great and paramount, stable, dependable and reliable. The hero (*heroic charisma*) is the juvenile counterpart of the patriarchal person, representing "what the father used to be: a hero well proven in courageous fights". The hero goes "his way unwavering and lonely" and defeats "all foes with super-human powers, gains admiration, appreciation and immortality". He "does not subordinate himself to others", but realizes the "collective dream of power and self-determination"; he can "do without company, fancies himself to be self-sufficient, mighty, strong, in short: magnificent". The savior (*missionary charisma*) is the "charismatic innovator, the great and magic transformer of the existing to the better". He holds the masses spellbound, breaks their own will, and makes them a willing tool. They readily subject themselves "to the extraordinary charisma of this luminous figure, so far removed from everyday life that it can no longer be measured by earthly standards" (Neuberger, 1990, p. 45 ff. passim).

The function and the position of the "savior", as exemplified by means of prophetic charisma by Weber, culminate in the statement, "This is what was laid down – but this is what I tell you" (Weber, 1976, p. 138).

In European folk tales, the figure of the king (*majestic charisma*) mostly is the target of the adventures and travels of the hero: the king is the final point of the hero's maturing process. Nobility by birth does not play a role here, but the message conveyed is that even central figures that have come from a simple background are capable of becoming kings. Especially in ancient cultures, the king ideally counted as the greatest of heroes but was not allowed to participate actively in fights. Finally, this figure manifests itself in the phenotype of the wise old man who is seen as the personification of the spiritual principle, where deeper insight and wisdom are inherited.

Accordingly, the metaphor of the king refers to the social reversion type of leadership in the sense of magnificence, tranquillity, introversion, and composure, which are opposed to the social dramatization types.

George Pullman is an example of paternalistic charisma, Steven Jobs of heroic charisma, and Donald Burr of missionary charisma. The form social reversion takes when manifesting itself in a king can be illustrated by the example of Hening Kagermann, the CEO at SAP. He was characterized as follows: "Kagermann is a man of small gestures, of being quietly different. He ... stands out more by what he doesn't do than by his own, mostly economical actions. ... He drives his car himself, without a chauffeur. His company car is the smallest amongst the top managers' big limousines. ... The 51-year-old appears as someone simple and unsensational, ... He is an exceptionally polite man and is courteous to the utmost, also towards his staff members. ... Kagermann does not build up a distance between himself and those he talks with. He is the first to take off his jacket in meetings. ... Kagermann does not heave himself through his company like someone who always knows what's what. His greatest ability is listening. ... He is a delicate man who you would rather think to be a cellist than a top manager. ... Hardly anybody knows that he is a humanist, that he would have liked to become a painter, and that he is an enthusiastic long distance runner. ... In fact, many in his line of business and even within his own company regard him as a 'softie'. He has always remained the same old Kagermann" (Manager, 1998, p. 106 ff.)

What appears as exceptional/exemplary with Kagermann is the eccentricity of his reserve and modesty. It has an irritating effect because, in his position, omnipotence is anticipated. He impresses by his introverted reserve, which is reminiscent of an artist's sensitivity. Accordingly, it is the unfamiliar that appears as the superlative of the non-sensational where the sensational is expected. Here, the focused reversion of what is anticipated into its positively connotated opposite manifests itself.

Finally, the archetypes of leadership can be understood as mythical super categories, which determine which basic forms of leadership exist in the first place and how leadership becomes symbolic and significant, by means of dramatization and reversion. At the same time, these mythical super categories function as symbolically charged representativity heuristics when perceiving leadership, and define imaginable and presentable polymorphic phenotypes of charisma.

Steyrer (2000) has been able to prove empirically that paternalistic charisma has high values in particular along the impression dimensions of loving care and sympathy as well as organization and control, subtlety and independence, and ego-strength and commitment. Conversely, heroic charisma is characterized by high values for the dimensions predominance and rigidity and ego-strength and commitment, while at the same time having low values for loving care and sympathy. As expected, missionary charisma had the highest values in the area of extraversion and effect calculation as well as capacity for enthusiasm and ambition. Conversely, majestic charisma was primarily distinguished by its high values for the introversion and authenticity dimension as well as for readiness to cooperate and empathy.

We should mention the problem that the derived archetypes are decidedly masculine. Here, we have to state that the social connotations connected with the concept of leadership are, to a large extent, influenced by patriarchy. Morgan (1986) has defined several female types of leadership (e.g. Great Mother, Amazone, Daughter, Jeanne d'Arc). We would have to examine whether, based on specifically feminine attributes, an attribution of charisma could be provoked, or whether leadership and charisma emerge only by means of masculine forms of self-representation.

NARCISSISM AND CHARISMA

Now we are dealing with the questions of who tends consciously/unconsciously towards wanting to appear to be a carrier of charisma by means of borderline behavior, and who is subject to the attraction of charisma to a special degree. We are also dealing with the question of how the interrelationship between the influencing processes between the protagonists can be described. We know by now that there seem to be two faces of charisma, in the sense of an ethical and an unethical phenotype (Howell, 1988). Furthermore, it has been proved empirically that the attribution of charisma to a leader correlates to a high degree with his or her level of narcissism (Deluga, 1997; O'Conner et al., 1995). Moreover, there are reliable empirical findings according to which charisma goes hand in hand with the leader's striving for power (House et al., 1991), a characteristic that is related to narcissism. Below, we will look more closely into the correlation between charisma and narcissism. For this purpose, we will use mainly models of narcissism such as those developed by Kohut and Kernberg in the 1980s.

Freud himself defines narcissism as a phenomenon where libido is withdrawn from the outside world and is concentrated on the ego. This is therefore an increased libidinous cathexis of the ego. He describes the narcissistic character type in the following words: "The subject's main interest is directed to self-preservation; he is independent and not open to intimidation.

His ego has a large amount of aggressiveness at its disposal, which also manifests itself in readiness for activity. In his erotic life loving is preferred above being loved" (GW XIV, p. 511).

In *Group Psychology and the Analysis of the Ego* (GW XIII), Freud provides an ontogenetic reason for leadership. There, he points out that triumphant satisfaction is always felt when something within the ego coincides with the ego-ideal. If, however, there is a pronounced gap between the two, this implies a state of depression, guilt, and inferiority. Freud then concludes that leaders and followers can complement each other in so far as the leader displays his or her self-centeredness due to a small discrepancy between the ego and the ego-ideal, which corresponds to the followers' need for perfect objects. As for the processes connected with this phenomenon, Freud says that, the "object has been put in the place of the ego ideal", with the idealization process at its core. A "considerable amount of narcissistic libido overflows on to the object" in the process, so that "the ego becomes more and more unassuming and modest, and the object more and more sublime and precious, until at last it gets possession of the entire self-love of the ego (. . .). We love it on account of the perfections which we have striven to reach for our own ego" (GW XIII, p. 113 passim).

If we look at the further theoretical development of the narcissism concept in more recent literature, it is evident that the libido is being given less importance in the concept (de-libidinization). The ego in the Freudian sense functions primarily as an intermediary between the id, superego, and reality. As Knapp states, this ego is a functional ego (Knapp, 1998, p. 90). Within this view, however, it is impossible to address narcissistic needs such as the affirmation of one's own self – in the sense of a feeling of one's own worth. Psychologically determined problems in regulating one's own worth are therefore difficult to grasp on the basis of physical urges/instincts, so that Freud's *Lust-Unlust-Prinzip* (pleasure-reluctance-principle) was subsequently replaced by the *Wert-Unwert-Prinzip* (merits-demerits principle) (Stimmer, 1987, p. 107). More recent definitions speak of a narcissistic personality system in this sense, with the adverbial or adjectival use of the concept referring to all those phenomena, which refer to the regulation of self-experience (Deneke et al., 1989).

Narcissistic people have the following personality characteristics, amongst others: feelings of superiority and uniqueness, high performance in schools and in their jobs; an extraordinary degree of self-centeredness; feelings of greatness and omnipotence alternating with feelings of inferiority; constant searching for satisfaction of their striving for brilliant success, admiration, wealth, power, and beauty; a strong desire to be loved and admired by others; a tendency to idealize or to devalue contemptuously; even being just average would be unbearable; lack of ability to love and to show sympathetic consideration for others; dependence on others is not accepted (e.g. Kernberg, 1988; Ronnigstam & Gunderson, 1996).

KOHUT'S CONCEPT OF NARCISSISM

Kohut's draft is based on an anthropology, which he formulated independently and in which he contrasts the guilty human being in the Freudian paradigm with the so-called tragic human being, in line with the de-libidinization of the concept mentioned above. Kohut defines two basic human needs, namely the need to be mirrored (mirror-needs), and the need to unify with a person who one deems to be strong (idealization-needs). According to Kohut, these needs are satisfied by so-called ego-objects. In analogy with the needs, he distinguishes between two self-objects, namely ". . . those who react to the child's innate feeling of vitality, greatness and perfection and confirm it, and those to whom the child can look up and with whose displayed tranquillity, infallibility and omnipotence it can unify" (Kohut & Wolf, 1980, p. 668). But what can the mirror-needs and idealization-needs and their varying intensity – also with adults – be attributed to?

Like Freud, Kohut also departs from a paradisiac primary narcissism, a state of complete self-sufficiency, but disturbed "by the unavoidable shortcomings of maternal care" (Kohut, 1986, p. 43). The child, however, replaces this previous perfection by establishing two basic configurations:

(1) by establishing a grandiose and exhibitionistic image of the self: *the grandiose self*; and
(2) by giving over the previous perfection to an admired, omnipotent (transitional) self-object: the *idealized parent imago*

(Kohut, 1986, p. 43). The human being's mental health subsequently is fundamentally dependent on the optimum integration and development of these concepts. In its verbalized form, the unconscious grandiose self manifests itself in the statement "I am perfect", whereas the idealized parent image culminates in the symbolic statement "You are perfect, but I am part of you" (Kohut, 1986, p. 45).

According to Kohut, the peculiarities of narcissistic disorders with human beings are the results of deficitary socialization conditions due to traumatizing insensitive self-objects who do not satisfy the mirror-needs and idealization-needs. In such cases, the infantile manifestations of the grandiose self or of the idealized parent imagines are not transformed into complex and efficient structures, but are preserved in their archaic/early childhood form. On the one hand, a mirror-hungry personality can result, in the sense of someone insatiably striving for admiration and exhibiting himself/herself; on the other hand, an ideal-hungry personality can result, in the sense of someone filling a void and compensating fear by idealized self-objects. If the parental self-objects are capable of reacting as mirrors, according to the principle of optimum denial (not too much and not too little), or of allowing idealizing unification, this depends on their own mature, coherent selves.

INTERACTIVE CIRCULAR CAUSALITY IN CHARISMATIC LEADERSHIP RELATIONS

The following model is based on the theory that the conscious/unconscious intention of a leader wanting to advance to become a carrier of charisma is due to fundamental narcissistic conflicts. The demonstration of borderline behavior that goes with it can be characterized psycho-dynamically as a compensation of ego deficits. The prospective carrier of charisma provokes the followers into mirroring him/her through social dramatization or reversion in order to maintain a weak narcissistic homeostasis.

Social dramatization/reversion of leadership attributes can trigger fascination, impression, emotional stimulation in the followers under specific contextual conditions. This leads to social affirmation in the shape of enraptured worship, admiration, and acclamation. Reinforcement and attention cause the intended increase in the feeling of the leader's own worth and in his/her self-assurance: his/her ego system gains coherence. Thus, an interactive building-up process is linked with a sequence of borderline behavior and idealization in charismatic leadership relationships. If the intended mirroring is provided, this feedback from the followers has a reinforcing effect. There is a vicious circle of self-presentation, idealization, and an increase in the feeling of the leader's own worth, as can be seen from Fig. 1.

However, this circle bears the inherent risk of escalation. Why? Through intended and activated feedback, borderline behavior can be reinforced even further, so that at some point, it falls into the being stigmative. Then, social dramatization/reversion degenerates to theatrically manipulative self-presentation. Fascination is replaced by a feeling of repulsion, disgust, and emotional dis-stimulation. Social aversion in the form of discrediting rejection, aversion, and contempt is articulated, causing insecurity and irritation on the part of the leader: his or her ego system loses coherence and becomes fragmented.

If we now try to attribute one psycho-dynamically oriented relation system each to the individual expressive and impressive qualities in charismatic leadership relationships, borderline behavior is based on a narcissistic mirror-

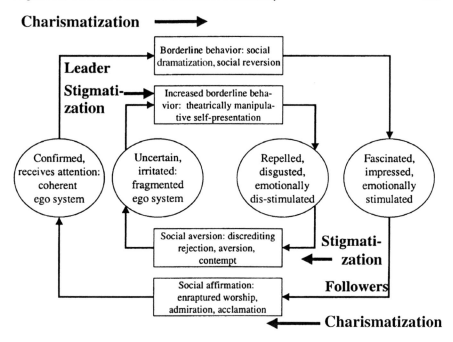

Charismatization ➡️

Leader

Stigmati-
zation

Borderline behavior: social dramatization, social reversion

Increased borderline behavior: theatrically manipulative self-presentation

Confirmed, receives attention: coherent ego system

Uncertain, irritated: fragmented ego system

Repelled, disgusted, emotionally dis-stimulated

Fascinated, impressed, emotionally stimulated

Social aversion: discrediting rejection, aversion, contempt

Social affirmation: enraptured worship, admiration, acclamation

Stigmati-
⬅️ zation

Followers

⬅️ Charismatization

Fig. 1. Interactive Circular Causality in Charismatic Leadership Relationships.

need, and enraptured worship, admiration, and acclamation on narcissistic idealization-needs and unification-needs. In connection with the emotional impressive quality, the leader's archaic grandiose self and the followers' idealized parent image are involved. In other words, the followers fill the expressive quality of the leader with narcissistic energy, which feeds from their idealized parent imagines and manifests itself in the shape of idealization-needs and unification-needs; the leader fills the expressions of the followers with narcissistic energy, which derives from his fixation on an archaic grandiose self. Fig. 2 illustrates this case.

It is difficult to explain specific destructive charismatic phenomena in the sense of unethical charisma from this model. One starting point is provided by Kernberg's narcissism theory (1988), which we cannot refer to in detail here. We would only like to say that, for Kernberg narcissism, there is a "highly pathological grandiose self" it "reflects a pathological condensation of some aspects of the real self (the specialness of the child reinforced by early experience), the ideal self (the fantasies and self images of power, wealth, omniscience, and beauty which compensated the small child for the experience

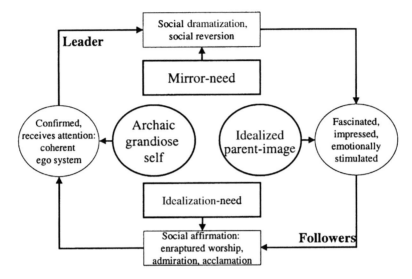

Fig. 2. Psychodynamic Frame of Reference and Interactive Circular Causality in Charismatic Leadership Relationships.

of severe oral frustration, rage and envy) and the ideal object (the fantasy of an ever-giving, ever-loving and accepting parent, in contrast to the child's experience in reality; a replacement of the devalued real parental object)" (Kernberg, 1988, p. 265 f.). This fusion of ideal self, ideal object, and actual self-images derives from a "defense against an intolerable reality in the interpersonal realm' with the aim "to deny normal dependency on external objects and on the internalized representations of the external objects" (Kernberg, 1988, p. 231).

Behind all this lies the deeply denied fundamental philosophy of a starving, angry, inwardly empty ego that emerges from impotent rage about suffered insults (e.g. narcissistic exploitation by an indifferent, aggressive mother) and enormous fear of hatred and revenge by others. Owing to their painful experiences, narcissistic people get caught in the image of their own greatness, which they have had to establish – not least helped by their parents' narcissism – until they can no longer distinguish between the image of who they think they are and the image of who they really are. If this aggression asserts itself – also reinforced reciprocally – a dangerous potential of destructiveness and destruction is set free (Steyrer, 1995, p. 307 ff.).

It seems likely that under normal ethical charismatic circumstances, a leader's mirror-needs play a central role in his or her desire to become the focus of social attention. However, under unethical conditions, the leader's pathological grandiose self in particular seems to be the starting point for the destructive consequences of his or her actions. The bifurcation in the outcomes associated with charismatic leadership can of course best be documented by means of the historical examples of Mahatma Gandhi and Adolf Hitler. Moreover, Gandhi's example shows how important it is to analyze the social reversion types of leadership in order to understand charisma, since, in his case, "introversion and authenticity" as well as "readiness to cooperate and empathy" in the sense of majestic charisma were particularly pronounced.

Finally, we can also refer here to the tragedy of 11 September 2001 in New York. We may assume that Osama Bin Laden – in contrast to Gandhi – represents a highly destructive type of majestic charisma where introversion and asceticism are combined with the highest degree of fanatacism and rigidity. The staged TV images of Bin Laden lead us to assume him to be a narcissist, and maybe we can also derive some hope from that: when he reads from a sacred text or is present at a wedding, or when he poses with his Kalashnikov, he conveys the camera awareness of an actor with his every self-loving gesture. He is tall and good-looking with soft eyes, elegant, ascetic, and introverted, and he conveys deep insight, wisdom, and knowledge. In addition, there is his secret vanity and deep narcissistic mirror-need, and this may be precisely the trait that will be his undoing, if he lets himself get carried away to a final act of self-destruction, with Osama Bin Laden as producer, director, script-writer, and actor.

SUMMARY AND OUTLOOK

Summing up the basic thesis of this chapter, we can say that the classification of a stimulus person as a charismatic leader results from the allocation of evaluative borderline attributes (symbolic codes in the sense of hyper/anti-representativity) to the leader. These attributes emerge from the prototypical core of leadership and are closely related to stigmatized characteristics. Social dramatization of prototypical attributes is perceived as attractive up to a certain level: the stimulus person appears as a paragon, as the incarnation of leadership (charisma). An additional intensification, however, can be perceived as an invalidating exaggeration (stigma). Social reversion of prototypical attributes makes a leader a significant personality because of his/her positively connoted manner of behaving differently (charisma): the significance lies in the reversion of what has been anticipated. Additional intensification evokes social aversion (stigma).

Therefore, leaders whose self-presentation is located in the border areas, i.e. outside the area showing prototypicality, always have to find the right balance – in the eyes of their followers, they are moving on a razor's edge. Too little social dramatization or social reversion means that they will not be distinguishable from the mass of their competitors. If there is too much mise-en-scène, charisma turns into stigma. The classic charisma-dilemma therefore is the dramatic/playful approximation to the corresponding border zones, without actually crossing the Rubicon. If borderline behavior turns into the direction of invalidating exaggeration, behavior that has been considered awe-inspiring for a long time becomes repulsive; what has long been impressive becomes grotesque and hypertrophic. In this sense, charismatic leaders in organizations are not border crossers who "turn social order inside out and turn it into its contrary" (Lipp, 1985, p. 44) (this is reserved for members of social fringe groups) but they are border crossers at the periphery of social expectations in the context of leadership: social dramatization and social reversion respectively are those modes of self-presentation from which charisma seems to emerge.

A building-up process is connected with the sequence of borderline behavior and idealization, where mirror-needs and idealization-needs are related to each other in a complementary manner. If the intended mirroring is provided, this followers' feedback has a reinforcing effect, so that there is a vicious circle of self-presentation, idealization, and reciprocal increase in the feeling of their own worth. It seems likely that the carriers of charisma, because of their personal history of socialization, have learned how to handle their narcissistic deficits productively, which means that they know how to organize for themselves what they need urgently. Behind all this, we have to assume a subtle learning process, on the basis of which they have learned which expressive quality receives the required amount of admiration from their followers. The truly tragic aspect of leaders is that their mirror-hungry personality can be satisfied only temporarily, and that this exclusively happens at the moment when they attract admiration. For the followers, identification and participation in the leader's power, built up by the leader himself/herself, mainly mean subordination and self-denial, in addition to increased commitment. A deep feeling of loyalty and unconditional readiness to follow are therefore the basis of the followers' becoming part of the projected omnipotence. What they can gain in feelings of their own worth and engagement, they can lose in independence.

After this analysis inevitably follows the question: Is charismatic leadership desirable at all? Compensatory energies such as those possibly emerging from narcissistic needs can motivate creative best performance. Entrepreneurial action is also fed by these energies, amongst others. In our opinion, societies organized on market principles have to rely on this potential for sublimation. They are kept moving also by their individuals' irrational delusions of grandeur and illusions of omnipotence. Therefore, charismatic leadership can be functional, in particular in pioneer phases and periods of transformational change in organizations. However, triumph and debacle are not far from each other if organizations tend to subject themselves to the dictate of one significant individual. This is not desirable in principle, but has to be classified as a functional process for the dynamics of market economy evolution and selection.

With a view to the risks of de-individuation connected with charisma, we have to qualify this statement by saying that such processes are limited in their development in the context of business organizations: followers are only partly integrated into the enterprise from the point of view of their overall existence. Furthermore, there is always the possibility of dissolving the relationship, at least potentially. In our view, this is different with carriers of political and social control functions. Especially because of the right of disposal over the monopoly on the use of force in this context, charismatic leadership can become totalitarian, and in the extreme, the psychopathology of an individual can become the measure of all things. However, there seems to be only one proven remedy against this, which is to prevent social conditions under which a critical mass of the population falls into collective regression and looks for salvation and solutions in a charismatic leader. In this sense, there are a sufficient number of narcissistic deformations left unexploited at any time, only waiting to transcend into the public limelight.

REFERENCES

Avolio, B. J. (1999). *Full leadership development: Building the vital forces in organizations.* Thousand Oaks, CA: Sage.

Bass, B. M. (1985). *Leadership and performance beyond expectations.* New York: Free Press.

Bass, B. M. (1995). Theory of transformational leadership redux. *Leadership Quarterly, 6,* 463–478.

Bass, B. M. (1998). *Transformational leadership: Industrial, military, and educational impact.* Mahwah, NJ: Lawrence Erlbaum Associates.

Bass, B. M., & Avolio, B. J. (1996). *Manual for the Multifactor Leadership Questionnaire.* Palo Alto, CA: Mind Garden.

Binning, J. F., Zaba, A. J., & Whattam, J. C. (1986). Explaining the biasing effects of performance cues in terms of cognitive categorization. *Academy of Management Journal, 29,* 521–535.

Bryman, A. (1992). *Charisma & leadership in organizations.* London: Sage.

Conger, J. A. (1999). Charismatic and transformational leadership in organizations: An insider's perspective on these developing streams of research. *Leadership Quarterly, 10,* 145–180.

Conger, J. A., & Hunt, J. G. (1999). Charismatic and transformational leadership: Taking stock of the present and future. *Leadership Quarterly, 10*, 121–129.

Conger, J. A., & Kanungo, R. (1987). Toward a behavioral theory of charismatic leadership in organizational settings. *Academy of Management Review, 12*, 637–647.

Conger, J. A., & Kanungo, R. N. (1998). *Charismatic leadership in organizations*. Thousand Oaks: Sage.

Deluga, R. (1997). Relationship among American presidential charismatic leadership, narcissism, and rated performance. *Leadership Quarterly, 8*, 49–65.

Deneke, F. W., & Hilgenstock, B. (1989). *Das Narzißmus-Inventar*. Bern: Schattauer.

Downton, J. V. (1973). *Rebel leadership: Commitment and charisma in the revolutionary process*. New York: Free Press.

Freud, S. (1955). *The standard edition of the complete psychological works of Sigmund Freud* (Vols XIII, XIV, XVIII). London: Hogarth Press.

Gardner, W. L., & Avolio, B. J. (1998). The charismatic relationship: a dramaturgical perspective. *Academy of Management Review, 23*, 32–58.

Goffman, E. (1963). *The presentation of self in everyday life*. New York: Doubleday.

Goffman, E. (1967). *Stigma*. Frankfurt: Suhrkamp.

Hartog, D. N. et al. (1999). Culture specific and cross-culturally generalizable implicit leadership theories: Are attributes of charismatic/transformational leadership universally endorsed? *Leadership Quarterly, 10*, 219–256.

House, R., J., & Aditya, R. N. (1997). The social scientific study of leadership: Quo vadis? *Journal of Management, 23*, 409–473.

House, R. J., & Shamir, B. (1993). Toward the integration of transformational, charismatic, and visionary theories. In: M. M. Chemers & R. Ayman (Eds), *Leadership theory and research. Perspectives and direction* (pp. 577–594). Orlando, FL: Academic Press.

House, R. J., Spangler, W. D., & Woycke, J. (1991). Personality and charisma in the U.S. presidency: A psychological theory of leader effectiveness. *Administrative Science Quarterly, 36*, 364–396.

Howell, J. M. (1988). Two faces of charisma: socialized and personalized leadership in organizations. In: J. A. Conger & R. N. Kanungo (Eds), *Charismatic leadership. The elusive factor in organizational effectiveness* (pp. 213–236). San Francisco: Jossey-Bass.

Howell, J. M., & Frost, P. J. (1989). A laboratory study of charismatic leadership. *Organizational Behavior and Human Decision Processes, 43*, 243–269.

Howell, J. M., & Higgins, C. A. (1990). Champions of technological innovation. *Administrative Science Quarterly, 35*, 317–341.

Hummel, R. P. (1972). *Charisma in politics: Psycho-social causes of revolution as pre-conditions of charismatic outbreaks within the framework of Weber's Epistemology*. New York: Dissertation.

Hunt, J. G. (1999). Transformational/charismatic leadership's transformation of the field: An historical Essay. *Leadership Quarterly, 10*, 129–144.

Hunt, J. G., & Conger, J. A. (1999). From where we sit: An assessment of transformational and charismatic leadership research. *Leadership Quarterly, 10*, 335–343.

Jermier, J. M. (1993). Introduction – charismatic leadership: Neo-weberian perspectives. *Leadership Quarterly, 4*, 217–233.

Kernberg, O. (1988). *Borderline conditions and pathological narcissism*. New York: Jason Aronson.

Knapp, G. (1988). *Narzißmus und Primär-Beziehung. Psychoanalytisch-anthropologische Grundlagen für ein neues Verständnis von Kindheit.* Berlin: Springer.

Kohut, H. (1986). *The analysis of the self. A systematic approach to the psychoanalytic treatment of narcissistic personality disorders.* New York: International Universities Press.

Kohut, H., & Wolf, E. S. (1980). Die Störungen des Selbst und ihre Behandlung. In: U. H. Peters (Ed.), *Die Psychologie des 20. Jahrhunderts* (pp. 650–687). Frankfurt: Kindler.

Lindholm, Ch. (1990). *Charisma.* Cambridge: Basil Blackwell.

Lipp, W. (1985). *Stigma und Charisma. Über soziales Grenzverhalten.* Berlin: Reimer.

Lord. R. G. (1985). An information processing approach to social perceptions, leadership and behavioral measurement in organization. In: B. M. Staw & L. Cummings (Eds), *Research in Organizational Behavior* (Vol. 7, pp. 87–128). Greenwich, CT: JAI Press.

Lord, R. G., & Foti, R. J. (1986). Schema theories, information processing, and organizational behavior. In: H. P. Sims & D. A. Gioia (Eds), *The thinking organization* (pp. 20–48). San Francisco: Jossey-Bass.

Lord, R. G., Foti, R. J., & DeVader, C. L. (1984). A test of leadership categorization theory: Internal structure, information processing, and leadership perceptions. *Organizational Behavior and Human Performance, 34,* 343–378.

Lord, R. G., & Maher, K. J. (1989). Cognitive processes in industrial and organizational psychology. In: C. L. Cooper & I. T. Robertson (Eds), *International Review of Industrial and Organizational Psychology* (pp. 49–91). Chichester: Unwin Hyman.

Lord, R. G., & Maher, K. J. (1989). Cognitive processes in industrial and organizational psychology. In: C. L. Cooper & I. T. Robertson (Eds), *International Review of Industrial and Organizational Psychology* (pp. 49–91). Chichester, UK: Wiley.

Lord, R. G., & Maher, K. J. (1990). Perceptions of leadership and their implications in organizations. In: J. S. Carrol (Ed.), *Applied social psychology and organizational settings* (pp. 129–154). Hillsdale, NJ: N. M. Erlbaum.

Lord, R. G., & Maher, K. J. (1991). *Leadership and information processing. Linking perceptions and performance.* Boston: Unwin Hyman.

Manager Magazin (1998). Der karge Mann Kagermann. *Manager Magazin, 12,* 106–109.

Meindl, J. R. (1990). On leadership: An alternative to the conventional wisdom. In: B. M. Staw & L. L. Cummings (Eds), *Research in Organizational Behavior* (Vol. 12, pp. 159–203). Greenwich, CT: JAI Press.

Meindl, J. R. (1995). The romance of leadership as a follower-centric theory: A social constructionist approach. *Leadership Quarterly, 6,* 329–342.

Miyahara, E. (1983). Charisma. From Weber to contemporary sociology. *Sociological Inquiry, 53,* 368–388.

Morgan, G. (1986). *Images of organization.* Thousand Oaks, CA: Sage.

Mummendey, H. D. (1990). *Psychologie der Selbstdarstellung.* Göttingen: Hogrefe.

Neuberger, O. (1990). *Führen und geführt werden.* Stuttgart: Enke.

O'Conner, J., Mumford, M., Clifton, T., C., & Gessner, T. (1995). Charismatic Leaders and destructiveness: An Historiometric Study. *Leadership Quarterly, 6,* 529–555.

Offermann, L. R., Kennedy, J. K., & Wirtz, P. W. (1994). Implicit leadership theories: content, structure and generalizability, *Leadership Quarterly, 5,* 43–58.

Pauchant, T. C. (1991). Transferential leadership. Towards a more complex understanding of charisma in organizations. *Organization Studies, 23,* 507–537.

Phillips, J. S., & Lord, R. G. (1982). Schematic information processing and perception of leadership in problem-solving groups. *Journal of Applied Psychology, 67,* 486–492.

Puffer, S. M. (1990). Attributions of charismatic leadership: The impact of decision style, outcome, and observer characteristics. *Leadership Quarterly, 3,* 177–192.

Ronnigstam, E., & Gunderson, J. (1996). *Deskriptive Untersuchungen zur narzißtischen Persönlichkeitsstörung.* In: O. Kernberg (Ed.), *Narzißtische Persönlichkeitsstörungen* (pp. 88–197). Stuttgart: Schattauer.

Schweitzer, A. (1984). *The age of charisma.* Chicago: Nelson Hall.

Shamir, B., Arthur, M. B., & House, R. J. (1994). The rhetoric of charismatic leadership. A theoretical extension, a case study, and implications for research. *Leadership Quarterly, 5,* 25–42.

Shamir, B., House, R. J., & Arthur, M. B. (1993). The motivational effects of charismatic leadership: A self-concept based theory. *Organization Science, 4,* 577–594.

Shamir, B. Zakay, E. Breining, E., & Popper, M. (1998). Correlates of charismatic leader behavior in military units: Subordinates' attitudes, unit characteristics, and superior's appraisals of leader performance. *Academy of Management Journal, 41,* 387–409.

Steyrer, J. (1995). *Charisma in Organisationen. Sozial-kognitive und psychodynamisch-interaktive Aspekte von Führung.* Frankfurt, New York: Campus.

Steyrer, J. (1998). Charisma and the archetypes of leadership. *Organization Studies, 19,* 807–828.

Steyrer, J. (2000). Die Archetypen der Führung – empirische Überprüfung eines Erklärungsmodells. *Die Unternehmung, 54,* 475–490.

Stimmer, F. (1987). *Narzissmus. Zur Psychogenese und Soziogenese narzißtischen Verhaltens.* Berlin: Duncker & Humbold.

Weber, M. (1976). *Wirtschaft und Gesellschaft.* Tübingen: Mohr Paul Siebeck.

Willner, A. R. (1984). *The spellbinders. Charismatic political leadership.* New Haven: Yale University Press.

Yagil, D. (1998). Charismatic leadership and organizational hierarchy: Attribution of charisma to close and distant leaders. *Leadership Quarterly, 9,* 161–176.

Yukl, G. (1999). An evaluation of conceptual weaknesses in transformational and charismatic leadership theories. *Leadership Quarterly, 10,* 285–306.

A CLOSER LOOK AT THE ROLE OF EMOTIONS IN TRANSFORMATIONAL AND CHARISMATIC LEADERSHIP

Shane Connelly, Blaine Gaddis and
Whitney Helton-Fauth

ABSTRACT

Emotion and emotion-related concepts are interspersed throughout theories of charismatic and transformational leadership. Existing research in this area articulates expected relationships of global emotion constructs such as emotional intelligence, positive affect, and negative affect to leadership. However, there has been little attention to the potential roles of more specific emotions. This chapter describes some of the existing theoretical and empirical research on leadership and emotion, and proposes a framework to examine more systematically how specific emotions may influence transformational and charismatic leadership. The emotion framework is applied to two theories to demonstrate its utility in gaining a more in-depth understanding of how emotions influence leader communication, motivation, interpersonal relations, and relationship management with followers.

INTRODUCTION

Some of the most salient moments in the career histories of presidents, military leaders, CEOs, and world leaders are remembered as emotional, inspiring

Transformational and Charismatic Leadership, Volume 2, pages 255–283.
ISBN: 0-7623-0962-8

actions or decisions leading to critical turning points, fundamental system changes, or radically new perspectives that have changed national policy, organizational adaptation, and military history. Likewise, seemingly more mundane organizational leadership events, such as when a manager's coaching and personal appeals for excellence turn an average performing sales team into a thriving one, can also be inspiring and emotionally salient. These forms of outstanding leadership are often characterized as transformational and charismatic, defined this way, in part, by their emotional content and emotional appeals to followers.

While it is often recognized when seen, emotion is an elusive element of leadership that is difficult to define and measure. This is perhaps one of the reasons that it is not widely examined in the general leadership literature, or in theories and research on transformational and charismatic leadership. The general intent of this chapter is to summarize and extend the thinking on the roles of leader and follower emotions in transformational and charismatic leadership. We review existing research on emotion and leadership, proposing a framework that can be used to explore systematically how specific types of emotions may impact leader-follower interactions and behavior. This framework is used to define further how leaders and followers appraise, use, and react to emotions within transformational and charismatic leadership paradigms. Additional ways in which the framework can be applied to increase our understanding of the complex linkages between emotions and leadership are also discussed.

LEADERSHIP THEORIES AND EMOTION

Theories of transformational and charismatic leadership allude to the importance of emotion without providing much detail about what emotions are most central or what roles they play in the types of leadership behavior and processes characterizing these types of leadership. References to providing emotional support to followers, making emotional appeals to followers, and communicating visions that evoke strong emotions in followers leave many aspects of emotion and leadership open to interpretation.

Charismatic and transformational leadership paradigms articulate exemplary leader characteristics and behaviors that inspire followers and enable them to accomplish great things (Bass, 1985; Conger & Kanungo, 1987, 1998; House, 1977; Shamir, House & Arthur, 1993). Various theories and lines of research on charismatic and transformational leadership have evolved, some emphasizing the conceptual similarities of these two paradigms, others maintaining distinct differences across these approaches to understanding leadership (Yukl, 1999).

Brief descriptions of several predominant theories are provided here to exemplify the broad level at which emotion is typically incorporated into charismatic and transformational leadership approaches.

Charismatic Leadership and Emotion

The theory of charismatic leadership described by House (1977) proposed that leadership arises from the interaction of leader capacities (self-confidence, dominance, moral conviction) leader behavior (successful role modeling one's beliefs and values, articulation of goals and visions, communicating high expectations, tapping into followers motives), follower characteristics (motive compatibility, identification with leader), and situational factors (crises, need for social change). These factors work together, enabling charismatic leaders to inspire trust, loyalty, devotion, and commitment in their followers.

Extensions of this theory further articulate and clarify how these factors give rise to leadership influence processes, emphasizing the collective (vs. dyadic) nature of this process (Shamir, House & Arthur, 1993). Shamir et al. (1993) describe how leaders exert motivational effects through linking followers' self-concepts to organizational visions and goals in an effort to get followers to internalize the importance of supporting and achieving these goals. Leaders do this by:

(1) increasing the intrinsic value of the cause or effort, making followers more aware of its importance generally and its importance to their own individual and collective identities;
(2) expressing confidence in followers' abilities to meet high expectations, boosting self-esteem and self-efficacy;
(3) increasing the value of goal accomplishment, making actions more meaningful to followers;
(4) providing hope for a better future and faith that this can be attained; and
(5) creating personal commitment to a common vision and mission by linking it to followers' personal goals, values, and morals.

One of several assumptions underlying this theory is that all of these leadership behaviors involve the expression of emotions, values, and self-concepts, which help to align leaders and followers in pursuing shared goals.

Another theory of charismatic leadership, proposed by Howell (1988) and her colleagues (House & Howell, 1992), describes two basic types of charisma – personalized and socialized. Through the use of emotional and other types of tactics, personalized leaders maintain psychological distance from followers, seeking their submission and obedience. Their visions are expressed in terms of their own personal values, regardless of the desires of the followers. Howell (1988) notes that followers are typically looking to identify with these leaders on a personal level, more than to identify with their ideas. Alternatively, socialized charismatic leaders develop shared goals with followers, using emotions and other methods to inspire acceptance and internalization of ideas and to work towards mutual goals. These leaders strive to reduce psychological distance from their followers, and followers derive their satisfaction from the ideas and goals of the leader.

House and Howell (1992) note that these may not be distinct types of leaders, but that leaders may behave both ways at different points in their relationships with followers (Conger, 1999). Accordingly, Weierter (1997) reframes these not as leader types, but as socialized or personalized relationships with followers. Bass and Steidlmeier (1999) take a stronger stand, distinguishing authentic charismatic leadership from personalized or pseudo charismatic leadership. Although leaders with a personalized style may exert considerable influence over followers, they are inauthentic, untrustworthy, unethical, manipulative, self-interested, and self-enhancing. Regardless of whether leader influence occurs through personal identification or internalization, emotions undoubtedly play a role in the interactions of leaders and followers. Moreover, the types of emotions and emotional exchanges present with these two leadership styles or relationships are likely to be very different.

Conger and Kanungo (1987, 1998) have articulated a third major theoretical approach to charismatic leadership, emphasizing that leadership is attributed to leaders by followers, based on their perception of the leader's behavior. These authors describe three stages of charismatic leadership (Conger, 1999). In stage 1, the leader evaluates the situation and followers, identifying shortcomings in the status quo and determining the needs and satisfaction levels of the followers. Emphasizing deficiencies enables the leader to be seen as an organizational reformer or change agent.

Stage 2 involves forming and relaying a vision or idealized goals for the organization that are discrepant from the status quo in a way that makes the leader seem out-of-the-ordinary. Using verbal and non-verbal behavior, the leader makes clear distinctions between the status quo and the new vision, focusing on negative aspects of the status quo and positive aspects of the new vision. Various positive and negative emotions are likely to be part of the process of ushering out the old and bringing along the new. In stage 3, leaders gain followers' trust in the vision and goals, showing how goals can be accomplished by personal example, risk-taking, and complete dedication, all of which are appraised emotionally and cognitively by followers.

The types of emotions and their manner of expression by leaders and followers have the potential to impact the motivational and influence processes in all of these theories in bi-directional ways. For example, leaders displaying positive emotional regard for followers may help to increase their feelings of self worth, particularly in instances where followers are experiencing frustration or hopelessness regarding aspects of their work. Affectively speaking, leaders may respond differently to followers exhibiting different patterns of emotion.

In fact, the model of individualized leadership developed by Dansereau, Yammarino, and colleagues supports this idea. Leaders who possess this aspect of leadership seek followers who will perform well, developing a unique relationship and mode of interacting with each follower. In turn, followers seek leaders who will contribute to, and enhance their feelings of self-worth. Followers develop and increase their sense of self-worth when leaders focus on each individual, empowering followers by supporting their achievement and autonomy needs, beliefs, values, integrity, ideas, etc. (Dansereau et al., 1995; Yammarino & Dansereau, 2002). Dansereau, Mumford and Yammarino (2000) note that individualized leadership may be a key mediating mechanism between exceptional leadership and follower effectiveness, with the potential to bring about good and bad outcomes. Connecting with followers on an emotional level initially, and continuing to understand and meet their emotional needs, may very well be one way that charismatic leaders exhibit individualized leadership.

The specific emotions and intensity levels that a leader exhibits with followers exhibiting positive emotions, who are seeking additional and new challenges, may be very different than those exhibited with followers who are feeling disenfranchised, angry, or powerless. Leader emotions can facilitate followers' psychological identification (with ideas or with the leader) or create psychological distance, either intentionally or unintentionally. Likewise, emotions can be used as impression management tools in building trust, articulating positive aspects of a vision, and emphasizing unappealing aspects of the status quo. Finally, leaders may use both negative and positive emotions to communicate the seriousness and level of their commitment to certain ideals, visions, and goals.

Transformational Leadership and Emotion

Theories of transformational leadership arose initially from Burn's (1978) distinction between transactional leaders, or those who use exchanges to meet follower needs, and transformational leaders, or those who bring followers to increased levels of effort and performance by encouraging them to transcend self-interests. A predominant theory of transformational leadership proposed by Bass (1985) and his colleagues (Avolio & Bass, 1988; Bass & Avolio, 1990, 1993) contains four defining behavioral components through which leaders help followers to internalize high personal standards and align their values to be consistent with the leader's own vision and broader ideals (Bass, 1985; Kuhnert & Lewis, 1987). Transformational leaders are characterized by:

(1) charisma or the ability to communicate their vision;
(2) inspirational motivation or making emotional appeals to followers to build or increase awareness of shared goals;
(3) intellectual stimulation or encouraging followers to think outside the box; and
(4) individual consideration or recognizing that different followers have different needs

(Bass, 1985; Bass & Avolio, 1993).

As with charismatic leadership, emotions clearly have the potential to play a role in communicating vision and inspiring followers in transformational leadership. Leaders may use both positive and negative emotions when appealing to followers to transcend self-interests and strive towards more difficult goals. Leaders may change their emotional orientation when interacting with different followers, depending on what is needed to increase levels of effort and performance. Alternatively, follower perceptions of a leader may be influenced by their emotional appraisals of the leaders' intentions, communication, and actions. In fact, some research has begun to emerge on emotion and leadership processes. The following section reviews existing theoretical approaches and empirical studies linking emotion and leadership.

RESEARCH ON EMOTION AND LEADERSHIP

Generally speaking, three different approaches have been taken in studying emotion and leadership. Some of this research examines the relationship of emotional intelligence to leadership processes and outcomes. Other research focuses on the impact of global positive and negative affect on leadership. A third approach looks at the presence of specific emotions in leaders, such as optimism, with respect to follower reactions or other leadership outcomes.

Emotional Intelligence and Leadership

The potential relevance of emotional intelligence for leadership has recently been noted by a number of scholars (Bass, 2002; Caruso, Mayer & Salovey,

2002; George, 2000; Megerian & Sosik, 1996; Sosik & Megerian, 1999). Emotional intelligence is characterized by a set of abilities and attributes enabling individuals to accurately identify and monitor their own and others' feelings and internal states and to use this information to guide cognition and behavior (Goleman, 1995; Mayer & Salovey, 1997; Salovey & Mayer, 1990). Important aspects of emotional intelligence include self-awareness, emotional management, self-motivation, empathy, and relationship management.

Megerian and Sosik (1996) and Sosik and Megerian (1996) suggest that leaders possessing emotional intelligence are more likely to be transformational. They note that self-awareness may result in leaders having stronger convictions in their beliefs and that emotional management enables leaders to consider the needs of others over their own. Emotional management and relationship management provide leaders with the capabilities to use emotionally expressive language and non-verbal behavior to promote positive affect and inspire followers to less self-centered, higher levels of performance. Additionally, empathy is likely to influence leaders' individual consideration for follower needs.

In a study examining the empirical relationships of these attributes to transformational leadership behavior, Sosik and Megerian found that self-awareness, self-motivation, relationship management and empathy were positively related to followers' ratings of transformational behavior for self-aware leaders. In leaders with lower self-awareness, empathy was negatively related to followers' ratings of transformational behavior. These results suggest that the self-awareness component of emotional intelligence may be particularly important, influencing the manifestation and impact of other aspects of emotional intelligence on leaders' transformational behavior.

Others have also proposed ideas about how emotional intelligence may influence leadership processes, although empirical tests of these models have not yet surfaced. Using an ability-oriented model of emotional intelligence proposed by Mayer and Salovey (1997), Caruso, Mayer and Salovey (2002) describe how emotional intelligence influences leadership. The ability model proposed by Mayer and Salovey (1997) involves:

(1) identifying or accurately perceiving emotion in oneself and others;
(2) using emotions to redirect attention, facilitate decision-making, consider multiple points of view, and promote alternative approaches to problem-solving;
(3) understanding the complexity of emotions and what causes them as well as how different emotions are interrelated; and

(4) managing emotions, including being aware of one's emotions, engaging or detaching from emotions, and integrating emotions and actions.

Caruso et al. (2002) discuss why it is important for leaders to identify, use, understand, and manage emotions. Accurate identification of one's own emotions improves self-awareness, which positively influences leader performance and allows a better interpretation of follower emotions and evaluation of their authenticity. Using emotions can help leaders to motivate others or direct followers to engage in appropriate activities congruent with their emotions. Leaders can also use emotions in symbolic management or the relaying of stories, etc. to orient followers to a specific vision. Being able to understand emotions will help leaders get a better read on follower points of view. Managing emotions will enable leaders to cope more effectively with failure and to form relationships that will enhance individual and group relationships. Effective leaders are aware that expressing emotions in an extreme or intense manner can create barriers that will inhibit relationships and understanding between the leader and followers, or may very well inspire individuals and groups to perform in extraordinary ways.

Ashkanasy and Tse (2000) view transformational leadership as management of emotion, describing the relevance of various aspects of emotional intelligence to transformational leadership in organizational settings. They make several propositions regarding the emotional qualities of transformational leaders and how the experience, perception, and management of emotions impacts leader-follower exchange processes and outcomes. Their view of the emotional make-up of transformational leader is summarized as follows. Transformational leaders engage followers and relay vision through emotional language and communication. They have a positive, optimistic outlook, and understand and have good intuition about others' needs, leading to greater sensitivity and high-quality exchanges with followers. These types of leaders are in touch with, and regulate, their emotions, making them more emotionally stable and able to understand others' emotions. Finally, they are affectively committed to their roles and responsibilities as a leader.

George (2000) also describes how various aspects of emotional intelligence contribute to leadership effectiveness, focusing on the appraisal and expression of emotion, use of emotions in cognitive processes and decision-making, knowledge about emotions, and management of emotions. She indicates how each of these elements of emotional intelligence influences five types of effective leadership behavior, including developing collective goals with subordinates, communicating the importance of work activities to followers, motivating subordinates by generating and maintaining their enthusiasm, confidence, optimism, cooperation, and trust, encouraging flexible decision-making and change, and maintaining organizational identity.

Constructs closely related to the concept of emotional intelligence have also been explored with respect to leadership. Dubinsky, Yammarino and Jolson (1995) hypothesize that leaders who possess emotional coping skills have a greater self-awareness and self-confidence, are able to control their emotions in interacting with others, and can reduce feelings of inner conflict, thus enabling them to tolerate stressful situations better. Their study showed positive but non-significant correlations of emotional coping with the four dimensions of transformational leadership (charismatic leadership, inspirational leadership, intellectual stimulation, and individualizes consideration) in a sample of 34 sales managers. Third-order partial correlations (controlling for length of managerial experience in the organization and in the job and education) showed a similar trend. However, these correlations may be attenuated given the nature of the sample and number of managers. Additionally, in light of Sosik and Megerian's work, unmeasured moderators such as self-awareness may have masked the relationship between emotional coping and transformational leadership here. An alternative explanation for these findings may be gleaned from Bass (2002), who argues that transformational leaders are less emotional and more behavioral in coping with stress and conflict, although he notes that emotions are more important to leaders who are high on the charismatic component and are more individually considerate.

While theories and studies of emotional intelligence and leadership suggest general ways in which accurate identification and management of emotion helps leaders understand, relate to, motivate, support, and manage followers, they do not identify what emotions are likely to be most prevalent or important in leader-follower interactions. Some emotions may be present in leaders and followers much more frequently than others, requiring greater attention and management. Additionally, different levels of intensity and forms of expression of certain emotions may make them more difficult to appraise and manage than others. In a related vein, individual differences in the emotional dispositions of leaders may facilitate understanding and management of certain emotions, both in themselves and in others, but inhibit the interpretation and control over other emotions.

The emotional intelligence literature assumes that individuals who possess and exhibit emotional intelligence do so with equal adeptness across a wide range of positive and negative emotions when, in fact, this may not be the case. Some leaders may be more comfortable with, and deal much more effectively with, positive emotions than with negative emotions and vice versa. Finally, there is an implied emphasis on positive emotion in the literature on emotional intelligence and leadership. It is presumed that fostering and maintaining positive affect in followers are desirable for effective communication and smooth, conflict-free relationships. Not only is this goal unrealistic, but it may be potentially detrimental for effective leadership depending on the circumstances, as indicated in some of the literature on global affect, specific emotions, and leadership. This is one reason for examining a full-range theory, as there are instances where contingent punishment makes sense and would not be perceived as positive affect or emotion.

Global Affect and Leadership

The study of emotion and leadership has also been approached by examining positive and negative affect – two broad factors of emotion that have been endorsed by a number of researchers as useful in studying and understanding emotion (Diener & Larsen, 1984; Isen, 1987, 1993; Watson & Clark, 1984, 1992; Watson & Tellegen, 1985). Positive affectivity is a personality disposition where people experience positive emotional states, feel an overall sense of well-being, and see themselves in a positive light (Tellegen, 1985). Negative affectivity is an aspect of personality where people experience negative emotional states such as being anxious, nervous, upset, and distressed (Tellegen, 1985; Watson & Clark, 1984) and are more likely to view themselves, others, and the world negatively.

In an experimental study, Price and Garland (1978) explored the effects of positively oriented failure feedback and negatively oriented failure feedback from a confederate leader on group attitudes and behavior following collective group failure. They found that the positive groups experienced increased group cohesion and greater endorsements of the leader relative to the negative groups. However, there were no significant differences in the impact of positive and negative approaches on task motivation or compliance with the leader's suggestions. Thus, while groups tended to like the positive leader better, this type of feedback did not have any effect on motivation or going along with the leader's suggestions.

Indirect evidence regarding the potential role of global affect in leadership situations was recently provided by George (1990) and others. George (1990) found that individual positive and negative affect was significantly related to the positive and negative affective tones of the groups and that group tone was significantly related to group behaviors. Negative group affect was negatively related to prosocial behavior, while positive group affect was negatively related to absenteeism. Interestingly, positive group affect was not significantly related to prosocial behavior. Related research by Totterdell and his colleagues

(Totterdell, 2000; Totterdell, Kellett, Teuchmann & Briner, 1998) reveals similar patterns of findings, where individuals' moods were significantly associated with the collective mood of their workgroup or team. Additionally, older, more committed members of a group are more susceptible to mood contagion. Evidence from these studies indicated that collective mood has facilitative and inhibitory effects on contextual and other forms of group performance (Totterdell, 2000).

Taken together, the results of these studies have some implications for the impact that leader affect may have on a group. Affective dispositions of leaders may have an even greater impact on the collective mood and subsequent performance of groups they work with because:

(1) leaders are particularly salient group members; and
(2) leaders tend to interact more with highly committed group members, potentially influencing their moods to a greater degree and increasing the likelihood that mood contagion will occur.

The relationship of global affect and leadership has also been examined in terms of degree of emotional reaction. A study by Mizuno, Matsubara and Takai (1994) looked at the level of subordinates' emotional reaction to the leader and its moderating influence on the relationship between task-oriented leadership and follower morale and commitment. Specifically, for subordinates low in emotional reaction, task-oriented leadership correlated positively with morale and commitment. However, task-oriented leadership was negatively related to morale and commitment for followers with a high emotional reaction to the leader. This implies that the intensity of follower emotions about the leader and potentially about other issues affects performance. In order to perform well, it appears that followers with greater levels of emotional intensity require different leadership approaches from those with lower levels of emotional intensity.

Studies examining global positive and negative affect do not clearly point to one or the other as being advantageous in all leadership contexts. When measured at this level, the impact of emotion and emotional intensity on leadership processes and outcomes appears to be context- and criterion-dependent, where positive leader and follower affect is positively related to some types of effective behavior and performance but not related to others. Additionally, global negative affect does not appear to hurt or help leadership in most of these studies, and emotional intensity moderates the effectiveness of leadership behavior on group outcomes. Findings regarding the role of positive and negative affect may become clearer as specific types of positive and negative emotions are explored with respect to leadership, especially as leader-follower relationships and reciprocal influence processes unfold over time. Perhaps one reason for the different patterns of findings in the literature to date is that affect and emotions are studied in an episodic manner rather than as they are exhibited and elicited over time.

Specific Emotions and Leadership

A limited number of researchers have hypothesized about the impact of specific emotions on leadership processes and outcomes, while others have conducted studies to test these types of relationships. One study conducted by Chemers, Watson and May (2000) found that optimism was positively related to faculty evaluations of leadership potential in a sample of ROTC Army cadets, but was not predictive of performance in an advanced leadership training camp. Thus, as was the case with general affect, specific emotions may be relevant for some criteria but not others. A second study revealed interesting findings with regard to negative emotions (Lewis, 2000). The relationships of leader emotional displays of sadness and anger with follower reactions were moderated by gender. Women leaders were rated as less effective when they displayed either sadness or anger (vs. no emotion), while men were rated less effective only when they displayed sadness. This implies that gender stereotypes regarding the expression of emotion may influence followers' views of leader effectiveness. Lewis (2000) also found that leader expression of sadness (a passive emotion) reduced follower arousal, while leader expression of anger (an active emotion) increased follower arousal, suggesting that some negative emotions might have motivating effects.

Along similar lines, Morrison (1998) proposes that different types of leader emotions have an impact on whether aggression is appropriately expressed and effectively directed, or not. When emotions such as distress, fear, or shame are linked to aggression, leaders' responses are more likely to be passive. When emotions such as anger, revenge, or envy are linked to aggression, leaders are more likely to have active, attack responses, which are appropriate in certain situations. When aggression is linked to interest, excitement, or challenge, leaders may show enthusiasm and energy, channeling their aggression in positive ways. Thus, a distinction is drawn between functional emotions, both positive and negative, and dysfunctional emotions. Morrison suggests that rather than shutting down all forms of negative affect, organizations need to focus on how these types of emotions can be used to generate effective leadership behavior.

Ball, Trevino and Sims (1992) propose that a number of variables, including the leader's management of punishment situations, influence subordinates' cognitive and affective reactions and subsequently their satisfaction, commitment, and performance. Propositions specifically related to emotions and leader follower interactions state that:

(1) a leader's negative demeanor during punishment incidents will lead to negative emotional responses from followers;
(2) a leader's consistency in applying contingent rewards and punishments will lead to perceptions of justice and will lessen negative affect from followers; and
(3) mutual liking between the leader and follower will lead to perceptions of justice and less negative emotions.

A number of observations regarding the research on specific emotions and leadership are worth mentioning. Given the range of possible human emotions, this literature has explored relatively few specific emotions in leadership contexts. There is a need for broadening the scope of this research to incorporate more diversity in positive and negative emotions and their roles in leadership processes. Additionally, assumptions that positive emotions will produce positive results and negative emotions will produce negative results should be questioned. For instance, anger is an emotion that is often suppressed or hidden by leaders in front of their followers for fear that displaying it will have negative consequences. In reality, not expressing anger may be counterproductive to accomplishing the goals at hand, because it may lead to putting off important, conflict-ridden issues, result in more destructive outlets of anger later, or shield followers from negative feedback potentially prolonging undesirable or ineffective behavior. These reactions will not help to empower followers to perform at higher levels and may do just the opposite – keep them functioning at current levels.

In addition to looking at the unique effects of a larger number of specific emotions, interactions among various emotions need to be explored, along with how the range of emotions and emotional intensity experienced and expressed by leaders and followers influences various behaviors and outcomes. For example, individuals who experience and express a wide range of emotions may be better able to relate to and understand a wider variety of individuals than those with more restricted emotional patterns.

To date, the literature on leadership and emotions has begun to identify some important issues likely to increase our understanding of how leaders and followers relate to each other and are affected by emotional experience. However, more research is needed to clarify and extend existing findings and to explore the roles of specific emotions with greater breadth and depth. A theoretical framework of specific emotions is presented next that may help to address this need.

AN EMOTION FRAMEWORK

There is a tremendous amount of diversity in theoretical approaches to defining and understanding emotion, ranging from evolutionary theories discussing the adaptive significance of emotion (Darwin, 1872; Izard, 1971; Plutchik, 1962; Tomkins, 1962) to theories emphasizing physiological and neurophysiological arousal (Cannon, 1927; Izard, 1993; LeDoux, 1995) to cognitive theories examining subjective appraisal processes causing emotions, eliciting events, and behavioral outcomes of emotion (Frijda, 1986; Lazarus, 1966, 1991; Roseman, 1984; Scherer, 1982). This diversity implies that a universally accepted theory capturing and integrating all perspectives and dimensions of emotion may never exist (Izard, 1977; Plutchik, 1980).

Ashkanasy, Härtel and Zerbe (2000) point out that no one theory best explains or maximizes prediction across the wide variety of criteria to which emotion can be related (Fell, 1977), and that the approach selected should depend on the nature of the issue being explored. In order to understand emotions as they impact leadership processes, we focus on a cognitive approach, emphasizing the appraisal of *emotion eliciting events*, the *experience of emotions*, and *possible outcomes* of emotional experience.

Cognitively oriented approaches have examined emotions in terms of both global affect and specific emotions. Several lines of evidence point to a need for continued research at the specific emotion level. Studies exploring the structure of emotion have supported hierarchical and circumplex structures of emotion, where specific emotions are identifiable beneath the broader categories of negative and positive affect or can be classified along positive and negative axes with respect to high and low activation (Diener, Smith & Fujita, 1995; Rosenberg, 1988; Russell, 1980; Watson & Tellegen, 1985). Additionally, different appraisal patterns have been observed for specific negative emotions and positive emotions, such as whether the emotion is self or other focused or whether it involves dealing with certainty or uncertainty about events in the environment (Arnold, 1960; Roseman, Spindle & Jose, 1990; Scherer, 1988). Different triggers, intensities, and behavioral responses have also been identified for different specific emotions. Research suggests that specific emotions do indeed exist apart from global positive and negative affect, operate in different ways, and may have different antecedents and consequences (Arnold, 1960; Frijda, 1986; Keltner & Buswell, 1997; Larsen, Diener & Emmons, 1986; Mesquita & Frijda, 1992; Scherer, 1988, 1997).

An emotion framework recently developed by Helton, Benavidez and Connelly (2000) draws from existing emotion research in an effort to extend and integrate some of the existing approaches and findings. This framework adds to the literature in three ways. First, it includes a wide range of specific positive and negative emotions. Second, it organizes emotions into different categories based on the types of antecedents and consequences likely to be associated with those emotions. Third, it aligns emotions within each category by degree of intensity, where the level of intensity is a characteristic of the emotion, in addition to being a function of an individual's interpretation or subjective experience of the emotion.

This framework makes a number of assumptions about emotional appraisals, experience, and reactions. Central to the framework is the assumption that a variety of specific positive and negative emotions are identifiable and unique from each other. This is based on numerous studies providing evidence for emotion differences (Frijda, 1986; Izard, 1977; Larsen & Diener, 1985, 1992; Roseman, 1984). Another assumption is that the appraisal and experience of specific types of emotion is both trait-based (driven by individual temperament) and state-based (induced by environmental stimuli). Thus, the particular label a person attaches to what he or she is feeling and the level of intensity of that feeling will depend on personality and other traits as well as the nature and salience of situational triggers. It is proposed that certain types of events or situations have a stronger probability than others to trigger certain types of emotions. In turn, these emotions have a stronger probability of leading to certain outcomes or consequences. Thus, the theory allows for generality or typicality of emotion appraisal and response but also considers that individuals will vary from what might be considered typical in their appraisals of, and responses to, antecedent events and felt emotions.

Sixteen positive emotions and 18 negative emotions are included in this framework, which is shown in Fig. 1. Positive emotions listed in the top half of the figure have been sorted into five categories, with likely antecedents presented in the far left column and likely outcomes or consequences presented in the far right column. Positive categories include:

(1) emotions associated with positive flow;
(2) emotions associated with realizing current possibilities;
(3) emotions associated with the anticipation of future possibilities;
(4) emotions associated with experiencing personal agency; and
(5) emotions reflecting accountability and responsibility to others.

Emotions within each category are listed from least to most intense. The categories are ordered in terms of the degree of passivity of outcomes.

NATURE OF ANTECEDENTS	POSITIVE EMOTION CATEGORIES	NATURE OF CONSEQUENCES	
Events that resolve problems or those that maintain or increase well-being or personal gain	Positive Flow Relief Contentment Happiness	Stay in and maintain current situation	P A S S I V E
Existing opportunities; novel or extraordinary people and events	Current Possibilities Interest Excitement Awe	Engage people, ideas, and events	
Perceived potential for future possibilities and opportunities	Future Possibilities Optimism Hope Determination	Persevere and persist towards future goals	
Events that are empowering or that encourage personal growth and development	Personal Agency Challenge Self-assurance Dominance Pride	Meet existing challenges and seek out opportunities for further self-enhancement	A C T I V E
Events that engender accountability for well-being of other individuals or social systems	Accountability Responsibility Caring Love	Embrace people and systems to facilitate their well-being and continued development	

NATURE OF ANTECEDENTS	NEGATIVE EMOTION CATEGORIES	NATURE OF CONSEQUENCES	
Loss of control over situation, events, people, or systems	Loss of Agency/Control Boredom Pessimism Powerlessness Meaninglessness	Surrender, become passive	P A S S I V E
Perception that events may lead to personal harm or loss	Anticipated Threat Anxiety	Avoid potential threats	
Events resulting in personal loss	Personal Loss Disappointment Sadness Despair	Withdraw from situation and other people, or, seek out others for comfort and support	
Events that threaten well-being, safety	Actual Threat Fear Distress Desperation	Escape existing threats	A C T I V E
Self-initiated events causing loss, pain, or harm to others or self	Self-focused Regret Guilt Shame	Make amends, change self	
Events or people that go against one's principles or that thwart one's efforts with potential or actual negative outcomes for self or others	Thwarted efforts/principles Frustration Dislike Envy Anger	Activate against events or people	

Fig. 1.   Emotion Framework.

The bottom portion of Fig. 1 contains the six negative emotion categories as well as their likely antecedents and consequences. Categories include:

(1) emotions associated with loss of control or personal agency;
(2) emotions associated with personal loss;
(3) emotions associated with anticipated threat;
(4) emotions associated with actual threat;
(5) self-focused emotions; and
(6) emotions associated with efforts or principles being thwarted by other people or events.

This theory of emotion suggests a variety of directions for research on the role of specific emotions and emotion categories in leadership processes. The next section of this chapter demonstrates how the framework can be used to understand better the potential roles of emotions for leader behavior including communication with followers, motivation of followers, interpersonal relationships with followers and the management of relationships with followers. Two theories were selected to examine how specific emotions impact these types of leadership behaviors – the theory of transformational leadership developed by Bass and Avolio (Avolio & Bass, 1988; Bass, 1985; Bass & Avolio, 1990, 1993) and the theory of socialized and personalized charismatic leadership developed by Howell (1988).

APPLYING THE EMOTION FRAMEWORK TO TRANSFORMATIONAL AND CHARISMATIC LEADERSHIP

The expression and use of emotions as part of leader-follower influence processes is expected to differ according to the type or style of leadership and the nature of the followers. Transformational leaders may manifest emotion and try to elicit followers' emotions in very different ways than leaders with predominantly socialized charismatic relationships or personalized charismatic relationships with their followers. These types of leaders employ different behavioral and psychological strategies to attract, inspire, and maintain the loyalty of followers in pursuing their visions. With respect to the emotion framework presented here, various behavioral and psychological strategies will reflect different antecedent events and thus are likely to trigger different emotional experiences and behavioral responses in followers. Additionally, the emotional predispositions of individual followers may serve to influence the particular behavioral or psychological strategies employed by leaders at certain points.

Transformational Leadership Relationships

Transformational leaders have the potential to intentionally and unintentionally convey emotions and elicit them in others when communicating vision, inspiring movement towards shared goals, stimulating intellectual thought and development, and attending to different follower needs and raising those needs to higher levels. Followers' own emotional appraisal and experience will, in turn, influence their perceptions of, and responses to, the leader. These types of leader behaviors might tap into positive emotions related to current possibilities, future possibilities, personal agency, and accountability – categories of emotions that are more likely to produce active responses rather than passive ones. Although theories of transformational leadership do not typically imply the presence of negative emotionality, transformational leaders and their followers undoubtedly experience these types of emotions, especially emotions related to thwarted efforts/principles (e.g. frustration, dislike) and self-focused emotions (e.g. regret, guilt). These categories, like some of the positive categories, are likely to trigger more active types of responses.

A variety of emotions may be operating at different points in the transformational influence process, as shown in Fig. 2. Sometimes, the leader may express and use emotions to influence followers as a collective, whereas at other times, the leader may express and use emotions differentially across followers, based on their unique emotional dispositions. When initially attracting or bringing followers on-board, transformational leaders may *de-emphasize* passive, positive flow emotions such as *relief*, *contentment*, and *happiness* so that followers experience dissonance in the current situation and a desire for change. However, transformational leaders will communicate their vision in a way that inspires *optimism* and *hope* in followers, future-oriented emotions associated with the desire to learn more about and pursue new opportunities and goals associated with the vision. This may be especially true under circumstances of organizational/system turnaround or radical shift in direction, where the leader's vision is one that simultaneously articulates viable new directions for the organization or group and convinces followers that there is a strong probability of realizing this vision.

When Desmond Tutu was asked how he kept South African blacks motivated during the darkest hours of apartheid, he said, "I told them you are already free in your mind, now the government must catch up with us." His inspirational appeals and selflessness exemplify key elements of the emotional influence of transformational leaders.

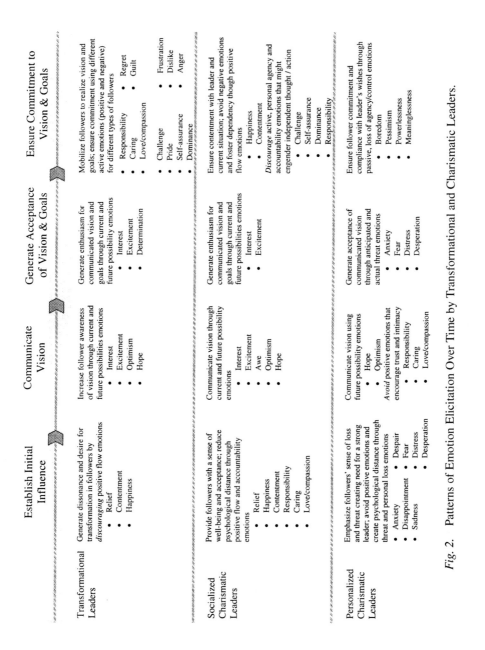

Fig. 2. Patterns of Emotion Elicitation Over Time by Transformational and Charismatic Leaders.

As the vision gains acceptance, the leader uses emotional appeals to present ideas, opportunities, and strategies that generate *interest, excitement,* and *determination* in followers. Experiencing these emotions helps to motivate followers to pursue ideas and to work with others to turn the vision into reality. Inevitably, both the leader and followers will encounter obstacles as well as unexpected opportunities in the broader environment. Leaders can make emotional appeals to followers at this point as well, motivating and challenging them to set higher standards and perform at higher levels. Leaders who carefully consider follower differences and needs will probably focus on different types of emotions in motivating different followers. For example, evoking personal agency emotions such as *challenge, self-assurance, dominance,* and *pride* will work well in motivating some followers to overcome obstacles, learn new skills, or tackle new projects.

The power of these emotions in stimulating action will not be as strong for other followers, who may be more responsive to *regret* or *guilt*. These emotions tend to induce greater self-reflection and awareness (Izard, 1993), increasing the probability that followers will take action to make amends for past failings and change to prevent experiencing these emotions again. Alternatively, other followers may be more motivated by emotions related to defending their principles against attack, whether real or perceived. Here, transformational leaders would ensure alignment of followers principles with the broader vision, and convince followers that there are events, circumstances, and people threatening the vision and its underlying principles. When managed correctly, emotions such as *frustration, dislike* and *anger* can activate followers to take steps to defend the vision. Anger is a very mobilizing emotion that can sustain and direct energy at high levels (Izard, 1993; Morrison, 1998). Anger has also shown a positive relationship to risk-taking, which can be both good and bad, depending on the circumstances (Leith & Baumeister, 1996).

Positive and negative emotions can also be instrumental in helping followers to transcend self-interests. In the positive domain, leaders can trigger accountability emotions such as *responsibility, caring,* and *compassion,* which, by their very nature, turn followers' focus towards other individuals, groups, or systems. Interestingly, self-focused negative emotions can also help followers to transcend self-interests. Emotions such as *regret* and *guilt* may initially cause followers to look inward but, if managed appropriately, can result in actions that set aside self-interests to serve the interests of other individuals or a broader group. Izard (1993) notes that self-focused emotions heighten awareness of one's weaknesses, which can motivate individuals to acquire additional skills to improve themselves. They can also be a force for social cohesion and conformity.

Socialized Charismatic Relationships

Leaders who have predominantly socialized charismatic relationships with their followers may exhibit emotions and elicit them in somewhat different ways than transformational leaders. One of the facets of charismatic leadership in general that may distinguish it from transformational leadership (despite the fact that charisma or idealized influence is a component of transformational leadership) is the nature of how charisma is intentionally displayed and used. Charismatic leaders may be more aware of the emotional impact they have on followers and consequently play to their audience with greater intentionality than transformational leaders. In other words, they are more consciously aware of how their own behavior and emotional displays impact or even manipulate followers, and they are willing to take advantage of this to achieve their vision. As such, it may be more difficult to separate real emotions from contrived emotions. Additionally, the emotional intensity of charismatic leaders may be perceived as higher than that of transformational leaders. Socialized charismatic leadership behavior also has a number of implications for specific emotions likely to be displayed by the leader and followers, as shown in Fig. 2.

When a charismatic leader emerges and begins developing socialized relationships with followers, s/he is likely to display and elicit emotions that will help to reduce psychological distance and foster dependency. The leader is likely to communicate accountability emotions such as *responsibility, caring* or even certain types of *love* or *compassion* for subordinates, communicating the message that s/he will facilitate the well-being and development of followers. Depending on the circumstances under which the leader comes into power, this can engender *relief, happiness*, and/or *contentment* in followers, making them want to go along with and support the leader. As leader-follower relationships develop, the leader learns more about follower goals, integrates these with his or her own vision or mission, and develops shared goals.

Like transformational leaders, socialized charismatic leaders will try to elicit future oriented emotions, such as *optimism* and *hope* to engage followers in the pursuit of long term goals, and will try to elicit emotions related to current possibilities, such as *interest, excitement*, and even *awe*. However, although these leaders will work to inspire followers' acceptance and internalization of goals and ideas embodying their vision, they do not necessarily seek to bring followers to higher levels of performance (Howell, 1988). It is more important that followers remain interested in the leader's ideas and in carrying out vision-related goals, and that they are happy in their current situation. Thus, socialized charismatic relationships will tend to emphasize positive, passive emotions rather than more active emotions, preferring contented followers to those who are always looking for the next challenge.

Research has shown that positive affect makes people more risk-aversive (Isen & Geva, 1987; Isen & Patrick, 1983) because it makes people more sensitive to the possibility of losing what they have. Over time, these emotional patterns will continue to foster dependency on, and therefore a continued need for, the leader's ideas as well as internalization of these ideas. When events within or outside the organization occur that elicit passive negative emotions such as *pessimism* or *powerlessness*, socialized leaders will try to alter the interpretation of these events so that followers will perceive them in a more positive light. Given the nature of socialized leader-follower relationships, leaders will avoid generating active negative emotions such as *frustration, dislike, envy,* or *anger* in their followers for fear of losing follower support.

Personalized Charismatic Relationships

Emotion patterns characterizing personalized charismatic relationships are markedly different from those characterizing socialized and transformational leadership. As with socialized charismatic leadership, personalized leaders are consciously aware that they can use emotions to shape people's behavior, and they are willing to take full advantage of this to achieve their vision. However, the types of emotions they display and elicit are likely to be more negative. Leaders fostering personalized relationships maintain psychological distance from followers, while simultaneously encouraging their dependence, submission, and obedience. Followers buying into this type of relationship are typically seeking to identify with the leader as a person rather than with the leader's ideas. This type of leader is more likely to play on negative emotions and suppress positive emotions to get desired responses out of followers.

Personalized leaders maintain psychological distance by avoiding positive emotions that encourage trust and intimacy such as *responsibility, caring* and *love* when interacting with followers, especially in one-on-one situations (see Fig. 2). In order to maintain the submission, obedience, and dependency of followers, these leaders are more likely to elicit threat-related emotions, loss of agency emotions, and personal loss emotions. By intentionally keeping followers half-informed about happenings within the organization and guessing about their status as employees, these leaders are likely to elicit feelings of *powerlessness, meaninglessness,* and *anxiety* in their followers.

Alternatively, these leaders may induce *fear* in followers through overt and subtle forms of coercion, providing ways for them to escape punishment that conveniently serve the leader's broader goals and vision. A secondary benefit of fear is that it can restrict attention to cues in the environment other than the source of fear (Izard, 1993), limiting the cognitive processing of information that might make followers reconsider their loyalties to the leader. They may enable or even orchestrate events that will result in personal loss for followers, causing them to withdraw or seek support from others. In the latter instance, leaders will make sure that the followers come to them for support, maintaining follower dependency by providing the illusion that the leader (or those doing his or her bidding) is the only one followers can turn to. By encouraging passive, negative emotions in followers, providing the impression of support, and promising better things in the long term for short-term sacrifices, personalized leaders generate sufficient follower satisfaction to remain influential. While leaders are likely to display a blend of personalized and socialized charismatic behaviors and attributes, it is still relatively easy to think of leaders with predominant emotional styles like the aforementioned patterns.

Implications of Specific Emotions for Leadership

Application of the emotion framework to these two theories highlights a number of interesting points with regard to the role of specific emotions in leadership behavior and influence processes. To begin, different types of leaders are likely to manifest different patterns of emotion, both consciously and subconsciously, that are consistent with their frames of reference for interacting with, and managing, followers. This is an important argument for studying emotions at a specific level because all three of the leader types described above would look the same in terms of overall levels of emotional intelligence.

A second point is that followers of leaders using different leadership approaches are likely to display different types of emotional dispositions. Thus, the nature of emotions involved in a leader's interactions with specific followers will depend in part on individual predisposition or emotional make-up driving the manifestation of certain emotions. However, the leadership situation or context, whether contrived by the leader or not, will also play a role in eliciting emotions. It is open to question whether individual emotional predispositions or situational influences will exert stronger forces on emotion appraisal and expression.

Third, specific emotions are targeted at different points in the leadership process, from the initial point when a vision is conceptualized and communicated to when vision-related goals have been realized, changed, or abandoned. While leaders may not always consciously realize that they are tapping into different emotions to accomplish different purposes with their followers, this may help to better explain the nature of leader influence processes.

CONCLUDING COMMENTS

The emotion framework outlined here explores only one avenue regarding how specific emotions impact transformational and charismatic leadership. While the focus here is on how leaders appraise and manage follower emotions in performing the types of leadership behaviors characterizing transformational and charismatic leaders, the framework could be applied to address a number of other topics. Influence is not unidirectional in leadership situations. Little is known about how followers intentionally and unintentionally influence or elicit leader emotions, or how they affect leaders' emotional appraisal.

Another issue that could be examined with this framework is differences in the emotional patterns of male and female leaders. Brody and Hall (1993) summarize findings from the research on emotion and gender, revealing that females tend to be more emotionally expressive than males, experience a greater intensity of emotions, are more likely to show certain types of emotions (e.g. sadness and love), and repress others (e.g. anger). There are also differences in the emotions that men and women appraise most accurately in other people. Gender differences have also been observed in verbal and non-verbal expressions of emotion.

This raises a third issue, of the extent to which leaders express different specific emotions verbally and non-verbally. What emotions are most amenable to non-verbal expression in leadership contexts (Riggio, 1998), and are there any differences in the impact or effectiveness of verbal and non-verbal emotional expression on leader-follower influence processes? Research is also needed in another area alluded to earlier. Specifically, are certain emotions more critical to emotional intelligence than others in leadership contexts? This question and how a leader's emotional disposition may impact his or her emotional intelligence are two areas for further exploration in this literature. A fifth potential area for research concerns the question of whether or not leadership processes shape patterns of emotion appraisal and expression over time and if it is possible to train or develop emotion management in leaders and followers.

Finally, the emotion framework, as well as other research on emotions in the workplace (Basch & Fisher, 2000), suggests that different work events elicit different types of emotions. Shamir and Howell (1999) propose that organizational factors such as technology, goals, structure, and culture can impact the emergence and effectiveness of charismatic leadership. Emotions may be one mechanism through which this occurs. Organizational factors such as policies or culture that are not necessarily under the control of a leader can have consequences for follower emotions that may foster passive or active emotional responses inappropriately, working against a leader's purposes. Exploring the role of specific emotions in these and other areas is one way that future research can further increase our understanding of leader-follower influence processes in transformational and charismatic leadership.

REFERENCES

Arnold, M. B. (1960). *Emotion and personality* (Vol. 1). *Psychological aspects.* New York: Columbia University Press.

Ashkanasy, N. M., Härtel, C. E., & Zerbe, W. J. (2000). Emotions in the workplace: Research, theory, and practice. In: N. M. Ashkanasy & C. E. Haertel (Eds), *Emotions in the workplace: Research, theory and practice* (pp. 3–18). Westport, CT: Quorum Books/ Greenwood Publishing Group.

Ashkanasy, N. M., & Tse, B. (2000). Transformational leadership as management of emotion: A conceptual review. In: N. M. Ashkanasy & C. E. Härtel (Eds), *Emotions in the workplace: Research, theory and practice* (pp. 221–235). Westport, CT: Quorum Books/Greenwood Publishing Group.

Avolio, B. J., & Bass, B. M. (1988). Transformational leadership, charisma, and beyond. In: J. G. Hunt, B. R. Baliga, H. P. Dachler & C. A. Schriesheim (Eds), *Emerging leadership vistas* (pp. 29–50). Lexington, MA: Lexington Books.

Ball, G. A., Trevino, L. K., & Sims, H. P. Jr. (1992). Understanding subordinate reactions to punishment incidents: Perspectives from justice and social affect. *Leadership Quarterly, 3,* 307–333.

Basch, J., & Fisher, C. D. (2000). Affective events-emotions matrix: A classification of work events and associated emotions. In: N. M. Ashkanasy & C. E. Haertel (Eds), *Emotions in the workplace: Research, theory and practice* (pp. 36–48). Westport, CT: Quorum Books/ Greenwood Publishing Group, Inc.

Bass, B. (1985). *Leadership and performance beyond expectations.* New York: Free Press.

Bass, B. M. (2002). Cognitive, social, and emotional intelligence of transformational leaders. In: R. E. Riggio, S. E. Murphy & F. J. Pirozzolo (Eds), *Multiple intelligences and leadership* (pp. 105–118). Mahwah, NJ: Lawrence Erlbaum Associates.

Bass, B. M., & Avolio, B. J. (1993). Transformational leadership: A response to critiques. In: M. Chemers & R. Ayman (Eds), *Leadership theory and research: Perspectives and directions* (pp. 49–80). San Diego, CA: Academic Press.

Bass, B. M., & Steidlmeier, P. (1999). Ethics, character, and authentic transformational leadership behavior. *Leadership Quarterly, 10,* 181–217.

Brody, L. R., & Hall, J. A. (1993). Gender and emotion. In: M. L. Lewis & J. M. Haviland (Eds), *Handbook of emotions* (pp. 447–460). New York: The Guilford Press.

Burns, J. M. (1978). *Leadership.* New York: Harper & Row.

Cannon, W. B. (1927). The James-Lange theory of emotions: A critical examination and an alternative theory. *American Journal of Psychology, 39,* 106–124.

Caruso, D. R., Mayer, J. D., & Salovey, P. (2002). Emotional intelligence and emotional leadership. In: R. E. Riggio, S. E. Murphy & F. J. Pirozzolo (Eds), *Multiple intelligences and leadership* (pp. 55–74). Mahwah, NJ: Lawrence Erlbaum Associates.

Chemers, M. M., Watson, C. B., & May, S. T. (2000). Dispositional affect and leadership effectiveness: A comparison of self-esteem, optimism, and efficacy. *Personality and Social Psychology Bulletin, 26*, 267–277.

Conger, J. A. (1999). Charismatic and transformational leadership in organizations: An insider's perspective on these developing streams of research. *Leadership Quarterly, 10*, 145–179.

Conger, J. A., & Kanungo, R. N. (1987). Toward a behavioral theory of charismatic leadership in organizational settings. *Academy of Management Review, 12*, 637–647.

Conger, J. A., & Kanungo, R. N. (1998). *Charismatic leadership in organizations.* Thousand Oaks, CA: Sage Publications.

Dansereau, F., Yammarino, F. J., Markham, S. E., Alutto, J. A., Newman, J., Dumas, M., Nachman, S. A., Naughton, T. J., Kim, K., Al-Kelabi, S. A., Lee, S., & Keller, T. (1995). Individualized leadership: A new multi-level approach. *Leadership Quarterly, 6*, 413–450.

Darwin, C. R. (1872/1985). *The expression of emotions in man and animals.* Chicago: University of Chicago Press.

Diener, E., & Larsen, R. J. (1984). Temporal stability and cross-situational consistency of affective, cognitive, and behavioral responses. *Journal of Personality and Social Psychology, 47*, 871–883.

Diener, E., Smith, H., & Fujita, F. (1995). The personality structure of affect. *Journal of Personality and Social Psychology, 69*(1), 130–141.

Dubinsky, A. J., Yammarino, F. J., & Jolson, M. A. (1995). An examination of linkages between personal characteristics and dimensions of transformational leadership. *Journal of Business and Psychology, 9*, 315–334.

Fell, J. P. (1977). The phenomenological approach to emotion. In: D. K. Candland, J. P. Fell, E. Keen, A. I. Leshner, R. Plutchik & R. M. Tarpy (Eds), *Emotion* (pp. 235–285), Monterey, CA: Brooks/Cole.

Frijda, N. H. (1986). *The emotions.* Cambridge: Cambridge University Press.

George, J. M. (1990). Personality, affect, and behavior in groups. *Journal of Applied Psychology, 75*, 107–116.

George, J. M. (2000). Emotions and leadership: The role of emotional intelligence. *Human Relations, 53*, 1027–1055.

Goleman, D. (1995). *Emotional intelligence.* New York: Bantam.

Helton, W. B., Benavidez, J. E., & Connelly, M. S. (2000). Emotion and emotional processes: A review and some new theoretical considerations. Technical Report for the Department of Defense (contract No. 1999*I033800*000). Norman, OK: University of Oklahoma, Department of Psychology.

House, R. J. (1977). A 1976 theory of charismatic leadership. In: J. G. Hunt & L. L. Larson (Eds), *Leadership: The cutting edge* (pp. 189–207). Carbondale, IL: Southern Illinois University Press).

House, R. J., & Howell, J. (1992). Personality and charismatic leadership. *Leadership Quarterly, 3*, 81–108.

Howell, J. M (1988). Two faces of charisma: Socialized and personalized leadership in organizations. In: J. Conger & R. Kanungo (Eds), *Charismatic leadership: The elusive factor in organizational effectiveness.* San Francisco: Jossey-Bass.

Isen, A. M. (1993). Positive affect and decision making. In: M. L. Lewis & J. M. Haviland (Eds), *Handbook of emotions* (pp. 261–278). New York: The Guilford Press.

Isen, A. M. (1987). Positive affect, cognitive processes, and social behavior. In: L. Berkowitz (Ed.), *Advances in Experimental Social Psychology* (pp. 203–253). New York: Academic Press.

Isen, A. M., & Geva, N. (1987). The influence of positive affect on acceptable level of risk: The person with a large canoe has a large worry. *Organizational Behavior and Human Decision Processes, 39,* 145–154.

Isen, A. M., & Patrick, R. (1983). The effect of positive feelings on risk-taking: When the chips are down. *Organizational Behavior and Human Performance, 31,* 194–202.

Izard, C. E. (1993). Organizational and motivational functions of discrete emotions. In: M. L. Lewis & J. M. Haviland (Eds), *Handbook of Emotions* (pp. 631–641). New York: The Guilford Press.

Izard, C. E. (1971). *The face of emotion.* New York: Appleton-Century-Crofts.

Izard, C. E. (1977). *Human emotions.* New York: Plenum.

Keltner, D., & Buswell, B. N. (1997). Embarrassment: Its distinct form and appeasement functions. *Psychological Bulletin, 122,* 250–270.

Kuhnert, K. W., & Lewis, P. (1987). Transactional and transformational leadership: A constructive/ developmental analysis. *Academy of Management Review, 12,* 648–657.

Larsen, R. J., & Diener, E. (1985). A multitrait-multimethod examination of affect structure: hedonic level and emotional intensity. *Personality and Individual Differences, 6,* 631–636.

Larsen, R. J., & Diener, E. (1992). Promises and problems with the circumplex model of emotion. In: M. S. Clark (Ed.), *Emotion* (pp. 25–29). Newbury Park, CA: Sage Publications.

Larsen, R. J., Diener, E., & Emmons, R. A. (1986). Affect intensity and reactions to daily life events. *Journal of Personality and Social Psychology, 51,* 803–814.

Lazarus, R. S. (1966). *Psychological stress and the coping process.* New York: McGraw-Hill.

Lazarus, R. S. (1991). Progress on a cognitive-motivational-relational theory of emotion. *American Psychologist, 46*(8), 819–834.

LeDoux, J. E. (1995). Emotion: Clues from the brain. *Annual Review of Psychology, 46,* 209–235.

Leith, K. P., & Baumeister, R. F. (1996). Why do bad moods increase self-defeating behavior? Emotion, risk-taking, and self-regulation. *Journal of Personality and Social Psychology, 71,* 1250–1267.

Lewis, K. M. (2000). When leaders display emotion: How followers respond to negative emotional expression of male and female leaders. *Journal of Organizational Behavior, 21,* 221–234.

Mayer, J. D., & Salovey, P. (1997). What is emotional intelligence? In: P Salovey & D. Sluyter (Eds), *Emotional development and emotional intelligence: Implications for educators* (pp. 3–31). New York: Basic Books.

Megerian, L. E., & Sosik, J. J. (1996). An affair of the heart: Emotional intelligence and transformational leadership. *Journal of Leadership Studies, 3,* 31–48.

Mesquita, B., & Frijda, N. H., (1992). Cultural variations in emotions: A review. *Psychological Bulletin, 112,* 179–204.

Mizuno, S., Matsubara, T., & Takai, J. (1994). Influences of emotional reaction and personal power on the leadership process: An examination of moderating and mediating effects. Japanese *Journal of Experimental and Social Psychology, 33,* 201–212.

Morrison, D. E. (1998). Leadership and aggression: Affect, values, and defenses. *Psychiatric Annals, 28,* 271–276.

Mumford, M. D., Dansereau, F., & Yammarino, F. J. (2000). Followers, motivations, and levels of analysis: The case of individualized leadership. *Leadership Quarterly, 11,* 313–340.

Plutchik, R. (1962). *The emotions: Facts, theories, and a new model*. New York: Random House.

Plutchik, R. (1980). *Emotion: A psychoevolutionary synthesis*. New York: Harper & Row.

Price, K. H., & Garland, H. (1978). Leader interventions to ameliorate the negative consequences of collective group failure. *Journal of Management, 4*(1), 7–15.

Riggio, R. E (1998). Charisma. *Encyclopedia of Mental Health, 1*, 387–396.

Roseman, I. J. (1984). Cognitive Determinants of Emotion: A structural Theory. *Review of Personality & Social Psychology, 5*, 11–36.

Roseman, I. J., Spindle, M. S., & Jose, P. E. (1990). Appraisals of emotion eliciting events: Testing a theory of discrete emotions. *Journal of Personality and Social Psychology, 59*, 899–915.

Rosenberg, E. L. (1988). Levels of analysis and the organization of affect. *Review of General Psychology, 2*, 247–270.

Russell, J. A. (1980). A circumplex model of affect. *Journal of Personality and Social Psychology, 39*, 1161–1178.

Salovey, P., & Mayer, J. D. (1990). Emotional intelligence. *Imagination, cognition, and personality, 9*, 185–211.

Scherer, K. R. (1982). Emotion as process: Function, origin and regulation. *Social Science Information, 21*, 555–570.

Scherer, K. R. (1988). Criteria for emotion-antecedent appraisal: A review. In: V. Hamilton, G. H. Bower & N. H. Frijda (Eds), *Cognitive perspectives on emotion and motivation* (pp. 89–126). Norwell, MA: Kluwer Academic Publishers.

Scherer, K. R. (1997). The role of culture in emotion-antecedent appraisal. *Journal of Personality and Social Psychology, 73*, 902–922.

Shamir, B., House, R. J., & Arthur, M. B. (1993). The motivational effects of charismatic leadership: A self-concept based theory. *Organizational Science, 4*, 577–594.

Shamir, B., & Howell, J. M. (1999). Organizational and contextual influences on the emergence and effectiveness of charismatic leadership. *Leadership Quarterly, 10*, 257–283.

Sosik, J. J., & Megerian, L. E. (1999). Understanding leader emotional intelligence and performance: The role of self-other agreement on transformational leadership perceptions. *Group and Organizational Management, 24*, 367–390.

Tellegen, A. (1985). Structures of mood and personality and their relevance to assessing anxiety, with an emphasis on self-report. In: A. H. Tuma & J. D. Maser (Eds), *Anxiety and Anxiety Disorders* (pp. 681–706). Hillsdale, NJ: Erlbaum.

Totterdell, P. (2000). Catching moods and hitting runs: Mood linkage and subjective performance in professional team sports. *Journal of Applied Psychology, 85*, 848–859.

Totterdell, P., Kellett, S., Teuchmann, K., & Briner, R. B. (1998). Evidence of mood linkages in work groups. *Journal of Personality and Social Psychology, 74*, 1504–1515.

Watson, D., & Clark, L. A. (1984). Negative affectivity: The disposition to experience aversive emotional states. *Psychological Bulletin, 96*, 465–490.

Watson, D., & Clark, L. A. (1992). Affects separable and inseparable: On the hierarchical arrangement of the negative affects. *Journal of Personality and Social Psychology, 62*, 489–505.

Watson, D., & Tellegen, A. (1985). Toward a consensual structure of mood. *Psychological Bulletin, 98*, 219–235.

Weierter, S. J. M. (1997). Who wants to play "follow the leader?" A theory of charismatic relationships based on routinized charisma and follower characteristics. *Leadership Quarterly, 8*, 171–193.

Yammarino, F. J., & Dansereau, F. (2002). Individualized leadership. *Journal of Leadership and Organizational Studies, 9,* forthcoming.

Yukl, G. (1999). An evaluation of conceptual weaknesses in transformational and charismatic leadership theories. *Leadership Quarterly, 10,* 285–300.

PART IV:
RELATED PERSPECTIVES

PYGMALION TRAINING MADE EFFECTIVE: GREATER MASTERY THROUGH AUGMENTATION OF SELF-EFFICACY AND MEANS EFFICACY*

Dov Eden and Roni Sulimani

ABSTRACT

Seven past field-experimental attempts to produce Pygmalion effects by training managers yielded meager results (Eden et al., 2000). The present effort bolstered the Pygmalion approach with special emphasis on means efficacy, defined as belief in the utility of the tools available for performing a job. Six randomly assigned anti-aircraft gunnery instructors received a one-day Pygmalion workshop with special emphasis on self-efficacy and means efficacy before beginning instruction in a new round of a course; eight control instructors received an interpersonal communication workshop. The trainees of the experimental instructors reported higher self-efficacy, means efficacy, and motivation, and obtained higher scores on written examinations and on performance tests than did the trainees of the control instructors. This is the first true-experimental confirmation of

* This article is based on the thesis submitted by Roni Sulimani as part of the requirements for his master's degree in organizational behavior at Tel Aviv University's Faculty of Management. Dov Eden served as thesis advisor.

  The Lilly and Alejandro Saltiel Chair in Corporate Leadership and Social Responsibility and the Israel Institute of Business Research supported part of Dov Eden's work on this experiment.

Transformational and Charismatic Leadership, Volume 2, pages 287–308.
ISBN: 0-7623-0962-8

the effectiveness of Pygmalion training among instructors of adults and the first replication of the means-efficacy findings.

INTRODUCTION

The Pygmalion effect is a special case of self-fulfilling prophecy (SFP) in which raising manager expectations boosts follower performance. After almost two decades of field experimentation, findings that looked promising elevated the Pygmalion paradigm to prominent standing within the industrial and organizational psychology community as well as among management and leadership scholars. It has become common knowledge that the Pygmalion approach "works," that is, raising manager expectations boosts follower performance. Research and application articles have been published in widely read scientific and practitioner journals, textbooks give routine coverage to the Pygmalion effect in organizations, and Pygmalion leadership training films are used extensively. This standing is based on the solid foundation of internally and externally valid field-experimental findings that confirm the Pygmalion paradigm in organizational settings (for narrative reviews, see Eden, 1990, 1993). For example, in his path-blazing *Leadership and performance beyond expectations*, Bass (1985) wrote, "Charismatics take advantage of the Pygmalion effect . . . and reciprocate in their confidence in their followers and in their optimistic expectations about their followers' performance. Follower self-esteem and enthusiasm are raised as a consequence, and the effort is increased among followers to fulfill the leaders' expressed expectations" (p. 47).

Cumulative analysis has fortified the empirical base accumulated over the last two decades. In recent meta-analyses of Pygmalion research in work settings, McNatt (2000) calculated an overall corrected estimate of the average effect size of $d = 1.13$ (58 effect sizes, $n = 2,874$) in 17 studies, and Kierein and Gold (2000), adopting somewhat different inclusion criteria, found an overall average effect size of $d = 0.81$ (13 effect sizes, $n = 2,853$) in nine studies. Thus, the accumulated results of experimental research in organizations have established that Pygmalion effects can be produced among adults in organizations and that these effects are of large magnitude. Nevertheless, Pygmalion research has reached a critical crossroads.

DECEPTIVE VERSUS NON-DECEPTIVE TREATMENT

Virtually all these confirmations were obtained using a deceptive experimental treatment. Typically, in an experimental procedure that lasts only a few minutes, managers are led into believing that some or all of their followers have high potential. Time and again, the results have confirmed that, once managers believe that their followers have high potential (corroborated by manipulation checks), they become unwitting prophets who fulfill their own expectations, and they lead the followers designated to be capable of more to achieve more. This occurs despite the fact that, unbeknownst to the managers, the designations were random from the start. The followers who were designated as having high potential were, on average, no more competent than the control followers toward whom no expectations were implanted. A question unanswered by these overwhelmingly confirmatory experiments is whether raising supervisors' expectations toward their followers *without* deception, say in consulting, coaching, or training, would be as effective as the 5-minute treatment and, if so, why such training works.

Early Pygmalion Application Quasi-experiments

The only previous published findings regarding the effectiveness of non-deceptive Pygmalion applications were from quasi-experiments conducted by King (1974) in the United States Navy and by Weinstein et al. (1991) in an elementary school. King (1974) pioneered applying the SFP approach in an organizational development study that involved Pygmalion training for all personnel involved. The leaders involved were fully informed that an experiment was taking place. The results showed that the followers of leaders trained in the Pygmalion approach outperformed the control followers. However, there were numerous methodological deficiencies in King's quasi-experiment, including non-random assignment of personnel to conditions and subjective post-experimental assessment of the followers' performance, the dependent variable, by the leaders whose expectations had been raised (Eden, 1990). Susceptibility to bias that could tilt the results in a confirmatory direction is obvious.

Weinstein and her colleagues involved teachers, parents, and school administrators in a collaborative, community-oriented, preventative intervention designed to apply the Pygmalion concept with the aim of changing school culture. The basic idea was to get all involved to communicate positive expectations to under-achieving ninth-graders at risk for school failure. They also changed such aspects of school functioning as student responsibility, curriculum, and evaluation in accord with the high-expectancy culture that they were trying to create. The authors described their results as "promising but not uniform" (p. 333). Pupils who were "at risk" attained higher grades, fewer disciplinary referrals, and better retention at the year's end. However, these improvements were not sustained the following year with teachers who were not involved in the project. Weinstein et al. suggested that their intervention may not have been strong enough to effect lasting change.

The strong internal validity that marked the previous 5-minute treatment experiments was lacking in both of these application studies. However, the results were encouraging as far as they went. Replication with greater rigor was needed before drawing any conclusions about the applicability of the Pygmalion paradigm.

The Seven Pygmalion Application Experiments

To clarify the applicability question with high internal validity, Eden et al. (2000) conducted seven field experiments in which they tested the effectiveness of training managers in Pygmalion Leadership Style (PLS). PLS is manager behavior that conveys high performance expectations to followers, creates a supportive climate, and attributes follower successes to stable, internal causes. The training workshop was developed across the seven experiments from a one-day familiarization experience to a three-day program that included learning Pygmalion concepts, behavioral skill-practice exercises, implementation planning, and follow-up sessions. The Pygmalion leadership workshop had three primary aims: first, to increase participating managers' *attributed efficacy*, that is, to get them to believe that their followers are indeed capable of achieving more; second, to increase participants' *managerial self-efficacy* by getting them to believe that they are capable of leading their followers to greater achievement; and third, several sessions were devoted to *behavioral skill acquisition* to raise participants' proficiency in enacting PLS.

The workshop opened with a 20-minute experiential warm-up exercise to demonstrate the meaning and strength of the leader-follower Pygmalion effect (see Eden, 1990c, p. 163). This was followed by an interactive lecture on SFP in economics, medicine, science, education, and management; Pygmalion, Galatea, and Golem effects; and leadership as the prime mediator of the effects of expectations on motivation and performance. The remaining two and a half days were interspersed with brief lecturettes on positive and negative SFP; general and specific self-efficacy, managerial self-efficacy, attributed efficacy, and collective efficacy; the effective management of attributions in the wake of success and failure; managing organizational culture to enhance organization-wide SFP. Analysis of famous Pygmalion-like leaders (e.g. Lee Iacocca) was supplemented by examples offered up by the participants.

Next, a session was devoted to identification of opportunities to exercise Pygmalion leadership. This set the stage for role playing to rehearse self-efficacy-enhancing leader behaviors in a variety of manager-follower situations suggested by the participants using VCR for instant replay and feedback. At the end of the role playing sessions, the facilitator emphasized how the role-playing exercise epitomized the Pygmalion leadership process by:

(1) encouraging participants to try something difficult;
(2) providing constructive feedback about their performance;
(3) getting them to try again, leading to improved performance; and
(4) providing feedback attributing the success to their ability to expand their mastery of PLS, thereby reinforcing their learning, enhancing their managerial self-efficacy, and augmenting their motivation to apply PLS.

The workshop concluded with implementation planning at the individual, departmental, and organizational levels using printed forms that led the participants through a process of defining Pygmalion leadership goals at different levels and for different time spans (immediate, several months, and a year). They were asked to foresee obstacles to transfer and implementation (e.g. overload, crises that demand immediate attention, follower resistance) and to plan how to overcome them. The workshop closed optimistically with a strong note of high expectations. Clearly, this training design shares some important elements with transformational leadership training conducted in the Bass transformational-leadership tradition.

In all seven experiments, questionnaires measured leader and follower perceptions; in three, objective performance data were also analyzed. There was little evidence that the workshops influenced the trained leaders or their followers. Meta-analysis of 61 effects ($n = 186$ groups) produced in the seven experiments yielded a small mean effect size, $r = 0.13$, $p < 0.01$. Using a conversion formula (Rosenthal & Rosnow, 1984, p. 361), McNatt's (2000) estimated effect size of $d = 1.13$ is equivalent to $r = 0.49$, and Kierein and Gold's (2000) $d = 0.81$ is equivalent to $r = 0.38$. Cohen (1988) defined $r = 0.10$ as a small effect, $r = 0.30$ as medium, and 0.50 as large. The disparity between the medium-to-very-large effect produced by the earlier 5-minute-treatment experiments and the much smaller effect produced in the seven training experiments constitutes Pygmalion's present crisis. The meager results of the training experiments led Eden et al. (2000) to question whether training can be used successfully to produce the Pygmalion effect. The discrepancy between the two sets of Pygmalion experiments requires explanation and resolution.

UNWITTING VERSUS WITTING PYGMALION EFFECTS

A major difference between the early confirmatory experiments and the seven training experiments is that, in the former, the managers were deceived. Once (mis)led to expect more, they unwittingly led their followers to achieve more. In contrast, the training experiments used no deception. In each of the seven training studies, as in King's and Weinstein et al.'s, the participating managers knew that a study was being conducted, and they were fully informed of the purposes of the research. The participants were actually invited to do wittingly back on the job what the participants in the previous studies had done unwittingly, that is, to treat their followers as though they were highly competent employees capable of excellent performance. Evidently, the participating managers did not implement this advice. Few of the measures that had detected significant and substantial pretest-posttest change in leader behavior in the 5-minute-treatment experiments detected such changes in the training experiments.

Echoing earlier speculation regarding the role of deception in producing the Pygmalion effect, Eden et al. (2000) suggested that deception may be an indispensable ingredient in the Pygmalion process. If so, this portends a dismal future for Pygmalion applications. Few applied psychologists will be willing to base their relations with their clients on routine deception. Ways must be found to make managers witting collaborators in producing worthwhile effects.

PYGMALION: EFFICACIOUS BUT NOT EFFECTIVE?

In the earlier "unwitting" experiments, it must have been non-conscious mental processes that led the managers to treat their followers in accordance with their expectations. Having internalized high expectations, the managers produced the Pygmalion effect unknowingly or "automatically." This converges with Bargh and Chartrand's (1999) explanation of how SFP can operate "entirely non-consciously" (p. 467). Bargh and Chartrand summarized experimental evidence for the automatic activation of stereotypes in which participants nonconsciously act in accordance with their expectations toward others and thereby get others to act as expected with no awareness of the process by either party. The "dual-process models" in social psychology (Chaiken & Trope, 1999) have established the fact that there are both conscious and non-conscious determinants of behavior.

It is possible that, despite its considerable internal and external validity, amply demonstrated by the meta-analyses, the Pygmalion approach may lack "application validity," that is, the purposive applicability that would render it an effective tool in the hands of practicing managers. This goes beyond Campbell and Stanley's (1966) "external validity." Seligman (1995, 1996; see also Holon, 1996 and Seligman & Levant, 1998) has used the terms "efficacy" and "effectiveness" to distinguish between recovery rates produced by psychotherapy in controlled experimental studies and in clinical practice, respectively. Evaluation research has shown that certain psychotherapeutic treatments achieve better recovery rates in controlled studies than in clinical practice, whereas other treatments work better in actual practice than in the highly controlled studies. Borrowing Seligman's terms, the meta-analyses of the unwitting Pygmalion experiments confirm that the Pygmalion approach has strong efficacy. However, the results of the Pygmalion training experiments show that it had yet to pass the effectiveness crucible.

Eden et al. (2000) concluded that a different approach must be taken to apply Pygmalion concepts effectively. They suggested a number of proposals for improving the design and increasing the likelihood of producing Pygmalion effects in future non-deceptive training applications. The present training experiment was an attempt to overcome the deficiencies that prevented the emergence of the Pygmalion effect in the previous seven attempts. In this sense, it was Experiment 8 in the series of Pygmalion training experiments. Its first purpose was to test, once again, the effectiveness of Pygmalion training.

THE INTERNAL-EXTERNAL EFFICACY MODEL: SELF-EFFICACY AND MEANS EFFICACY

Jim Harter of the Gallup organization passed on an observation about very large differences in performance between several hundred retail stores. What was interesting was that every store had exactly the same equipment; yet, when asked if they had the right equipment at Time 1, the best performing stores said their equipment was quite adequate and the worst performing stores said it was inadequate[1].

Self-efficacy is only half of the efficacy story. The Internal-External Efficacy model (Eden, 1996, 2000) is an expanded conceptualization of efficacy beliefs. It was introduced to broaden the conceptualization of efficacy beliefs and to encompass sources of work motivation overlooked by previous self-efficacy theory. Subjective efficacy is defined as one's *overall* assessment of *all* available resources that may be applied toward successful job performance. Some of these resources are *internal* and are encompassed within the *self-efficacy* construct. These include such talents, knowledge, resourcefulness, endurance, willpower, or other traits that the individual deems useful for performance. Subjective *external* efficacy is defined as the individual's belief in the utility of the means available for performing the job (Eden, 1996, 2000). Individuals attach utility value to the various means or tools that may facilitate- or hinder-performance. "Means efficacy" is the aggregate subjective utility of these external means. It is hypothesized that means efficacy is as motivating as self-efficacy; as high self-efficacy imbues one with expectations for success and thereby augments motivation to exert effort (Bandura, 1997), so a high level of means efficacy motivates a person to use the means energetically.

Furthermore, internal and external efficacy may interact; the motivating effects of a high level of internal efficacy ("I am an expert sharpshooter") can be offset by low external efficacy ("The weapon is miscalibrated"). Conversely, a marvelous tool may have little impact on motivation for the individual who has a low self-efficacy for using it ("I'm sure it's a great lap-top, but I'll never be able to learn how to use one"). It is hypothesized that synergistically maximal motivation results when workers believe themselves to be highly skilled at what they do *and* believe that they have at their disposal the best means for doing it, that is, when *total* subjective efficacy is high. The practical implication is that managers should motivate their employees by persuading them to believe not only that they are competent (self-efficacy), but also that their tools are effective (means efficacy).

Means Efficacy Complements Self-efficacy

So far, organizational psychologists have considered only internal efficacy (i.e. self-efficacy) in their theories of work motivation. Means efficacy adds the other, external, half of the subjective efficacy construct. Adding the external dimension expands the efficacy concept and leads to a greater understanding of what motivates effort. It also opens the way for practical applications not implied by previous self-efficacy theory. Means efficacy is not offered up as an alternative or replacement for self-efficacy; nor should self-efficacy and means efficacy be thought of as coming at the expense of one another. Rather, either or both can be raised without reducing the other. Thus, means efficacy complements self-efficacy. It is their separate and combined effects on motivation and performance that are of interest.

Previous Means Efficacy Research

Eden and Granat-Flomin (2000) reported the first, and so far the only, empirical test of the Internal-External Efficacy model. They showed that an experimental treatment designed to raise means efficacy can improve performance. They told employees in randomly assigned branches of a service organization that the new computer system that they were about to receive had proved to be the best of its kind. Control personnel were given the same computer system with no means-efficacy treatment. Means efficacy increased in both conditions, because branches in both conditions had received much improved computer systems. However, a significant Treatment × Occasion interaction indicated that the increase in the experimental condition was greater, attributable to the means-efficacy-boosting treatment.

Eden and Granat-Flomin had set out to demonstrate the effects of raising means efficacy; therefore, they focused their treatment on means efficacy but took no action to increase self-efficacy. As predicted, pretest-posttest comparisons showed that self-efficacy remained unchanged in both experimental and control conditions. Finally, the experimental branches surpassed the control branches significantly and substantially in service-time improvement, as predicted. This improvement could not be attributed to self-efficacy, which remained unchanged. Thus, Eden and Granat-Flomin showed that it is possible to measure means efficacy, to augment it experimentally, and thereby to produce a significant performance improvement. Moreover, they showed that means efficacy can have effects that are independent of self-efficacy.

Total Efficacy, Motivation, and Performance

The most important implication of efficacy beliefs is their effect on motivated effort (Bandura, 1997; Eden, 1996, 2000). The aim of efficacy raising is better performance. Stajkovic and Luthans' (1998) meta-analysis confirmed that there is a strong, positive relationship between self-efficacy and performance. Furthermore, field experimentation has established the causal effects of self-efficacy on performance in organizations (e.g. Gist, Schwoerer & Rosen, 1989). Therefore, based on the postulates of the Internal-External Efficacy model, we hypothesized that raising self-efficacy and means efficacy increases motivation and performance.

The Present Experiment

Summarizing, the present experiment came in the wake of Eden et al. (2000) and Eden and Granat-Flomin (2000). It was designed to test the effectiveness of Pygmalion training and of integrating the means-efficacy concept into a Pygmalion training model. We aimed at strengthening training effectiveness by teaching instructors to use both self-efficacy and means efficacy to motivate their trainees for better performance.

Thus, the present experiment differed from previous Pygmalion training experiments by adding means efficacy to the tools suggested for the participants to use in implementing Pygmalion style, and it differed from Eden and Granat-Flomin's experiment in being non-deceptive and in targeting both means efficacy and self-efficacy. Hypothesizing positive effects of total subjective efficacy on motivation and performance, we predicted that trainees of the experimental instructors, who were to be trained in Pygmalion and total-efficacy concepts, would have a greater self-efficacy, means efficacy, and motivation, and would outperform comparable trainees whose instructors got alternative training. We also tested the interaction hypothesis that performance would be disproportionately high among individuals who are high in both self-efficacy and means efficacy.

METHOD

Design and Sample

This was an after-only randomized field experiment among instructors and trainees at the Israel Defense Forces Anti-aircraft Gunnery School. The 16 instructors were non-commissioned officers who had completed command training and had been assigned to an instructor-training course to prepare them for their designated role as anti-aircraft gunnery instructors. As part of this 5-week preliminary instructor training, we assigned the instructors randomly to experimental and control conditions, eight instructors to each, and gave each group of eight a different one-day workshop. The experimental group received Pygmalion training emphasizing how to raise self-efficacy and means efficacy. This was the experimental treatment. The control group were trained in interpersonal communication. After this preliminary training, instructors were dispersed and assigned to training duty in a variety of courses. These were 7- to 8-week-long specialty courses for recruits who had successfully completed basic training. This advanced training is routinely delivered to small groups, with four to six trainees per instructor.

For administrative reasons that were unrelated to the experiment, two of the eight experimental instructors were subsequently assigned to other duties not comparable to the training done by the rest. Therefore, we omitted them from the sample. The final sample numbered the remaining six experimental instructors and their 27 trainees, and eight control instructors and their 40 trainees, all men.

Measures

General Self-efficacy (GSE) was assessed among managers and workers by the Hebrew version of Sherer et al.'s (1982) 17-item GSE scale used in several of the Eden et al. (2000) experiments, $\alpha = 0.91$. Illustrative items are "When I make plans, I am certain I can make them work" and "When unexpected problems occur, I don't handle them well." We devised a 15-item measure of *means efficacy* for anti-aircraft gunnery, $\alpha = 0.95$. The trainee indicated on a seven-point scale agreement with such statements as, "The system I have been trained on is one of the best in the world," "My system can bring victory to our forces," "My system is dependable in wartime," "My system is reliable," and "My system is accurate." Eden (1996) has proposed that the specificity of motivational measures should match the specificity of the task performed. Therefore, we measured motivation at two levels of specificity. *General motivation* was measured by four items dealing with overall willingness to serve in anti-aircraft units, $\alpha = 0.70$. *Means-specific motivation* was gauged by four items concerning desire to use the weapon system on which the respondent was being trained, $\alpha = 0.74$. *Performance* was assessed with the Anti-Aircraft School's routine written and practical tests.

The Workshops

The instructor training was rendered in two one-day workshops, one experimental and one control, each of which involved 6 hours of contact time two weeks into the preliminary course. The experimental workshop opened with a warm-up experiential exercise demonstrating the Pygmalion effect briefly, simply, and concretely (see Eden, 1990, p. 163). Next, a lecturette presented the theoretical model and research findings showing that the effect works and how it works.

The version of the Pygmalion model presented emphasized the role of augmenting self-efficacy and means efficacy in leading followers to effective performance. The facilitator stressed using verbal persuasion and model-ing, defined by Bandura as sources of self-efficacy, in boosting trainee self-efficacy and means efficacy. Several role-play exercises that simulated real-life instructor-trainee relationships had been prepared in advance. These role plays were conducted with one participant playing a Pygmalion-like instructor, another enacting the role of a trainee, the remaining participants observing. The facilitator led a discussion after each role play in which he and the participants provided feedback on the instructor's enactment of the Pygmalion role and contributed ideas for application of the behaviors practiced.

The participant then re-played the role, invariably much better than the first time, and received "congratulatory feedback" (Rowe & Kahn, 1998) on his improvement to bolster his self-efficacy.

The workshop conducted for the control group focused on common failures of interpersonal communication and how to avoid them. It included role-playing exercises in which the participants practiced effective communication as instructors with their future trainees. There was no mention of Pygmalion, self-efficacy, or means efficacy in the control workshop.

Procedure

It is routine in the preliminary course to split the group of instructors into two smaller groups for certain activities. During the previous two weeks of the preliminary course, several exercises had been conducted in subgroups. Unbeknownst to the personnel involved, at the outset, we had determined the composition of the subgroups at random. Therefore, random assignment of the participants to workshops was unobtrusive. After the preliminary course, the instructors were dispersed to instruct in various specialty courses. Trainees completed questionnaires during the final week of their specialty courses. We piggybacked our questionnaires on to a routine survey conducted near the end of every course at the base. Owing to a technical glitch, some of our measures were not administered to some of the courses. Therefore, the number of cases varies somewhat from variable to variable in the control condition.

Debriefing

After the specialty courses were finished and the grades submitted, a debriefing presentation was made for all the instructors and command staff of the school. This included a detailed description of the SFP and Pygmalion effects, the self-efficacy and means efficacy constructs, past research, and disclosure of the design and aims of the present experiment.

Analysis

We tested experimental-control mean differences using t-tests. Following Rosenthal and Rubin (1982; see also Rosenthal, Rosnow & Rubin, 2000), we computed the correlation coefficient, r, to estimate effect size and the binomial effect size display (BESD) to estimate the success-rate equivalent of r as an expression of the practical importance of the treatment.

RESULTS

Manipulation Check

Table 1 compares the experimental and control mean levels of all variables. The first two rows show that the experimental trainees reported significantly and appreciably higher levels of both self-efficacy and means efficacy, as predicted. This is the manipulation check; it shows that the treatment influenced the independent variables as intended. The impact of the treatment on means efficacy was stronger than its effect on self-efficacy, as evidenced by their respective effect sizes ($r = 0.43$ vs. 0.27, respectively). The BESD equivalent of the means-efficacy effect size, $r = 0.43$, is a success rate of 71.5% vs. 28.5% in the experimental vs. control conditions, respectively. For self-efficacy, the comparable percentages are 63.5% vs. 36.5%. Thus, the likelihood of an experimental participant compared to a control participant to score above median on means efficacy was 2.5 : 1, whereas for self-efficacy, it was less than 2 : 1. For both efficacy variables, BESD indicates a practically important effect.

Motivation

Line 3 of Table 1 shows that the treatment did not influence general motivation. Though somewhat higher, the experimental mean is not significantly greater than the control mean. In contrast, the next line shows that the treatment did affect means-specific motivation as predicted. The size of the effect of the treatment on means motivation, $r = 0.42$, translates to a BESD of 71% vs. 29%

Table 1. Comparison of Experimental and Control Participants.

| Variable | Experimental | | | Control | | | | |
	M	SD	*n*	*M*	SD	*n*	*r*	*t*
Self-efficacy	5.62	0.77	24	5.07	1.22	41	0.27	2.21*
Means efficacy	5.18	1.37	24	3.93	1.10	40	0.43	3.79**
General motivation	5.45	1.19	24	5.02	1.08	24	0.19	1.29
Means motivation	5.76	1.51	24	3.88	2.21	30	0.42	3.31**
Written test	85.43	6.19	24	80.67	9.48	37	0.27	2.17*
Performance test	86.55	6.18	23	79.21	4.30	32	0.57	5.04**

* $p < 0.05$; ** $p < 0.01$.

in favor of the experimental trainees, again, a large effect. Even the effect of the treatment on general motivation, although not statistically significant, is not trivial in BESD terms (59.5% vs. 40.5%), indicating about half again as great a chance for an experimental trainee to be above median in general motivation than a typical control trainee.

Pygmalion Hypothesis

The last two rows of Table 1 show that the experimental trainees outperformed the control trainees significantly on both tests. The effect size for the written test was $r = 0.27$ (63.5% vs. 36.5% in BESD terms). Moreover, the effect size for the performance test ($r = 0.57$) was exceptionally large. Cohen (1988) defined an r of 0.50 as "about as high as they come" (p. 81). The comparable success rates are 78.5% in the experimental group compared to only 21.5% for the control group; almost four times as many experimental trainees scored above the median on the performance test than control trainees. This is the largest effect produced in this experiment.

Mediation and Moderation Hypotheses

The efficacy and motivation variables were predicted to mediate the effects of the treatment on performance. Using Baron and Kenny's (1986) criteria, neither self-efficacy nor means efficacy and neither motivation measure mediated either performance outcome. Furthermore, stepwise multiple regression analyses did not confirm the interaction hypothesis. Regressing performance on both self-efficacy and means efficacy simultaneously revealed that means efficacy was a significant predictor of performance, whereas self-efficacy was not ($\beta = 0.44$, $F = 8.74$, $p < 0.005$ and $\beta = 0.11$, $F = 0.53$, $p = 0.47$, respectively). The interaction term added in the next step was not significant ($\beta = -0.44$, $F = 0.12$, $p = 0.73$). Thus, after accounting for the main effects of the two efficacy variables, they did not combine interactively to affect performance. However, the relatively small sample provided insufficient degrees of freedom for a powerful test of third-variable effects; therefore, it would be prudent not to rule out such effects on the basis of the present analyses.

DISCUSSION

Pygmalion Training Applications Can Work

The present results give Pygmalion training a new lease of life. Instructors trained to produce Pygmalion effects did so, and they did so consciously. After seven largely unsuccessful attempts to produce Pygmalion effects in real-world training experiments, the present application worked. This can be counted as Experiment 8 in the wake of Eden et al.'s (2000) seven attempts that produced, at best, a small effect. Furthermore, Experiment 8 moves us beyond "efficacy" and constitutes the most compelling evidence to date of the potential "effectiveness" of the Pygmalion approach. Thus, the most important implication of the present results is that applied psychological researchers and practitioners can move ahead with Pygmalion training applications without deceiving their clients, knowing that there is an empirical basis for expecting success.

Why Is This Experiment Different From All Other Pygmalion Training Experiments?

Several unique features of the present experiment may have facilitated its success. Most of these have been discussed in the Pygmalion literature (Eden, 1990, 1993, 2000; Eden et al., 2000; McNatt, 2000).

Means Efficacy
A feature that was new to the present experiment was its focus on means efficacy. The addition of means efficacy as a concept can strengthen leaders' arsenal with a new tool that previous leaders who received Pygmalion training did not receive. In the present experiment, it is clear that means efficacy made a difference. However, it is impossible to determine whether or not we would have produced a Pygmalion effect without the emphasis on the means-efficacy concept. The only previous test of means efficacy was not a fully informed leader training situation; Eden and Granat-Flomin's (2000) test of means efficacy was in the tradition of deceptive experimentation in which the participants had no awareness of the true nature of the treatment. Therefore, only further research will be able to sort out these effects and determine whether Pygmalion training can be effective without means efficacy.

Military Setting
McNatt's (2000) meta-analysis revealed stronger Pygmalion effects in military settings. Consistent with this, the most confirmatory of Eden et al.'s (2000) seven experiments was the only one that was conducted in the military, though that experiment was conducted in a combat unit and the present experiment was in a training context. (McNatt's meta-analysis did not include any of Eden et al.'s (2000) seven experiments.) Thus, the fact that the present experiment took place in a military setting might have been in its favor. More replication in

civilian organizations is needed. It is possible that military organizations nurture a culture for the transfer of leadership training that is not as prevalent in civilian organizations. This points to the more general need for appreciation of contextual factors when choosing when and where to conduct leadership training, be it Pygmalion, transformational, or any other kind (Day, 2000).

Instructors, Not Managers

In six of the seven earlier training experiments, the supervisors who were intended to become Pygmalions were *managers*. (Again, the exception is the military experiment in which the participants were commissioned and non-commissioned training officers.) In contrast, in the present study, the experimenter imparted the Pygmalion concepts to *instructors*. Perhaps the Pygmalion approach to training is more appropriate for training instructors than for training managers. The modern Pygmalion notion was born in the classroom (Rosenthal & Jacobson, 1968). Pygmalion's home court may be the classroom after all. The answer will be forthcoming from a future meta-analysis contrasting the effectiveness of Pygmalion applications in training vs. supervision.

Prior Experience

In five of the previous seven Pygmalion training experiments, the participants brought with them varying amounts of management experience. None was a management neophyte. (The two exceptions were the military experiment and the one among summer camp counselors, who were also young and new to their roles; these two experiments had more confirmatory results than the other five.) Their prior experience might have made these participants somewhat impervious to new ideas. Conversely, the present anti-aircraft instructors were young, inexperienced, and eager to learn whatever might help them in their new role. This may have maximized their receptiveness to the Pygmalion training.

After our debriefing presentation, several of the experimental instructors approached us informally and volunteered their enthusiastic opinions about the utility of the Pygmalion approach. Although we did not quantify them, such animated reactions confirmed our sense of their exceptional receptiveness. This instantiates what Avolio (1999, p. 69) has dubbed, "developmental readiness" for leadership training interventions in an organization. The practical implication is that Pygmalion trainees should be selected for their openness to new experiences or should be beginners who naturally approach their roles with the earnest passion that the cynicism born of experience so often extinguishes.

Prior Acquaintance

Raudenbush (1984) has discussed the problem of overcoming prior expectations in producing Pygmalion effects among teachers. In five of the seven training experiments, after the Pygmalion workshop, the managers returned to continue leading the same employees they had known for some time. This means that they entered and left the Pygmalion training with prior knowledge of their followers' performance potential. Months and years of working together undoubtedly had created expectations in the managers' minds regarding what those followers were capable of achieving. Effective training must supplant existing low expectations and with higher expectations commensurate with the Pygmalion approach, undoubtedly a formidable task. The "only" task before the workshop facilitator for participants with no prior acquaintance is to implant generalized high expectations.

The much more daunting task for the facilitator training participants who have intimate knowledge of their followers' capability involves, first, uprooting or unfreezing their crystallized low expectations toward some of their followers and then replacing them with higher expectations. Judging by remarks made by workshop participants, many managers cling to their low assessment of some of their followers and resist the idea that everyone can improve (Eden et al., 2000). A recent experimental attempt to overcome prior acquaintance did not produce a Pygmalion effect (Eden & Aloni, 2000). Thus, the absence of prior acquaintance gave the present replication an advantage shared by few of the previous Pygmalion training experiments.

All experiments are artificial to some extent and therefore relatively context-free, even those conducted in the field. Artificiality reduces the impact of contextual sources of variation. The 5-minute-treatment experiments among leaders who had not met their followers were more context-free than the training experiments among managers who knew the followers to whom they would soon return. This prior acquaintance constitutes a cognitive background that is part of a context against which new information is weighed. Therefore, one more explanation for the difference between the results of the two genres of experiments is that participants exposed to the 5-minute treatment do not invest cognitive energy in analyzing various aspects of the followers and of other contextual factors; they simply accept the expectation-boosting information, remain cognitively unengaged, and go on from there.

In contrast, when given Pygmalion information about individuals they know, participants "process" it in ways that take into account numerous contextual variables that may disrupt creation of the Pygmalion effect. Depending on the nature of the contextual factors at work in particular circumstances, context may facilitate or inhibit training effects. Prior acquaintance is only one such contextual factor. Others need to be delineated and studied (Day, 2000).

Summarizing, the differences between the present successful experiment and most of its unsuccessful predecessors include:

(1) the emphasis on means efficacy;
(2) the military setting;
(3) training instructors rather than managers;
(4) the participants' lack of prior experience; and
(5) the lack of prior acquaintance between them and their followers.

These five variables could comprise an agenda for future Pygmalion application research. Each is a potential moderator of the Pygmalion effect, worthy of further study. How they interact to inhibit or facilitate creating the Pygmalion effect is for future research to discover.

Meantime, practitioners should bear in mind that these moderators have been confounded in previous research. Many Pygmalion experiments in military settings have involved personnel who were new to their roles and had no prior experience and acquaintance. There does not seem to be anything inherently "military" about Pygmalion. It is "at home" in the elementary school classroom, and civilian managers in training workshops seem to resonate to the Pygmalion approach no less than their military counterparts (Eden et al., 2000). It is more likely the experience and prior acquaintance of the personnel involved in these studies, in both military and civilian settings, that moderate attempts to create the Pygmalion effect. Therefore, pending future research to disentangle these effects, practitioners in civilian and military settings alike should focus their Pygmalion applications on inexperienced managers slated to supervise employees they do not know, and to include means efficacy in their training. Finally, as Eden et al. (2000) surmised, the potential moderators discussed here may be relevant to leadership training at large, not only Pygmalion training.

Too Much Training?

The present experiment shares one more characteristic with the two most successful of Eden et al.'s (2000) replications: the training lasted only one day. Eden et al. started out with a one-day workshop and increased it to two and then to three days. It was the first two of the seven, one with military trainers and one with summer camp counselors, both of which received one day of training, that produced the most confirmatory results. Eden et al. concluded that the longer the training became, the less effective it was. Similarly, Smoll, Smith, Barnett and Everett (1993) trained Little League coaches in building players' self-esteem for two and a half hours, and Barling, Weber and Kelloway (1996) trained bank branch managers in transformational leadership for one day. Most recently, Frayne and Geringer (2000) trained sales personnel in self-management for eight hours. All three of these studies reported significant, hypothesis-confirming training effects. The evidence shows that one day of training can be more effective than three days. *Have we been overtraining?* Would more of Eden et al.'s experiments have succeeded had they been briefer? A meta-analysis of leadership training with length of training as a moderator is in order.

Means Efficacy

This is the first replication of the means-efficacy effect. Coming in the wake of Eden and Granat-Flomin's (2000) experimental confirmation of the Internal-External Efficacy model, the present results show that the impact of boosting means efficacy is replicable. Moreover, this is the second experiment in which means efficacy had a sizable effect on performance, and self-efficacy had none. Eden and Granat-Flomin did not attempt to raise self-efficacy, and its lack of effect in their study was expected. However, in the present experiment, the instructors had been trained in raising both means efficacy and self-efficacy. Therefore, we did expect self-efficacy to play a role. Nevertheless, regression showed that raising means efficacy influenced performance, whereas raising self-efficacy did not. The fact that it did not may be idiosyncratic to the particular circumstances. Perhaps in jobs that involve heavy use of tools, means efficacy overshadows self-efficacy in motivating performance.

The Internal-External Efficacy model suggests that tasks that differ in the extent to which they are tool-dependent may differ in the extent to which means efficacy plays a role in motivating their performance (Eden, 2000). Some tasks, such as auto repair, nursing, and air traffic control, require continual use of tools, whereas other tasks, such as proofreading, playing chess, and most kinds of retail sales, require little or none. Both confirmatory experiments to date involved highly tool-dependent jobs. These are the types of jobs in which practitioners should seek to apply this motivation booster.

Mediation and Moderation

The mediation and moderation hypotheses were not supported. One explanation for this is the dearth of statistical power for testing third-variable hypotheses. The relatively small number of degrees of freedom did not obscure the potent treatment effects or the strong influence of means efficacy. Thus, what is clear is that training instructors in the Pygmalion approach did culminate in their trainees' having a higher self-efficacy, means efficacy, means-specific motivation, and performance. We leave it to future research with greater statistical power to sort out the mediating and moderating relationships.

Specificity Matching

We predicted that instructors trained in total efficacy concepts would be able to increase trainee motivation. Means-specific motivation was influenced by the treatment, whereas general motivation was not. Because our treatment and performance measures were specific to particular weapon systems, these results bear out Eden's (1996) call for matching the specificity of the motivational measure to the specificity of the treatment and of the task performance predicted. This replicates for motivation what Davidson and Eden (2000) showed for self-efficacy, namely, that a measure that matches the specificity of the domain being studied confirms more hypotheses than measures that are either too general or too specific. Specificity matching of measures of self-efficacy, motivation, and performance should increase hypothesis confirmation in studies involving these variables.

CONCLUSION

The results of the present experiment should serve to augment means efficacy of a higher order. The Pygmalion approach is a tool or means in the practitioner's hands. Knowledge of these results should reinforce practitioners' confidence in the applicability of the Pygmalion concept as an effective means to aid them in their attempts to improve their clients' effectiveness. This may generalize to leadership training at large.

NOTE

1. Bruce Avolio, personal communication.

ACKNOWLEDGMENT

We thank Lieutenant Colonel Zvi Volk, chief training officer, for help in conducting the experiment.

REFERENCES

Avolio, B. J. (1999). *Full leadership development: Building the vital forces in organizations.* Thousand Oaks, CA: Sage.

Bandura, A. (1997). *Self-efficacy: The exercise of control.* New York: Freeman.

Bargh, J. A., & Chartrand, T. L. (1999). The unbearable automaticity of being. *American Psychologist, 54,* 462–479.

Barling, J., Weber, T., & Kelloway, E. K. (1996). Effects of transformational leadership training on attitudinal and financial outcomes: A field experiment. *Journal of Applied Psychology, 81,* 827–832.

Baron, R. M., & Kenny, D. A. (1986). The moderator-mediator variable distinction in social psychological research: Conceptual, strategic, and statistical considerations. *Journal of Personality and Social Psychology, 51,* 1173–1182.

Bass, B. M. (1985). *Leadership and performance beyond expectations.* New York: Free Press.

Campbell, D., & Stanley, J. (1966). *Experimental and quasi-experimental designs for research.* Chicago: Rand McNally.

Chaiken, S., & Trope, Y. (Eds) (1999). *Dual-process theories in social psychology.* New York: Guilford Press.

Cohen, J. (1988). *Statistical power analysis for the behavioral sciences* (2nd ed.). Hillsdale, NJ: Lawrence Erlbaum.

Davidson, O. B., & Eden, D. (2000). Remedial self-fulfilling prophecy: Two field experiments to prevent Golem effects among disadvantaged women. *Journal of Applied Psychology, 85,* 386–398.

Day, D. V. (2000). Leadership development: A review in context. *Leadership Quarterly, 11,* 581–613.

Eden, D. (1990). *Pygmalion in management: Productivity as a self-fulfilling prophecy.* Lexington, MA: Lexington Books.

Eden, D. (1993). Leadership and expectations: Pygmalion effects and other self-fulfilling prophecies in management. *Leadership Quarterly, 3,* 271–305.

Eden, D. (1996, August). From self-efficacy to means efficacy: Internal and external sources of general and specific efficacy. Presented at the 56th Annual Meeting of the Academy of Management (Organizational Behavior Division), Cincinnati, OH.

Eden, D. (2001). Means efficacy: External sources of general and specific subjective efficacy. In: M. Erez, U. Kleinbeck & H. Thierry (Eds), *Work motivation in the context of a globalizing economy* (pp. 65–77). Hillsdale, NJ: Lawrence Erlbaum.

Eden, D., & Aloni, G. (2000). Pygmalion effects among blue-collar supervisors and subordinates: Is prior acquaintance a barrier? (Working Paper No. 18/2000). Tel Aviv, Israel: Tel Aviv University, Faculty of Management.

Eden, D., Geller, D., Gewirtz, A., Gordon-Terner, R., Inbar, I., Liberman, M., Pass, Y., Salomon-Segev, I., & Shalit, M. (2000). Implanting Pygmalion leadership style through workshop training: Seven field experiments. *Leadership Quarterly, 11,* 171–210.

Eden, D., & Granat-Flomin, R. (2000, April). Augmenting means efficacy to improve service performance among computer users: A field experiment in the public sector. Presented at the Fifteenth Annual Meeting of the Society for Industrial and Organizational Psychology, New Orleans.

Frayne, C. A., & Geringer, J. M. (2000). Self-management training for improving job performance: A field experiment involving salespeople. *Journal of Applied Psychology, 85,* 361–372.

Gist, M. E., Schwoerer, C., & Rosen, B. (1989). Effects of alternative training methods on self-efficacy and performance in computer software training. *Journal of Applied Psychology, 74,* 884–891.

Holon, S. D. (1996). The efficacy and effectiveness of psychotherapy relative to medications. *American Psychologist, 51,* 1025–1030.

Kierein, N. M., & Gold, M. A. (2000). Pygmalion in work organizations: A meta-analysis. *Journal of Organizational Behavior, 21,* 913–928.

King, A. S. (1974). Expectation effects in organization change. *Administrative Science Quarterly, 19,* 221–230.

McNatt, D. B. (2000). Ancient Pygmalion joins contemporary management: A meta-analysis of the result. *Journal of Applied Psychology, 85,* 314–322.

Raudenbush, S. W. (1984). Magnitude of teacher expectancy effects on pupil IQ as a function of the credibility of expectancy induction: A synthesis of findings from 18 experiments. *Journal of Educational Psychology, 76,* 85–97.

Rosenthal, R., & Jacobson, L. (1968). *Pygmalion in the classroom: Teacher expectation and pupils' intellectual development.* New York: Holt, Rinehart & Winston.

Rosenthal, R., & Rosnow, R. L. (1984). *Essentials of behavioral research: Methods and data analysis.* New York: McGraw-Hill.

Rosenthal, R., Rosnow, R. L., & Rubin, D. B. (2000). *Contrasts and effect sizes in behavioral research: A correlational approach.* Cambridge: Cambridge University Press.

Rosenthal, R., & Rubin, D. B. (1982). A simple, general purpose display of magnitude of experimental effect. *Journal of Educational Psychology, 74,* 166–169.

Rowe, J. W., & Kahn, R. L. (1998). *Successful aging.* New York: Dell.

Seligman, M. E. P. (1995). The effectiveness of psychotherapy: The Consumer Reports study. *American Psychologist, 50,* 965–974.

Seligman, M. E. P. (1996). Science as an ally of practice. *American Psychologist, 51,* 1072–1079.

Seligman, M. E. P., & Levant, R. F. (1998). Managed care policies rely on inadequate science. *Professional Psychology: Research & Practice, 29,* 211–212.

Sherer, M., Maddux, J. E., Mercadante, B., Prentice-Dunn, S., Jacobs, B., & Rogers, R. W. (1982). The Self-efficacy Scale: Construction and validation. *Psychological Reports, 51,* 663–671.

Smoll, F. L., Smith, R. E., Barnett, N. P., & Everett, J. J. (1993). Enhancement of children's self-esteem through social support training for youth sport coaches. *Journal of Applied Psychology, 78,* 602–610.

Stajkovic, A. D., & Luthans, F. (1998). Self-efficacy and work-related performance: A meta-analysis. *Psychological Bulletin, 124,* 240–261.

Weinstein, R. S., Soule, C. R., Collins, F., Cone, J., Mehlhorn, M., & Simontacchi, K. (1991). Expectations and high school change: Teacher-researcher collaboration to prevent school failure. *American Journal of Community Psychology, 19,* 333–363.

THE ROLE MOTIVATION THEORIES OF ORGANIZATIONAL LEADERSHIP

John B. Miner

ABSTRACT

The essential message set forth here is that if we are to truly understand leadership processes, they need to be couched in the form of the organizational system within which they occur. These organizational systems are understood to include the hierarchic (managerial), professional (specialized), task (entrepreneurial), and group (team). Research results reported in this chapter support the tie between leadership and organizational form, and a role motivation theory of leadership is proposed. Implications are drawn for charismatic/transformational theorizing and future research. On a number of grounds, it appears that these theories need to be tested in a much broader set of organizational types than has been the case to date.

The purpose of this presentation is to demonstrate that macro-structural variables can, and in fact should be, incorporated into leadership theories. The primary vehicle for this demonstration is an elaboration of role motivation theory extending beyond organizational motivation into the leadership domain, and the presentation of research on the theory as thus elaborated. At the same time, implications are drawn for the extension of the charismatic/transformational cluster of theories and how these theories might benefit from the

Transformational and Charismatic Leadership, Volume 2, pages 309–338.
ISBN: 0-7623-0962-8

inclusion of similar macro variables – consonant with the theme of this book, and looking to the "road ahead" for these theories.

Role motivation theory traces its origins back to the beginnings of organizational behavior. At that time, however, it was a theory with a rather small domain; it dealt only with managerial motivation and with managerial roles in hierarchic organizations. In the 1970s, this theoretical picture began to change, and a considerable expansion occurred. Consonant with this theoretical expansion, significant problems with the then-existing concept of leadership were raised, but not fully resolved. The essence of this critique was that ". . . our current theories of leadership tend to exist in an organizational vacuum. Some either explicitly or implicitly assume a bureaucratic context; some do not even do that . . . we have gone as far as is possible in the leadership area without forging a strong link between leadership on the one hand and the particular organizational context in which leadership behavior occurs on the other" (Miner, 1982, p. 295).

Now, some 20 years later, I hope to cement this bonding of leadership with its various organizational forms – not to minimize the leadership construct, as was my original idea, but to give it additional strength by welding it on to the organizational context of which it is an inherent part. In the process, I present data from a previously unpublished study of former Princeton University undergraduates, which extends across their entire subsequent careers and the findings from certain re-analyses of data from a number of other studies that were published previously in different forms.

THE CORE OF ROLE MOTIVATION THEORY

Role motivation theory's central constructs are four organizational forms, institutionalized role requirements for key performers (managers, professionals, entrepreneurs, and group members in good standing) that follow from these forms, and motivational patterns that are congruent with these roles. Each organizational type represents a theoretical domain; thus there are four parallel theories. The role requirements are derived logically and/or empirically from the form of organization involved and from the relationship the key performers have with that form. A matching set of motive patterns is posited, one for each role requirement. If the role-motive pattern match is congruent (theoretically specified), the likelihood that the role requirements will be carried out increases, and the potential for positive outcomes becomes greater. The roles and matching motive patterns of the four role motivation theories are outlined in Table 1.

Table 1. Roles and Matching Motive Patterns of the Four Role Motivation Theories.

Role	Matching Motive Pattern
Hierarchic (Managerial) Theory	
1. Positive relations with authority	A favorable attitude toward people in authority
2. Competitive with peers	A desire to compete
3. Imposing wishes on those at lower levels	A desire to exercise power over others
4. Assertive parental	A desire to assert oneself
5. Standing out from the group	A desire to assume a distinctive, differentiated status
6. Performing routine administrative functions	A desire to perform routine managerial duties in a responsible manner
Professional (Specialized) Theory	
1. Acquiring knowledge	A desire to learn and acquire knowledge
2. Acting independently	A desire to exhibit independence
3. Accepting status	A desire to acquire status
4. Providing help	A desire to help others
5. Exhibiting professional commitment	A value-based identification with a profession or specialized occupation
Task (Entrepreneurial) Theory	
1. Individual achievement	A desire to achieve through one's own efforts
2. Risk avoidance	A desire to minimize risk
3. Seeking results of behavior	A desire to receive feedback on performance
4. Personal innovation	A desire to introduce innovative solutions
5. Planning and goal setting	A desire to think about the future, plan and establish goals
Group (Team) Theory	
1. Interacting with peers effectively	A desire to interact socially and affiliate with others
2. Gaining group acceptance	A desire for continuing belongingness in a group
3. Positive relations with peers	A favorable attitude toward those viewed as peers
4. Cooperating with peers	A desire to have cooperative/collaborative relationships
5. Acting democratically	A desire to participate in democratic processes

The Four Organizational Forms

An organizational description questionnaire has been developed that participants may use to describe the unique features of an organization in which they

work (see Oliver, 1982). The median correlation between scores for each type is –0.30, a figure that is without question influenced by the forced-choice nature of the instrument. Although many organizations represent a mix of forms, it is typically true that one form predominates within a given work component or unit. The scales match a priori classifications for organizational units with a 90% hit rate.

Hierarchic

Size is what most aptly characterizes hierarchic organizations. These are the bureaucratic forms that Weber (1968) describes. They possess multiple levels of hierarchy, and they often overlay other forms of organization. This mixing with professional, entrepreneurial, and group forms does not make the bureaucratic components any the less hierarchic. Typically, the hierarchic components appear at the top and assume control. However, hierarchic units may be embedded in other types of organizations, such as a hierarchic support staff unit in a professional organization. Wherever the hierarchic component is found, control resides in the managerial positions. The organization may be in the private sector, government, or non-profits.

Professional

The seminal type of professional system is individual private practice. This has increasingly expanded to group practice, and still further to professional organizations or units. The distinctive feature is that a substantial measure of control remains with the professionals. However, in many respects, this control reflects the external influence of professional associations. Service to some type of client is always involved. When professional components are embedded in hierarchic organizations, there is a single client, the surrounding organization, and lacking client diversification, the professional unit may face considerable competition for control, and thus substantial conflict.

Task

In the task form, key performers such as entrepreneurs are embedded directly in the pushes and pulls of the work system. Control resides in the task itself, which imposes the threat of business failure and offers the prospect of sizable financial reward. The prototype of a task system is the entrepreneurial startup. However, growth is an essential component of this form, or at least intended growth. Thus, family businesses that pass from one generation to another and even purchased small businesses may be of a task nature. Within the task system, the entrepreneur operates as an individual moving to deal with crises and grasping opportunities without reference to hierarchic or professional constraints. The entrepreneur may be plural, but typically, a lead entrepreneur exists. Entrepreneurial components may be embedded in other organizational forms, and when this occurs, with the venture dependent on resources supplied by the surrounding organization, control conflicts may escalate.

Group

The group may be free-standing or embedded in some other type of organization. Examples are many voluntary organizations, musical groups, and autonomous or self-managing work teams. The key performers are members in good standing, leadership is emergent and at the will of the majority, and both cohesion and stability are important. Control resides in the group as a whole, and normative pressures derive from this source. As originally conceived, this form was envisioned as encompassing relatively small face-to-face groups. Nevertheless, town meetings, legislative components of government, and political parties including election campaign teams appear to share many features with these small groups.

Roles and Motive Patterns

The role motivation theories emerged over a considerable time span and the motivational variables have been operationalized, so that research could be conducted, at different points in time as well. There is as yet no motivational measure for the group theory; only the organizational level measure exists. The roles and their matching motive patterns as set forth in Table 1 have been the subject of substantial theoretical and empirical development (see Miner, 1993 for an overview). It is important to note that the motives of role motivation theory are assumed to operate at below the conscious level on occasion.

Hypotheses

Using these concepts of organizational forms, their inherent roles, and the motive patterns that match them, four standing hypotheses have been formulated (Miner, 1982, 1993). The first three of these hypotheses were tested in the present research.

Hypothesis 1: In hierarchic systems, managerial motivation should be at a high level in top management, and it should be positively correlated with other managerial success indexes; managerial motivation should not differentiate in these ways within other types of systems.

Hypothesis 2: In professional systems, professional motivation should be at a high level among senior professionals, and it should be positively correlated with other professional success indexes; professional motivation should not differentiate in these ways within other types of systems.

Hypothesis 3: In task systems, task motivation should be at a high level among task performers (entrepreneurs), and it should be positively correlated with task-success indexes; task motivation should not differentiate in these ways within other types of systems.

Hypothesis 4: In group systems, group motivation should be at a high level among emergent leaders, and it should be positively correlated with other group-determined success indexes; group motivation should not differentiate in these ways within other types of systems.

These hypotheses are domain-specific, and they reflect a causal effect from the appropriate motives to outcome variables. Within a theoretical domain, indexes of motive strength are combined additively to obtain comprehensive measures of managerial, professional, task, and group motivation. Thus, motivational deficiencies of one kind may be offset by high levels of motivation of some other type. In hypotheses 1 through 4, the assumption is that individuals with the appropriate motives will indicate a preference for work of a congruent kind and will make job and career choices accordingly. Those with higher congruent motives will perform better in these positions, will be more likely to stay in positions of the appropriate kind, and will achieve greater career success within the domain that best fits their motivational pattern.

DEVELOPMENT OF THE LEADERSHIP THEORY

The four standing hypotheses of role motivation theory make reference to top management in the case of the hierarchic theory and to emergent leadership in the case of the group theory, thus indicating a concern with leadership issues. Yet the professional theory hypothesis refers to senior professionals, not necessarily leaders among professionals, and in the case of task theory, entrepreneurs are mentioned, but without reference to entrepreneurial leadership. In fact, leadership theory to date has shown little inclination to incorporate entrepreneurship within its domain, and vice versa.

As noted previously, during the 1970s and into the early 1980s, I was quite critical of leadership theory, in part at least on the grounds that it was too narrowly defined to deal effectively with the phenomena that in my view should be its central focus. The problem as I saw it was inherent in the fact that the study of leadership had its origins within social psychology as a component of the larger field of group dynamics. Its major concerns in this early period were with the effects of leadership on small group performance, the emergence of leadership within such groups, and with the positive effects of democratic (as opposed to autocratic) leadership behavior. Much of the research was of a laboratory nature with extensions to the lower, work group levels of hierarchic organizations. This was a very narrow focus; yet it prevailed for a number of years, and served to limit the scope of leadership theory in a way that I believed (and still believe) made the field much less useful than it could have been. In particular, it failed to recognize that leadership is a function of the larger organizational form within which it operates. This seems like an obvious conclusion, especially for a field labeled organizational behavior, but it has continued to escape us to this day. Charismatic/transformational theory continues to show signs of its early origins in the group dynamics way of thinking up to the present; it needs to escape this bondage more fully.

Recently, however, a degree of broadening has taken hold within leadership, which, although still not sufficient, has the potential to move the field in the right direction. Thus:

> . . . a meeting of eighty-four scholars representing fifty-six countries from all regions of the world was conducted. In that meeting a consensus and universal definition of organizational leadership emerged: "the ability of an individual to influence, motivate, and enable others to contribute toward the effectiveness and success of the organizations of which they are members" (House, Wright & Aditya, 1997, p. 548).

Notice that this definition does not utilize the term "group" at all, and that it specifically engages the organizational context – although still failing to consider particular organizational forms.

In a previous publication, I have touched upon the ways in which my theoretical views speak to leadership (Miner, 2000). As a prelude to the presentation of the research on this topic, let me now amplify this earlier discussion.

Hierarchic Leadership

A frequent distinction in the leadership literature is between managers and leaders, with the former term often carrying negative connotations and the latter having something of a heroic quality (Terry, 1995). This distinction goes back at least to Zaleznik (1977). Both terms tend to be used with reference to the hierarchic or bureaucratic domain. Given the variations in usage here, it seems essential to provide a view of role motivation theory's take on this issue.

Managers are those who hold managerial positions in hierarchic systems. In most cases, they have followers. Managers holding positions in the upper reaches of the hierarchic chain, often referred to as "top managers," are theoretically defined as organizational leaders. Attaining such positions represents the goal of hierarchic career success. There is nothing particularly good or bad about this achievement, only being more or less successful within a hierarchic system. These leaders may be heroic, but they need not be. In this context, managers below the top level are considered to be in a pre-leadership role, and of course many careers end in this zone. Hierarchic role motivation theory of leadership clearly indicates that, for its purposes, the study of top management should be the focus of leadership research (not the study of first level supervision). There is a managerial continuum extending from the early pre-leadership stages to the very top of the bureaucratic hierarchy. At some point in this continuum, an individual breaks into top management and is considered to be a hierarchic leader.

Since role motivation theory has been a theory of motivation and personality, it is important to specify how such a theory might relate to leadership *behavior*, a long-standing concern of leadership theory. Role motivation theory takes the position, consistent with Victor Vroom's normative decision process theory and Frank Heller's influence-power continuum theory but not with Fred Fiedler's contingency theory, that leaders are not tied to a single set of behaviors by their strong motives. Rather, each manager has the capability to vary his or her behaviors over a wide range, in pursuit of motivationally based goals, depending on the nature of the situations and constraints faced.

The research surrounding Vroom's and Heller's theories certainly supports this view, as does the research conducted by Zaccaro, Foti and Kenny (1991). Thus, the hierarchic theory, and the other three theories as well, do not specify any particular behaviors (such as directive behavior), but they do anticipate that this behavior will be consistent with the goals inherent in the strong motives held by a person and with the demands of the situation faced. Note that, in contrast, existing charismatic/transformational theories have tended to continue to focus on explicit leader behaviors.

Professional Leadership

Professional, or intellectual, leadership has been given practically no attention by leadership theory, although within the sociological literature, the distinction between administrative elites and rank-and-file practitioners within a profession is discussed. It is these elites that the professional theory considers as its leaders. Intellectual leadership of this kind may be of either a cosmopolitan or local nature. In the former instance, the focus is on achieved professional status and recognition in the professional community as a whole; in the latter case, the focus is on achieved rank and status in the employing organization.

Many professionals rise to leadership positions or status of both kinds. The key is that the person must be a professional and must have given evidence of high professional status, which often involves having rank-and-file professionals or pre-professionals who depend upon him or her in some manner. In hypothesis 2, the term "senior professionals" should be changed to "professional leaders" to make the statement consonant with the present view. Although the concept of mentoring has been studied most extensively within the hierarchic domain, it is an important function of professional leaders as well.

Since acquiring knowledge is so important to becoming a professional, and takes considerable time as well, the professional career tends to extend across various degrees of training, to the early career stages, and then for some to true intellectual leadership. Thus, the idea of a continuum holds for professionals, too. Leadership tends to be defined by such factors as publications, professional compensation levels, professional rank, signs of recognition, administrative position, status within the educational context, professional organization activity, and the like, depending on the particular profession and its organizational context.

Task Leadership

Task or entrepreneurial leadership involves the concept of a lead entrepreneur, who typically owns a larger share of the venture or holds a more dominant position, and the existence of a growth orientation; both must be present for task leadership to occur. Entrepreneurs who are not leaders are venture team members who do not hold lead status and/or who are involved in ventures not evidencing commitment to organizational growth. The lead entrepreneur concept is especially important in team entrepreneurship of the kind that characterizes high technology ventures. In the team context, the concept of a lead entrepreneur has been shown to be a viable entity, and the vision of that person has been found to play an important strategic role (Ensley, Carland & Carland, 2000).

Growth orientation, the second requirement, has been operationalized as a demonstrated record of organizational growth (measured in years) over which the firm has increased substantially in number of employees and/or dollar volume of sales. This growth need not be maintained under all circumstances, such as during a period of recession, but it must have occurred, and under the guidance and vision of the same lead entrepreneur.

Entrepreneurial leadership is typically achieved following a period of intentional and/or unintentional training for the position as reflected in educational experiences, part-time entrepreneurship, other employment, non-leader entrepreneurial work, and even other entrepreneurial leadership. Thus, again, a continuum of career development exists.

Group Leadership

For lack of an inductive empirical base from which to operate, defining group leadership in the manner of the other three types is difficult. Yet, some dimensions can be established to represent group leadership. Group leadership is emergent from within the group; it is not appointive from the outside, and it is not based on criteria held outside the group. It fits the model obtained from ad hoc laboratory groups, but it may appear in autonomous or self-managed teams as well, and in other similar settings. This is where leadership theory began, and it should be retained as a more limited domain of study.

Emergent leadership of this kind can be quite unstable in that group leaders may be replaced at any time by others who fit group norms better. Any group member in good standing is a potential candidate for group leadership. Group leaders receive a substantially greater amount of interaction with others than mere members (Cohen & Zhou, 1991). Furthermore, a given group may well have several of these emergent leaders, each with a different role to play.

Hypothesis

Thus, we have four types of leadership based in four different organizational forms, with four different categories of institutionalized role prescriptions, and four different sets of motivational patterns needed in the leaders for effective performance to occur. This results in:

> *Hypothesis 5*: Leadership roles take different forms in different organizational contexts and require different types of people to perform in these roles effectively – people whose motives are strongly congruent with the particular organizational type involved; thus, leadership careers vary in important ways with the organizational forms in which they occur.

Yet, in all instances, leadership involves the ability "to influence, motivate, and enable others to contribute toward the effectiveness and success of the organizations of which they are members." This is a very different, and much broader, concept of leadership than that with which leadership theory began, and in which it persevered for many years. Some time ago, however, Etzioni (1961) espoused a similar concept of leadership, covering both formal position holders and informal leaders, as well as power inherent in a position and personal power.

Leadership in any of its various organizational forms is essentially a developing process of career identification in which the individual increasingly takes on a set of institutionalized roles, which are viewed as personally compatible (Ashforth, 2001). For some, a leadership career represents the whole or the major part of a total career. More frequently, a long period of career preparation and socialization precedes entering into the true leadership career.

METHOD

The primary source of data for the research reported here, although only part of the total, was a mail survey of the surviving members of the class of 1948 at Princeton University conducted on the occasion of the fiftieth anniversary of the class's graduation (1998). This was my class, and I am sure that facilitated data collection. However, the sample is important because it permitted studying careers across their full duration, contained a large number of leaders in the various domains, and represented a balanced sample in that hierarchic, professional, and task forms of organization were all well represented. In addition, a number of previously published studies yielded samples whose data were reanalyzed to provide findings relevant to the leadership hypotheses.

The Princeton Study

The addresses and much of the career data for this sample were obtained from a yearbook published to commemorate the class's fiftieth anniversary (Princeton University Class of 1948, 1998). This was a wartime class, and members actually graduated from college over a period starting in the latter 1940s and extending well into the 1950s; their ages spanned a roughly 10-year period.

The yearbook provided varying degrees of information on class members. Of the 778 individuals listed, 239 (31%) had no biographical data, or the career information was insufficient to make a career designation, or, less frequently, the apparent career did not fit into the manager, professional, or entrepreneur categories required by the research design. Another 143 of those listed had died at the time of mailing (plus 54 not listed). When eight honorary class members were subtracted, 388 individuals remained to whom the initial mailing was sent – just 50% of those listed. Subsequent information indicated that 17 more people could not have responded (owing to death, severe illness, or inadequate addresses), so the operative base sample was 371 – and perhaps smaller owing to deaths and illnesses of which we were unaware.

Through two rounds of mailings, 110 individuals provided usable data, for a 30% return rate. The response to the first mailing was 18%, and to the second mailing (sent roughly three months later) 12%. This reflects a reasonably good response rate, especially to the second mailing (Roth & BeVier, 1998). A comparison of the first and second round respondents to check on the representativeness of the sample utilized (see Rogelberg & Luong, 1998) was carried out, and the conclusions are reported subsequently.

The 110 members of the respondent sample are all male, reflecting the fact that Princeton did not admit females until a number of years later. Although this limitation of the sample's composition might seem to represent a deficiency, it may well have been fortuitous in that female career patterns have been found to differ substantially from those of males (Melamed, 1996). In any event, it should be understood that the findings of this research are generalizable only to males.

The mean age of sample members at the time of response was 72 with a range of 70 to 80; however, almost three-quarters were either 71 or 72. Within the sample, 74% listed themselves as retired, meaning that they had passed the point of disengagement from their main careers. Nevertheless, considering the partially retired and the not-yet-retired numbers, a case can be made that the sample did not contain only individuals whose careers were completely behind them, and in that sense deal entirely with whole careers. Yet, whole careers were the prevailing mode, and all who were not fully disengaged were clearly in the last stages of their careers. For 44% of the sample, this career was managerial in nature, for another 34%, it was professional or highly specialized, and for 22%, it was entrepreneurial.

Motivational Measures
The independent variables of the research were the total scores and subscales measuring the first three sets of variables in Table 1. The total score measures are the sums of the subscale scores. Each item is scored –1, 0, or + 1, using the scoring guides, to indicate whether the response deviates from theoretical expectations, is equivocal, or supports theoretical expectations. The item scores of a subscale are summed to obtain the subscale score. When necessary, for a given analysis, total scores for each sentence completion scale were converted to standard scores with a mean of 50 and the standard deviations set equal to 10. The appropriate normative sample data were used for the purpose of standardization.

Scorer reliability studies have been conducted where the author, who devised the measures and the scoring procedures, was one participant, and an experienced scorer was the other. With only a few exceptions, these reliabilities are in the 0.90s; the total score values are all 0.95 or higher, and the subscale median is 0.91. These figures are relevant given that all of the tests used in the Princeton research were scored and then checked by the author. The test-retest reliabilities of the total scores, based on 35 to 40 items, appear to be at least 0.85. Subscale reliabilities, based on five to eight items, average 0.65, were considerably lower because of the smaller number of items. For most purposes, the total scores would seem to provide the measures of choice simply because of their much greater reliability. Additional evidence on psychometric properties is given in Miner (1993).

The Miner Sentence Completion Scales are projective measures and thus permit the incorporation of motives below the level of consciousness in the measurement process. Projective measures such as this have been shown to yield outcome correlations that are significantly larger than those obtained with self-report measures intended to measure the same variables (Spangler, 1992). Sentence completion indexes are widely used by clinical psychologists (Holaday, Smith & Sherry, 2000). A recent major review of projective technique validities (Lilienfeld, Wood & Garb, 2000) notes that a sentence completion measure, developed and scored in much the same manner as the MSCSs, proves far superior to other projective measures (including most indexes from the Rorschach and the Thematic Apperception Test); when based on sound psychometric procedures, such approaches can yield substantial validities.

The research design used would ideally call for administration of all three scales to all subjects. This, however, requires the completion of 12 pages of items, when evidence indicates that after four pages, the response rate to surveys begins to fall off substantially (Roth & BeVier, 1998). To deal with this problem, subjects were initially sent only the MSCS form (hierarchic, professional, or task) that matched their career as initially determined from the yearbook information (Princeton University Class of 1948, 1998); they were also asked if they would be willing to complete the additional two forms.

The result of this process was that 51 first wave respondents and 23 second-wave respondents, for a total of 74 out of the 110 subjects, completed all three forms. The remainder provided either one form (33) or, in a few cases, two (3). All in all, we received 92 Form Hs, 85 Form Ps, and 84 Form Ts. These represent the base data used in the analyses.

Outcome Measures
The analysis called for comparing the respondents with various career types on the motivational measures to provide a test of the core theoretical hypotheses; thus, managerial careers vs. other careers on Form H, professional/specialists

careers vs. other careers on Form P, and entrepreneurial careers vs. other careers on Form T. The theory, of course, would anticipate higher scores in the theoretically congruent samples than in the incongruent (other career) samples. In this design, the career is the dependent outcome variable.

Initially, as indicated previously, a career classification was made based on the yearbook information only. However, we solicited additional data of this nature in our letter to the subjects, and a number provided it. Furthermore, a 25-year book on the class (Princeton University Class of 1948, 1974), which contained biographical information, was located. With these latter data, career histories at two points in time at a 25-year interval became available for 74% of the subjects. There were no significant differences among the three career types in this regard. When supplemented with *Who's Who* listings and subject-provided information, 80% of the subjects had career data from at least two sources. The consequence was that more precise career classifications became possible – 91% of the respondents remained unchanged, but 9% were shifted to a new category.

The managerial career sample was constituted of 43 corporate managers and five non-profit managers. The managerial careers most typically started below the managerial level, but still in a hierarchic system. There were a few instances where the early period was spent in a professional capacity subsequent to a professional education before the move into hierarchic management.

The professional career sample of 38 was very diverse. Most frequently represented were the law, the clergy, teachers (at both the private school and university levels), and practicing physicians, but there were research scientists, professional engineers, librarians, accountants, and others as well. Also included with these professionals were certain individuals who had made a career of some specialty, which, although not generally recognized as a profession, involved advanced education and/or specialized experience. Included here were technical editors, writers, therapists, international specialists, and financial experts.

The entrepreneurial career sample contained 24 individuals who had developed a firm (usually one they had started) and often several firms, and spent most of their careers in this type of activity. The actual entrepreneurial careers more often than not were initiated after a stint in hierarchic or professional systems, but these stints may well have been part of the entrepreneurial careers in that they provided the learning needed to start a particular venture. These entrepreneurs invariably headed their firms, but the ventures themselves were quite varied in nature; the major concentrations were in oil and gas exploration and in the financial area.

Leadership Careers

In an effort to test theoretical expectations regarding leadership, those subjects who were leaders in their respective career fields were compared with those who did not achieve this status using the standardized total scores. The leaders were identified using the criteria presented previously.

Of the 48 managers, 38 achieved the status of hierarchic leader, and 10 had not. Of the 38 professionals and specialists, 27 were professional or intellectual leaders, and 11 were not. Of the 24 entrepreneurs, 19 were task leaders, and five were not. Overall, 76% of the subjects achieved a leader role in their careers and this was as likely to occur in one career domain as another. Among the leaders, 15 were listed in *Who's Who in America* at some point during the 1990s.

Sample Representativeness

Evidence on the probability of non-response bias in surveys such as this (where 70% did not respond) may be obtained by comparing the responses on the study variables of the first-wave respondents with those of the second-wave respondents. If differences were minimal, it is likely that no differences would be found comparing the respondents and non-respondents either. If differences were found from wave one to wave two, this trend should be perpetuated into the non-respondent group, and the representativeness of the respondent sample comes into serious question (Rogelberg & Luong, 1998).

Comparisons were made between wave one and wave two data for all MSCS measures (numbering 20), age, retirement status, career type, and leadership status. There was only one significant difference, on value-based identification (professional commitment) at $p < 0.05$ with the second-round respondents scoring higher. This finding would have been anticipated on the basis of chance alone, given that 24 comparisons were made. Thus, the evidence obtained supports the representativeness of the respondent sample.

Intercorrelations

Within instruments, the subscales correlate significantly with the total scores of which they are part. These values range from 0.41 to 0.73 with an average of 0.58. The subscales themselves are generally positively correlated within instruments, with median values of 0.19, 0.22, and 0.18 for Forms H, P, and T, respectively – 19 of these positive correlations are significant; almost half of the total. The same pattern occurs across all three measures – generally positive, but not large relationships. Comparing these findings with those from other studies (see Miner, 1993), the present data appear entirely consistent with previous results, and with theoretical expectations.

Across instruments, where the theory would expect values close to 0.00, the three total score correlations are –0.12, 0.04, and 0.12 – none significant; the median subscale correlations across instruments in each data set are –0.04, 0.02, and 0.07. Overall, there are 61 positive correlations and 67 negative, with eight of the positive values significant and six of them negative. This looks very much like the total lack of relationships across instruments that was expected.

These results across measures stand in contrast to what has been obtained in previous studies (Miner, 1993). There, a positive relationship, not large but consistent, has been obtained across all three measures. The present results, obtained with balanced samples and using whole career data that do not include any subjects who subsequently will be involved in career turnover are more compatible with theory and would seem to be more valid as well.

Other Leadership Data Sources

The samples used in these re-analyses all derive from previously published studies, which permit the leadership hypotheses to be investigated – that is there are both leaders and members involved. Results were calculated in correlation form, whereas in the prior publications, they typically were not. The re-analyses involve not only the calculation of these correlations, but also the actual establishment of criterion groups.

In addition to the Princeton study, two other investigations dealt with congruent hierarchic motivation. One was an analysis of 101 human resource managers from a Bureau of National Affairs (BNA) panel, obtained in the mid-1970s. The leaders were in charge of the human resource function and often carried a vice-presidential title. Several publications have appeared dealing with this data set; they are brought together in Miner (1977).

The other source utilizing congruent hierarchic motivation was Berman and Miner (1985). This study contained, in the leadership group, 49 chief executives, chief operating officers, executive vice-presidents, and group vice-presidents. The comparison group was selected from the same companies to achieve age matching, but utilizing lower and middle managers of varied performance levels. Top executives with an entrepreneurial role in their companies were deleted from this analysis. The data were obtained during the latter 1970s.

Professional motivation was the focus of a study of 112 Academy of Management members, also sampled in the latter 1970s, who served as university professors (Miner, 1980). Leaders tended to be of senior rank, active publishers, with higher total professional compensation, and they often held administrative positions. This sample provided information on hierarchic motivation as well, thus permitting non-congruent analyses.

Task motivation was studied in two entrepreneurial samples, the first of which yielded non-congruent data for both hierarchic and professional motivation. In this instance, the sample was accumulated over some seven years in the late 1980s and early 1990s. Most of the lead entrepreneurs had started their firms initially, but some had taken over a family business or purchased a going operation. All leaders had experienced substantial growth under their tutelage, although in some instances, this growth was not maintained subsequently during a period of economic downturn in the Buffalo area (Miner, 1997). The sample contained 100 entrepreneurs, but in 11 cases, the data were insufficient to determine leadership status. Comparing the 89 cases where leader status could be established with the 11, no evidence of meaningful differences was found.

The second entrepreneurial sample consisted of 118 high-tech entrepreneurs who applied for National Science Foundation (NSF) grants during the late 1970s and early 1980s (Miner, Smith & Bracker, 1989). All were lead entrepreneurs, but some firms had substantially poorer growth records than others. The sample was split at the median on growth to establish leadership status. The low-growth firms included a number that subsequently failed.

A final leader analysis was conducted using hierarchic motivation as applied to non-congruent professional leadership (Miner, 1977). This sample of 49 professors was from three different business schools with a wide range of disciplines represented. Leadership level was determined using professorial rank and administrative position.

In two of these samples, the human resource managers and the Buffalo, NY area entrepreneurs, data could also be obtained on validities against the leader-member criterion using other predictors that have been supported in the literature; thus, an index of relative effectiveness vs. the MSCS measures could be obtained in the same samples.

For the human resource managers (Miner, 1977) these alternative predictors were:

Ghiselli Self-Description Inventory – the Supervisory Ability measure; reported to be the best index of managerial talent found in the Ghiselli research.

Adorno F-Scale – a 28-item abbreviated version; widely viewed as an appropriate measure of authoritarian management.

Kuder Preference Record Supervisory Interest Scale – found to be an effective predictor of management appraisal ratings.

For the Buffalo, NY area entrepreneurs (Miner, 1997), the alternative predictors were:

Shure and Meeker Risk Avoidance Scale – a 17-item abbreviated version; found to provide an index of bargaining effectiveness.

Gallup-Thorndike Vocabulary Test – Forms A & B – a 40-item measure that correlates highly with measures of general intelligence.

Matteson-Ivancevich Individual Behavior Activity Profile – an index of Type A behavior, which is widely reported as characteristic of successful entrepreneurs.

Levenson Internal-External Control Instrument – Internal, Powerful Other, and Chance measures; positive validities for the first scale and negative correlations for the other two are widely reported in the entrepreneurship literature.

Rowe-Mason Decision Style Inventory – Directive, Conceptual, and Behavioral measures; the first two scales, but not the latter, are reported by the authors to be high among successful entrepreneurs.

Data on these instruments are reported in Miner (1977, 1997).

RESULTS

The findings that follow derive from the Princeton study, which provides a test of the core hypotheses of role motivation theory, and from a series of tests of the leadership hypothesis including one using the Princeton data.

The Princeton Study

Table 2 presents the Princeton results in correlational form. Significance was established using t-tests to compare the means. All of the congruent findings are highly significant; none of the non-congruent findings were significant. When these congruent data are combined, using standard scores, the resulting correlation is 0.64. Given the comprehensiveness of the Princeton data, this appears to be the most definitive test of the core hypotheses of role motivation theory obtained to date; these total score findings are completely in accord with theory.

At the subscale level, the correlations characteristically substantiate the total score results. All five congruent Form T correlations are significant at $p < 0.01$ ranging from 0.32 to 0.53 (median 0.42). All five congruent Form P correlations are also similarly significant ranging from 0.24 to 0.43 (median 0.36). With Form H, the hierarchic chain subscales – authority (upward), competitiveness (lateral), and power (downward) – yield similar congruent

Table 2. Relationships Between MSCS Total Scores and Various Congruent and Non-congruent Career Indexes in the Princeton University Class of 1948 Sample.

MSCS Form	Comparison	Point Biserial Correlation
Congruent Analysis		
H	Managers ($n=48$); $M=6.65$) vs. Professionals + Entrepreneurs ($n=44$; $M=-2.00$)	0.65**
P	Professionals ($n=38$; $M=12.84$) vs. Managers + Entrepreneurs ($n=47$; $M=4.17$)	0.56**
T	Entrepreneurs ($n=24$; $M=13.71$) vs. Managers + Professionals ($n=60$; $M=0.67$)	0.75**
Non-congruent Analysis		
H	Professionals ($n=28$; $M=-2.50$) vs. Entrepreneurs ($n=16$; $M=-1.13$)	−0.11
P	Managers ($n=31$; $M=2.81$) vs. Entrepreneurs ($n=16$; $M=6.81$)	−0.27
T	Managers ($n=32$; $M=1.16$) vs. Professionals ($n=28$; $M=0.11$)	0.10

** $p<0.01$.

correlations, significant at $p<0.01$ and ranging from 0.41 to 0.53 (median 0.45). This is the pattern anticipated by Nystrom (1986). Consistent with Nystrom's hypothesis, the remaining Form H subscales yield correlations in the 0.10s, usually significant ($p<0.05$), but relatively low. This type of finding has not been characteristic previously (Miner, 1993).

Tests of the Leadership Hypothesis

Table 3 contains descriptive data and correlations for the six studies in which congruent motives were related to a leadership measure. Two involve hierarchic systems, one professional, two task, and one all three combined. The latter, the Princeton University study, yields the lowest correlation, and that may be a function of using combined data standardized on different samples; however, the low proportion of non-leader, rank-and-file members may be a factor as well. In all three components, the directionality is as hypothesized. Note also that the member MSCS scores are still above the expected mean of 50, thus introducing some restriction of range.

Table 3. Relationships Between MSCS Total Scores and Various Congruent Leadership Forms.

Sample (Prior Description)	MSCS Form	Leadership Form	Method of Analysis	Correlation
1. Princeton University class of 1948	H, P & T	Managerial, Professional & Entrepreneurial	Biserial correlation using combined standard scores Leaders – $n = 84$; $M = 58.34$ Members – $n = 26$; $M = 52.45$	0.44**
2. Personnel and industrial relations managers (Miner, 1977)	H	Managerial	Biserial correlation using total scores Leaders – $n = 41$; $M = 6.18$ Members – $n = 60$; $M = 0.95$	0.54**
3. Top managers and age-matched comparison managers (Berman & Miner, 1985)	H	Managerial	Biserial correlation using total scores Leaders – $n = 49$; $M = 6.76$ Members – $n = 49$; $M = 0.86$	0.72**
4. Academy of Management members (Miner, 1980)	P	Professional	Biserial correlation using total scores Leaders – $n = 46$; $M = 11.70$ Members – $n = 66$; $M = 1.30$	0.87**
5. Buffalo, NY area entrepreneurs (Miner, 1997)	T	Entrepreneurial	Biserial correlation using total scores Leaders – $n = 45$; $M = 12.93$ Members – $n = 44$; $M = 7.11$	0.71**
6. High-technology entrepreneurs – NSF grant applicants (Miner, Smith, & Bracker, 1989)	T	Entrepreneurial	Biserial correlation using total scores Leaders – $n = 59$; $M = 10.95$ Members – $n = 59$; $M = 0.92$	0.77**
			Median value	0.715

** $p < 0.01$.

Even with this relatively low correlation from the Princeton sample, the median value in Table 3 is in the low 0.70s. This is a very high figure for an uncorrected average validity coefficient. Something clearly quite important is going on here. The analyses that follow are intended to give some insight into what might be involved.

One possibility is that the MSCS measures inevitably yield such high correlations within their appropriate domains irrespective of the criterion. To determine whether this is the case, both the concurrent and predictive studies considered in Miner (1993), plus a few more recent studies, were culled. For Form H, dealing with hierarchic motivation, 50 relevant correlation coefficients were found; the median value was 0.24 (18 using a rating criterion for which the median was 0.24, 30 using a managerial level or compensation criterion for which the median was 0.25, and two using a job satisfaction criterion for which the median was 0.20). For Form P, dealing with professional motivation, there were 19 coefficients spread across a wide range of criteria, but with too few in any one category to break out separately; the median correlation was 0.35. For Form T, dealing with entrepreneurial motivation, the number of correlations found was down to 13; for these varied criteria, the median value was 0.36.

Taken as a whole, when leadership and career criteria are excluded, the average validity coefficient runs just under 0.30 for total scores – less than half of what Table 3 reports for leadership criteria. It seems evident that the MSCSs themselves do not invariably produce such high values.

Another question involves the extent to which various subscales may be operating. In this analysis, the Princeton study had to be excluded because of small ns for individual subscales in the leadership analysis. The median correlation for the Form H subscales is somewhat lower, presumably because of the smaller number of items (5) in contrast to Forms P and T (8). Clearly, the limited reliability of the subscales (0.65 on average) is a consideration throughout this analysis. Nevertheless, every single subscale yields at least one significant correlation; there are no non-contributing factors. The highest contributors to leadership appear to be attitude to authority within Form H, acquiring status within Form P, and achieving on one's own within Form T. The median subscale correlations with leadership for Forms H, P, and T, respectively are 0.30, 0.49, and 0.40. Of the 29 values, 24 are significant ($p < 0.05$ or better).

The Table 4 findings deal with the question of whether the results of Table 3 apply only to congruent relationships, or to non-congruent relationships as well (which they should not according to theory). The data overall are consistent with theoretical expectations – the median correlation is a non-significant 0.125. Yet there is one unexpected significant relationship, involving

Table 4. Relationships Between MSCS Total Scores and Various Non-congruent Leadership Forms.

Sample (Prior Description)	MSCS Form	Leadership Form	Method of Analysis	Correlation
Academy of Management members (Miner, 1980b)	H	Professional	Biserial correlation using total scores Leaders – $n = 46$; $M = -1.59$ Members – $n = 66$; $M = -2.80$	0.11
Buffalo, NY area entrepreneurs (Miner, 1997)	H	Entrepreneurial	Biserial correlation using total scores Leaders – $n = 45$; $M = 3.18$ Members – $n = 44$; $M = 2.16$	0.13
	P	Entrepreneurial	Biserial correlation using total scores Leaders – $n = 45$; $M = 11.13$ Members – $n = 44$; $M = 7.82$	0.33**
Business school faculty from three schools (Miner, 1977)	H	Professional	Pearson correlation with leadership level ($n = 49$)	0.12

** $p < 0.01$.

the prediction of entrepreneurial leadership from professional motivation; the significant subscales here are acquiring knowledge (0.28*), acquiring status (0.37**), and professional commitment (0.29*). There are a number of professionals among the Buffalo area entrepreneurs, and the Form T vs. Form P total score correlation is 0.26* (vs. only 0.12 in the more balanced Princeton sample). When the effects from Form T are controlled, the resulting partial correlation of Form P with entrepreneurial leadership drops to a non-sigificant 0.21, a figure more consistent with theoretical expectations.

Table 5 presents information bearing on the question of whether the Table 3 findings might reflect something inherent in the samples involved. Although data are available for only two samples, the median correlation for the predictors studied is only 0.14 (vs. 0.715 for the congruent MSCS predictors); there are only two of the 12 relationships that achieve significance. It seems unlikely that the samples utilized are in and of themselves particularly likely to yield high correlations.

Rather the implication of the data is that something about the match of the theoretical motives and their congruent indexes of organizational leadership is responsible for the very high validities obtained.

DISCUSSION

A considerable amount of evidence now exists to the effect that leadership is a set of organizational variables that often behave much like career variables. However, the really significant finding reported here is not that these motives predict; that had been reasonably well established previously. The major finding is that they can predict at a level well above that for other predictors, and above those obtained with non-leadership criteria. With these findings, a sizable proportion, although certainly not all, of the variance associated with leadership is accounted for.

How might this occur? To provide a possible explanation, I turn to a finding by Martell, Lane, and Emrich (1996), originally developed to explain the effects of sex bias on organizational careers. Using computer simulations, they were able to demonstrate that in hierarchic systems, very small relationships at the lowest levels tend to escalate, as multiple career decisions were made over time, into very large relationships at the top of the hierarchy. It would seem likely that in other types of organizations beyond the hierarchic, this same process may occur, at least to the extent that the organization is of substantial size, that leadership is a scarce commodity, and that an underlying leadership continuum exists.

Table 5. Relationships Between Various Predictors and Leadership Forms in Samples Where Congruent MSCS Correlations are Available.

Sample (Prior Description)	Predictor Measure	Leadership Form	Method of Analysis	Correlation
Personnel and industrial relations managers (Miner, 1977)	Ghiselli Self-Description Inventory – Supervisory	Managerial	Biserial correlation	
	Ability		Leader – n = 41; Member – n = 60	
			Leader – M = 30.39; Member – M = 28.19	0.25*
	Adorno F-Scale		Leader – M = 72.98; Member – M = 70.19	0.14
	Kuder Preference Record Supervisory Interest		Leader – M = 35.73; Member – M = 34.33	0.14
Buffalo, NY area entrepreneurs (Miner, 1997)	Shure and Meeker Risk	Entrepreneurial	Biserial correlation	
	Avoidance		Leader – n = 45; Member – n = 44	
	Scale		Leader – M = 31.87; Member – M = 32.14	–0.03
	Gallup-Thorndike Vocabulary Test:			
	Forms A & B		Leader – M = 25.02; Member – M = 25.43	–0.06
	Matteson-Ivancevich Individual Behavior Activity			
	Profile – Type A		Leader – M = 54.15; Member – M = 57.20	–0.17
	Levenson Instrument			
	Internal Control		Leader – M = 40.73; Member – M = 38.98	0.28*
	Powerful Other Control		Leader – M = 18.87; Member – M = 20.16	–0.14
	Chance Control		Leader – M = 16.60; Member – M = 15.73	0.11
	Rowe-Mason Decision Style Inventory			
	Directive Scale		Leader – M = 79.91; Member – M = 79.43	0.02
	Conceptual Scale		Leader – M = 81.29; Member – M = 76.00	0.21
	Behavioral Scale		Leader – M = 60.44; Member – M = 60.34	0.00

* $p < 0.05$.

If escalation of this kind does occur, it could well account for the high correlations reported for leadership variables. These relationships have been established well into the subjects' careers, and in some cases for whole careers, at a point where many career decisions have had an opportunity to compound. Whatever small advantage having a congruent motivational pattern may have given in the early years, and our data suggest that it is indeed small, is translated later into the results noted in Tables 2 and 3. What these leadership and career variables appear to measure is the end result of a career process, involving many decisions, that has unfolded over a considerable period of time.

Use of Organizational Forms in Leadership Theory

In a book now in the process of publication (Miner, 2002), I review, among other organizational behavior theories, 16 major leadership theories. It may prove instructive to see how the constructs of the role motivation theories of leadership relate to this general body of knowledge in the field.

One such question involves the extent to which the four forms or systems of role motivation theory enter into the theoretical formulations of these other leadership theories; to what degree are these theories organizationally based? A tabulation indicates that all 16 utilize the hierarchic form in some manner, although this incorporation is frequently more implicit than explicit. The next most frequently incorporated is the group form, with half of the theories employing it. This is consistent with the group dynamics origins of leadership theory. Professional and task forms are embodied in several theories, but these types of organizational leadership play a much less significant role than do the other two.

The only theory that introduces constructs from all four organizational systems is substitutes for leadership theory – with professional, task, and group attributes appearing as substitutes for hierarchic leadership. This orientation is most manifest in a paper by Kerr and Slocum (1981).

The typical pattern is for two organizational forms to be incorporated in certain of their aspects. Among these forms, the dominant combination is some mix of hierarchy and group variables. Fiedler's contingency theory illustrates this approach. The key LPC factor is at least on occasion viewed as an index of people orientation on the high end, and thus contains a variable from group systems, as does the leader-member relations construct. Yet, position power is construed as a hierarchic component (Fiedler & Chemers, 1974). Fiedler's research, which provided the inductive base for theory development, has been conducted primarily within small groups and/or within the very hierarchic military. Other theories of the time often take this same tack, emphasizing both hierarchic and group forms.

Another approach in leadership theory has been to emphasize some construct, which by its nature cuts across the various organizational forms and could manifest itself in one form just as well as in another. Typically, however, these multi-organizational constructs are actually treated by the theory as present in hierarchic organizations and at best in one other form. Degrees of participation and/or delegation can be varied, for instance, in any type of organization, even the group form, where, under certain circumstances, the emergent leader can assume increasingly unilateral powers. Charismatic leadership behavior and its variants need not be limited to hierarchic systems but can appear through the visionary leadership of entrepreneurs, the god-like qualities of emergent sect leaders, and the intellectual brilliance of professional (intellectual) leaders.

Transformational leadership (Bass, 1985) is generally treated as a factor that occurs in hierarchic systems or in the professional context, where empirically it has been found to act somewhat differently. Yet, there is no reason why entrepreneurial and group systems should not be permeated with the same type of leadership on occasion; in fact, we know that they often are, although transformational leadership has rarely been studied in these contexts.

My point here is that looking at leadership as it occurs in different organizational forms, as the role motivation theories of leadership do, could well extend the leadership field into new domains and new kinds of knowledge. The processes involved may not be unlike what has occurred as the multi-level approaches have come to permeate the field (Dansereau, Yammarino & Markham, 1995).

Implications for Charismatic/Transformational Theorizing

In closing, I want to extend these ideas with reference to the development of the charismatic/transformational cluster of theories. In doing so, I will draw on the literature review contained in Miner (2002). Two points seem to be important. The first deals with the distinction between leader personality and leader behavior; the second with the extent to which charismatic/transformational leadership extends to lower levels of organization, or in role motivation theory terms into the ranks of organization members who are not leaders, at least as yet.

Both the House (1977) propositions and those that have followed, as well as the Bass (1985) propositions, are concerned with leader personality *and* leader behaviors. These represent two distinct levels within the individual level of analysis. They are not the same thing and in fact, they would be expected to be only minimally correlated, because behavior (but less so personality) should be more strongly influenced by contextual forces and constraints. The House theory, especially in its research, has placed much more emphasis on personality; the Bass theory, using the Multi-factor Leadership Questionnaire (MLQ) and consistent with the theory's origins, has tended to focus primarily on behavior in the research conducted.

Research on charismatic personality in the context of the House theory has been concerned with executive leadership in hierarchic organizations and with laboratory studies. The latter, being short-term, have often lacked a strong organizational form induction of any kind. Within hierarchic organizations, the personality pattern that emerges in conjunction with charisma is very similar in a number of its aspects to that of the hierarchic leader. These are contexts, such as the U.S. presidency, where charismatic behaviors, if available to a leader, should work well; thus one cannot help wondering whether this research may only demonstrate the use of charismatic behavior by hierarchic leaders whose personalities are congruent with the organizational form in which they find themselves.

Charismatic leaders in other, non-bureaucratic contexts, according to this hypothesis, should prove to be very different types of people. But since we have only research, which looks at congruent leaders in one type of organization, it is easy to conclude that we have *the* charismatic personality. This is an alternative interpretation of the research, which needs testing; will role motivation theory of leadership serve to explain the charismatic results in so far as personality is concerned?

Research on the Bass theory, as indicated, has had little to say about personality. It has focused on the *behaviors* of transformational leaders, again in hierarchic organizations, although many of these "leaders" are in what I would view as pre-leadership positions. There has been considerable focus on military organizations and business bureaucracies. On the few occasions when research has strayed outside the hierarchic form, to the professional for instance, it has not produced results that are as consistent with transformational leadership theory, even for behavior; there appears to be something operating behind the charismatic behavior that is different here. Again, we need to conduct more research outside the bureaucratic form, if we are to understand fully the nature of charismatic/transformational leadership. Do we simply have a cluster of theories dealing with a limited aspect of hierarchic leadership?

The second point I wish to raise also calls for research outside the hierarchic domain. Since Weber (1968), charisma has been associated with the upper levels of bureaucracies. Yet, Etzioni (1961) places it throughout all levels of normative (professional) systems as well, and Bass too has found charisma at lower (member) levels, although, in his view, it is identified primarily with lower levels of hierarchic systems. House appears to hold closer to the Weberian position. The role motivation view would be that charismatic behavior could be exhibited by leaders, or even pre-leaders, in any type of organization; its use would, however, be constrained by the potential willingness of those who are dependent on the leader to follow his or her dictates. Since potential follower responsiveness could vary across organization types, being greater for instance in certain professional systems, charismatic behavior could well exhibit an uneven pattern as it cuts across different kinds of organizations. In any event, there is a great need for research in multiple organizational domains to disentangle the existing theoretical perspectives here.

In a similar vein, we need to deal with the matter of the routinization of charisma. Routinization would seem to represent a normal leadership process, whatever accounts for the emergence of charisma. Thus, in role motivation theory terms, it should follow a different route in different types of organizations. There has been little research (or theory either) in this regard. Within task systems, however, it appears that hierarchy may be introduced to routinize the entrepreneur's vision (Miner, 1997). Perhaps similar phenomena operate in other organizational contexts as well. Again, the operation of charismatic/transformational processes within clearly specified organizational forms needs to be given much greater attention than it has been given in the past.

REFERENCES

Ashforth, B. E. (2001). *Role transitions in organizational life: An identity-based perspective.* Mahwah, NJ: Lawrence Erlbaum Associates.

Bass, B. M. (1985). *Leadership and performance beyond expectations.* New York: Free Press.

Berman, F. E., & Miner, J. B. (1985). Motivation to manage at the top executive level: A test of the hierarchic role motivation theory. *Personnel Psychology, 38,* 377–391.

Cohen, B. P., & Zhou, X. (1991). Status processes in enduring work groups. *American Sociological Review, 56,* 179–188.

Dansereau, F., Yammarino, F. J., & Markham, S. E. (1995). Leadership: The multiple-level approaches. *Leadership Quarterly, 6,* 97–109, 251–263.

Ensley, M. D., Carland, J. W., & Carland, J. C. (2000). Investigating the existence of the lead entrepreneur. *Journal of Small Business Management, 38*(4), 59–77.

Etzioni, A. (1961). *A comparative analysis of complex organizations: On power, involvement, and their correlates.* New York: Free Press.

Fiedler, F. E., & Chemers, M. M. (1974). *Leadership and effective management.* Glenview, IL: Scott, Foresman.

Holaday, M., Smith, D. A., & Sherry, A. (2000). Sentence completion tests: A review of the literature and results of a survey of members of the Society for Personality Assessment. *Journal of Personality Assessment, 74*, 371–383.

House, R. J. (1977). A 1976 theory of charismatic leadership. In: J. G. Hunt & L. L. Larson (Eds), *Leadership: The cutting edge* (pp. 189–207). Carbondale, IL: Southern Illinois University Press.

House, R. J., Wright, N. S., & Aditya, R. N. (1997). Cross-cultural research on organizational leadership: A critical analysis and a proposed theory. In: R. C. Earley & M. Erez (Eds), *New perspectives on international industrial/organizational psychology* (pp. 535–625). San Francisco, CA: New Lexington Press.

Kerr, S., & Slocum, J. W. (1981). Controlling the performances of people in organizations. In: P. C. Nystrom & W. H. Starbuck (Eds), *Handbook of organizational design* (Vol. 2, pp. 116–134). New York: Oxford University Press.

Lilienfeld, S. O., Wood, J. M., & Garb, H. N. (2000). The scientific status of projective techniques. *Psychological Science in the Public Interest, 1*, 27–66.

Martell, R. F., Lane, D. M., & Emrich, C. (1996). Male-female differences: A computer simulation. *American Psychologist, 51*, 157–158.

Melamed, T. (1996). Career success: An assessment of a gender-specific model. *Journal of Occupational and Organizational Psychology, 69*, 217–242.

Miner, J. B. (1977). *Motivation to manage: A ten year update on the "Studies in management education" research* (pp. 50–94). Eugene, OR: Organizational Measurement Systems Press.

Miner, J. B. (1980). The role of managerial and professional motivation in the career success of management professors. *Academy of Management Journal, 23*, 487–508.

Miner, J. B. (1982). The uncertain future of the leadership concept: Revisions and clarifications. *Journal of Applied Behavioral Science, 18*, 293–307.

Miner, J. B. (1993). *Role motivation theories*. New York: Routledge.

Miner, J. B. (1997). *A psychological typology of successful entrepreneurs*. Westport, CT: Quorum.

Miner, J. B. (2000). Testing a psychological typology of entrepreneurship using business founders. *Journal of Applied Behavioral Science, 36*, 43–69.

Miner, J. B. (2002). *Organizational behavior: Foundations, theories, and analyses*. New York: Oxford University Press.

Miner, J. B., Smith, N. R., & Bracker, J. S. (1989). Role of entrepreneurial task motivation in the growth of technologically innovative firms. *Journal of Applied Psychology, 74*, 554–560.

Nystrom, P. C. (1986). Comparing beliefs of line and technostructure managers. *Academy of Management Journal, 29*, 812–819.

Oliver, J. E. (1982). An instrument for classifying organizations. *Academy of Management Journal, 25*, 855–866.

Princeton University Class of 1948 (1974). *The book of the Princeton University class of 1948 on the occasion of its twenty-fifth anniversary*. Princeton, NJ: Princeton University.

Princeton University Class of 1948 (1998). *Going back: 50 years of the class of 1948*. Princeton, NJ: Princeton University.

Rogelberg, S. G., & Luong, A. (1998). Nonresponse to mailed surveys: A review and guide. *Current Directions in Psychological Science, 7*, 60–65.

Roth, P. L., & BeVier, C. A. (1998). Response rates in HRM/OB survey research: Norms and correlates, 1990–1994. *Journal of Management, 24*, 97–117.

Spangler, W. D. (1992). Validity of questionnaire and TAT measures of need for achievement: Two meta-analyses. *Psychological Bulletin, 112*, 140–154.

Terry, L. D. (1995). The leadership-management distinction: The domination and displacement of mechanistic and organismic theories. *Leadership Quarterly, 6*, 515–527.

Weber, M. (1968). *Economy and society.* New York: Bedminster Press.

Zaccaro, S. J., Foti, R. J., & Kenny, D. A. (1991). Self-monitoring and trait-based variance in leadership: An investigation of leader flexibility across multiple group situations. *Journal of Applied Psychology, 76*, 308–315.

Zaleznik, A. (1977). Managers and leaders: Are they different? *Harvard Business Review, 55*(3), 67–78.

FOUR PHENOMENOLOGICALLY DETERMINED SOCIAL PROCESSES OF ORGANIZATIONAL LEADERSHIP: FURTHER SUPPORT FOR THE CONSTRUCT OF TRANSFORMATIONAL LEADERSHIP

Ken W. Parry

ABSTRACT

One recent direction for leadership research has been the use of purely qualitative data and qualitative analysis. One analytical method used in this phenomenological research has been the full grounded theory method. That method has generated social process theories about leadership in organizational settings. The present research operationalizes those theories into questionnaire format. This operationalized work gives support to a one-factor model for social processes of leadership (SPL) in organizations. It also identifies four lower-order social processes of leadership. Concurrent validity is concluded from a high correlation with Bass & Avolio's and Podsakoff's transformational leadership constructs. The correlations are so high that the SPL scale might be tapping the same underlying construct as transformational leadership. The augmentation effect of transformational leadership over (transactional) management is

Transformational and Charismatic Leadership, Volume 2, pages 339–372.
ISBN: 0-7623-0962-8

also supported. Support has been obtained for ongoing grounded theory-based research into the social processes of leadership and influence, and related phenomena, in organizations.

INTRODUCTION AND PROBLEM STATEMENT

Leadership may be conceptualized as a social influence process (Conger, 1998; Parry, 1998). First, leadership is about influence – of that there is consensus within the literature. Second, it is social because it is about relationships and interactions between people, usually within the context of a society. For the purposes of the present chapter, the society in question is an organizational society. Third, leadership is processual. It is about 'doing' as much as it is about a person, a personality, a rank or position, a set of competencies, or behaviors. Hence, the processual nature of leadership can be thought of in terms of verbs, invariably ending with the suffix ". . . ing", and is about activity within the organizational society in question. An example is the basic social process of enhancing adaptability (Parry, 1999). Finally, that influencing activity is between and among people as much as it emanates from individuals.

Organizational *processes* have been researched exhaustively over the years, mainly via the discipline of psychology, but also via sociology. More specifically, *social processes* such as cohesion and citizenship have also been determined via that research. However, the subjects of the present research are social processes *of leadership* and of influence. These have not been well researched over the years.

Therefore, leadership should be researched with methodologies that generate social processes as their outcomes. Although most mainstream leadership research has utilized objectivist methodologies, Parry (1998) and Conger (1998) have argued for greater use of non-objectivist methodologies that generate social process and social process theory as their research outcomes. One such methodology utilizes the grounded theory (Glaser & Strauss, 1967) data analytic method. This method uses qualitative data mainly, and fully qualitative analysis of those data. Grounded theory analysis follows an iterative format based around theory emergence rather than theory testing. The emergent theory is based around the determination of a "basic social process" that explains the phenomenon under investigation – leadership in this case. Although many authors have conducted research under the grounded theory rubric, often it is not the full grounded theory method that is actually employed. In the present case, I reiterate the criticality of using the full method.

Although traditionally used in research into observable phenomena like teaching and nursing, Parry and Conger argued that the grounded theory method can and should be used in the research of less observable phenomena like leadership. Such research has been undertaken. Examples are the work of Irurita (1994, 1996), Parry (1999), and Harchar and Hyle (1996). Although not strictly using the grounded theory method, other authors have also theorized about the social processes of leadership that are present in organizational settings (Bass, 1985; Bennis & Nanus, 1985; Boyd & Taylor, 1998; Kent et al., 1996). The conceptual interpretation of these qualitatively derived theories indicates they have much in common with transformational leadership (Bass, 1985; Irurita, 1996; Parry, 1999). The transformational leadership body of literature is the most researched, validated, and comprehensive explanation of leadership available today (den Hartog et al., 1997).

The issue that has arisen in recent years is that the relationships between qualitatively derived social process theories of leadership and the mainstream psychometrically derived theories of leadership have not been equated other than conceptually. Therefore, there is a need to empirically test the relationships between both bodies of knowledge. The present research commences this task. In this case, the theoretical framework used is to operationalize the qualitatively derived theory into questionnaire format. Alternate theoretical frameworks would utilize qualitative data and qualitative analysis to test the psychometrically derived theories.

I will now outline the social processes of leadership that have been derived from purely qualitative research in recent years. Discussion will include how those processes are similar to constructs of leadership that have been derived from nomothetic epistemologies and methods. Further discussion will include how those qualitatively derived social processes of leadership have been translated into questionnaire format for the purpose of validation and reliability testing.

Optimizing

Irurita (1996) recently presented one example of important research into the leadership process. In this, Irurita conducted a qualitative analysis of nursing leadership using grounded theory methodology (see Glaser, 1978, 1992; Glaser & Strauss, 1967; Strauss, 1987; Strauss & Corbin, 1990). Grounded theory enables theory generation from data rather than using data to support already formed theories (Irurita, 1996). From data collected over four years, and analyzed with the grounded theory method, Irurita determined a theory of *optimizing* (Irurita, 1992, 1994). Optimizing is a term given to the effective leadership process of "making the best of the situation, making the most effective or optimal use of all available and potential resources to compensate for the state of retardation and to move beyond mediocrity toward excellence" (Irurita, 1996, p. 129). Irurita's identification and theorizing of optimizing is important, as it is explicitly a theory of social process in leadership. It considers the three aspects of social process highlighted above, that is, change and transformation over time, the linking of interactional sequences, and the associated human relation dynamics (Parry, 1998).

Optimizing involves three progressive phases of process, where an organization may be in a period of *surviving*, *investing*, or *transforming*. The transforming phase is conceptually similar to Burns' (1978) socio-political process theory of the same name. Leaders who successfully generate the process of optimizing will help their organization move through these phases. This takes the organization from retardation and mediocrity in which basic survival is the focus, through turbulence, in which investing is key, and on towards excellence, a period of continuous development and transformation (Irurita, 1996). Contextual variables impact upon the leadership process of optimizing. These variables include environmental and organizational aspects such as culture, the characteristics of followers, and the leader's values, attitudes, knowledge, skills, and traits. The leader attributes that are clearly important for the optimizing process include optimism, caring, commitment, determination, courage, articulate communication, and self-esteem. Importantly, in the context of Irurita's study, such attributes of successful leaders were found to be guided by values and strong morals (Irurita, 1996, p. 130).

Irurita's model of optimizing is conceptually more similar to Transformational Leadership than to other leadership theories. Leaders who work on the basis of contingent reward and management by exception are classified in the optimizing model as survivors. Moreover, leaders who are transformers in the optimizing model are clear examples of successful leaders as described in the transformational leadership theory. However, there are some important differences between these theories. The optimizing model involves a third level, *investors*, in between survivors and transformers. Irurita (1996) suggests that investors have strengths in individual consideration and intellectual stimulation, two aspects of the transformational leader.

Of particular importance, Irurita explicitly mentions that because the process of optimizing is cumulative, in which one level is built upon the previous level, a transformer will also be an investor and a survivor. When this model is related to transformational theory, one sees that a successful leader should have both transactional (survival) and transformational leadership qualities. As discussed earlier, this augmentation effect is an important characteristic of transforma-tional leadership theory (Waldman, Bass & Yammarino, 1990).

Personal Adaptability • Resolving Uncertainty • Enhancing Adaptability

Like Irurita, Parry (1999) used qualitative methods and grounded theory to explore the leadership processes occurring amid turbulent change in Australian local government settings. Through this work, two social processes were found to occur in relation to leadership, change and following. These social processes involve *resolving* the *uncertainty* and *enhancing* the *adaptability* of the followers and the leaders in their organizations. Again, in parallel to Irurita's optimizing model, Parry's theory is important because it explicitly focuses on aspects of a social leadership process – changes occurring over time, and the interaction sequences arising between human individuals in the organization.

Parry identified two major moderators of the relationship between leaders and followers. First, *change*, incorporating turbulence and uncertainty, is found to be a key moderating variable. The second moderator was found to be the degree of *personal adaptability* of the followers to the change process.

Personal adaptability to change becomes important because low adaptability accentuates one's experience of the complexity and turbulence of change. This in turn exacerbates the stress felt by followers and leaders. Also, the inertia generated by change may be accentuated. However, high adaptability reduces the stress experienced due to change, increases teamwork and harmony, and may in fact aid in the manifestation of leadership. The adaptability of followers is influenced by several factors including experience, personality, knowledge of change outcomes, and leader interventions (Parry, 1999).

RESOLVING UNCERTAINTY

Parry (1999) found that where effective leadership was present, the uncertainty of change experienced by both followers and leaders could be resolved through strategies, behaviors, and activities demonstrated by the leaders. Moreover, in the absence of effective leadership, both leaders and followers became consumed with uncertainty, and their knowledge, performance, and morale reduced while inaccurate perceptions were maintained. Thus, the resolution of uncertainty due to change and turbulence may directly reduce the degree to which the change becomes threatening to individuals in the organization.

Therefore, it is important for leaders to have a clear understanding of their leadership role in the resolution of uncertainty. From this, leaders themselves will be more adaptable and can then help increase the personal adaptability of their followers through strategies such as identifying positive outcomes of the change, and giving followers the experience of success through the change. Identification and understanding of this process are important because traditionally many managers have dealt with the negative humanistic effects of change by simply shielding subordinates from the disruption and pain that are removed from change (Cabana, 1996). However, such a strategy is ineffectual in an organization that deals with continuous change, as it is a strategy that becomes impossible to maintain. Rather, Cabana (1996) maintains that it is more effective to help followers deal with, adapt to, and process the negative effects of change as they arise.

Enhancing Adaptability

Parry (1999) recognized that the process of resolving uncertainty lacked important strategies required by leaders to help enhance their own and followers' adaptability to turbulence and change. Through a deeper analysis of the data, Parry identified some key strategies within the process of enhancing adaptability. Leaders can help resolve uncertainty through slowly implementing changes and giving followers the experience of success. Resource provision is also used as an important strategy leaders use to help a follower's transition during change – including workplace changes, benchmarking, competency-based costing and removing blockages. In order to enhance followers' adaptability, leaders can influence change in their follower's perceptions, create reciprocal commitment, improve knowledge of reciprocal benefits of changes, consistently and clearly communicate desirable messages, facilitate experiences of different change situations for followers, and achieve complementarity of values (Parry, 1999, p. 145).

Relationship Between Enhancing Adaptability, Transformational Leadership, and the Leadership Process
The theory of enhancing adaptability can be related to literature describing transformational leadership, and to leadership theory more generally. First, just as transformational leaders need to be self-confident and clear of their purpose and direction in order to motivate, stimulate, and inspire (Avolio, 1996), so too do leaders who want to enhance the adaptability of others and the self. Parry (1999) highlighted that it is important for leaders to engage in some self-development, and to reflect and be clear in their minds of their role, direction, and required action. Also, Parry highlighted the importance of the transformation of follower's confidence, communication of vision for the future, and heightening the sense of follower self-efficacy, to the process of enhancing

adaptability. Each of these leadership qualities may be located among important transformational strategies (Bass, 1998). Therefore, enhancing adaptability and transformational leadership are conceptually similar, and both theories are supported by the wider leadership theory.

The fourth and final social leadership process under consideration in the present research is the promulgating of vision. Like optimizing, resolving uncertainty, and enhancing adaptability, promulgating vision is a process that involves relationships, trust, and communication, and is a dynamical social process, occurring over time.

Promulgating Vision

Bennis and Nanus (1985, p. 89) stated that, "a vision articulates a view of realistic, credible, attractive future of an organization, a condition that is better in some important ways than now exists". Moreover, Bennis and Nanus believe that "attention to vision" is a major strategy of effective leadership. Through communication of vision, leaders will create focus, compel attention and action, and bring about confidence in their followers. Vision may also increase a follower's sense of direction and his or her sense of empowerment, and enhance his or her motivation (Bryman, 1992). An important aspect of this is the effect of reducing the uncertainty of employees during times of change (Nicholls, 1993). If followers know in which direction they are headed, they will no longer feel stress due to operating in the unknown. Thus, visioning is clearly related to the social process of resolving uncertainty. Nanus (1992) summed up the positive effects of vision into four components when he suggested that the right vision:

(1) attracts commitment and energizes people;
(2) creates meaning in worker's lives;
(3) establishes a standard of excellence; and
(4) bridges the present with the future.

Therefore, vision becomes a very important aspect of effective organizational leadership. This message is reflected in other literature. For example, when Bryman (1992) conducted a review of the literature concerning "new leadership" and charismatic leadership, every author who was considered used *vision* as a central theme in their discussion.

However, if visioning is to be seen as a social process, it is not adequate to simply create a vision. The vision must be meaningfully communicated between the leader and their followers. In other words, promulgation of vision must occur. Conger (1992, p. 96) stated that, "for leaders to be influential, they must be able to articulate their 'vision of the future' in ways that uplift and attract others". Nanus (1992) highlighted that if employees do not feel that they themselves have *chosen* to adopt the vision, they will eventually revert back to their old ways.

A tactic given by Nanus to aid the sharing of vision is for leaders to connect "with people in a way that resonates with their own deepest feelings about what is right and worth doing" (Nanus, 1992, p. 135). Further, Nanus suggested that this is done best by leaders who listen carefully to followers and attend to subtle cues. Promulgating vision, therefore, relies on good relationships, a high degree of trust, and excellent communication skills. In addition, Rowsell and Tony (1993) suggest that to do this, a leader must "live their vision". This point reflects that it is not only through verbal communication that a vision will become a central motivating and guiding force of an organization: it is also through the leader's actions. Therefore, like the core social processes of trust, relationships and communication, a leader promulgating vision must have some degree of behavioral integrity in which their actions match their words (Simons, 1999).

In the descriptions of the social processes above, there is an obvious contradiction between these theories and the aforementioned theoretical foundation and research objectives of this project. These theories of social processes are based upon the dyadic relationship of leader-follower and therefore overlook critical dimensions of the social process of leadership such as leadership between many people and at all levels. However, these theories provide a strong basis for extension of theory because they concentrate on the dynamic and process-based nature of leadership, rather than on specific qualities possessed by the leader, of the behaviors of individual "leaders".

Item Generation and Development

Content validity or "a clear link between items and their theoretical domain" (Hinkin, 1995, p. 971) is a fundamental requirement of quality scale development. The present research uses a deductive process to ensure content validity of items generated for the scale. Deductive scale development utilizes previous understanding and theoretical classification of constructs in question to inform development of the items (Hinkin, 1995).

The current scale is founded in grounded theories that have previously identified key social processes of effective leadership (Irurita, 1996; Parry, 1999). Three of the social process constructs used in this scale – *enhancing adaptability, optimizing*, and *resolving uncertainty* – were derived through this grounded theory work. The fourth construct investigated, *promulgating vision*, emerged from qualitative analysis within organizations and is supported by a considerable literature base, although not using the grounded theory method per se to generate theory.

Grounded theory provides a strong theoretical footing for scale development because it is theory that has been developed and abstracted from within contextually relevant data. In addition, accounts of grounded theory process draw on the literature for the support of the newly generated theories, and therefore the content validity of subsequent scales is reinforced.

However, where grounded theory is often criticized is that it is necessarily context-specific and substantive, and is not generalizable to organizational situations other than that studied. Thus, there is an argument for attempting to extend grounded organizational theory into generalized organizational theory by the development of widely applicable measurement scales.

Using grounded theory as a basis for empirical scale development, the current design knits together methodologies to develop a stronger theoretical position than either qualitative identification or quantitative testing of the social processes of leadership in isolation would allow.

Intended Outcomes

There are four intended outcomes from this line of research:

(1) To validate the existing social process of leadership (SPL) work that has been done using the mainly grounded theory method.
(2) To ascertain whether existing scales measure the SPL adequately without the need for a new SPL scale.
(3) To test for the presence of separate constructs of SPL, in other words, to discriminate between SPL sub-factors.
(4) To validate a new SPL instrument, if there is indication of a need for it.

Design Objective

A critical guideline of the SPL development was to design a tool that was applicable to a range of organizational and industrial settings, and thus extend primarily substantive work to a broader scope of organizational leadership. As such, the items were developed to avoid industry- or organization-specific language and were based on behavioral social processes rather than detailed descriptions of work roles.

In addition, the central position of leadership *process* in this investigation required items to describe *leadership in action*, and therefore, items were developed using verbs with the suffix "–ing". For example, words such as encourage became encouraging, as in "encouraging others to share in the work unit's vision", and enhance became enhancing as in "enhancing others' adaptability". Such expression indicates "action" and reflects the change in organizational research emphasis around the world. For example, Ruigrok, Pettigrew, Peck and Whittington (1999) research "organizing" and "strategizing" rather than "organization" and "strategy".

Stage 1: Pilot Study of Social Process Items

A pilot study was conducted as a preliminary stage of scale development. This pilot study used a small social processes scale within a larger survey investigating leadership practices (Proctor & Parry, 1999). This scale comprised nine items derived from the grounded theory work described above. The scale items were designed to measure a focal leader's capability to create or support effective social processes of leadership. Such a design was in keeping with the larger survey that required respondents to report leadership styles and capabilities of focal leaders.

The item response scale chosen was a five-point ratio scale of frequency, ranging form "not at all" to "frequently, if not always". Five points were selected because previous research suggests that the reliability of scales increases up to the use of five points but then levels off (Lissitz & Green, 1975). In addition, Bass et al. established support for the use of this frequency scale as an interval scale (Bass, Cascio & O'Connor, 1974).

All of the components of this small scale were significantly related to each other, and an adequate internal consistency of the social process construct was demonstrated (Cronbach's alpha 0.91). Item-to-total analysis supported the inclusion of all items in the scale, with the lowest correlation being $r = 0.59$. A factor analysis using principal components with promax rotation indicated that the construct was unidimensional. Only one factor was indicated, giving an eigenvalue of 5.36, which was over five times larger than the nearest factor (eigenvalue = 0.96). This factor explained 59.6% of variance. Convergent validity was supported by correlational patterns following predicted relationships between the social process constructs and related constructs including leadership style (transformational and transactional) and outcomes of effective leadership. This pilot study provided adequate support for testing the SPL more widely and in more detail.

Stage 2: Current Analysis

The preliminary analysis supported the development of a broader social processes scale, but during this stage, three issues were identified that required further theorizing and development:

- Investigation of social process at *all* organizational levels.
- Investigation of social process *between* and *among* people (not just by individuals).
- Constructs de-jargonized and broken down into discernible and quantifiable processes.

(Proctor & Parry, 1999).

The pilot study of the SPL began by focusing on individual people who contribute to the social process of leadership, but prior theorizing suggested that the social process of leadership, by definition, should be investigated in the social context, that is *between* people. Therefore, in the current stage of development, the SPL items are designed to measure the social process of leadership involving multiple potential origins of behavior. Therefore, all items begin with the stem "Using the scale above, please indicate how frequently the following behaviors occur within your team or work unit . . .".

Results from the pilot study also suggested that some of the items used may have been be too "jargonistic", and consequently poorly understood concepts by many practicing managers. The item response frequency for each item varied, with two items in particular demonstrating a low frequency of response. The items were "enhancing the adaptability of others" and "enhancing one's own adaptability". In addition, qualitative indications of unclear meaning were apparent in the form of question marks, or comments such as "meaning?" that were at times written beside these items.

In the original pilot scale, only a few items were used to measure a very large behavioral domain, and therefore, abstracted theoretical ideas were used as items to ensure coverage of this domain. The low frequency of response for some items appears to indicate that these theoretical concepts were not easily grounded in management practice or observable and discernible behavior. However, in the original grounded theory research, the abstracted constructs *were* grounded in observable behavior, and therefore, it was suggested that an expanded group of behavioral items relevant to the wider and more detailed background information of the social process constructs may be useful.

The current analysis attempts to address these issues in two ways. First, it returns to the original grounded theory work to derive a fuller list of items describing the particular behaviors within relevant social processes. Second, it develops the items to reflect collective practices of leadership that may occur within a group context.

Item Development

A list of 54 items was derived from the published social processes of leadership to describe the four main constructs of the SPL. This list was then subjected to a process of refinement through a focus group consisting of a selection of experts, including two professors of management, postgraduate management students, and a leadership researcher, as well as several laypeople, including those in administrative management roles within the management department.

In light of this focus group, it was decided that all items would be changed to reflect *behaviors of members* of the work unit, rather than items that described general behaviors of the group but gave no reference to the people involved in the actions. Thus, the original items using the suffix "-*ing*" were dropped, and replaced with items that implied actions by individuals, but within a collective context. Continuous use of "-ing" words was found to be cumbersome and confusing. For example, items such as "Prioriti*zing* work tasks" and "encoura*ging* others to share in the work unit's vision" were changed to "People in our work unit . . . 'prioritize work tasks' and 'encourage others to share in the work unit's vision'". In addition, some items were dropped either because of their ambiguous nature or because they were deemed inconsistent with the theoretical domain they were representing. Certainly, most of the items relate mainly to behaviors by individuals, but I was looking for the extent to which these behaviors were exhibited in the work unit overall, rather than by each individual.

The focus group analysis suggested that by using -*ing*, the items were asking people about behavior that occurs *out there, among* people. This appeared to conflict with the fact that we live in a world where *behaviors* have their origin in individuals. After all, it is individual people who act, do, and behave. This is not to imply a philosophical stance against useful theories such as social constructionism. In fact, the concept of social process assumes that behavior can be constructed *between* people, such that humans react, collude, collaborate, and interact. However, behavior cannot be said to be present if there is no individual actually acting out the behavior. The very definition of behavior involves the prescription of a doer, or someone who behaves. Anything above or outside "behavior" within the social world is assigned different terminology such as "climate", "atmosphere", or perhaps "aura". By contrast, this research investigates the social processes that occur between and among people.

Use of the five-point frequency scale used in the pilot study was continued in the final version. Eight reverse-coded items were also included in the final scale representing all four of the social process constructs: optimizing, resolving uncertainty, enhancing adaptability, and promulgating vision. Although the literature has mixed conclusions about this practice (Jackson, Wall, Martin & Davids, 1993), it was decided that some reverse-scored items should be included to attenuate response bias (Idaszak & Drasgow, 1987). The final scale included 44 items.

METHOD

Sample and Procedure

Data were collected from 719 useable surveys completed by middle and senior managers drawn from a membership list of the national Institute of Management in New Zealand. The sample was the combination of respondents of two parallel questionnaires sent out simultaneously to different members of same population. The two versions of the questionnaires varied slightly in the instruments that were included in the survey to provide construct validity to the SPL. To minimize questionnaire size and therefore to minimize respondent fatigue, each questionnaire was kept to just over 100 items. The SPL items were on both questionnaires, and related instruments were spread across both questionnaires. This sample came from a potential 3720 questionnaires sent out, and therefore the response rate was approximately 19%. This is quite a good response rate historically for this population. Also, as Waldman, Ramirez, House and Puranam (2001) have claimed, the response rate is not crucial for broad-brush population research such as this. Moreover, I am researching the constructs, not the population, so representativeness of the sample was not an issue. The sample represented a range of organizations with varying size and industry focus.

During initial analysis, there appeared to be a small proportion of respondents who indicated that they were reporting about organizational groups of 200 members or more. The results given by these respondents were potentially problematic for two reasons. First, in comparison with the USA, New Zealand is made up of a small-medium business economy. Organizations or work units that have in excess of 200 people are a distinct and small group. Therefore, they are likely to have qualities that are specific to big business in contrast with the majority of New Zealand companies. Second, our unit of analysis was the work group, unit, or team rather than the entire organization. Therefore, from the results, I found that comparing responses from "work units" of greater than 200 people with responses from smaller work units was qualitatively comparing organizations such as the New Zealand Army with an isolated Rifle Company, or the entire Michael Hill Jeweller Franchise chain with one retail outlet. Using less than 200 members in the work unit as a filter criterion, 14 responses (1.9%) were withdrawn from the original 719 useable surveys.

Approximately two-thirds of the remaining sample of 705, were involved in mainly private sector enterprise, and the remaining 36% worked mainly in the public sector. Seventy-five per cent of survey participants had been in their work units for more than 1.5 years, whereas only 6% had worked in their unit for less than six months. The average work unit size had approximately 19 members with a relatively even split of men and women (58% and 42%, respectively). The age of respondents ranged between 21 and 79 years, with a mean age of 47.8 years.

The sample data contained rater evaluations of "team" or "work unit" leadership processes and behaviors. The first section of the questionnaire consisted of the new scale under evaluation. This section was followed by established measures of other leadership processes that were conceptually similar to the construct of the *social process of leadership*. The total number of items in Questionnaire 1 and 2 were 113 and 111, respectively. Questionnaires were mailed to members with a letter of support from the Chief Executive of the National Institute of Management. Surveys were self-administered and, when completed, returned in reply-paid envelopes.

Measures
There is a vast selection of measurement scales that *partially* reflect the process of leadership. By using some of these in the present research, it was hoped that the new scale and theory could be compared and contrasted to a comprehensive range of constructs within the current literature. However, the majority of these scales were developed to measure individual leadership characteristics. For the purposes of this investigation, it was necessary to reword some scales to reflect a team context. For example, the item "Does not take extra breaks" from the Organizational Citizenship Behavior Scale (Podsakoff, MacKenzie, Moorman & Fetter, 1990) was changed to "people do not take extra breaks", to incorporate the collective behavior. The reliabilities of the new "team" scales were assessed to ensure the use of appropriate measures. Presentation of the new scale was standardized by retaining the Social Processes of Leadership items within both questionnaires.

Transformational Leadership
Two measures of transformational leadership were utilized in this study because of previously identified conceptual similarity with the grounded theory-determined social processes of leadership (Irurita, 1996; Parry, 1999).

Questionnaire 1: Three of the six key behaviors of transformational leadership identified by Podsakoff et al. (1990) were measured. The three behaviours were *identifying and articulating vision, providing an appropriate model*, and *fostering the acceptance of group goals*. These constructs were chosen because of their theoretical similarity to some of the social processes of leadership measured in the SPL. For example, *identifying and articulating a vision* is conceptually related to promulgating vision, whereas fostering the acceptance of goals is similar to, although distinct from, enhancing adaptability to change and to the development of strategic directions. The seven-point response scale used by Podsakoff et al. (1990) was shortened in this analysis to five-point Likert scale that ranged from "strongly disagree" to "strongly agree". The results suggested reasonable reliability of all three scales with alpha coefficients all exceeding the recommended value of 0.7 (Nunnally, 1978) (see Table 5).

Questionnaire 2: Three constructs measuring transformational and trans-actional leadership, as measured by the Multi-factor Leadership Questionnaire-Team (MLQT) (Bass & Avolio, 1993), were included in Questionnaire 2. The three constructs are *inspirational motivation, contingent reward*, and *management-by-exception-passive*. For the sake of parsimony, inspirational motivation was included as the measure of transformational leadership. Inspirational motivation tends to correlate so closely with the other transformational leadership factors that the presence of one factor indicates the concurrent presence of the other transformational leadership factors. Indeed, Avolio, Bass and Jung (1999) have confirmed the presence of a higher-order transformational leadership construct that contains inspirational motivation, idealized influence and intellectual stimulation, each correlating in excess of 0.70 with the other. Hence, by measuring inspirational motivation, transformational leadership is being represented in the survey. Contingent reward is a measure of *constructive transaction*, and management-by-exception-passive is a measure of *corrective-avoidant transactional* leadership (Avolio, Bass & Jung, 1999). Because management-by-exception-passive is passive and corrective, and because it correlates negatively with transformational leadership (den Hartog et al., 1997), it is used in this research to test the discriminant validity of the SPL.

The MLQ is the most researched measure of organizational leadership in use today (den Hartog et al., 1997). Although, in the past, there have been some criticisms of the MLQ (Bycio et al., 1995; Carless et al., 1998; Tepper & Percy, 1994; Tracey & Hinkin, 1998, 1999; Yammarino & Dubinsky, 1994), there has also been substantial evidence to support its use. For example, Lowe et al. (1996) conducted a meta-analysis of MLQ literature and found the transformational leadership scales to be reliable and to have a good predictive validity. Strong evidence in this volume provided by Antonakis and House also supports the construct validity of the MLQ. The MLQ is now widely accepted as a key tool for the investigation of transformational and transactional leadership styles (den Hartog et al., 1997).

Again, a five-point frequency scale, from 0 (not at all) to 4 (frequently, if not always), was used. The reliability estimates for inspirational motivation, contingent reward, and management-by-exception in the current analysis were acceptable (see Table 4).

Innovation

A measure for the *Climate for Innovation* (Scott & Bruce, 1994) was used to describe the degree to which the collective environment of the work unit supports innovative thinking and implementation. Scott and Bruce (1994) describe innovation as a *process* representing the generation and implementation of ideas that requires a wide variety of behaviors on the part of individuals, but is critically related to the degree of support for innovation within the collective context. Therefore, the social processes of leadership occurring within work units become central to the development of innovation, as claimed by Bass (1998). Moreover, innovation is meaningfully connected to the social processes of optimizing and enhancing adaptability. The Climate for Innovation measure consists of 22 items, using a five-point Likert scale ranging from "strongly disagree" to "strongly agree". Two reliable measures are included in the Climate for Innovation scale: *support for innovation* (16 items, alpha = 0.92) and *resource supply* (6 items, alpha = 0.77) (Scott & Bruce, 1994). The current study supported these reliabilities (see Table 5).

Humor

Recently, humor has gained increased recognition as a potential domain of enhanced leadership effectiveness (Avolio et al., 1999; Barsoux, 1996; Crawford, 1994). Humor has been found to enhance group cohesiveness, facilitate communication (Duncan, 1982), improve morale (Gruner, 1997), and disturb status differentials (Vinton, 1989), and has been positively related to individual and unit performance measures (Avolio, Howell & Sosik, 1999). Moreover, Avolio et al. (1999) have found humor to be significantly related to various leadership styles, including transformational, contingent reward, and avoidant leadership.

Although the consideration of humor has been somewhat neglected in previous years (Duncan, Smeltzer & Leap, 1990), it has had the advantage of being considered as necessarily social, and as such has been investigated primarily within a collective context (e.g. Duncan & Feisal, 1989; Vinton, 1989). Despite the study of leadership itself tending to be restricted in the past to the leader and the follower, the management implications of humor have been located freely within the social domain.

Because humor has been meaningfully related to leadership and has a history of social analysis, a measure of workplace humor was included in the current study of the social process of leadership. The scale used is a unidimensional measure of five items demonstrating reliability alphas around 0.90 (Avolio, Howell & Sosik, 1999; Dubinsky, Yammarino & Jolson, 1995). In the present study, the scale also demonstrated adequate reliability (see Table 4).

Organizational Citizenship
Five organizational citizenship behavior constructs were measured in the current study, including *Conscientiousness, Sportsmanship, Civic virtue, Courtesy,* and *Altruism* (Podsakoff, MacKenzie, Moorman & Fetter, 1990). These scales were developed by Podsakoff et al. to measure the constructs of Organizational Citizenship Behavior (OCB) described by Organ (1988). Organ identified organizational citizenship behavior as incidents of discretionary behavior by an individual that in aggregate, improve the functioning of organizations. Factors related to OCB include job satisfaction (Bateman & Organ, 1983; Smith, Organ & Near, 1983), attitudes, and individual differences. Traditionally, OCB has been investigated at an individual level of analysis (Organ & Ryan, 1995), which is represented in Organ's definition above. However, more recently, the benefit of considering OCB as a group-level phenomenon has been identified (George, 1990; George & Brief, 1992; Organ & Ryan, 1995). For example, team cohesiveness has been related to prosocial or organizational citizenship behavior (O'Bannon & Pearce, 1999), which in turn has been related to motivating increased participation in team activities (Cartwright & Zander, 1968). The re-worded OCB "team" scales generally demonstrated reasonable reliability (see Tables 4 and 5).

Cohesion
Group cohesion is an established component of effective process within team or work group contexts (see Evans & Dion 1991; Mullen & Cooper, 1994 for meta-analyses). However, this relationship has been shown to be moderated by a range of variables, including expectation norms of productivity (Munroe, Estabrooks, Dennis & Carron, 1999), task norms, organizational context (Langfred & Shanley, 1997), and surface and deep level diversity within groups (Harrison, Price & Bell, 1998). Alternately, group cohesion itself has been found to moderate the relationship between leadership and team perfor-mance (Carless, Mann & Wearing, 1998) and between motivation and performance (Chia, 1998). Therefore, it appears that work group cohesion is

firmly embedded within the social processes occurring within collective environments.

Recently, the multi-dimensional nature of cohesion has been identified (Carless & DePaola, 2000). In particular, a distinction between "commitment to task", the central focus of Mullen and Cooper's meta-analysis, and more social aspects of cohesion has been drawn (Langfred & Shanley, 1997). Recent measurement validation by Carless and DePaola has incorporated this distinction into a three-dimensional scale measuring *Task Cohesion, Social Cohesion*, and *Individual Attraction to the Group*. These authors demonstrated adequate reliability of the first two dimensions (alpha = 0.74 and 0.81, respectively), but only marginal consistency of the third construct (alpha = 0.63). In addition, the third construct was found to be unrelated to most relevant variables within the study. For this reason, the current study uses the task and social cohesion dimensions of the Work-Group Cohesion Scale (Carless & DePaola, 2000) in questionnaire 2. The results herein suggested adequate reliability of both cohesion measures (see Table 4).

Work Group Characteristics

Three process-oriented work group characteristics with established links to effectiveness (Campion, Medsker & Higgs, 1993) were included in Questionnaire 1. The first of these was *social support* including items such as, "members of my work unit help each other out at work when needed" and "my team increases my opportunities for positive social interaction". This construct is conceptually related to social cohesion, as measured in Questionnaire 2, and is also relevant to aspects of the social processes of leadership construct.

Workload sharing is the second work group characteristic measured in the present study. This scale measures the degree to which all members of the group contribute to work done. This is an important dimension of social process within teams because it distinguishes between groups in which all members are active in effective processes and those groups in which one or two people act as drivers or leaders while the rest withdraw from the collective team process.

The third dimension measured here is the degree of *communication and cooperation* within work groups. Communication is a more general aspect of group dynamics but is nevertheless fundamental to effective social processes. The SPL attempts to measure communication issues such as sharing information about change and cooperation between team members. Therefore, measurement of these issues via Campion et al.'s scale will assist with the interpretation of the scale. Each of these scales demonstrated adequate reliability (see Table 5).

Trustworthiness

Trust is an important dimension within the organizational context. However, although trust has been recognized as central in dyadic corporate relationships, its emphasis in collective contexts is much less obvious (Kramer, Brewer & Hanna, 1996, p. 358). Jarvenpaa et al. (1998) highlight the importance of trust in new organizational arrangements in which previous hierarchical and highly structured forms are replaced by flexible, flatter, and more collaborative systems such as project teams, and work units involving diversified and changing work roles.

However, understanding trust as a social process is not simply a matter of patching past, predominantly dyadic, trust theory on to new organizational relationships. Collective trust is made more complicated because of the multiplicity of trustees of which some but not all may demonstrate trustworthy attributes (Jarvenpaa et al., 1998; Kramer et al., 1996). Moreover, the dynamics and implications of trust within the collective context are also divergent from traditional trust patterns. For example, Jarvenpaa et al. (1998) found that teams demonstrating high trust levels would rotate leadership roles. The leader was neither consistent nor chosen throughout the project, and each individual member demonstrated certain leadership strengths during the course of the project. Thus, trust and the social process of leadership appear to be closely connected.

The current study used a scale developed by Pearce et al. (1994) to measure trustworthiness in an organizational context. However, the scale was then modified by Jarvenpaa et al. (1998) to make the *team*, the unit of analysis. The current study used the "team" version by Jarvenpaa et al. (1998) but adapted the response scale to obtain consistency with the other measurements in the investigation using a measure of agreement ranging from 1 (strongly disagree) to 5 (strongly agree). The trustworthiness scale has previously demonstrated adequate reliability estimates (Cronbach alpha = 0.92; Jarvenpaa et al., 1998), and this was supported in the present study (see Table 4).

Outcomes

Five leadership outcomes were measured in the present research. They were satisfaction, effectiveness, morale, productivity and extra effort. The first four of these were measured by a single item each and were included in both versions of the survey. The fifth outcome, extra effort, was included as part of the MLQ measure in Questionnaire 2 and was assessed using three items.

Demographics

A selection of demographic items was placed in the front and back section of each questionnaire. These items requested data about work unit: function, size, gender distribution, main sector type (public/private), industry, and the length of time the work unit had been working together. The respondents' own organizational level, gender, age, and ethnicity were also considered.

RESULTS

Response Rate

Owing to the relatively low response rate of 19%, cross-tabulations of early (within the first 2 weeks), medium (2–3 weeks), and late (after 3 weeks) responses against all demographic characteristics were performed. Identification of systematic response trends may indicate a non-response bias. This type of analysis is based on the premise that very late respondents in the research sample are the most akin to those that do not respond at all (Moser & Kalton, 1971).

No significant demographic differences were found between early and late response distributions of gender, age, ethnicity, and industry-type distributions; nor did there appear to be any significant differences in ratings on any of the new or previously validated measures of the early and late responses. These results suggest a low probability of response bias (Moser & Kalton, 1971).

Non-response is probably a function of high workload, the time of year (coming up to Christmas), and questionnaire burnout (the population had another questionnaire distributed to them shortly before this one). It is probably not an issue of any systematic problem with questionnaire content. Testing for non-response bias seems to bear this out.

Initial Factor Analysis

The scale under investigation was first subjected to exploratory factor analysis using principal components with promax rotation. Promax is an oblique rotation, which assumes correlated factors. In view of the conceptual similarity of the SPL constructs, correlated factors were assumed. Factors were extracted if eigenvalues were greater than 1. From this analysis, there appeared to be a very strong single factor with an eigenvalue six times larger than the second factor. Five factors in total were identified initially.

Further analysis demonstrated a distinct group of reverse-coded items with poor item-to-total correlations. Four of these demonstrated item-to-total correlations < 0.4, and were therefore withdrawn from further analyses.

Subsequent factor-analyses, constraining factor solutions to one, two, three or four factors, demonstrated that although the remaining reverse-coded items were designed to span all four components of the scale, they consistently factored together rather than loading on to the predicted factors. These results suggest that the clustering of the reverse-scored items was more a function of wording or possible systematic response bias (Jackson, Wall, Martin, & Davids, 1993), rather than a replicable factor of the social process of leadership. For this reason, all nine reverse-scored items were withdrawn from further analyses. Accordingly, four factors remained after EFA.

Exploratory and Confirmatory Factor Analyses
In order to determine the *optimal* model solution, a comparative analysis of competing models was necessary. Therefore, further exploratory factor analyses using the remaining 36 items of the scale derived factor solutions of one, two, three, or four factors, which were assessed using confirmatory factor analysis (CFA). Confirmatory factor analyses used the AMOS 4 Structural Equation Modeling procedure (Arbuckle & Wothke, 1999) in SPSS 10. Five measures of goodness of fit were used. These measures were the Goodness of Fit Index (GFI) (Jöreskog & Sörbom, 1984; Tanaka & Huba, 1985), the Adjusted Goodness of Fit Index (AGFI), which takes into account the degrees of freedom available for testing the model, the Normed Fit Index (NFI) (Bentler-Bonnet, 1980), the Tucker-Lewis coefficient (TLI) (Bentler-Bonnet, 1980), and the Comparative Fit Index (CFI) (Bentler, 1990). In all of these, 1 indicates a perfect fit, and values over 0.9 are generally thought to indicate a very good fit (Arbuckle & Wothke, 1999). The Root Mean Square Residual (RMR), and Root Mean Square Error of Approximation (RMSEA) (Browne & Cudeck, 1993) were also measured. Like Chi-square, these latter indices measure how badly the proposed model fits the data; thus, the lower the value, the better the fit. For both RMR and RMSEA, 0.0 indicates a perfect fit, but models that score 0.8 or less on RMSEA are also usually thought to indicate a reasonable fit (Browne & Cudeck, 1993).

When a one-factor solution was imposed on all 36 remaining items, all items loaded more than 0.30 on to that one factor. However, this solution provided a poor fit to the data, with an AGFI of 0.78 (Table 2). A two-factor solution provided 33 items loading adequately on to the two factors. The AGFI of 0.82 indicated a better, but still inadequate, fit. Three- and four-factor solutions indicated that 28 items would fit adequately but with AGFI scores of only 0.86 and 0.88, respectively. This pattern of results demonstrated that the four-factor model provided the best fit for the data. However, some of the goodness-of-fit indices were lower than optimal (<0.9), suggesting that a better model could be developed. Although there are guidelines when interpreting fit indices, there are no absolutes, and therefore small deviations of fit values across models may be difficult to interpret accurately. For example, although guidelines of 0.9 or larger are used for goodness-of-fit measures, Cuttance (1987) suggests that models with an AGFI greater than 0.8 are acceptable. Therefore, the collection of eight fit indices was expected to produce a more easily interpretable result.

Correlation matrices within each of the four factors were constructed in order to investigate how each item contributed to their explanatory factor. From this analysis, seven items were eliminated because of low correlations with their indicative factor. A final four-factor solution of the remaining 21 items was submitted to confirmatory factor analysis producing fit indices well within suggested limits (see Table 2). The factor loadings of this optimum four-factor solution are provided in Table 1. The four lower-order processes are:

(1) active management processes;
(2) team goal alignment;
(3) resolving uncertainty to change; and
(4) reciprocity/interdependence.

To the extent that the first of the four factors presented a very strong first factor with eigenvalue six times greater than that of the second factor, a one-factor solution was possible. Theoretically, it is also plausible that the single dimension of effective social processes of leadership overrides the distinction between lower-order constructs of the SPL. However, the remaining 21 items, when subjected to a confirmatory factor analysis, provided an AGFI of only 0.84, indicating a weak fit. Therefore, a one-factor solution was possible, but less persuasive than a four-factor solution.

The originally proposed factor solution was a four-factor model consisting of 36 items that represented the constructs of optimizing, enhancing adaptability, resolving uncertainty, and promulgating vision. This proposed model was also tested but provided a poor fit to the data with an AGFI of only 0.80 (see Table 2). In other words, four factors emerged from the data analysis but not the same four that the grounded theory research proposed.

Within the context of confirmatory factor analysis, chi-square values are difficult to interpret, as significant results are likely when assessing large sample data (Kline, 1998). However, unlike all of the other fit indices, chi-square values may be used to determine the significance of the difference between competing models (Spittal, Siegert, McClure & Walkey, 2001), and therefore provide useful information for analysis. The observed differences between all models were found to be significant at the 0.05 level.

Table 1. Principal-components Factor Loadings on to Four Factors (Final 21 Items) Using Promax Rotation.

"People in my work unit . . ." [1]	Factors (Lower-order Processes)			
	1 Active Management Processes	2 Team Goal Alignment	3 Resolving Uncertainty to Change	4 Reciprocity/ Inter- dependence
Effectively plan for workload variation	0.96			
Take responsibility to educate selves	0.78			
Display perception of own leadership role	0.76			
Attempt to move work unit forward	0.74			
Display sound management practice	0.63			
Prioritize own work tasks	0.43			
Facilitate flow of information	0.34			
Distribute tasks and responsibilities	0.30			
Take advantage of opportunities		0.87		
Persist in efforts		0.85		
Co-operate to get things done		0.83		
Share information		0.65		
Try to provide rational explanations		0.52		
Display personal values that complement those of the organization		0.41		
Have face-to-face discussions			0.90	
Discuss where the organization is heading			0.89	
Resolve uncertainty of others			0.62	
Resolve personal uncertainty			0.62	
Rely on each other for information				0..98
Rely on each other for support				0.76
Motivate each other to work hard				0.70
Eigenvalues	8.70	1.31	1.02	1.01
Variance explained %	41.41	6.26	4.87	4.75
Cumulative Variance explained %	41.41	47.67	52.54	57.29

[1] Individual items have been abbreviated.

As Table 2 demonstrates, the fit indices generally become more favorable as the number of factors in the model are increased, and the total number of items-

Table 2. Eight Structural Equation Modeling Indices of Fit for Seven Alternate Model Factor Structures for the Social Process of Leadership (SPL) Scale.

Index	Number of Factors in Model						
	1 Factor 36 Items	2 Factors 33 Items	3 Factors 28 Items	4 Factors 28 Items	4 Factors Final 21 Items	1 Factor Final 21 Items	Proposed Model – 4 Factors 36 Items
Chi-square	2551.55	1877.75	1245.28	1028.90	591.02	997.69	2346.19
df	594	494	347	318	183	189	588
p	0.00	0.00	0.00	0.00	0.00	0.00	0.00
GFI	0.80	0.85	0.88	0.90	0.92	0.87	0.83
AGFI	0.78	0.82	0.86	0.88	0.90	0.84	0.80
CFI	0.85	0.88	0.90	0.92	0.94	0.89	0.86
NFI	0.81	0.84	0.87	0.89	0.92	0.86	0.83
TLI	0.84	0.87	0.90	0.91	0.93	0.87	0.85
RMSEA	0.07	0.06	0.06	0.06	0.06	0.08	0.07
RMR	0.04	0.04	0.03	0.03	0.03	0.04	0.04
Cronbach alpha range	0.96	0.87–0.94	0.84–0.91	0.78–0.89	0.75–0.89	0.90	0.81–0.90

Table 3. Correlation Matrix Between Total SPL Measure and Four
Sub-processes (21 items).

	Total	1	2	3	4
Total 21 items SPL measure	(0.94)				
1. Active management processes	0.93	(0.89)			
2. Team goal alignment	0.89	0.75	(0.83)		
3. Resolving uncertainty	0.81	0.65	0.65	(0.80)	
4. Reciprocity	0.81	0.67	0.67	0.58	(0.75)
Mean	2.82	2.86	2.94	2.69	2.65
SD	0.57	0.64	0.57	0.72	0.78

Note: Figures in parenthesis are Cronbach alphas.

included in the analysis are decreased, such that the four-factor solution
provides the best fit. The method of exploratory factor analysis followed by
item trimming and then confirmatory factor analysis automatically ensures
increasing fit as more factors are added to the model. In other words, as items
are withdrawn, the variance decreases, and with each additional factor added to
the model, a greater percentage of the variance is explained.

Each of the four factors (21 items) demonstrates adequate internal
consistency, with the lowest alpha coefficient of 0.75 (see Table 3). Correlation
patterns with established measures are given in Tables 4 and 5. As is shown, the
total SPL scale and the four lower-order processes correlated positively with all
other leadership scales except management-by-exception-passive. This result
was as expected since each of the constructs other than management-by-
exception-passive have previously been related to effective leadership. These
results suggest the convergent validity of the SPL.

Discriminant validity was also supported. Correlations between SPL
constructs and established measures were positive and significant, as expected,
they did not exceed $r = 0.77$, suggesting differing underlying constructs. Higher
correlations with transformational leadership (0.78 and 0.86), especially with
Podsakoff et al.'s (1990) measure, indicate that transformational leadership and
the SPL may be the same underlying construct.

DISCUSSION AND CONCLUSIONS

The grounded theory-derived SPL work carried out in recent years has
been validated. Consequently, one could advocate that the present work

Table 4. Correlation Matrix of SPL Factors and Established Measures in Questionnaire 2.

	1	2	3	4	5	6	7	8	9	10
1. Humor	(0.87)									
2. Constructive transaction	0.41	(0.79)								
3. Transformational l-ship (Bass & Avolio)	0.38	0.70	(0.86)							
4. Corrective-avoidant transactional l-ship	−0.12*	−0.34	−0.46	(0.76)						
5. Sportsmanship	0.22	0.44	0.57	−0.57	(0.86)					
6. Civic virtue	0.20	0.40	0.45	−0.40	0.37	(0.69)				
7. Altruism	0.44	0.60	0.57	−0.39	0.48	0.51	(0.82)			
8. Task cohesion	0.34	0.50	0.59	−0.53	0.66	0.40	0.60	(0.75)		
9. Social cohesion	0.28	0.37	0.42	−0.37	0.36	0.33	0.45	0.40	(0.82)	
10. Trustworthiness	0.30	0.54	0.61	−0.57	0.65	0.43	0.65	0.71	0.42	(0.88)
11. Active management processes	0.39	0.67	0.72	−0.49	0.54	0.45	0.62	0.60	0.41	0.67
12. Team/goal alignment	0.42	0.63	0.69	−0.44	0.53	0.44	0.65	0.66	0.44	0.67
13. Resolving uncertainty to change	0.31	0.56	0.62	−0.34	0.38	0.34	0.46	0.44	0.36	0.47
14. Reciprocity/interdependence	0.41	0.67	0.64	−0.39	0.45	0.39	0.59	0.53	0.45	0.57
15. 21-item SPL	0.44	0.73	0.78	−0.49	0.56	0.47	0.68	0.65	0.48	0.70

Notes: Figures on the diagonals represent Cronbach alphas. All correlations are significant at the 0.01 level, except for *, which is significant at the 0.05 level (two-tailed).

Table 5. Correlation Matrix of SPL Factors and Established Measures in Questionnaire 1.

	1	2	3	4	5	6	7	8	9	10	11
1. Transformational l-ship (Podsakoff)	(0.94)										
2. Articulates vision	0.91	(0.90)									
3. Provide appropriate model	0.89	0.66	(0.91)								
4. Fosters acceptance goals	0.90	0.69	0.84	(0.87)							
5. Support for innovation	0.53	0.48	0.46	0.49	(0.85)						
6. Resource supply	0.47	0.41	0.44	0.44	0.69	(0.79)					
7. Conscientiousness	0.52	0.40	0.52	0.53	0.41	0.39	(0.83)				
8. Courtesy	0.56	0.44	0.54	0.58	0.45	0.43	0.67	(0.86)			
9. Communication and co-operation	0.59	0.47	0.56	0.62	0.45	0.39	0.52	0.54	(0.78)		
10. Workload sharing	0.52	0.43	0.50	0.53	0.31	0.30	0.54	0.45	0.52	(0.75)	
11. Social support	0.55	0.44	0.53	0.55	0.45	0.40	0.48	0.51	0.57	0.48	(0.74)
12. Active management processes	0.82	0.70	0.76	0.78	0.42	0.42	0.53	0.56	0.58	0.55	0.55
13. Team/goal alignment	0.77	0.66	0.72	0.72	0.48	0.44	0.49	0.51	0.59	0.48	0.56
14. Resolving uncertainty to change	0.65	0.64	0.53	0.56	0.45	0.41	0.37	0.42	0.48	0.35	0.48
15. Reciprocity/interdependence	0.70	0.66	0.60	0.63	0.34	0.27	0.44	0.50	0.50	0.42	0.51
16. 21-item SPL scale	0.86	0.77	0.77	0.79	0.50	0.46	0.54	0.58	0.63	0.54	0.61

Notes: Figures on the diagonals represent Cronbach alphas. All correlations are significant at the 0.01 level (two-tailed).

has supported the ongoing use of the grounded theory method as an important source of insight into leadership phenomena in organizations and elsewhere.

Second, not only have I concluded validation of the work that has been done, but I can support the reliability of the findings from that work. I can conclude this because the four factors tested were the four factors confirmed, albeit not the same four. I acknowledge that the factor structure that has been confirmed does not fit exactly to the GT-derived SPL factor structure that was being tested. However, one must remember that because there is a high conceptual overlap between the four GT-derived SPLs, one would expect some overlap between the four confirmed factors. Such overlap does exist, both conceptually and statistically. Indeed, no new constructs have emerged from the confirmatory work, and no existing constructs disappeared during the confirmatory work. For example, the active management of one's human and other resources is an important characteristic of "optimizing". This active management was confirmed as an independent factor, and the other components of optimizing were found to be a part of "team goal alignment" and "resolving uncertainty". Therefore, I may conclude that the GT-derived SPLs have been validated and confirmed.

It would appear that there is one overarching construct associated with the social processes of leadership, as well as one subsidiary layer of abstraction associated with that overarching construct. The presence of the one overarching construct of social processes of leadership is supported via exploratory factor analysis, confirmatory analysis, and theoretically. The one overarching construct is difficult to make sense of, other than to say that the social process of leadership is a phenomenon in its own right. However, it is refreshing to see that there is support for the one construct of the "social process of leadership". Such support hitherto has come only from theoretical argument, and not from empirical investigation. The second layer of abstraction is useful in terms of the sense-making associated with the macro-level challenges of leadership. For example, managers may make sense of their leadership role by appreciating the imperative of actively managing resources as the basis of any further leadership initiative. As another example, managers may make sense of the leadership role they must fulfill in resolving the uncertainty that followers and colleagues experience as a result of the turbulence and uncertainty of change.

Transformational leadership (whether Podsakoff's or Bass & Avolio's) may well be an existing measure of the construct of the social process of leadership. However, the links are stronger with active management and team goal alignment than with resolving uncertainty and reciprocity. Therefore, while transformational leadership will explain much of the social processes of leadership that go on in "work units", there may be other processes taking place that are not explained by transformational leadership. Remember that the present research did *not* come from the transformational leadership genre. It came from purely qualitative phenomenological research. Yet, transformational leadership is the best *existing* construct to measure and operationalize it, as demonstrated by the tests for the convergent validity of the SPL constructs.

Finally, this research has found some support for the augmentation effect of leadership over management. Inasmuch as the "active management" of one's resources was found herein to be the major factor associated with the social processes of leadership, the present research lends support to Seltzer and Bass (1990) and Waldman, Bass and Yammarino's (1990) augmentation effect. This finding was not tested. Rather, it emerged from the factor structure, which separated "active management processes" from the other constructs of the social process of leadership.

Future Research Directions

Leadership researchers must continue to undertake social process investigations of leadership, as advocated by Conger (1998) and Parry (1998). The data gathering for such research can and must put the full range of qualitative and quantitative data into the analysis. One's analysis need not use the full grounded theory method, but this method is probably the most rigorous qualitative method of analysis, and the most likely to generate explanatory theory. This theory will be valuable in its own right. It will need also to be tested quantitatively, as was done here, and compared with existing findings both conceptually and empirically. This iterative process must proceed at least until the theoretical workings of the social process(es) of leadership are saturated conceptually. Last, and most importantly, future grounded theory leadership research should concurrently analyze qualitative data (gathered via interview, observation, and participation) and data gathered with the use of the MLQ, MLQT, and ODQ. In this way, researchers will gain the best insight into how transformational and charismatic leadership, as measured by these instruments, operates in conjunction with the social processes of leadership that are present in organizations.

ACKNOWLEDGMENTS

The author would like to acknowledge the support of Sarah Proctor-Thomson, Research Assistant with the Centre for the Study of Leadership. The research reported in this chapter was funded by the New Zealand College of Management.

REFERENCES

Arbuckle, J. L., & Wothke, W. (1999). *AMOS 4.0 User's Guide*. Chicago, IL: SmallWaters Corporation.

Avolio, B. J. (1996). What's all the karping about down under? Transforming Australia's leadership systems for the 21st century. In: K. Parry (Ed.), *Leadership research and practice; Emerging themes and new challenges* (pp. 3–16). Melbourne: Pitman Publishing.

Avolio, B. J., Bass, B. M., & Jung, D. I. (1999). Re-examining the components of transformational and transactional leadership using the multifactor leadership questionnaire. *Journal of Occupational and Organizational Psychology, 72*, 441–462.

Avolio, B. J., Howell, J. M., & Sosik, J. J. (1999). A funny thing happened on the way to the bottom line: Humor as a moderator of leadership style effects. *Academy of Management Journal, 42*(2), 219–227.

Barsoux, J. L. (1996). Why organizations need humor. *European Management Journal, 14*(5), 500–509.

Bass, B. M. (1985). *Leadership and performance beyond expectations*. New York: Free Press.

Bass, B. M. (1998). *Transformational leadership; Industry, military, and educational impact*. Mahwah, NJ: Lawrence Erlbaum Associates.

Bass, B. M., & Avolio, B. J. (1993). Transformational leadership: A response to the critics. In: M. M. Chemers & R. Ayman (Eds), *Leadership theory and research: Perspectives and directions*. Sydney: Academic Press.

Bass, B. M., Cascio, W. F., & O'Connor, E. J. (1974). Magnitude estimations of expressions of frequency and amount. *Journal of Applied Psychology, 59*(3), 313–320.

Bateman, T. S., & Organ, D. W. (1983). Job satisfaction and the good soldier: The relationship between affect and employee 'citizenship'. *Academy of Management Journal, 26*, 587–595.

Bennis, W., & Nanus, B. (1985). *Leaders; The strategies for taking charge*. New York: Harper & Row.

Bentler, P. M. (1990). Comparative fit indexes in structural models. *Psychological Bulletin, 107*, 238–246.

Bentler, P. M., & Bonnet, D. G. (1980). Significance tests and the goodness of fit in the analysis of covariance structures. *Psychological Bulletin, 88*, 588–606.

Boyd, N. G., & Taylor, R. R. (1998). A developmental approach to the examination of friendship in leader-follower relationships. *Leadership Quarterly, 9*(1), 1–25.

Browne, M. W., & Cudeck, R. (1993). Alternative ways of assessing model fit. In: Bollen, K. A. & Long J. S. (Eds), *Testing structural equation models* (pp. 36–162). Newbury Park, CA: Sage.

Bryman, A. (1992). *Charisma and leadership in organizations*. London: Sage.

Burns, J. M. (1978). *Leadership*. New York: Harper Torchbooks.

Bycio, P., Hackett, R. D., & Allen, J. S. (1995). Further assessments of Bass's (1985) conceptualization of transactional and transformational leadership. *Journal of Applied Psychology, 80*, 468–478.

Cabana, S. (1996). Leadership for turbulent times. *Journal for Quality & Participation, 19*(2), 76–79.

Campion, M. A., Medsker, G. J., & Higgs, A. C. (1993). Relations between work group characteristics and effectiveness: Implications for designing effective work groups. *Personnel Psychology, 46*, 823–850.

Carless, S. A., & DePaola. C. (2000). The measurement of cohesion in work teams. *Small Group Research, 31*(1), 71–88.

Carless, S. A., Mann, L., & Wearing, A. J. (1998). Leadership, managerial performance and 360-degree feedback. *Journal of Applied Psychology: An International Review, 47*, 481–496.

Cartwright, J. A., & Zander, A. (1968). *Group dynamics: Research and theory* (3rd ed.). New York: Harper Row.

Chia, Y. M. (1998). Motivation and junior supervisors' performance: The moderating role of work-group cohesion. *International Journal of Management, 15*(4), 441–453.

Conger, J. (1992). *Learning to lead: The art of transforming managers into leaders.* San Francisco: Jossey-Bass.

Conger, J. A. (1998). Qualitative research as the cornerstone methodology for understanding leadership. *Leadership Quarterly, 9*(1), 107–121.

Crawford, C. B. (1994). Theory and implications regarding the utilization of strategic humor by leaders. *Journal of Leadership Studies, 1*, 53–67.

Cuttance, P. (1987). Issues and problems in the application of structural equation models. In: P. Cuttance & R. Ecobs (Eds), *Structural modeling by example: Applications in educational, sociological and behavioral research* (pp. 241–279). Cambridge: Cambridge University Press.

den Hartog, D. N., Van Muijen, J. J., & Koopman, P. L. (1997). Transactional vs. transformational leadership: an analysis of the MLQ. *Journal of Occupational and Organizational Psychology, 70*(1), 19.

Dubinsky, A. J., Yammarino, F. J., & Jolson, M. A. (1995). An examination of linkages between personality characteristics and dimensions of transformational leadership. *Journal of Business and Psychology, 9*, 315–335.

Duncan, W. J. (1982). Humour in management: prospects for administrative practice and research. *Academy of Management Review, 7*, 136:278.

Duncan, W. J., & Feisal, J. P. (1989). No Laughing matter: Patterns of humor in the workplace. *Organizational Dynamics, 17*(4), 18–30.

Duncan, W. J., Smeltzer, L. R., & Leap, T. L. (1990). Humor and work: Applications of joking behavior to management. *Journal of Management, 16*(2), 255, 279.

Evans, C. R., & Dion, K. L. (1991). Group cohesion and performance: A meta-analysis. *Small Group Research, 22*, 175–186.

George, J. M. (1990). Personality, affect, and behavior in groups. *Journal of Applied Psychology, 75*, 107–116.

George J. M., & Brief, A. P. (1992). Feeling good-doing good: A conceptual analysis of the mood at work-organizational spontaneity relationship. *Psychological Bulletin, 112*, 310–329.

Glaser, B. (1978). *Theoretical sensitivity.* Mill Valley, CA: Sociology Press.

Glaser, B. (1992). *Emergence vs. forcing: Basics of grounded theory analysis.* Mill Valley, CA: Sociology Press.

Glaser, B., & Strauss, A. (1967). *The discovery of grounded theory.* Chicago: Aldine Press.

Gruner, C. R. (1997). *The game of humor: A comprehensive theory of why we laugh.* New Brunswick, NJ: Transaction.

Harchar, R. L., & Hyle, A. E. (1996). Collaborative power: A grounded theory of administrative educational leadership in the elementary school. *Journal of Educational Administration, 34*(3), 1–29.

Harrison, D. A., Price, K. H., & Bell, M. P. (1998). Beyond relational demography: Time and the effects of surface- and deep-level diversity on work group cohesion. *Academy of Management Journal, 41*(1), 96–107.

Hinkin, T. R. (1995). A review of scale development practices in the study of organizations. *Journal of Management, 21,* 967–988.

Idaszak, J. R., & Grasgow, F. (1987). A revision of the Job Diagnostic Survey: Elimination of a measurement artefact. *Journal of Applied Psychology, 64,* 349–371.

Irurita, V. F. (1992). Transforming mediocrity to excellence: A challenge for nurse leaders. *The Australian Journal of Advanced Learning, 9*(4), 15–25.

Irurita, V. F. (1994). Optimism, values, and commitment as forces in leadership. *Journal of Nursing Administration, 24*(9), 61–71.

Irurita, V. F. (1996). Optimizing: A leadership process for transforming mediocrity to excellence. In: K. Parry (Ed.), *Leadership research and practice; Emerging themes and new challenges.* Melbourne: Pitman Publishing.

Jackson, P. R., Wall, T. D., Martin, R., & Davids, K. (1993). New measures of job control, cognitive demand, and production responsibility. *Journal of Applied Psychology, 78,* 753–762.

Jarvenpaa, S. L., Knoll, K., & Leidner, D. E. (1998). Is anybody out there? Antecedents of trust in global virtual teams. *Journal of Management Information Systems, 14*(4), 29–64.

Jöreskog, K. G., & Sörbom, D. (1984). *LISREL-VI User's Guide* (3rd ed.). Mooresville, IN: Scientific Software.

Kent, T., Johnson, J. A., & Graber, D. R. (1996). Leadership in the formation of new health care environments. *Health Care Supervisor, 15*(2), 27–34.

Kline, P. (1998). *The new psychometrics: Science, psychology, and measurement.* London: Routledge.

Kramer, R. M., Brewer, M. B., & Hanna, B. A. (1996). Collective trust and collective action: The decision to trust as a social decision. In: R. M. Kramer & T. R. Tyler (Eds), *Trust in organizations: Frontiers of theory and research* (pp. 357–389). Thousand Oaks, CA: Sage.

Langfred, C., & Shanley, M. (1997). The importance of organizational context, I: A conceptual model of cohesiveness and effectiveness in work groups. *Public Administration Quarterly,* (Fall), 349–369.

Lissitz, R. W., & Green, S. B. (1975). Effect of the number of scale points on reliability: A Monte Carlo approach. *Journal of Applied Psychology, 60,* 10–13.

Lowe, K. B., Kroeck, K. G., & Sivasubramaniam, N. (1996). Effectiveness correlates of transformational and transactional leadership: A meta-analytic review of the MLQ literature. *Leadership Quarterly, 7*(3), 385–425.

Moser, K., & Kalton, G. (1971). *Survey methods in social investigation.* London: Heinemann Educational Books.

Mullen, B., & Cooper, C. (1994). The relation between group cohesiveness and performance: An integration. *Psychological Bulletin, 115,* 210–227.

Munroe, K., Estabrooks, P., Dennis, P., & Carron, A. (1999). A phenomenological analysis of group norms in sports teams. *The Sports Psychologist, 13,* 171–182.

Nanus, B. (1992). *Visionary leadership.* San Francisco: Jossey-Bass.

Nicholls, J. (1993). Rescuing leadership from Humpty Dumpty. *International Review of Strategic Management, 4,* 127–140.

Nunnally, J. C. (1978). *Psychometric theory* (2nd ed.). New York: McGraw-Hill Book Company

O'Bannon, D. P., & Pearce, C. L. (1999). An exploratory examination of gain sharing in service organizations: Implications for organizational citizenship behavior and pay satisfaction. *Journal of Managerial Issues, 11*(3), 363–378.

Organ, D. W. (1988). *Organizational citizenship behavior; The good soldier syndrome.* Toronto: Lexington.

Organ, D. W., & Ryan, K. (1995). A meta-analytic review of attitudinal and dispositional predictors of organizational citizenship behavior. *Personnel Psychology, 48,* 775–802.

Parry, K. W. (1998). Grounded theory and social process: A new direction for leadership research. *The Leadership Quarterly, 9*(1), Spring, 85–105.

Parry, K. (1999). Enhancing adaptability: Leadership strategies to accommodate change in local government settings. *Journal of Organizational Change Management, 12*(2), 134–156.

Pearce, J. L., Branyiczki, I., & Bakacsi, G. (1994). Person-based reward systems: A theory of organizational reward practices in reform-communist organizations. *Journal of Organizational Behavior, 15,* 261–282.

Podsakoff, P. M., MacKenzie, S. B., Moorman, R. H., & Fetter, R. (1990). Transformational leader behaviors and their effects on followers' trust in leader, satisfaction, and organizational citizenship behaviors. *Leadership Quarterly, 1*(2), 107–142.

Proctor, S. B., & Parry, K. W. (1999). Social Processes of Leadership (SPL) Scale: The development of an instrument to identify the presence of social processes in organizations. Monograph of the Centre for the Study of Leadership. Wellington: Victoria University, p. 28.

Rowsell, K., & Tony, B. (1993). Leadership, vision, values and systemic wisdom. *Leadership and Organization Development Journal, 14*(7), 18–22.

Ruigrok, W., Pettigrew, A., Peck, S., & Whittington, R. (1999). Corporate restructuring and new forms of organizing: Evidence from Europe. *Management International Review, 39*(2), 41–64.

Scott, S. G., & Bruce, R. A. (1994). Determinants of innovative behavior: A path model of individual innovation in the workplace. *Academy of Management Journal, 37*(3), 580–607.

Seltzer, J., & Bass, B. M. (1990). Transformational leadership: beyond initiation and consideration. *Journal of Management, 16*(4), 693–703.

Simons, T. L. (1999). Behavioral integrity as a critical ingredient for transformational leadership. *Journal of Organizational Change Management, 12*(2), 89–104.

Smith, C. A., Organ, D. W., & Near, J. P. (1983). Organizational citizenship behavior: Its nature and antecedents. *Journal of Applied Psychology, 68,* 653–663.

Spittal, M. J., Siegert, R. J., McClure, J. L., & Walkey, F. H. (2001). The spheres of control scale: The identification of a clear replicable three-factor structure. *Personality and Individual Differences,* in press.

Strauss, A. L. (1987). *Qualitative data analysis for social scientists.* Cambridge: Cambridge University Press.

Strauss, A. L., & Corbin, J. (1990). *Basics of qualitative research: Grounded theory procedures and techniques.* Newbury Park, CA: Sage Publications.

Tanaka, J. S., & Huba, G. J. (1985). A fit index for covariance structure models under arbitrary GLS estimation. *British Journal of Mathematical and Statistical Psychology, 38,* 197–201.

Tepper, B. T., & Percy, P. M. (1994). Structural validity of the Multifactor Leadership Questionnaire. *Educational and Psychological Measurement, 54*, 734–744.

Tracey, J. B., & Hinkin, T. R. (1998). Transformational leadership or effective managerial practices? *Group and Organization Management, 23*(3), 220.

Tracey, J. B., & Hinkin, T. R. (1999). The relevance of charisma for transformational leadership in stable organizations. *Organizational Change Management, 12*(2), 105.

Vinton, K. L. (1989). Humor in the workplace; It is more than telling jokes. *Small Group Behavior, 20*(2), 151–166.

Waldman, D. A., Bass, B. M., & Yammarino, F. J. (1990). Adding to contingent reward behavior: The augmenting effect of charismatic leadership. *Group and Organization Studies, 15*, 382–395.

Waldman, D. A., Ramirez, G. G., House, R. J., & Puranam, P. (2001). Does leadership matter? CEO leadership attributes and profitability under conditions of perceived environmental uncertainty. *Academy of Management Journal, 44*(1), 134–143.

Yammarino, F. J., & Dubinsky, A. J. (1994). Transformational leadership theory: Using levels of analysis to determine boundary conditions. *Personnel Psychology, 47*, 787–811.

PART V:
THE ROAD AHEAD

FORECASTING ORGANIZATIONAL LEADERSHIP: FROM BACK (1967) TO THE FUTURE (2034)

Bernard M. Bass

ABSTRACT

During the first week of May 1967, I addressed a conference of the American Management Association in Hamilton, New York on the subject of management, leadership, and organizations in the year 2000. I was right about some things to come such as that in 2000, organizations would be more nimble and that I would be 33 years older. After reviewing the accuracy of my predictions in 1967, I will forecast what organizations and leadership will be like 33 years from now in the year 2034, but one of the folks younger than me will have to check the accuracy of the forecast.

FLEXIBLE ORGANIZATIONS

I stated in 1967 that in the year 2000, "organizations will be more flexible. Developments will continue in the understanding and skill with which we apply ourselves to the dynamics of organization change. The flexible organization will be the rule rather than the exception, and we will see more attention to both short- and long-range efforts by management to gear itself to a world of fairly continuous change. Likely to be common in the year 2000 are internal feedback mechanisms and training programs of various types that lead people to be flexible, to be ready for change, and to be helpful in changing a process."

Transformational and Charismatic Leadership, Volume 2, pages 375–384.
© 2002 Published by Elsevier Science Ltd.
ISBN: 0-7623-0962-8

Importance of Challenging Work

I was right about another trend that looked possible in 1967, which was seen to be inherent in the new approach to motivation – new in the sense that only in the 1950s and 1960s had sensory deprivation studies experiments suggested that important basic human drives included curiosity and information seeking.

The inability of individuals to tolerate a complete lack of stimulation in the environment around them paralleled the then current interest in making jobs more challenging. In 1967, I saw an increasing tendency for management to try to make jobs and careers more challenging and stimulating.

None the less, like other commentators at the time, I foresaw correctly that more of both sorts of new jobs – stimulating and boring – would appear as we become more automated. The trend would be toward both more simple jobs and more complex jobs with fewer in-between in complexity. In manufacturing in the year 2000, blue-collar employees would now be tending, adjusting, and monitoring automated equipment instead of carrying out "hands on" work on the line.

On-line Computers

In 1967, I was right in stating that, "the on-line computing possibilities that are becoming available to management lead directly to dialogues between management and the computer". (The computer I had in mind was a centralized giant, not a yet-to-be invented desktop PC.) "This already has begun; and, in the forthcoming years, we expect that the behavioral scientist will be able to provide further input which will make these dialogues between the manager and the computer more meaningful. Furthermore, the speed with which communications flow into top management will be greatly increased. The executive will have the problems of coping with these speeded-up communications, of deciding when it is appropriate to simplify matters with a computer, when it is appropriate to try to deal with things himself, and how to avoid information overload."

"As managers attempt to simulate the environment, one of the big issues will be how much weight to give the computer in the total decision process. Are managers to relegate the problem to the computer, or are they to make their decisions primarily on the basis of the weight they attach to the computer simulation and the assumptions that go into it? Are their own personalities going to be a determining factor in these interactions? The question of how much computer and how much human judgment there is to be in higher-level decision processes should be an interesting one for at least the next 33 years." At the time of writing, the questions still are not resolved.

Management Education

In 1967, I indicated that "a world of 100 million managers has been envisaged by experts in international labor organizations – and why not? If you anticipate a world of six to seven billion people, you must figure on needing a proportionate number of people to manage them. So it is rather obvious that we will need to package education techniques in a way that we are not doing now. The teacher plus 20 students in a classroom, or one teacher and one student at the opposite ends of a log, are clear impossibilities in terms of future volume and demand. No matter what we think about packaged techniques, in order for even a small number of these 100 million managers to have an opportunity for managerial education, there will have to be great increases in programmed instruction, in television and videotape innovations, in the use of small-group exercises of various types, in self-study techniques, in the simulation of workers and organizations, and in the effective confrontation of managers with situations and environments." However, I did not foresee interactive distance learning via the internet, nor corporate universities.

Sensitivity Training

In 1967, I suggested that, by 2000, sensitivity training was likely to become a lot more proficient. "In comparing some of my own experiences with this technique, during the past decade (1957 to 1967), I am struck by what appear to be considerable increases in the efficiency with which it is conducted. Of course, the biggest problem that we still face is that of transferring the effects of sensitivity training from the laboratory to actual practice in the organization itself. Generally speaking, our success to date has been relatively low in this respect. It is to be expected that we will learn how to be more successful in the years to come." In 2000, much of this has come to pass, but we now call it team building.

The Manager as Knowledge Worker

In 1967, I noted that, "Management is becoming increasingly an intellectual process featuring rational planning, mathematization of decision making and systematic problem solving. The manager processes information as blue-collar employees process materials. He is a knowledge worker. His interest is likely to grow in the psychology of problem solving and decision-making. In the future, I expect an accentuation of these trends."

"Intellectual processes will be of greater importance to future managers than to their present-day counterparts; they will spend more time on intellectual activities. The managerial job will have many more intellectual and educational requirements. It will involve more technical, scientific and engineering problems, as well as more complex budgeting and financial planning. Managers will function in a world where their performance will be evaluated even more than it is today on their intellectual skills in bringing about increases in rate of growth, in quality of services and output."

"If the prognosticators are right, upper-level managers will be involved in fewer day-to-day decisions – decisions that can be programmed for the computer. As a result, they will be less involved in 'fire fighting'; rather, they will be more able and more willing to take intellectual, generalized views of the business environment with which they must deal. At the same time, they will face increasingly intricate technologies, organizational forms, and marketing phenomena again which places a premium on intellectual prowess."

Increased Focus on Behavioral and Social Sciences
In 1967, I noted that "like many other graduate business schools, the Graduate School of Business at the University of Pittsburgh has opted to make a heavy investment of student time in study of the behavioral sciences. The investment seems to be paying off. In a follow-up survey of MBA graduates of the 1961–1966 classes, respondents singled out courses in the behavioral sciences as among the most valuable to them on the job. Probably the most obvious and most general kind of statement that can be made safely is that managers are going to be big users of whatever behavioral sciences happen to be around in the year 2000."

"The manager in the year 2000 will be seeking out information about different kinds of people, about different cultures, about different styles of living. This will be even more important for the manager than it is today in the sense that the world of the future will contain within it more managers who are pursuing – or attempting to pursue – democratic and participative rather than authoritarian methods. They will have to know more about people in order to be successful in this respect."

"More managers will see themselves in teaching roles vis-à-vis their subordinates. Teacher managers whose evaluation will depend to some extent on how much they develop their subordinates will become more commonplace. And community leadership will be expected of managers. I noticed in today's paper a strong message offering support from General Motors' management to the mayor of Detroit, indicating that the company's resources are available to aid in Detroit's post-riot rebuilding. Managers and their organizations will involve themselves in community problem solving much more in the future than in the past. The broad-gauge manager-citizen will certainly be of greater significance in the year 2000 than he is today."

"Other areas of environmental change will call for the manager to be knowledgeable about behavioral and social problems, social change, and particularly cross-cultural and intercultural matters. Foreign markets are growing faster than domestic markets. It has been suggested that 60% of all the world's business will eventually be done by international firms. Tariffs are likely to be lower; there will be more countries in common markets. Capitalist and socialist ideologies will have come closer together; the typical American manager will have to face up to a world of mixed economies, not necessarily like his own, in the many countries in which he will do business. The trend toward devoting a greater proportion of national income to health, education, and welfare will continue. The businessman either is going to be a very frustrated person or will necessarily acquire an appreciation of the society in which he lives – and its problems which will require 21st century solutions."

"By 2000, managers will be more willing and able to transfer from business to hospitals, to government, to research foundations, and back again. In doing so, they will be likely to seek and keep up with a wide spectrum of information about sociology, psychology, social issues, cultural matters, and political affairs. Correspondingly, behavioral scientists will increase their efforts to help make this information available to managers. Highly readable journals and magazines will present in digested form the current findings of the behavioral sciences. It is likely that there will be an increase in this kind of communication, making possible a more rapid dissemination of behavioral science information to managers."

Supervision and the Computer

In 1967, over a decade had passed since Leavitt and Whisler (1958) had predicted that the use of electronic data processing for information gathering, storage, and retrieval and for decision-making would make a substantial impact on organizations of the 1980s, especially on the supervisory process and management structure. Top managers would take on increasingly creative functions. Middle line management would become more structured as its functions become increasingly suited to the use of electronic data-processing systems. A relative decline in the numbers of middle managers was foreseen.

In 1967, I proposed that the computer would affect lower management as well as middle management. "Early predictions generally forecast greater job routinization for these lower levels. Some observers now believe, however, that a computer-based information system can aid middle and lower managers to furnish detailed information to higher levels. Thus middle and lower management may spend less, not more, time in routinized activities."

"Students today receive minimal instruction on computer use; tomorrow's students will probably be thoroughly indoctrinated in the uses and benefits of computers. Typical supervisors in the year 2000 are thus likely to use the computer as a tool to give them not only better and faster information but more time to concentrate on other aspects of their jobs, such as solving human relations problems."

LOOKING AHEAD 33 YEARS FROM 2001 TO 2034

Many of the trends in management and leadership we see today will have become commonplace in 2034. Theories, if they are any good, are meant to be displaced by better ones. Transformational/transactional leadership theory should have been replaced by a better theory by 2034 or at least continued to evolve. When Burns (1978) began, he conceived transforming leadership as opposite to transactional leadership. They were opposite ends of a single dimension. In Bass (1985a), I had shown that each was factorially complex and argued that most leaders did some of both. Transformational leadership added to transactional leadership in better leaders and much more so in the best of leaders (Bass, 1985b, 1990; Bass, Waldman & Yammarino, 1990). Numerous factorial studies in the 1990s found variations in factor outcomes, but basically the transformational factors of idealized influence (charisma) and inspirational motivation, intellectual stimulation, and individualized consideration held up. The transactional leadership factors included contingent reward, active management by exception and passive leadership (passive management by exception and laissez-faire leadership) (Avolio, Bass & Jung, 1999).

For the past 20 years, my confidence has grown that the factors form a hierarchy of associations with the effectiveness of leadership. In most of the many studies to date in business, military, educational, religious, governmental, and not-for-profit organizations, the transformational factors correlate highest with the leader's effectiveness, contingent reward next highest, followed by active management by exception. Passive leadership is negatively correlated with effectiveness. The theory in 2034 will have been built on advances in understanding leadership at different levels in organizations, in virtual team leadership, in developments in the ethics of leadership (Bass & Steidlmeier, 1999), and in improved methodologies for triangulation of quantitative and qualitative research. It will allow for some cultural differences yet be widespread in applications in developing and developing countries (Bass, 1997).

TRENDS FOR THE NEXT 34 YEARS

I will conclude by envisioning 24 trends in applications of transformational leadership as well as more general developments between now and 2034.

(1) We see increasing studies of multiple levels of analysis. WABA will be the procedure of choice in examining supervisor-subordinate relations as well as group and larger entities such as at the departmental level. Basically, testing for level of analysis will become a routine part of scientific inquiry in the organizational sciences. I expect that as individualized consideration becomes routinized, and each individual follower is treated individually, the effect of the group led will decline in favor of individual follower differences (Avolio & Bass, 1995).

(2) Development of leaders will be the rule. Organizations, large and small, as well as their consultants, will make heavy use of on-line web-based programs. More of a premium will be placed on managers' individualized consideration, as demonstrated by their effective coaching and mentoring.

(3) Organizational barriers will continue to fall with increasing organizational alliances, trade shows, and cooperation. The "not-invented here" syndrome will have disappeared in a total global economy. Purely transactional bureaucracies will have given way to more transformational organizations with greater flexibility and informality (Bass & Avolio, 1993).

(4) Second careers after retirement will become commonplace, as will 85-year-old employees. Diversity in age of working teams will be greater than now, again favoring individuation by leaders in relation to their followers.

(5) In 2034, in the industrial world, women MBA students and middle managers in business organizations, service industries, and government agencies will be in the majority in the USA. They will also be in the majority in NGOs, legislatures, city governments, and ownership of small businesses. With their six-year-longer lifespan compared to men, women will become the majority of shareholders, directors, and leaders in many organizations. Patterns of leadership behavior are likely to change by 2034 as women tend to be more transformational than their male counterparts (Bass, Avolio & Atwater, 1996), do more networking, are more focused on relationships, and are more concerned than men about social justice, equity, and fairness.

(6) Given current population tends in America, by 2034, a considerably larger percentage of CEOs in the USA compared to today will be women,

Hispanics, Asian and African Americans, and those of Eastern and Southern European ethnicity.

(7) Many more longitudinal field studies will have been completed, contrasting economic agency theory with various human-relations approaches with results favoring the latter.

(8) Ethical codes will have been established for managers based on a wide range of inputs about borderline behavior and judgments of them by samples of managers, ethicists, and employees.

(9) In 2034, empowerment, collaboration, and continuing change in organizations matching a changing organizational environment will be usual and ingrained in the values and beliefs of most senior leadership. Adaptability at all levels in the organization will be required. Again, we will see more transformational and less transactional leader behavior.

(10) Artificial intelligence will be used for guidance when senior leaders need to deal with important decisions.

(11) Leaders will be prized for their innovativeness, responsiveness and flexibility, all linked to their greater frequency of transformational leadership behavior.

(12) Continuing advances in biotechnology will have an impact on selection and development of leaders. For example, the linkages between testosterone level (now known to affect libido, boldness, focused attention, and dominance) will be included in the study of leadership. Leader perceptions, cognitions, and behavior as a function of hormonal levels will have been studied.

(13) Genetic profiling will similarly have been introduced into the study of leadership.

(14) Brain scans (much more precise than now) of more and less effective leaders and at different times will provide a better understanding of what is innate in leader perception, cognition, and behavior, and what requires learning.

(15) Robert Crowley suggested that, "Disease has to be counted on as one of the wild cards of history." We still do not know how President Reagan's Alzheimers disease affected the second Reagan Administration. But given the continuing medical advances, disease, incapacitation, death, and dying will be less important in executive succession in 2034.

(16) In looking ahead to 2034, we will seriously underestimate the speed of development and application of information technology, particularly as related to nanotechnological advances and many other improvements in information technology between now and then.

(17) Multiple organizational charts will be used to describe the hierarchies and networks of leadership, accountability, responsibility, and communications.

(18) There will be a return to focus on the personalities of leaders especially in changing and stressful environments. Much will be learned about traits that discriminate between the highly transformational leader and the highly transactional leader. Positive psychology will be focused on the strengths in leaders' personalities. Personality flaws that cause leaders to fail will continue to be examined.

(19) In 2034, we will know much more about the true and false memories that shape the ratings of leaders by self and others.

(20) Mathematical operations will be used to optimize the outcomes of negotiations among leaders and leaders and followers.

(21) The trend will continue that transforms rule-driven bureaucracies into mission-oriented organizations aided by more transformational and less transactional leadership.

(22) We will pay more attention to ethical considerations in management and leadership. The need for authenticity, integrity, and honesty will be seen as more important for the long-term success of organizations than hidden agendas, bluffing, and ingratiation, as these will be exposed more easily with the availability of information at all organizational levels and the requirements of financial transparency.

(23) I cannot specify the future, unresearched fads in managerial and leadership development, but there certainly will be some fads still going strongly in 2034. They will start in a popular book, be advanced by consultants and senior managers, and then be routinized by external and internal consultants. But they will slowly fade away and decline in adoption when costs exceed perceived benefits, and some serious evaluations are publicized.

(24) This is a "no-brainer". In 2034, virtual teams and e-leadership will be the rule rather than the exception.

REFERENCES

Argyris, C. (1967). How tomorrow's executive will make decisions. *Think, 33*(6), 18–23.
Avolio, B. J., Bass, B. M., & Jung, D. I. (1999). Reexamining the components of transformational and transactional leadership using the multifactor leadership questionaire (Form 5X). *Journal of Organizational and Occupational Psychology, 72*, 441–462.
Bass, B. M. (1985a). *Leadership and performance beyond expectations.* New York: Free Press.
Bass, B. M. (1985b). Leadership: Good, better, best. *Organizational Dynamics, 13*, 26–41.

Bass, B. M., & Avolio, B. J. (1993). Transformational leadership: A response to critiques. In: M. M. Cehmers (Ed.), *Leadership theory and research: Perspectives and directions*. New York: Academic Press.

Bass, B. M., Avolio, B. J., & Atwater, L. (1996). The transformational and transactional leadership behavior of men and women. *International Review of Applied Psychology, 45*, 5–34.

Bass, B. M., & Steidlmeier, P. (1999). Ethics, character and authentic transformational leadership behavior. *Leadership Quarterly, 10*, 181–217.

Bellamy, E. (1967). *Looking backward 2000–1887*. Cambridge, MA: Harvard University Press (Belknap Press).

Bennis, W. (1967). Organizations of the future. *Personnel Administration, 30*(5), 6–19.

Burns, J. M. (1978). *Leadership*. New York: Harper & Row.

Galbraith, J. K. (1966). *The new industrial state*. Boston, MA: Houghton Mifflin.

Jenkins, R. L. (1967). The supervisor of the future. *Training and Development Journal, 20*(8), 28–30, 32–36.

Kirkpatrick, F. H. (1968). Implications of the behavioral sciences on management practices in the year 2000. In: L. A. Appley & A. W. Angrist (Eds), *Management 2000*. Hamilton, NY: American Foundation for Management Research.

Leavitt, H. J., & Whisler, T. L. (1958). Management in the 1980s. *Harvard Business Review, 36*, 41–48.

Levinson, H. A. (1962). A psychologist looks at executive development. *Harvard Business Review, 40*(5), 69–75.

Likert, R. (1967). *The human organization: Its management and value*. New York: McGraw-Hill.

Schein, E. H. (1966–1967). Attitude change during management education. *Administrative Science Quarterly, 11*, 601–607, 614–628.

Waldman, D., Bass, B. M., & Yammarino, F. J. (1990). Adding to contingent reward behavior: The augmentation effect of charismatic leadership. *Group & Organizational Studies, 15*, 381–394.

Yammarino, F. J., & Bass, B. M. (1990). Long-term forecasting of transformational leadership and its effects among Naval officers: Some preliminary findings. In: K. E. Clark & M. B. Clark (Eds), *Measures of Leadership*. Greensboro, NC: Center for Creative Leadership.

REFLECTIONS, CLOSING THOUGHTS, AND FUTURE DIRECTIONS

Bruce J. Avolio and Francis J. Yammarino

INTRODUCTION

On the back cover of Bass's (1985) book entitled, "Leadership and Performance Beyond Expectations", Abraham Zaleznik was quoted as saying, "This book will recast leadership for the next decade or more." It is clear from the chapters in this book, and work appearing throughout the leadership literature, that we are now into the "more" part of Zaleznik's quote. Bass's work, coupled with many other ground breaking contributions in leadership such as Burns' (1978) research on transformational leadership, and House's (1977) work on charismatic leadership, have ignited a whole new wave of research on the "higher end" or "new genre" of leadership. These ideas are represented in part by the contributions made in this book.

BASS'S CONTRIBUTIONS

Reflecting back to 1985, there were several major contributions made by Bass's work that have significantly advanced theory and research on leadership (see Yammarino, 1993). First, he identified the qualities of leadership that the general public typically thought about, admired, or in some cases reviled when they thought about "leaders." Until the early 1980s, most leadership work in psychology and management was focused on the more managerial aspects of leadership that Bass labeled "transactional." This work paralleled what House (1971) discussed in his path-goal theory of leadership, as well as what Hersey

Transformational and Charismatic Leadership, Volume 2, pages 385–406.
© 2002 Published by Elsevier Science Ltd.
ISBN: 0-7623-0962-8

and Blanchard (1977) referred to in their situational theory of leadership. By moving the construct of transformational leadership to the foreground, Bass was able to bring the field of leadership research closer to what the layperson had in his or her mind when asked to describe exemplary leadership. Indeed, Bass and Avolio (1994) reported that what constituted ideal leadership in the minds of people was almost always the four components of transformational leadership.

Second, Bass brought into focus leadership orientations that were more dynamic, visionary, and unfortunately more dangerous. For example, there are charismatic and transformational leaders who think of ways to build their community and can be called "authentic" leaders (Bass & Steidlmeier, 1999). Alternatively, with the "personalized charismatics," we observe the same level of emotion, identification, and willingness on followers' part to sacrifice for the leader, but their efforts are typically directed towards the leaders' gain at the expense of the community or organization.

Bass (1985) shifted his position on transformational leadership to include a moral component that was later described as the "idealized," not "idolized," component. The inclusion of the moral component, which was prominent in Burns' (1978) reference to transforming leaders who were "morally uplifting," has motivated a very important discussion on what differentiates charismatic leaders from inspirational or transformational leaders; what differentiates 'good' charismatic leaders from 'bad' ones; what impact the situation or context has in terms of the emergence of personalized vs. socialized charismatic leaders; and what understanding and concerns we should have about developing charismatic leadership.

In a recent issue of the *Journal of Applied Psychology*, Turner, Barling, Epitropaki, Butcher and Milner (2002) reported that leaders rated as more transformational had higher moral reasoning scores. This sort of empirical evidence reinforces Bass' inclusion of higher moral reasoning associated with transformational leadership.

Third, Bass's work has helped to make the more colorful aspects of leadership more measurable, albeit with some degree of controversy over how best to assess what constitutes transformational leadership. For example, some authors such as Beyer (1999) have argued that charisma is not something that can be measured like other styles of leadership. Yet, in Bass's (1985) book, and in subsequent work with his associates, he has developed ways to measure what constitutes all of the components of transformational leadership, including charisma.

The whole area regarding the measurement of transformational leadership has stimulated much healthy debate about how it should be measured, by what, by whom, and when. This discussion has most recently crossed over into examining how to triangulate measures using both quantitative and quantitative methodologies to assess all of the components of transactional and transformational leadership (Berson, 1999).

Paralleling the debate regarding how best to measure transformational leadership, there has been considerable discussion concerning how levels of analysis should shape the new emerging theories of leadership, and the ways we must conceptualize and measure leadership. Leadership theory and research are now emerging at multiple levels of analysis (see Dansereau & Yammarino, 1998a, b), including the strategic (Waldman & Yammarino, 1999), collective or shared (Sivasubramaniam, Murry, Avolio & Jung, 2002), and the individual and dyadic levels (Dansereau et al., 1995), which, in combination, have substantially enriched the domains of leadership investigation.

Fourth, an unintended consequence of Bass's idea that transformational leaders develop followers into leaders is that there is now much greater attention to the follower as a significant and interesting player in the leadership process. For example, there has been some recent discussions about what changes in followers when leaders transform them, as well as discussions about how followers can mediate the impact of leadership on performance depending on their needs, expectations, desires, and so forth (Dvir, Eden, Avolio & Shamir, in press).

Fifth, research on transformational leadership and the full-range theory of leadership (Avolio & Bass, 1991) has extended to nearly every continent on earth and continues to provide support for Bass's (1997) contention that transformational leadership is universal. Indeed, as noted by Antonakis and House in this volume, In support of Bass's position, Den Hartog, House, Hanges, Ruiz-Quintanilla and Dorfmann (1999) confirmed that elements of transformational and charismatic leadership were universally reported as highly effective across 62 cultures. Never before has there been such a global approach to leadership research with some of the most outstanding research coming from countries other than the USA.

Perhaps a remaining question is, why did Bass's work so ignite the field of leadership when earlier work by Downton (1973), Burns (1978), House (1977), Weber (1924/1947), and Zaleznik (1977) failed to do so? It may be that Bass placed transformational leadership in the context of other models, demonstrating where it augmented those theories. Alternatively, it may have been timing. In the USA during the 1980s, many industries were at what Gladwell (2000) called a "tipping point." *In Search of Excellence* had been published just a few years earlier by Peters and Waterman (1982), highlighting the importance of managing and leading people. The personal computer was infiltrating organizations, and information technology would begin to transform what was conceived of and called "organizations." U.S. industries were losing the war to Japan Inc., and it was time to transform the way our organizations functioned, leading to the emergence of a focus on process in programs like TQM and six-sigma. At the same time, Tichy and Devanna (1986) were writing about transforming leadership, and CEO Jack Welch was beginning his journey to reshape and transform General Electric. Or, perhaps there is a much simpler explanation: when the author of the *Handbook of Leadership* spoke, the field of leadership scholars listened.

Regardless of the reasons, it seems fair to say that transformational leadership theory has now gone from being novel and interesting; to initial acceptance; to critiques of what is missing (see Bass & Avolio, 1993; Yukl, 1999); and now to a much deeper investigation of what constitutes the constructs of transformational leadership and how can it be measured, developed, and projected through technology in virtual teams and organizations.

BUILDING THE NEXT GENERATION OF RESEARCH

Starting with the chapter by *Antonakis and House* in this volume, these authors examined what Avolio, Bass and Jung (1999) discussed as a "fuller" range theory of leadership. Specifically, the full-range theory was put forth to encompass leadership that ranged from the highly passive-avoidant to the inspiring and idealized. The term "full range" was chosen to intellectually stimulate the field to consider what else in this particular range of activity coupled with effectiveness was missing that could enhance our understanding of leadership. It was not meant to be "the full range," but rather "a full range."

Antonakis and House examined whether the full-range model and its nine basic components could be reliably measured and was universal. They identified studies that reported results on the nine theoretically distinct components comprising the full range theory. These components included: Laissez-Faire, Passive Management-by-Exception, Active Management-by-Exception, Contingent Reward, Individualized Consideration, Intellectual Stimulation, Inspirational Motivation, and Idealized Influence (Attributed and Behaviors).

Antonakis (2001), as summarized in the chapter by Antonakis and House, "affirmed that the nine-factor model consistently represented the data better in homogenous conditions than eight other competing models. Thus, the nine-factor model was found to be invariant – a very strong test for the construct validity of a psychometric instrument – within homogenous conditions, suggesting that the FRLT is context sensitive, but universal across conditions".

Although the evidence presented by Antonakis and House strongly supported the nine-factor model, they also argue that this model should be used as a stepping stone to a more enhanced, comprehensive model of leadership. Arguing that the full-range model can be used as a framework for expanding leadership theories and measures, Antonakis and House state, "We believe that this scaffolding is the FRLT, to which other theories of leadership should be compared and attached, so that lacunae in the FRLT are identified and filled. In this way, a more complete full-range theory will emerge." Indeed, their main point is that the full-range model now needs to be expanded to include leadership styles and behaviors not yet included to make the range more comprehensive.

One of the challenges set forth in Bass's (1985) book title was leadership that created "performance beyond expectations." To some degree, this has set in motion nearly 20 years of research linking transformational leadership to higher levels of performance in the military, industry, public schools, government agencies, churches, sport teams, volunteer agencies, hospitals, financial institutions, and broad range of service organizations. There has been relatively little controversy over the hypothesized linkage between transformational leadership, extra effort, and performance.

Lowe, Kroeck and Sivasubramaniam (1996) provided some of the strongest evidence in the first meta-analysis of this literature. They showed that the transformational scales measured by the Multi-factor Leadership Questionnaire positively predicted rated and objective performance in both public and private organizations. Subsequent research and a meta-analysis conducted by Gaspar (1992) have produced the same level of support for Bass's main notion that connects higher performance to transformational leadership.

Dumdum, Lowe, and Avolio set out to examine the literature generated since the Lowe et al. (1996) article was published, going back to 1995 and moving forward to the present. Their primary goal was to replicate these earlier findings examining linkages between transformational and transactional leadership with both rated and objective measures of performance. In this meta-analysis update, they have reported confirming evidence to support the earlier findings of Lowe et al. (1996). Transformational leadership clearly had more positive relationships with measures of effectiveness, satisfaction, and performance as compared to transactional and non-transactional leadership. Similar to earlier results, these relationships were moderated by organizational type and the type of outcome measure included in the meta-analysis.

Providing some recognition for the validity of the full-range model constructs leads naturally to the next basic question posed by *Kark and Shamir*. Specifically, these authors were interested in examining the identification processes associated with transactional and transformational leadership that impact followers, and how individual and collective identification impact motivation and performance. The work of Kark, Shamir, and others in this volume, highlights the sort of "drilling down" to more specific levels of explanation regarding how, for example, transformational leaders "transform" followers. Stated differently, we know that transformational leaders are associated with higher levels of commitment, motivation, and performance, and now we need to examine why.

Kark and Shamir's chapter builds on earlier theoretical work published by Shamir, House, and Arthur (1993), which examined how leaders impact the self-concept of followers to create identification with the leader. To the extent that identification underlies intense commitment, motivation, and support for the leader, Kark and Shamir are starting to address what constitutes the core processes that explain how leaders transform followers into leaders and how they get them to identify with the unit/organization's mission and vision.

It has been said many times that leaders must first be willing to change themselves to change others. Kark and Shamir add to this idea, stating that to change followers, the followers must change how they view themselves and, in turn, their units. For example, new recruits to the New York City fire department come to understand that, over time, how they view themselves as individuals will become a reflection of who they represent in terms of the institution to which they belong. Their self-concept becomes defined in part by their identification with the institution, which in turn builds among followers a collective identification with the organization. All become connected via identification "on the inside."

How leaders build such identification and sustain it over time is a question leaders have asked themselves since the very beginning of civilization. It is a core question that Bass (1985) came to when he addressed the construct of transformational leadership and how it impacted follower motivation and performance "beyond expectations." Kark and Shamir use the work of Pratt as a basis for discussing ways that personal identification transforms followers' views of themselves, their roles, and their relationship with the leader and unit: Pratt (1998):

(1) evoking follower's self concept in the recognition that they share similar values with the leader; and

(2) giving rise to followers' desire to change their self-concept so that their values and beliefs become more similar to those of the leader" (p. **??**).

Elevating the identification process to the group level, they argue that transformational leaders are able to create a sense of self-identity, which also includes a level of social identification with the follower's unit or organization. By altering the self-concepts of individuals, transformational leaders ostensibly reconnect the self-identity of followers to a collective identity, creating alignment around purpose, mission, and vision.

Kark and Shamir's work helps to identify what goes on within the "black box" of transforming a disaffected or even alienated group of followers, into a unit that is highly aligned, committed, and supportive of one another's efforts. They do so by combining the self-concept theory of charismatic leadership developed by Shamir et al. (1993) and the self-concept theory of Lord, Brown and Fieberg (1999). They state that, "transformational leadership exerts its effects by strongly engaging two levels of follower's social-self concepts – the relational self and the collective self – leading to followers' identification with the leader and the organizational unit". Further, they say that, "certain behaviors of transformational leaders may simultaneously increase not only relational aspects of the self and identification with the leader, but also followers' collective identities and identification with the unit".

Kark and Shamir also raise some very compelling questions regarding whether leaders can be taught to "influence" or "manipulate" the self and/or relational concepts of their followers. Without doubt, there have been charismatic leaders throughout history that have been able to do so; however, they learned to do so. Yet, there has been relatively little research demonstrating how transformational leaders change the self and collective concepts of followers. Recently, Paul, Costley, Howell and Dorfman (2002) examined the effects of charismatic leadership messages on followers in a simulated experimental context, reporting that charismatic leadership enhanced the accessibility of followers' collective self-concept. Undoubtedly, there will be much more to say about how transformational and charismatic leaders affect the "internal" processes of identification, which in turn positively impacts the external outcomes we have typically associated with transformational leadership.

Couto addresses the issue of how charismatic leaders influence others in a compelling analysis of the Founding Fathers' leadership in the USA. He discusses the concerns that the Founding Fathers had with charismatic leaders and the checks and balances they put into place in the event that a charismatic leader turned out to be "personalized" rather than "socialized." He points to the willingness of the Founding Fathers to put controls in place that may inhibit the "common" follower from emerging and having his or her voice heard. This cost of maintaining control and order in society raises an interesting point about the balance between leadership and the use of power. In some sense, many aspects of leadership can be viewed as either directly or indirectly addressing the issue of balancing control/order with flexibility and change.

The balance that Bass proposed between transactional and transformational leadership is another attempt at dealing with this pivotal issue. Transactional leaders provide the control and order to enhance stability, whereas transformational leaders change the rules, challenge the status quo, and move individuals, groups, and organizations to new ways of performing. Interestingly enough, often it is the same leader who exhibits both transactional and transformational leadership "in balance" depending on the circumstances and challenges. Indeed, building on Couto's observations, it is the optimal balance of transactional and transformational leadership that likely leads to highly effective performance over time, varying circumstances and challenges.

When forming a government and country following a revolution, it seems reasonable for the Founding Fathers to seek to establish a basis for order and control. Yet, building in the opportunity for challenge and change sustains organizational systems and countries. This intent seems to be reflected in Couto's following comments on leadership: "You gave us bold directions but modest means of government to pursue them. We have had to amend what you gave us to keep going in the direction of democratic liberty that you provided and to overcome some of the prejudices that you built into the Constitution". Today, "all men are created equal," means blacks and whites, men and women, the newest immigrant groups, and the oldest inhabitants. Amendments are always needed to adapt to change, and one might say that transformational leaders are the promoters of amendments to adapt to change in organizations and societies.

Mumford and Strange extend the work discussed on transformational and charismatic leadership by delving into the concept of visionary leadership. Whenever anyone discusses charismatic or transformational leadership, invariably the construct of vision comes to the foreground. Vision is part of outstanding leadership in all models of leadership whether they discuss the "good" leaders or the "bad" leaders.

Mumford and Strange articulate a core argument about vision's place in the overall leadership framework, stating that, "we will argue that the formation of a viable prescriptive mental model provides the cognitive foundation for the vision that lies at the heart of outstanding leadership". Paralleling Couto's arguments, they use George Washington's vision for a new nation as an example of how his mental prescriptions affected the development of the U.S. government. They also make a distinction between ideological leaders and charismatic leaders, which parallels the distinction made by Howell (1988) between personalized and the socialized charismatic leaders.

To some extent, the work by Kark and Shamir is directly relevant to the work of Mumford and Strange. In particular, once a leader articulates a "mental picture" for the future, and that mental picture becomes shared among followers, we would expect that the group, organization, community or nation's collective self-concept would include or represent that mental image or picture. Thus, part of the change in self-concept is likely motivated by linking an individual's self-concept to a vision, which in turn helps build the collective concept of the followers. This new collective concept ultimately provides the basis for a new sense of meaning and direction for the leader and his or her followers.

Perhaps the unique contribution that Mumford and Strange make to the leadership literature is the way they describe charismatic leaders tying their visions to either pro-social or self-serving values, and how that linkage is then reflected in what they say and do with followers. Mumford and Strange studied world-class leaders using a psycho-historical content coding methodology to distinguish ideological from charismatic leaders. Specifically, they state, "ideological leaders were identified, in accordance with our foregoing propositions, based on the leaders' consistent expression of strongly held beliefs and values while charismatic leaders were identified based on their expression of a future-oriented vision". Visions are part of outstanding leadership, but some leaders use visions to achieve self-serving ends, whereas other leaders who are willing to sacrifice for the good of the community use the articulation of a vision to serve the community.

In their concluding comments, Mumford and Strange state, "charismatic, and mixed style leaders were more likely than ideological leaders to take into account the needs of the organization in generating a vision, adjust their vision to the needs of followers, and maintain a close relationship with followers whose interpersonal reactions provided a basis for establishing the meaningfulness of their vision".

The chapter by *Kim, Dansereau, and Kim* also reflects the type of "drilling down" that is occurring in the leadership literature concerning attempts to deepen our understanding of individual constructs put forth in Bass's (1985) model as well as in the work of House (1977) on charismatic leadership. Kim et al. not only focus on what are the various unique behavioral components comprising charismatic leadership but also address the other side of the equation by examining the type of followers who are more or less likely to follow charismatic leaders. Specifically, they explore charismatic followership building on earlier theoretical work by stating, "Charismatic effects on followers may take various forms such as trust in the correctness of the leader's beliefs, unquestioning acceptance of the leader, affection for the leader, willing obedience to the leader, identification with the leader, and emotional involvement in the mission (Conger & Kanungo, 1988, 1998; House, 1977)." Among these characteristics, we view follower acceptance of the charismatic leader as a key factor in defining charismatic followership.

Two different types of acceptance have been suggested in the literature. Followers respond to charismatic leaders by unquestioning acceptance (House, 1977) or voluntary acceptance (Graham, 1988). Again, along the lines discussed above, there typically appears to be a balance between creating followers who fail to question the leadership vs. followers that question leaders too much, resulting in chaos and revolution. Some leaders simply prefer order and compliance and will seek and/or develop followers who are not willing to question them. Many examples exist throughout history where such followers existed, including most recently the ongoing saga of Enron. Many followers described key leaders at Enron as charismatic and people who one dare not question. One wonders to what extent charismatic leadership in this situation and at Anderson Consulting contributed to the downfall of both of these organizations, and to what extent it will facilitate their re-emergence, if they do indeed survive.

Both directly and indirectly, Kim et al. also address how the self-concepts of followers contribute to their identification with the leader, and how the self-concept emerges into a collective concept. They focus on the role of the context in the emergence of charismatic followership, going back to the notion proposed by Weber on crisis-induced charisma. For example, building on Mumford and Strange's work, Kim et al. argue that followers are more willing to comply with personalized charismatic leaders' wishes when the situation is uncertain or chaotic vs. in more stable periods of time.

They also argue that the same follower across different situations may be more or less likely to be influenced by a charismatic leader; again linking context, follower characteristics and leadership style, concluding that, "followers with different characteristics (i.e. high and low self-esteem) voluntarily or unquestioningly accept charismatic leaders with different characteristics under different environmental situations. . . . our view is consistent with Shamir and Howell's (1999), who point out that crisis facilitates the emergence of charismatic leader, but is not a necessary factor in defining charisma".

Finally, Kim et al. integrate the three main components that make up what constitutes the leadership process by stating, "we propose that charismatic leaders must display the three behaviors (i.e. vision-related, personal, and empowering behaviors) to some degree in order to be perceived as charismatic. However, we also propose that it depends on the characteristics of followers (high and low self-esteem) and the environment (crisis and non-crisis) whether individuals become followers of charismatic leaders". Again, we see an extension of Bass' original theory examining these three essential and interrelated components comprising the leadership process.

The chapter by *Waldman and Javidan* represents a trend in the leadership literature to begin examining the qualities, behaviors, and styles of strategic leaders in organizations. Most of the literature on leadership has focused on individual leadership, with only recent attention being given to collective or shared leadership and strategic leadership. Although there has been some attention to strategic leaders in organizations, most of this research has focused on the demographic qualities of such leaders, as opposed to their dispositions, styles, and behaviors. Using upper echelon theory as a guiding framework, Waldman and Javidan build on the strategic leadership literature to explore a gap in this literature. This gap is reflected in the following quote cited in Waldman and Javidan: "As Finkelstein and Hambrick stated: As yet, we know of no evidence of a generally advantageous functional profile for top executives. Instead, the external environment and the company's chosen strategy create a context in which certain functional orientations may have distinct but conditional benefits" (1996, p. 99). Waldman and Javidan have set out to examine what constitutes the profile of successful executives by focusing on styles of leadership and behavior in addition to demographics.

Citing earlier work by Waldman, Ramirez, House, and Puranam (2001), the authors point out how assessing the charismatic leadership qualities of CEOs, coming from a broad cross-section of Fortune 500 firms, they were able to demonstrate the relationship between CEO charisma and firm net profit margin in unstable vs. stable market conditions. Extending these results to both Canadian and U.S. firms, Waldman and Javidan reported in the current chapter that perceptions of strategic change in organizations had an impact on the leader's charisma, which in turn affected net profit.

The work by Waldman and Javidan further opens the door to exploring the links between transformational and strategic leadership in organizations, either with respect to the CEO or in terms of senior management team leadership. A logical extension of their work could involve examining how leadership close-up and at a distance affects organizational performance. Specifically, to what extent does the CEO's strategic leadership cascade throughout the organization and impact followers very distant to that leader? And more importantly, how does such leadership impact followers directly and indirectly?

The work of *Popper and Mayseless* takes us in a rather different leadership direction – into the psycho-dynamic processes associated with transformational leadership development. Bass (1985) discussed the importance of examining some of these psycho-dynamic processes to get a better handle on how charismatic and transformational leadership emerges. The focus of Popper and Mayseless's approach to explaining the development of transformational leaders is best captured in the following comment: "We further argue that the origins of the ability and motivation to be a transformational leader lie in childhood experiences, and that the development of this ability and motivation can be understood and conceptualized by means of major developmental theories such as attachment theory (Bowlby, 1969, 1973, 1977, 1988)."

Having identified that there are transformational leaders and that they generate more positive organizational outcomes, we expect the next new horizon for leadership research will likely be focused on where they come from and how more of them can be developed. Examining the basic factors underlying the motivation to lead in a transformational way seems like a fruitful area to pursue in future research. In this regard, Popper and Mayseless draw parallels between transformational leadership and exemplary parenting to demonstrate how the optimism, empathy, openness, and confidence of the leader come from his or her earlier relationships with parents, attachments, and general social upbringing.

People who are secure with themselves are able to explore others and their environment, learning when and where to transform. Perhaps the key issue right now is whether individuals who were not trained by effective parents to be transformational can be trained later in life. Preliminary evidence accumulated over the last several years (see Dvir et al., 2002) suggests that experimental training interventions can create transformational leadership, but much more needs to be done to evaluate systematically how far one can change individuals to become transformational leaders. In some cases, the trainer may be able to build on an effective base to elevate the individual to become more transformational. In other cases, it may take a complete recovery of the individual to enhance his or her transformational potential. The conditions in which training can be successful, and with whom, remain wide-open areas for future research. Indeed, the weakest area today in terms of rigorous leadership research is leadership development (Avolio, 1999).

Steyrer's chapter takes a more in-depth look at the perceptions of charismatic leadership, also using a psycho-dynamic framework, where he specifically focuses on the construct of stigma. In a very intellectually stimulating way,

Steyrer uses the construct of stigma to help explain why charismatic leaders stand out from the crowd, arguing that it is these "borderline" characteristics that help charismatic leaders come to the foreground. The borderline characteristics become what Steyrer refers to as qualities that distinguish charismatic from non-charismatic leaders. These include ego-strength and commitment; capacity for enthusiasm and ambition; predominance and rigidity; subtlety and independence; extraversion and effect calculation; organization and control; and loving care and sympathy. Yet, he also notes the importance of balancing these borderline qualities:

> Therefore, leaders whose self-presentation is located in the border areas, i.e. outside the area showing prototypicality, always have to find the right balance – in the eyes of their followers they are moving on a razor's edge. Too little social dramatization or social reversion means that they will not be distinguished from the mass of their competitors. If there is too much mise-en-scène, charisma turns into stigma. The classic charisma-dilemma therefore is the dramatic/playful approximation to the corresponding border zones, without actually crossing the Rubicon.

Perhaps what is most intriguing about Steyrer's work is the idea that the same qualities that caused followers to revere the leader over time may cause them also to revile the leader. This may be one way of explaining how President Clinton's expressions of vulnerability and empathy came to be seen over time as inauthentic manipulations on his part to curry favor with his constituency. He represents a prototypical example of a "border crosser" that may have got stuck on the wrong side of stigma!

Again, along the lines of exploring internal processes, *Connelly, Gaddis and Helton-Fauth*, address a topic that is receiving more and more attention in the leadership literature – the link between emotions and leadership. These authors offer a framework to examine how emotions impact the leader and follower dynamic, suggesting that charismatic and transformational leadership in particular involve the expression of certain emotions that have an effect on followers. For example, demonstrating their emotional commitment to a cause that followers deeply believe in is expected to result in inspiring leadership. The authors specifically link their conceptual framework to earlier work on individualized leadership stating that:

> Mumford, Yammarino and Dansereau (2000) note that individualized leadership may be a key mediating mechanism between exceptional leadership and follower effectiveness, with the potential to bring about good and bad outcomes. Connecting with followers on an emotional level initially, and continuing to understand and meet their emotional needs, may very well be one way that charismatic leaders exhibit individualized leadership.

Leaders can choose to exhibit certain emotions that signal followers about the importance of their message, how deeply committed they are, what they desire from followers, and what followers are expected to do. A related issue is how leaders choose to use emotions as part of their impression management strategy and why it is easier vs. more difficult for certain leaders to use emotions and have the impact on followers that they desire.

The capability to choose emotions and express them relates to the emerging interest and work on emotional intelligence (Goleman, 1995; Mayer & Salovey, 1997; Salovey & Mayer, 1990). Such intelligence is expected to provide the leader with the capacity to be aware of the emotional needs of others and to adjust their presentation of themselves to accommodate those needs. In line with some of Bass's (1985) descriptions of transformational leaders, Megerian and Sosik (1996) and Sosik and Megerian (1996) argue that leaders who are more transformational are also likely to have higher levels of emotional intelligence, including self-awareness.

Caruso, Mayer and Salovey (2002) discuss why it is important for leaders to identify, use, understand, and manage emotions. By being able to accurately identify one's own emotions, the leader is more capable of improving his or her self-awareness, which can then positively impact the leader's performance and his or her interaction with followers. Knowing one's followers is a key component of transformational leadership, referred to by Bass as individualized consideration. The core message here is that to fully know others' means, you must also know yourself.

Connelly et al. make the basic argument that the leadership literature has not extensively explored how both positive and negative emotions influence the leader's impact on a particular follower or a group of followers. Issues such as which emotions will sustain follower perseverance, get them to question the status quo, and reflect on and challenge their own development represent critical areas for future research to pursue. For example, how can anger be used positively to ignite compassion in followers? Extending these questions to examining how leaders will express emotions at a distance through technology becomes an intriguing research area for situations in which many leaders now lead.

Connelly et al. note that the use of emotions can have a different impact at different points in the leadership process: ". . . specific emotions are targeted at different points in the leadership process, from the initial point when a vision is conceptualized and communicated to when vision-related goals have been realized, changed, or abandoned. While leaders may not always consciously realize that they are tapping into different emotions to accomplish different purposes with their followers, this may help to better explain the nature of leader influence processes". This statement leads to the same question that we have raised throughout this chapter. Specifically, now that we understand the importance of emotions to the leadership process, do we understand how it can be developed to enhance overall leadership potential?

Eden and Sulamani take on the issue of leadership development directly, examining one aspect of motivation and leadership – the Pygmalion effect – that Eden has examined over the last 20 years. Eden confronted an interesting dilemma in his life's work: the only time he was able to create the Pygmalion effect was when he engineered a ruse or deception, telling subjects something that was not true (e.g. "we are assigning to you, a group of high potential followers", when in fact, the followers were randomly assigned).

Eden et al. (2000) had conducted seven field experiments to test the effectiveness of training managers in Pygmalion Leadership Style (PLS). This style is characterized as conveying high performance expectations to followers, building a supportive climate, and viewing followers' success as being attributed to the followers' personal qualities. The training workshops that he and his colleagues constructed ranged from a one-day familiarization experience to a three-day intensive program that included learning Pygmalion concepts, behavioral skill-practice exercises, implementation planning, and follow-up sessions. Unfortunately, none of these training experiments worked in that the leaders were no more capable following training to create the Pygmalion effect.

Stepping back to explore this conundrum further, Eden and his colleagues realized that perhaps leaders not only have to build self-efficacy to be successful, but also may need to know the means to success or what they called "means-efficacy." Eden and Granat-Flomin showed that it was possible to measure means efficacy, to augment it experimentally, and to enhance performance outcomes. They also demonstrated that means efficacy had an independent impact on performance apart from self-efficacy.

In the current chapter, the Eden and Sulamani tested the following: "Hypothesizing positive effects of total subjective efficacy on motivation and performance, we predicted that trainees of the experimental instructors, who were to be trained in Pygmalion and total-efficacy concepts, would have greater self-efficacy, means efficacy, and motivation, and would outperform comparable trainees whose instructors received alternative training". The authors demonstrated that it was actually possible to train managers to create the Pygmalion effect if it included a focus on means efficacy in training. They also demonstrated that it was not necessary to deceive participants to create the Pygmalion effect.

Eden and Sulamani's results have implications for training leaders in general, in that most training efforts have focused more on what behaviors transformational leaders should exhibit as opposed to the means of transforming followers. Attention to such means can help to take the abstract constructs associated with transformational leadership and make them more action-oriented and applicable to change.

Miner's chapter reminds us of the importance of examining the context in which we study leadership. He takes us back to the early 1980s when he made his first call for not examining leadership in a vacuum, as House and Aditya (1997) did nearly 15 years later. Taking Miner's call one step further, we would argue that leadership is by its very nature contextually based. For example, the very same behaviors in crisis and stable conditions can have dramatically different effects. Moreover, evidence is emerging that the stability of factor structures for survey measures of leadership are in part dependent on the context in which the survey is used. In other words, the factor structure may or may not be invariant, depending on the context in which it is administered. So, to study transformational, charismatic, and inspiring leadership, it is essential that we include the context in our analysis of these leadership styles.

Miner makes the point of emphasizing the context very clearly in the following statement: "Now, some 20 years later, I hope to cement this bonding of leadership with its various organizational forms – not to minimize the leadership construct, as was my original idea, but to give it additional strength by welding it on to the organizational context of which it is an inherent part". Miner extends this point by examining how different motive patterns serve leaders in working across different contexts and settings. He argues that those leaders with motive patterns congruent to the situation will perform better and stay with that situation longer.

Miner reports on a follow-up study with a group of Princeton alums over a 50-year time span, in which he examined the types of their terminal career positions. Miner reports that the motive patterns of these leaders had very high predictive validities for the type of leadership careers members enjoyed over a 50-year time span. He concluded by saying that, "My point here is that looking at leadership as it occurs in different organizational forms, as the role motivation theories of leadership do, could well extend the leadership field into new domains and new kinds of knowledge".

Parry addresses leadership as a social influence process, and in effect considers Miner's challenge to examine leadership in context by pursuing a phenomenological strategy to leadership styles. Parry places particular emphasis on examining the social interactions between leaders and followers. He then explores how leaders address uncertainty in context to enhance their adaptability and the adaptability of their followers. Parry's focus goes to the core of what transformational leaders do, i.e. take on uncertainty as an opportunity for change and adaptation.

Parry examined how leaders enhance adaptability, optimize, resolve uncertainty, and promulgate a vision as the four key social dynamic processes associated with leadership. He creates and attempts to validate a new survey entitled, "Social Processes of Leadership" (SPL). His results demonstrated that the SPL tended to tap into many of the same constructs and dimensions that have been associated with transformational leadership. Generally, Parry found, in this initial study, that there is one global factor representing the social influence processes associated with leadership. Parry's exploration into the general social processes associated with leadership represents a broadening of the theoretical approaches used to understand the dynamics of leadership, as well as the use of both qualitative and quantitative means for construct validation of survey measures of leadership.

In the final chapter, *Bass* goes back to 1967 to examine some of the main trends he envisioned would shape leadership and organizations up to the year 2000. He said in 1967 that, "organizations will be more flexible. Developments will continue in the understanding and skill with which we apply ourselves to the dynamics of organization change. The flexible organization will be the rule rather than the exception, and we will see more attention to both short- and long-range efforts by management to gear itself to a world of fairly continuous change". It took nearly 15 years to explore the type of leadership that would be most suitable to the type of organizational context that Bass had envisioned – transformational leadership. It was also clear in his projections that understanding people and their contribution to organizational effectiveness, now termed "human capital," would be a core competency that would grow in importance for leaders to be successful. In the context of the full-range theory, individualized consideration is closset to representing this deeper focus on understanding and developing followers.

Bass closes his chapter by projecting into the future and highlights the importance of multiple levels of analysis issues and the role that technology will play in the social process of leadership. He refers to the changing demographics of leaders and how that will impact organizations, as well as what an organization will be in a world of interconnected systems and boundaryless markets. He emphasizes the need to explore what constitutes authentic leadership and unethical leadership. Indeed, as we move to the more profoundly influential forms of leadership, we will also need to understand the ethical boundaries that guide such leaders. This understanding clearly is becoming more relevant as industrial organizations become more powerful entities in our communities and nation-states.

Bass also raises some interesting notions about using technology such as genetic profiling, artificial intelligence, and brain scans in the selection and development of leaders. These approaches raise their own unique ethical dilemmas. And as he did in 1967, he re-emphasizes the need to enhance the adaptability of every single employee at every single level of the organization to remain effective as an organization.

CLOSING THOUGHTS

With the closing of Bass's chapter, we ourselves are left with some final observations oriented toward future perspectives. First, it is clear to us that leadership theory and research is no longer the stepchild of organizational research. It has moved to the foreground of interest within many theoretical models and has become an obsession in organizations throughout the world. It is critical to identify, place, and develop correctly leaders at all levels in all types of organizations. Never before has there been so much attention directed towards leadership and such high expectations for its impact on organizational performance.

Second, the construct of leadership has matured from the transactional to the transformational, and in this process of maturation, it has been extended across multiple levels of analysis. We now discuss organizational leadership as comprising at least four essential elements: individual, dyadic, shared or collective, and strategic.

Third, how leadership is mediated through advanced information technology is a field in its infancy, even though there are many managers who are being asked to lead anytime/anywhere through advanced information technology. Clearly, the rapid advances in information technology are changing what we conceived of as being an organization and what we conceive of as leadership in these new organizational settings.

Fourth, leadership research has become increasingly cross-cultural, and we see this pace continuing as the global community becomes a reality. Exploring whether transformational leadership is universal will continue, but we believe that more research attention will be given to how such leadership is moderated and mediated by cultural differences.

Fifth, our understanding of leadership in different ethnic and racial groups is also in its infancy. As a field, we are presented with some great opportunities to explore whether leaders of color lead differently from white leaders; how women leaders lead differently from men leaders; how leaders in one culture lead differently from leaders in another culture, etc. So much of our work in leadership has been conducted with primarily samples of white male and some white female leaders and followers. We see this changing dramatically over the next 10 years or more.

Sixth, there have been a handful of studies that have examined how to develop transformational leadership. Indeed, many of these studies have shown through rigorous experimental applications how to "create" constructs like transformational leadership. We envision that there will be considerably more attention to systematically manipulating leadership through such experimental interventions because managers looking for the "total solution" to leadership development will demand evidence for the efficacy of training programs. Such demonstrations will come about through rigorous experimentation, which will be an important contributing factor to advancing the field of leadership.

Finally, as Bass aptly notes, the field of leadership has now been characterized in a multi-level framework. Future work on transformational leadership will no doubt examine how individual-, dyad-, group-, and organizational-level transformational leadership impacts followers, and how such leadership is embedded and affected by the context in which it is observed. Such multi-level theories of leadership will require that we expand our use of both qualitative and quantitative methods for study leadership. Using both approaches vs. one or the other will no doubt become the norm in the field of leadership research.

In closing, it is truly remarkable how far the field of transformational and charismatic leadership has come in the last 15 years. Building on where we started, and what Zaleznik correctly noted, there is much "more" to come in the next 15 years that we suspect will transform the field of leadership. We are delighted to be a small part of this "road ahead."

REFERENCES

Antonakis, J. (2001). The validity of the transformational, transactional, and laissez-faire leadership model as measured by the Multifactor Leadership Questionnaire (MLQ5X). Dissertation Abstracts International (University Microfilms No. 3000380).

Avolio, B. J. (1999). *Full leadership development: Building the vital forces in organizations.* Thousand Oaks, CA: Sage.

Avolio, B. J., & Bass, B. M. (1991). Full range leadership development manual. Center for Leadership Studies Report, Binghamton, NY.

Avolio, B. J., Bass, B. M., & Jung, D. I. (1999). Re-examining the components of transformational and transactional leadership using the Multifactor Leadership Questionnaire. *Journal of Occupational and Organizational Psychology, 72,* 441–462.

Bass, B. M. (1985). *Leadership and performance beyond expectations.* New York: The Free Press.

Bass, B. M. (1997). Does the transactional-transformational leadership paradigm transcend organizational boundaries? *American Psychologist, 52*(2), 130–139.

Bass, B. M., & Avolio, B. J. (1993). Transformational leadership: A response to critiques. In: M. M. Chemers & R. Ayman (Eds), *Leadership theory and research: Perspectives and directions* (pp. 49–80). San Diego: Academic Press.

Bass, B. M., & Avolio, B. J. (Eds) (1994). *Improving organizational effectiveness through transformational leadership*. Thousand Oaks, CA: Sage Publications.

Bass, B. M., & Steidlmeier, P. (1999). Ethics, character, and authentic transformational leadership behavior. *Leadership Quarterly, 10*, 181–217.

Berson, Y. (1999). A comprehensive assessment of leadership using triangulation of qualitative and quantitative methods. Unpublished Doctoral Dissertation, SUNY-Binghamton.

Beyer, J. M. (1999). Taming and promoting charisma to change organizations. *Leadership Quarterly, 10*, 30–330.

Bowlby, J. (1969). *Attachment and loss* (Vol. 1). *Attachment*. New York: Basic Books.

Bowlby, J. (1973). *Attachment and loss* (Vol. 2). *Separation*. New York: Basic Books.

Bowlby, J. (1977). The making and breaking of affectional bonds. *British Journal of Psychiatry, 130*, 201–210.

Bowlby, J. (1988). *A secure base: Clinical applications of attachment theory*. London: Routledge.

Burns, J. M. (1978). *Leadership*. New York: Harper & Row.

Caruso, D. R., Mayer, J. D., & Salovey, P. (2002). Emotional intelligence and emotional leadership. In: R. E. Riggio, S. E. Murphy & F. J. Pirozzolo (Eds), *Multiple intelligences and leadership* (pp. 55–74). Mahwah, NJ: Lawrence Erlbaum Associates.

Conger, J. A., & Kanugo, R. N. (Eds) (1988). *Charismatic leadership: The elusive factor in organizational effectiveness*. San Francisco: Jossey-Bass Publishers.

Conger, J. A., & Kanugo, R. N. (1998). *Charismatic leadership in organizations*. Thousand Oaks, CA: Sage Publications.

Dansereau, F., & Yammarino, F. J. (Eds) (1998a). *Leadership: The multiple-level approaches (Part A: Classical and new wave)*. Stamford, CT: JAI Press.

Dansereau, F., & Yammarino, F. J. (Eds) (1998b). *Leadership: The multiple-level approaches (Part B: Contemporary and alternative)*. Stamford, CT: JAI Press.

Dansereau. F., Yammarino, F. J., Markham, S. E., Alutto, J. A., Newman, J., Dumas, M., Nachman, S. A., Naughton, T. J., Kim, K., Al-Kelabi, S. A., Lee, S., & Keller, T. (1995). Individualized leadership: A new multiple approach. *Leadership Quarterly, 6*, 413–450.

Den Hartog, D. N., House, R. J., Hanges, P. J., Ruiz-Quintanilla, S. A., & Dorfmann, P. W. (1999). Culture specific and cross-cultural generalizable implicit leadership theories: Are attributes of charismatic/transformational leadership universally endorsed? *Leadership Quarterly, 10*(2), 219–256.

Downton, J. V. (1973). *Rebel leadership: Commitment and charisma in the revolutionary process*. New York: The Free Press.

Dvir, T., Eden, D., Avolio, B. J., & Shamir, B. (in press). Impact of transformational leadership on follower development and performance: A field study. *Academy of Management Journal*.

Eden, D., Geller, D., Gewirtz, A., Gordon-Terner, R., Inbar, I., Liberman, M., Pass, Y., Salomon-Segev, I., & Shalit, M. (2000). Implanting Pygmalion Leadership Style through workshop training: Seven field experiments. *Leadership Quarterly, 11*, 171–210.

Eden, D., & Granat-Flomin, R. (2000, April). Augmenting means efficacy to improve service performance among computer users: A field experiment in the public sector. Presented at the Fifteenth Annual Meeting of the Society for Industrial and Organizational Psychology, New Orleans.

Finkelstein, S., & Hambrick, D. C. (1996). *Strategic leadership: Top executives and their effects.* Minneapolis/St. Paul: West Publishing Company.

Gasper, J. M. (1992). Transformational leadership: An integrative review of the literature. Dissertation Abstracts International (University Microfilms No. 9234203).

Gladwell, M. (2000). *The tipping point: How little things can made a big difference.* Boston, MA: Little, Brown and Company.

Goleman, D. (1995). *Emotional intelligence.* New York: Bantam.

Graham, J. W. (1988). Chapter 3 commentary: Transformational leadership: Fostering follower autonomy, not automatic followership. In: J. G. Hunt, B. R. Baliga, H. P. Dachler & C. A. Schriesheim (Eds), *Emerging leadership vistas* (pp. 73–79). Lexington, MA: Lexington Books.

Hersey, P., & Blanchard, K. H. (1977). *Management of organizational behavior: Utilizing human resources.* Englewood Cliffs, NJ: Prentice-Hall.

House, R. J. (1971). A path-goal theory of leadership effectiveness. *Administrative Science Quarterly, 16*, 321–328.

House, R. J. (1977). A 1976 theory of charismatic leadership. In: J. G. Hunt & L. L. Larson (Eds), *Leadership: The cutting edge* (pp. 189–207). Carbondale, IL: Southern Illinois University Press.

House, R. J., & Aditya, R. N. (1997). The social scientific study of leadership: Quo vadis? *Journal of Management, 23*(3), 409–474.

Howell, J. M. (1988). Two faces of charisma: Socialized and personalized leadership in organizations. In: J. A. Conger & R. N. Kanugo (Eds), *Charismatic leadership: The elusive factor in organizational effectiveness* (pp. 213–236). San Francisco: Jossey-Bass Publishers.

Hunt, J. G. (1999). Transformational/charismatic leadership's transformation of the field: An historical essay. *Leadership Quarterly, 10*(2), 129–144.

Lord, R. G., Brown, D. J., & Feiberg, S. J. (1999). Understanding the dynamics of leadership: The role of follower self-concepts in the leader/follower relationship. *Organizational Behavior and Human Decision Processes, 78*(3), 167–203.

Lowe, K. B., Kroeck, K. G., & Sivasubramaniam, N. (1996). Effectiveness correlates of transformational and transactional leadership: A meta-analytic review of the literature. *Leadership Quarterly, 7*(3), 385–425.

Mayer, J. D., & Salovey, P. (1997). What is emotional intelligence? In: P Salovey & D. Sluyter (Eds), *Emotional development and emotional intelligence: Implications for educators* (pp. 3–31). New York: Basic Books.

Megerian, L. E., & Sosik, J. J. (1996). An affair of the heart: Emotional intelligence and transformational leadership. *Journal of Leadership Studies, 3*, 31–48.

Mumford, M. D., Yammarino, F. J., & Dansereau, F. (2000). Followers, motivations, and levels of analysis: The case of individualized leadership. *Leadership Quarterly, 11*, 313–340.

Paul, J., Costley, D. L., Howell, J. P., & Dorfman, P. W. (2002). The effects of charismatic leadership on followers' self-concept accessibility. *Journal of Applied Psychology, 31*, 1821–1844.

Peters, T. J., & Waterman, R. H. (1982). *In search of excellence.* New York: Harper & Row.

Pratt, M. G. (1998). To be or not to be: Central questions in organizational identification. In: D. A. Whetten & P. C. Godfrey (Eds), *Identity in organizations: Building theory through conversation* (pp. 171–207). Thousand Oaks, CA: Sage Publications.

Salovey, P., & Mayer, J. D. (1990). Emotional intelligence. *Imagination, Cognition, and Personality, 9*, 185–211.

Shamir, B., House, R. J., & Arthur, M. B. (1993). The motivational effects of charismatic leadership: A self-concept based theory. *Organization Science, 4*(4), 577–594.

Shamir, B., & Howell, J. M. (1999). Organizational and contextual influences on the emergence and effectiveness of charismatic leadership. *Leadership Quarterly, 19*(2), 257–283.

Sivasubramaniam, N., Jung, D. I., Avolio, B. J., & Murry, W. D. (2002) A longitudinal model of the effects of team leadership and group potency on group performance. *Group and Organization Management, 27,* 66–96.

Sosik, J. J., & Megerian, L. E. (1999). Understanding leader emotional intelligence and performance: The role of self-other agreement on transformational leadership perceptions. *Group and Organizational Management, 24,* 367–390.

Tichy, N. M. & Devanna, M. A., (1986). *The transformational leader.* New York: John Wiley.

Turner, N., Barling, J., Epitropaki, O., Butcher, V., & Milner, C. (2002). Transformational leadership and moral reasoning. *Journal of Applied Psychology, 87,* 304–310.

Waldman, D. A., Ramirez, G. G., House, R. J., & Puranam, P. (2001). Does leadership matter?: CEO leadership attributes under conditions of perceived environmental uncertainty. *Academy of Management Journal, 44,* 134–143.

Waldman, D. A., & Yammarino, F. J. (1999). CEO charismatic leadership: Levels-of management and levels-of-analysis effects. *Academy of Management Review, 24,* 266–285.

Weber, M. (1947). *The theory of social and economic organization* (T. Parsons, Trans.). New York: The Free Press. (Original work published 1924.)

Yammarino, F. J. (1993). Transforming leadership studies: Bernard Bass' Leadership and performance beyond expectations. *Leadership Quarterly, 4,* 379–382.

Yukl, G. (1999). An evaluation of conceptual weaknesses in transformational and charismatic leadership theories. *Leadership Quarterly, 10,* 285–305.

Zaleznik, A. (1992). Managers and leaders: Are they different? *Harvard Business Review* (March-April), 126–135. (Original work published 1977.)

INDEX

NOTE: Many terms have been used in the text to describe different and similar styles of leadership, and it would not be appropriate to provide cross-references between them all. In each context the particular term used has been indexed. To access related information the reader should consult entries for the following leadership styles:

CEO, charismatic, contingent reward, FRLT, group, heroic, hierarchic, ideological, inspirational, instrumental, laissez-faire, mixed style, professional, role motivation, socialized, socialized charismatic, strategic, task, transactional, transactional contingent reward, transformational, visionary.